THE ONE YEAR

IMPACT FOR LIVING

MEN'S DEVOTIONAL

DAILY COACHING FOR A LIFE OF SIGNIFICANCE

SCOTT WHITAKER & NATHAN WHITAKER

Tyndale House Publishers, Inc.
Carol Stream, Illinois

To our family—Lynda (Mom), Amy, Hannah, and
Ellie Kate, and to our loving God, who created them
and blessed us by placing them in our lives

Visit Tyndale online at www.tyndale.com.

TYNDALE, Tyndale's quill logo, *The One Year,* and *One Year* are registered trademarks of Tyndale House Publishers, Inc.

The One Year logo is a trademark of Tyndale House Publishers, Inc.

The One Year Impact for Living Men's Devotional: Daily Coaching for a Life of Significance

Copyright © 2016 by Scott Whitaker and Nathan Whitaker. All rights reserved.

Cover photograph of mountain copyright © fotoVoyager/iStockphoto. All rights reserved.

Designed by Jacqueline L. Nuñez

Published in association with Yates & Yates, LLP (www.yates2.com).

Unless otherwise indicated, all Scripture quotations are taken from the *Holy Bible*, New Living Translation, copyright © 1996, 2004, 2015 by Tyndale House Foundation. Used by permission of Tyndale House Publishers, Inc., Carol Stream, Illinois 60188. All rights reserved.

Scripture quotations marked KJV are taken from the *Holy Bible*, King James Version.

Scripture quotations marked NKJV are taken from the New King James Version,® copyright © 1982 by Thomas Nelson, Inc. Used by permission. All rights reserved.

Scripture quotations marked MSG are taken from *THE MESSAGE* by Eugene H. Peterson, copyright © 1993, 1994, 1995, 1996, 2000, 2001, 2002. Used by permission of NavPress Publishing Group. All rights reserved.

Scripture quotations marked NIV are taken from the Holy Bible, *New International Version,® NIV.®* Copyright © 1973, 1978, 1984, 2011 by Biblica, Inc.® (Some quotations may be from the earlier NIV edition, copyright © 1984.) Used by permission. All rights reserved worldwide.

Scripture quotations marked ESV are taken from *The Holy Bible*, English Standard Version® (ESV®), copyright © 2001 by Crossway, a publishing ministry of Good News Publishers. Used by permission. All rights reserved.

Scripture quotations marked NASB are taken from the New American Standard Bible,® copyright © 1960, 1962, 1963, 1968, 1971, 1972, 1973, 1975, 1977, 1995 by The Lockman Foundation. Used by permission.

ISBN 978-1-4143-7632-5

Printed in the United States of America

22   21   20   19   18   17   16
7   6   5   4   3   2   1

WHAT'S NEXT?

Can anything ever separate us from Christ's love? Does it mean he no longer loves us if we have trouble or calamity, or are persecuted, or hungry, or destitute, or in danger, or threatened with death? . . . No, despite all these things, overwhelming victory is ours through Christ, who loved us. **Romans 8:35, 37**

WHAT'S NEXT? It seems like an obvious question as we move into the new year.

There is a loftiness and fearlessness to the words *What's next?* They could almost be considered a dare: ready to fly beyond a week of subzero temperatures, the past year's disappointments, old anxieties, lingering fears, and ever-present doubt into a new day with its promise of opportunities, friendships, challenges, and uncertainty.

What's next? With blinding clarity the words stop you in your tracks.

It's a question we have too often turned away from. Or if we don't turn away from it, we ask it quietly, under our breath, and with a spirit of timidity, hoping no one will hear.

What's next?

Too much suspense is wrapped in whatever answer comes tumbling over the wall. What's next?

We remember when we asked it before, and we still remember some of the results. The disappointment and heartache of past results are still raw, too painful, and too recent to chance another foray into a world where failure seems to be the majority rule. But there were some good results also, and, well, here we stand ready to ask it again.

For you see, *what's next* is the only path from yesterday—through whatever is going on today—and into tomorrow. It's the only path from who we were—through who we are—to who we are meant to be.

As we march into a new year, maybe we should consider exactly who we are meant to be. Very simply and for all eternity, we are meant to be victorious children of God.

The apostle Paul had been beaten, shipwrecked, and jailed, and yet he had the audacity to ask, "What's next?" Or as Paul put it, "I am convinced that nothing can ever separate us from God's love. Neither death nor life, neither angels nor demons, neither our fears for today nor our worries about tomorrow—not even the powers of hell can separate us from God's love. No power in the sky above or in the earth below—indeed, nothing in all creation will ever be able to separate us from the love of God that is revealed in Christ Jesus our Lord" (Romans 8:38-39).

So where do we find the passion to stand in the sunrise of each new day and boldly ask the question, "What's next?" We find it in the assurance that as children of God, Christ has our future—all the way to and through eternity—in His hands.

IMPACT APPLICATION: What if we approached the "what's next?" in the rest of our lives, knowing that we are the victorious children of God?

JANUARY 2

IN THE TIME LEFT

Teach us to number our days aright, that we may gain a heart of wisdom. **Psalm 90:12**, NIV

IT'S HARD TO BELIEVE another year has passed. Last year was so full of stuff, it could have easily been counted as two. Not that I will.

Maybe you had one of those years also, where time flew by so fast you barely noticed the year was gone or had time to notice all the things you should have.

You know, all the things that really count and that put a smile on your face and warmth in your heart when your perspective is clear and not muddled by the worrisome stuff. Things like family, time with trusted friends, and perhaps even— or especially—regular quiet time with your Creator.

I was reading an old and favorite book of mine, *Growing Strong in the Seasons of Life* by Chuck Swindoll, and came across this story. It seems a young lady had the common problem a lot of college students face—low grades and no money. In any case, she was forced to let her parents know of her plight and was sure they would not understand. So she tried a unique approach with this letter:

> *Dear Mom and Dad,*
>
> *Just thought I'd drop you a note to clue you in on my plans. I've fallen in love with a guy named Jim. He quit high school after grade eleven to get married. About a year ago he got a divorce.*
>
> *We've been going steady for two months and plan to get married in the fall. Until then, I've decided to move into his apartment (I think I might be pregnant).*
>
> *At any rate, I dropped out of school last week.*

On the next page she came clean:

> *Mom and Dad, I just want you to know that everything I've written so far in this letter is false. NONE of it is true. But Mom and Dad, it IS true that I got a C in French and flunked math. It IS true that I'm going to need some more money for my tuition payments.*

I've got to believe her parents were okay with what really happened. It all depends on your perspective when the circumstances of life come barreling your way.

I suspect this year will move along just as quickly as the last.

But let me suggest a way to slow it down and fill it with more meaning: keep your perspective on the things that God tells us really matter.

 IMPACT APPLICATION: Today, tomorrow, and throughout this year, think about this—if this were the last year you had on earth, what would you fill it with?

JANUARY 3

KEEP RUNNING!

You take over. I'm about to die, my life an offering on God's altar. This is the only race worth running. I've run hard right to the finish, believed all the way. All that's left now is the shouting—God's applause! Depend on it, he's an honest judge. **2 Timothy 4:6-8,** MSG

AS THE MORNING UNFOLDS in all its radiant promise, the reality of another year of birthday celebrations—mine, my granddaughters', and other family members'—begins to settle deeper into my consciousness. Time seems to be flying by.

There will be many more such occasions, I have assured myself, though the pragmatic reality of the swift passing of time and remembering we are not promised tomorrow weighs a bit heavier on my heart. I tend to wonder what I might have missed and what else I need to be about. Already another year has gone by, with another about to do the same.

So what do we do when time seems to fly by faster than we are able to reach out and hold on to the fullness of each day that evaporates into tomorrow? What do we do when we realize that all our planning, running, celebrating, and living may end up short of the dreams and goals we have set in our hearts? What do we do when the hands on the clock not only won't stop but seem to be a blinding whir, spinning faster and faster with each passing day?

In the passage above from his letter to his beloved Timothy, Paul makes it very clear what the answer is—simply to keep running and live. "Run hard right to the finish," or as the New International Version puts it, continue to "[fight] the good fight" all the way with and to God's applause.

Feeling older than you ever thought you would? Not quite as spry as you envisioned? Children and grandchildren growing faster than you like to admit? Still hanging on to that passion to wrap your career around?

Time may seem to be flying by or just passing at the same pace as the day we were born. Yet it's not the time that has passed that matters but the time we have left. And the admonition of Scripture is clear: run hard to the finish. If plans fail, plan again. If we fall, get up and run again. Celebrate, and then celebrate again. Live, live, and live again, all the way to the finish.

My granddaughters turn another year older this year. Me too. I can't believe it. Time seems to be flying by. And the lesson we can take from that is this: keep running—all the way to the finish.

 IMPACT APPLICATION: It's a great finish we're heading toward, with God waiting and applauding! In the time line of your eternal life with Him, you've got a lot left. So act like it! Keep running. Keep running!

JANUARY 4

SOMEWHERE OUT THERE

"Interpreting dreams is God's business," Joseph replied. **Genesis 40:8**

I FIND MYSELF MARVELING at how quickly the calendar changes from one year to the next. I wonder if growing older has anything to do with it, or is it that being busier tends to blur the lines of each passing day, month, and year? Or maybe I'm just not paying much attention.

I wonder if this is the year I will do the things I have long felt I should do.

It was early in a brand-new year, and Lynda and I decided to underscore it by watching the movie *An American Tail*. It's an animated story about a mouse, Fievel, and his family who emigrate from Russia to America because they hear that there are no cats in America. Dreams of freedom from the tyranny of the chase for survival—fulfilled at last!

Early in the movie, during the voyage across the Atlantic, Fievel becomes separated from his family, and most of the rest of the movie follows Fievel through his efforts to reconnect with his family. One night, while looking out the window of his temporary tenement room at the full moon high in the sky above him and dreaming of finding his family once again, he realizes that they—wherever they are—might be looking up at that same moon at that very moment, and he sings, "Somewhere out there, if love can see us through / then we'll be together somewhere out there / out where dreams come true."

Maybe this is the year where those dreams become reality as we realize that . . .

Somewhere out there is the person you've always dreamed you would be.

Somewhere out there is a child dreaming dreams that may never come true, unless someone steps in to help.

Somewhere out there is an elderly person with only their memories to get them through the day.

Somewhere out there is all you have wanted to do in your life.

Joseph's words in the Scripture above should echo in our lives. God is the One who places dreams in our hearts, and He's the One who will lead us through the "somewhere out there" to our destination of those dreams and all who He created us to be.

Upon further reflection, I suppose the years aren't really going by any faster than before. Maybe it's just that the time that's left to us in this, our one moment of history, is becoming shorter.

Think about that for a moment—but not too long. There is too much to do!

IMPACT APPLICATION: May you feel God's arms around you today and throughout this year, and may you feel His gentle nudge toward becoming all He created you to be today.

A LIGHT IN THE DARKNESS

The people who walk in darkness will see a great light. For those who live in a land of deep darkness, a light will shine. **Isaiah 9:2**

I WONDER what it would have been like living in those days when people were depicted as walking in darkness.

One might wonder if the darkness of which the prophet spoke in Isaiah 9:2 was born out of despair, economic hardships, or oppression. Actually, though, the times about which the Scripture speaks—around 700–680 BC—were none of those but instead were fairly affluent times in which the people had experienced relative peace and prosperity. Isaiah himself had come from the side of affluence, was well educated, and had influence in all the right places.

Yet he depicted those times as times of darkness. And for good reason.

They were times when people had forgotten God, when idols and idolatry in many forms had taken over day-to-day living. They were times when people had what they wanted and then some and when temptations were assuaged in nearly every corner of their lives, times when comfort ruled and callousness set in. The times were marked by abuses of power, self-dealing, extortion, drunkenness, idleness, and corrupt government.

The people of the day had forsaken their God—the one true God—and had sought "refuge" in the things of the world. That is what the darkness looked like—a falling away from the guiding hand of God. Sound familiar? All too familiar.

Here we are today, more than two thousand years later, and I wonder if we are able to hear that call of the prophet Isaiah from across the ages. A call crying through the centuries about a Light that is coming again.

I wonder if we can hear it. I wonder if other things we are listening to will instead drown out its message of hope. I wonder what the voice is saying or to whom we are listening. Who do we hear speaking into our lives and the lives of our children and grandchildren? What are our television sets tuned to—for viewing by ourselves and our families? What do we let in through the "doors" of our homes and our hearts?

In the midst of all these competing voices of disillusionment, despair, false teachings, and destructive temptations, all trying to get our attention, the one voice we need to hear is still calling out to us. And we need to hear that one true voice from so long ago telling us once again about a Light that is coming. A Light that has and will again penetrate the darkness of our world and make all the difference in our lives. It is here.

IMPACT APPLICATION: The Light is here, always. Perhaps this year we, and those we love, will spend more time with the One the prophet calls out to us about—the great Light, the Light that is Christ.

JANUARY 6

YOUR SECRET PLACE

Those who live in the shelter of the Most High will find rest in the shadow of the Almighty. This I declare about the LORD: He alone is my refuge, my place of safety; he is my God, and I trust him. **Psalm 91:1-2**

LOOKING AT THE LANDSCAPE through double-pane windows from the warmth of a safe place where I am, I see a desolate picture. The mountains in winter. Snow pushed in piles along the side of the road, sustained for weeks by never-ending subzero temperatures. Barren tree limbs revealing places hidden throughout the rest of the year. Empty streets and shops. A quiet that casts doubt that there are seasons when it is different.

Moses faced it too. Substitute searing temperatures and blowing sands for the numbing cold and snow. Wandering around monotonously in the desert, leading a bunch of whining wimps complaining about how much longer they would have to brush the sand from someone else's sandals out of their teeth. Forty years following a plume of cloud during the day and fire at night. Forty years of feeling abandoned, disappointed, anxious, frustrated, alone, worried, and empty, waiting for greener grasses or, for that matter, any grass at all.

In his moments of frustration, doubt, anxiety, and worry, Moses returned to his secret place—to his God in whom he put all his trust—the safe place Moses sought and abided in through the valleys of searing temperatures and unending expanses of desert sand and in those times when he couldn't find his way.

How's it going for you today? Is any part of you sitting in a cold place or on a hot seat? Are you facing a seemingly never-ending expanse of desert or the isolation and sting of a frigid winter? Perhaps you are feeling the monotony of life and the seemingly never-ending reign of repetition. Same problems, heartaches, disappointments as before . . . or worse? Wondering whether tomorrow will bring the same—and feeling a bit left out of what the plan for your life should be? Perhaps you've forgotten that the next step in your valleys of discouragement could very well lead to the most encouraging view from the top of the mountain.

Let me suggest that you do what Moses did. Seek that secret place of the Most High. Abide under the shadow of the Almighty. Say to the Lord, "You are my refuge and my fortress; my God, in You I will trust."

 IMPACT APPLICATION: Whether today or tomorrow brings a great day or one of struggles, either way, return to that secret place, that place of refuge that will sustain and restore you, that will move you through moments of discouragement onto the peaks of impact.

A STILL SMALL VOICE

He went on alone into the wilderness, traveling all day. He sat down under a solitary broom tree and prayed that he might die. "I have had enough, LORD," he said. "Take my life, for I am no better than my ancestors who have already died." **1 Kings 19:4**

WE'VE ALL BEEN THERE—overwhelmed by despair, our purpose in life seemingly vanished.

Elijah understood these feelings well. During one of Israel's darkest hours of sin and separation from God, the people were encouraged to worship Baal (a false god). These "worship" times were often accompanied by drunken orgies and degrading rituals. Seeing the moral decline of the people, Elijah stepped forward with passion and a sense of purpose, pointing the people back to the God who had delivered them from so much already.

But King Ahab and his wife, Jezebel, had had enough of Elijah, and so they set about to have him killed. When Elijah got wind of their plan, he fled and eventually found himself under a broom tree in the wilderness. Depressed, not knowing which way to turn, he threw a full-blown pity party and attempted to cash in his life with God.

And God's response?

He sent an angel to care for Elijah, to comfort and encourage him. The angel brought him water and food and stayed with him until he was renewed. After the angel ministered to him, Elijah went to look for God. He needed help. He needed to know why he had done such great things for God yet was being hunted. And he wondered why God seemed not to be around.

But God showed up. He came to Elijah in a still, small voice.

And that's the way God is with us. His response is always calm, always providing comfort and peace.

So where do we look for that still, small voice of God when we feel as Elijah did, when we need comfort and direction? I'll bet we've all listened to the winds of dissension, objection, and criticism; submitted to the earthquakes of broken relationships or tragedy; or have been burned by the fires of doubt, which often follow us like heat-seeking missiles. Those are the voices of the world.

Instead, we'll find God's voice of assurance, direction, and peace in the quiet of our thoughts as we study His Word and offer prayers of concern and requests for guidance. We'll find it in the encouraging voices of loved ones and trusted friends—never far away and always ready to pick us up when we're down.

Listen for that still, small voice—it's there, always.

IMPACT APPLICATION: God sees us and stands with us in those difficult moments. Often His voice of calm guidance comes quietly to us in the voices of those we trust. God doesn't speak to us in a voice of doubt or criticism. When He speaks to us, we have a sense of peace—that's Him.

JANUARY 8

A FEW GOOD MEN

The only thing necessary for the triumph of evil is for good men to do nothing. **Attributed to Edmund Burke**

I HEARD EDMUND BURKE'S famous words again the other night, and they have swirled in the unused spaces of my brain since.

This morning I wondered as I posted the American flag if simply hanging our nation's symbol of all we stand for is enough to move me past the point of Burke's "doing nothing." After all, hanging the flag is making a statement of what I believe. I wondered if just identifying and commenting (or in some cases criticizing) what should be different in our world, our nation, our communities, and our individual lives is enough. I suspect not.

It takes more than thinking and believing to overcome evil. It requires doing something. Think about this for a moment:

- In your personal life, what *one thing* would you like to be different? What steps can you take to change that one thing?
- In our nation or in the world, what *one thing* would you like to see changed, fixed, or cured? What steps can you take—alone or perhaps mobilizing others to your cause—to change that one thing?
- Then finally—what are we doing about this? Are we "good men doing nothing"?

Just a few good men doing whatever they can to change the world around them—that was what Christ was looking for in His ministry on earth more than two thousand years ago. He started with twelve good men. I suspect He is still looking for good men today:

- Within the walls of our homes and hearts;
- On the streets where gangs roam and children are abused;
- In the midst of the poverty, disease, and despair we see on the evening news;
- Where genocide occurs because of the world's apathy;
- Wherever and whenever we find ourselves looking into the face of need.

"The only thing necessary for the triumph of evil is for good men to do nothing." What have you done today to improve our world?

 IMPACT APPLICATION: Opportunities to make an impact encircle us each and every day. Grab one of them, and do something to make this world a better place.

A LEGACY OF MESSAGES

Your life is an occasion. Rise to it! **Mr. Magorium, from** *Mr. Magorium's Wonder Emporium*

LATE ONE NIGHT a surgeon was awakened by another doctor calling to ask if he could come to the hospital to operate on a young boy because no one else in town could perform that surgery.

The surgeon, of course, agreed, quickly got dressed, and started toward the hospital. Several blocks down the street, while he was waiting for a traffic light to change, a desperate-looking man in a brown leather jacket, with a cap pulled down almost over his eyes, and holding a revolver suddenly opened the car door and demanded that the surgeon get out.

The surgeon pleaded with the man, "I've got to have the car! It's an emergency!" But the other man insisted he needed the car instead, jerked the surgeon out, and drove off, leaving the surgeon in the street.

By the time the surgeon arrived at the hospital, the other doctor was waiting at the curb to tell him the boy had died. The surgeon tried to explain the delay, and the other doctor said, "I know you tried to get here, and his parents know that too. They will want to speak to you."

The surgeon went into the waiting room to meet the dead boy's parents. The boy's mother sat crying, and beside her sat the boy's father, wearing a brown leather jacket and a cap pulled down almost over his eyes.

That man had shoved out of his life the only person who could have saved his son. And with that action he threw away his child's life.

Though our choices probably won't be as dramatic as in this story, every day we have the opportunity to change lives for the better or to shove those around us out of our lives—and the choices we make, whether we realize it or not, determine our legacy. And usually it's the overall cumulative effects of the smaller, everyday choices that have a profound impact on the lives of our children and others.

Our words, our demeanor, our response to adversity, and our priorities all repeatedly convey to our children and others around us our perception of their value. We send clear messages to them about how to deal with adversity, disappointment, and challenges—and in those messages we tell them whether their lives are a wonderful occasion to rise to. And most likely, our legacies will be determined by the way these others turn out.

Tell them, *show* them that their life is an occasion. Rise to it!

 IMPACT APPLICATION: Do you realize the immense impact you have on your children and other loved ones? Remind them of their value in everything you do for them.

JANUARY 10

FRIENDS IN A PASSING STORM

[God] comforts us in all our troubles so that we can comfort others. When they are troubled, we will be able to give them the same comfort God has given us. **2 Corinthians 1:4**

IT SEEMED LIKE ANY OTHER Saturday. I called a longtime friend—on the wedding day of the younger of his two daughters—to make sure he knew I was thinking of him and praying for him.

My friend's wife told me he was in the yard picking up the debris from a storm that had passed through the night before. I wasn't aware of this latest storm but knew he was probably dealing with a different "storm": the mixture of joy and the difficulty of letting go on this day of beginnings and endings in his family.

He and I have been accountability prayer partners, along with two other men, for more than thirty years, and together we have weathered, shared, and picked up the rubble from most of the storms in our lives, sweeping the landscape clean each time for the next day's arrival of the dawning sunshine, which always came.

We knew we never handled life alone. On any given Saturday. On any given day. We always knew we were never alone.

They're all around us. Family, friends, and others going through storms, trying their best to pick up the rubble that those storms tend to leave behind, trying to move on into tomorrow. Career changes, lack of a clear direction for the next step, uncertainty in tomorrow, broken relationships, illness, the loss of a loved one— storms that too often and for too long block our sight of the rainbow at the end of the rain. If we aren't careful, in the busyness of our own lives, we can neglect-fully pass others by who need someone to help with the debris. We may miss the moment to assure them they are not alone, that they are never alone.

It seemed like any other Saturday. They all do. But it turned out to be a special affirming moment. I recognized that in the same way I can and should be there for my friend in the midst of his storms, God is always there for me in the midst of mine.

I wonder if on any Saturday, on any given day, we truly understand that the One who was there when we were born and when our child was born, the One who knows whether we were rocked as a child, who knows what our childhood was like, and who was with us in our happiest moments and in our deepest disappointments, is always there in the storms of our lives, helping us to pick up the debris they leave behind.

IMPACT APPLICATION: In all the storms of our lives, we are never separated from the One who will never leave us. Use your platform today to help someone pick up the debris of a passing "storm."

A FLICK FOR LIFE

Let's not get tired of doing what is good. At just the right time we will reap a harvest of blessing if we don't give up. **Galatians 6:9**

YOU'VE BEEN THERE. Maybe you're there now. You're surrounded by voices of doubt or discouragement. Sometimes you want to just quit. That option recently crossed my mind.

Until God sent a reminder that He is still in control. And He did it, as He so often does, through one of my granddaughters. They were spending the night with my wife and me not too long ago, and while we were putting them to bed, our younger granddaughter, Ellie Kate, asked to say prayers for both herself and her older sister, Hannah.

I don't recall what it was now, but something was troubling me, and Ellie Kate must have sensed it. And so, amidst thanking God for a beautiful day, and for her sister, and for other things she was thankful for, she prayed, "And Jesus, if Satan is talking in Granddaddy's ear, please just flick him off his shoulder!"

There it is—the remedy for discouragement when you want to throw in the towel. Just flick Satan off your shoulder. Don't let him have a place to stand and whisper in your ear his message of doom, defeat, and discouragement. Instead, replace his messages with a message of encouragement, hope, and victory for whatever you're going through.

Legend has it that many years ago, a renowned pianist and composer was to perform in Philadelphia. It was the social highlight of the year, and men and women arrived dressed in their finest tuxedos and evening gowns. While the audience was milling in the aisles, a fidgety little boy wriggled free from his mother, climbed onto the stage, and began to play "Chopsticks." The crowd was furious and shouted for him to stop.

Offstage, the pianist heard the commotion, and he walked onstage behind the boy. Then he leaned over him at the piano and began to play the most beautiful melody around the tune the boy was playing. As he did, he whispered in that little boy's ear, "Don't stop; keep going. Don't quit; I'll stay right here by your side."

That's what the Master, Jesus Christ, is saying to each of us as we awaken to a brand-new day, weighed down at times with discouragement, disappointment, defeat, and uncertainty: "Don't stop, keep going. Don't quit, I'll stay right here by your side."

And He will.

If you find the voices of defeat and discouragement from Satan talking too loudly in your ear, take a lesson from a brilliant little girl's prayer, and "just flick him off your shoulder!"

It works.

 IMPACT APPLICATION: In the midst of the discouraging voices, listen for that still, small voice of God telling you to keep going and offering the promise that He'll stay right by your side. And He will.

JANUARY 12

BEGIN WITH THE FOUNDATION

Jesus told her, "I am the resurrection and the life. Anyone who believes in me will live, even after dying. . . . Do you believe this?"
John 11:25-26

IT'S ONE OF THOSE MORNINGS swirling with emotions amidst a confluence of internal and external struggles and all-too-distant hopes. Maybe it is the sobering reminder through a video I saw of the tragedy of September 11, 2001, when all the insanity and the reality of the existence of evil in the world was captured forever in one horrific morning.

And then a smile breaks through as I look at a photo of my elder granddaughter as it flashes onto my digital photo frame. In the photo she proudly wears her "Future President" T-shirt I bought her a few years earlier. Then another picture flashes on the screen, bringing another smile across my face. This time it is of my younger granddaughter—a few years ago—sitting contentedly on the kitchen floor eating from bags of chocolates she retrieved from the pantry nearby when no one was around to monitor her dietary selections.

The future belongs to those two precious girls and others like them—and at times I worry what it will look like. I wonder if we realize that the brushes and paints to determine the look of the canvas of the future—their future—have been entrusted into our hands.

So what, then, do we paint?

Standing with paintbrushes and paints in our hands before the blank canvases of our tomorrows—where do we look for the inspiration and guidance to paint the portrait for today and for the rest of our lives and for the futures of the generations to follow?

We find our hope in the resurrection. As the capstone to his explanation of Jesus' resurrection and what it means for believers, Paul writes, "My dear brothers and sisters, be strong and immovable. Always work enthusiastically for the Lord, for you know that nothing you do for the Lord is ever useless" (1 Corinthians 15:58). Because of the resurrection, we have hope that this world will be renewed. We know that the good work we do in the present will have value for ages to come—even eternally.

So where do we look for inspiration and guidance? We look to the Foundation of all the world. We look to the One who provides stability, clarity, truth, and hope.

Jesus says to each of us, "I am the resurrection and the life. Do you believe this?" Do you? Where do we begin? Begin there.

 IMPACT APPLICATION: There will be days when life piles up around you and living with purpose seems daunting. Place your trust on the unshakable foundation of Christ, and He will help you to rise above it all.

ALL THE POSSIBILITIES

The thief's purpose is to steal and kill and destroy. My purpose is to give them a rich and satisfying life. **John 10:10**

IT'S OVERCAST OUTSIDE my window, and my bride, Lynda, has just driven off with our two granddaughters, Hannah and Ellie Kate, to return them to their home. The gray cloud cover has pretty well blocked the morning sunshine, even though recollections from my better moments remind me that somewhere up there the sun is waiting to break through into my day.

But not now. I'm having trouble imagining that this morning.

Each night our granddaughters were with us was dedicated to watching a movie produced by Walden Media. Positions and blankets on the couch and overstuffed chairs were secured, while trays full of drinks, "fudge-stickles" (Ellie's favorite), chocolate ice cream (Hannah's choice), and Granddaddy's world-famous popcorn (everybody's favorite) were spread out for all to enjoy. Last night was the second viewing of *Bridge to Terabithia*.

One of our favorite songs from the movie—a movie that all the world should see—offers this reminder: "You've got to keep your mind wide open, all the possibilities."

Bridge to Terabithia is a movie of hope, reminding us of the wonder and power of imagination and the warm, safe place of true friendship. It's a movie for "children of all ages," for all the days before them. And as much as there is in the movie—in scene after scene and message after message—that will offer encouragement for the living of each day, I want to mention again the line from the movie's song for you to cling to in all the days ahead:

"You've got to keep your mind wide open, all the possibilities."

There it is. The key to open the door to the rest of your life. It's the bridge to the abundant life Christ speaks of in the Scripture verse above. An abundance of life in all the possibilities before us, which is the life God intended for us to live each day. A life of depth and substance for today, and a life that is long and lasting and sustained not just for today but throughout eternity.

It's a life that's not just as good as it can be—or as wonderful as we can imagine—but it's an abundance of life even *beyond* anything that we can imagine!

Keep your mind wide open—to all the possibilities.

IMPACT APPLICATION: When was the last time that you were wide open to all the possibilities that lay before you? And not just the ones you can think of, but all of the possibilities that may not have crossed your mind yet? Go ahead. Cross the bridge. Your impact just may be on the other side.

JANUARY 14

DECISIONS AND PRIORITIES

My help comes from the LORD, who made heaven and earth! He will not let you stumble; the one who watches over you will not slumber.
Psalm 121:2-3

I'LL NEVER FORGET the moment when a number of friends and professional acquaintances were twisting my arm to run for the open circuit court judge seat in our district. It had been a position of service I had always thought I would occupy one day. From my early years after graduating from law school, I always felt it was a position I would enjoy and do well in. The demands on my time and lack of flexibility would not be optimal, though I had never shied away from those before.

So I decided to consider it further, and I gathered more information to help me decide whether it was the right time to seek to serve in that position. *Why not?* I figured.

I was also coaching my son Nathan's high school baseball team, and his mom and I were both involved in helping with various high school activities. As a circuit judge, of course, all of that would change. Time in the courtroom presiding over various cases would not permit me to coach his team, and I would also miss being able to simply attend many of his games and other activities. Nathan and I had always spent a lot of time together, and that would be significantly altered.

All that led to a period of uncertainty as to what was the right course for me to pursue.

It's in those times between uncertainty and certainty—of not understanding and then finally comprehending—that God always appears, if we'll just look around. As the psalmist points out in Psalm 121, the guidance for those decisions comes from the wisdom of our God, who never slumbers and will never allow us to stumble under His leadership.

As I drove home from a meeting about that judgeship, I realized that God's priorities for my life were clear—the time with my son had to prevail over an advancement of my own career. Instantly, in a divine moment, a sense of peace overcame me as the decision I had struggled with for weeks became clear.

I was honored that many thought I should serve as a judge, but that decision would be a clear departure from the priorities of my life—the values Lynda and I held dear—and the meaningful life I would experience by continuing to follow those priorities I knew were grounded in the absolute truth of God's Word and wisdom.

What values and priorities are guiding your decisions today? Look to the Lord, "who made heaven and earth," for guidance.

 IMPACT APPLICATION: Maybe you're at a juncture in the road and are not sure which way to go. Let me suggest that you rephrase the issue in terms of the values and priorities God has called you to.

ANGELS AND INNOCENCE

You, O LORD, are a shield around me; you are my glory, the one who holds my head high. I cried out to the LORD, and he answered me from his holy mountain. **Psalm 3:3-4**

I'M SURE IT WON'T TAKE you by surprise when I suggest that little children seem to have an innate sense about and trust in all things and values that are innocent and eternal. Yet their perceptions change as they grow, as they begin to listen to and notice everything else in the changing world around them. We can only hope that what they hear and see are things that honor and glorify the God who created them.

The other night my granddaughter Ellie Kate demonstrated that sense of innocence and trust in the eternal once again.

We had just spent another day helping my son and his family unpack boxes as part of their move to Gainesville, Florida. My wife, "Mimi," as our granddaughters call her, had just given Ellie Kate her bath, and Ellie Kate was now working her way toward bed—or, from her vantage point, employing as many delaying tactics as possible to forestall that inevitability.

As part of that bedtime process, I went into her bedroom to say goodnight, to get lots of hugs and kisses, and to pray for her. As part of my prayers for both granddaughters, I always pray that God would keep angels around them to protect them and care for them. They have heard me pray that for as long as they have lived.

As I finished praying—calling forth angels and all—Ellie Kate looked up at me, and with a confidence born out of security, love, protection, and perhaps even through a direct line to God, she offered these words of assurance to me: "Gran, don't worry about me. Take care of yourself. I have angels around me."

She believes it. Our elder granddaughter, Hannah, believes it. It's what they've heard over and over from me, Mimi, and their parents and have now internalized in their approach to life. Do we still believe in angels and other things of God? Or did there perhaps come a time when we stopped believing in the promises, assurances, and counsel of a God who will surround us with angels to protect us? Could our unbelief have begun to creep in when we unwittingly or intentionally chose the ways of the world over God's ways?

It might be that we need to look to the littlest of His creations all around us to help us reclaim a sense of innocence, of eternal values, and of a change in our lives, a change that will not only remind us of His presence with us but which will also glorify Him.

 IMPACT APPLICATION: Reclaim the innocence and trust in the eternal that you had in your childhood— He is still the same today as He was then.

JANUARY 16

BROADER THEMES
OF LIGHT

The light shines in the darkness, and the darkness can never extinguish it. **John 1:5**

AS I SIT IN MY OFFICE early this morning, the room is dark, except for the glow from my laptop's screen. No light anywhere.

I know from experience that the darkness will be lifted before too long as the sun rises across the landscape. But right now, I'm haunted by the vision of the "dark rooms" around the world that will never see light. Places where millions sit waiting. "Crooked places" where the sunrise will bring no light for these people, no change to straighten them, no hope—where it would seem that the glory of the Lord has yet to be revealed.

I suspect that even on the day Martin Luther King Jr. rose to render his "I Have a Dream" speech from the steps of the Lincoln Memorial in Washington, DC, he experienced his own sunrise, perhaps prodding him to believe anew in the possibilities of change, in the possibilities of hope. I suspect that light filled that day for him, and the next, and most of the rest of his days. And I suspect that the light he experienced that morning was sufficient to allow him to journey beyond any self-centered places that would have limited his life and calling.

Instead, Dr. King's life reflected a broader theme than self. It reflected empathy, passion, and compassion for those who continued to sit in darkness long after the sun had risen on the rest of the world. It reflected a continuing belief in the better chapters of mankind's history, lifting the least, the lost, the left behind, and the forgotten among us to reveal the sunshine of a brand-new day.

And even though Martin Luther King Jr. experienced opposition, hatred, and abuse along his journey to bring light to the "dark rooms" of those lives around the communities, slums, tenements, churches, streets, and back alleys of this country and the world, he continued to embrace—and never allowed himself to be surprised by—the possibilities that could flow from the hearts of people who were willing to step out of their own self-centered lives. He knew that stepping out would penetrate the darkness and make a difference in the lives of those isolated in the "dark rooms" of all their days.

 IMPACT APPLICATION: I pray that you and I are never surprised by the hearts of people willing to reach for the broader themes of their lives. The themes our Creator envisioned we would live out when He formed us. The themes that will bring light to the "dark rooms" of the lives around us, in this country, and the world.

JANUARY 17

ABOVE THE CLOUDS

Come close to God, and God will come close to you. **James 4:8**

THE SCORE WAS KNOTTED at zero in the fifth inning of the baseball game, pitting our all-star players from North Florida against those from a team in Central Florida. The winner of the game would play the next day for the right to go to the State of Florida Pony League championships. I was doing my best to coach them toward that goal.

With my focus on the game and on each pitch, I never saw the clouds forming high in the sky behind the backstop.

But he did. Of course.

He was our spectacular center fielder with an always unpredictable approach to life. As I watched a routine fly ball heading toward him, I realized he wasn't moving toward the ball. He was looking at the clouds, oblivious to what was happening in the game.

From the dugout, I screamed his name as the ball fell at his feet. The other team scored. When our team came off the field at the end of the inning, I asked him what happened.

"Coach," he said, while pointing to the clouds. "Don't those clouds look like a *huge* pinball game?" I told him to get ready, doing my best to hide a smile.

We clawed our way back into the game to win and then played well enough—with no more distractions—to win the next day to go to the state championships. Our center fielder played well and was a key component to our success.

But he hasn't seen many good days since that game, making some choices that got him on the wrong roads for a time, and he has been clawing his way back into the life he was meant to live ever since.

Others and I will be there to help as he does. But the One who will help that young man the most is the One we all need to draw nearer to forever. He is the same One available to each of us as we claw our way back into the life we are meant to live. The same One who will walk with us, listen to us, laugh with us, cry with us, heal our broken hearts and lives, and lift us to the glorious sunshine of all the promise and potential Christ places in our lives.

Look up. You may not see a huge pinball or video game forming in the clouds, but you will always see Him, sense His presence, and be able to touch His face smiling down upon you, as He draws you closer to His precious side.

Look up.

 IMPACT APPLICATION: You will have successes and failures, but always remember to look up. And when those you influence need a reminder, help them to look up as well.

JANUARY 18

ALWAYS THERE

Always be joyful. Never stop praying. Be thankful in all circumstances.
1 Thessalonians 5:16-18

THE APOSTLE PAUL wrote the verses for today. This is the same guy who was imprisoned regularly, lashed five times, beaten with rods three times, stoned, shipwrecked three times, constantly on the move, in danger from bandits or friends who betrayed him, and was always hungry, thirsty, and sleep deprived.

And Paul's advice to us: "Always be joyful. Never stop praying. Be thankful in all circumstances."

The man obviously had a few screws loose.

Why would we listen to a guy who went through all of that and was probably writing out of exhaustion, dehydration, blurred thinking, and anger and who was an obvious candidate for long-term psychological counseling?

A hurricane heads toward Florida. A tornado whacks the Midwest. You've lost a job. A young friend dies unexpectedly. Your boss continues to prove the power of his ego. You anxiously await the doctor's word on whether he removed all the cancer or if it has migrated to other areas. Your parents are aging and changing right before your eyes. Your children are beginning to attend schools where guns are found in lockers. Your wife has just told you she is leaving you. Your children are on a mission trip in a dangerous part of the world.

In the midst of life's shipwrecks, we discover that our brains are not big enough, our arms are not strong enough, and our reach isn't long enough to control what we are facing.

And Paul says: "Always be joyful. Never stop praying. Be thankful in all circumstances."

Ugh! That's it? Paul is either a lunatic or delusional! There has to be something else we can do, someone else we can listen to, and somewhere else we can find relief.

But there it is again, in the midst of whatever we face: "Always be joyful. Never stop praying. Be thankful in all circumstances."

Why? Because God has never left us. Whatever we are going through, God is still at work. God still sees us. He still cares. He still controls eternity. He still walks beside us, behind us, before us, and carries us when we need to be carried.

It may be hard to admit that our brains are not big enough, nor our arms strong enough, nor our reach long enough to control what we or our loved ones are facing. And yet God, through Paul, tells us: "Always be joyful. Never stop praying. Be thankful in all circumstances."

When we remember the One we're looking to, we realize that He is more than enough—for today and all eternity.

IMPACT APPLICATION: The apostle Paul was able to maintain an enduring passion to build God's Kingdom despite great suffering and persecution. I suppose it's ultimately a matter of trust—a trust in the God who created you and me and those we love, a trust in the God who is always there.

CLIMBING WITH HOPE

The optimist fell ten stories, And at each window bar
He shouted to the folks inside, "Doing all right so far!"
Unknown

SHE HADN'T ANNOUNCED her plan to scale the mountain. If she had, I would have at least rushed to her side to provide a human safety net for the climb.

As the moment began to unfold, I wasn't really watching my then three-year-old granddaughter Ellie Kate as she moved some of her reading books with her foot from the lower level of the built-in media center in her family room. With other folks around, I was mildly aware of where she was but was busy with something else. Then I saw her. Ellie Kate was now one good leg up from the top of the media center and—before I or anyone else could reach her—was sitting on top of it, grinning from ear to ear.

I suppose it was a naïveté to the dangers of falling and splitting her head wide open on the tile floor below, combined with the adventure of seeing whatever was on top of the media center, along with an optimistic confidence in her three-year-old ability that led her to believe she could accomplish whatever she purposed to do.

Not that I want her to engage in such perilous endeavors. But if such an approach to life—exemplified in the littlest miracles who walk among us—could be bottled, I wonder what difference it would make in our approach to each day and to dealing with the perils and uncertainties that we know, from too many years of experience, lay ahead. Ellie Kate taught me again what it means to live with purpose.

"All right so far, Gran!" Worry wasn't a part of the tenor of her voice.

Think about that for a minute. Here we are claiming to believe in the everlasting Hope of all the world—Jesus Christ—and many of us live our lives under a cloud of worry. In the midst of whatever we face, isn't God still on the throne? Isn't He standing with us as the doctor gives us the chilling news that it's cancer? Isn't He still standing next to us as we say our good-byes to loved ones in the cemetery? Isn't He still waiting for us in the rest of today and all of our tomorrows? Isn't He with that crazy optimist from today's quote, falling ten stories? Wasn't He with Ellie Kate as she climbed that media center? And wouldn't He still have been with her had she fallen?

The Hope of the risen Christ.

The Hope from the God who is still on the throne.

The Hope that holds us, walks with us, and will catch us in the midst of all the stuff of our days.

You can climb anything with that.

 IMPACT APPLICATION: Fully embracing the hope that is ours through Jesus Christ will dispel fear and allow us to embrace our God-given purpose in life. Happy climbing!

NEVER DOUBT—
CHANGE THE WORLD

Never doubt that a small group of thoughtful, committed citizens
can change the world; indeed, it's the only thing that ever has.
Margaret Mead

WHAT ONE THING in your life do you want to change?

If his answer was related to golf, I'm sure Bubba Watson, the 2012 Masters champion, would not change much about his final round of the tournament, winning on the second playoff hole after a nearly miraculous shot from the woods to within twenty feet of the hole on the tenth green.

But maybe he would have his bride, Angie, there with him, along with their newly adopted son, Caleb—instead of their staying home. But there was a good reason for why they weren't at the tournament. It was just two weeks earlier that this couple changed Caleb's life forever. For Bubba and Angie, adopting him was something well beyond playing in or even winning golf tournaments.

Tony and Lauren Dungy, when asked why they adopt children—they now have adopted seven—respond, "Because we can." I suspect that Bubba and Angie Watson might say something similar. There are things in life that are so much more substantive and meaningful than winning trophies, building résumés, earning money, and acquiring things. Tony and Lauren Dungy are the kind of folks who understand that.

Okay, you've had some time to think about the question I asked as we began. So what is your answer to the question, What one thing in your life do you want to change?

While you're thinking some more about that, here's another question: What one thing *in the world* do you want to see changed?

Some things that come to mind are:

- Eliminating world hunger, poverty, and genocide. But that's three things.
- Eliminating AIDS and homelessness. Two things.
- Eliminating human trafficking. One thing.
- Developing further adoption alternatives for children and new mothers.

Are these too big to tackle at the moment? Then what can each of us do now? What about some things like teaching a young child to read? Or taking an underprivileged child to lunch and the museum? Or helping a homeless person find a job? Or spending an afternoon conversing with an elderly friend?

But I'm getting ahead of you. These are questions for you to find your own answers to. I won't make any more suggestions.

What are your answers? And what are you going to do about those questions? And more important, what are you going to do about your answers?

 IMPACT APPLICATION: Let me suggest that *today* you write down the answers to these questions, and then begin to act on those answers by doing whatever it takes to effect the change you want to see.

EXPECT A MIRACLE

Jesus traveled throughout the region of Galilee, teaching in the synagogues and announcing the Good News about the Kingdom. And he healed every kind of disease and illness. **Matthew 4:23**

HOW WAS LAST WEEK FOR YOU? Anything special happen in your family? Any miracles? Did you even notice? Or in the midst of your busyness, would you have even had a chance to notice any?

Reflect with me on these moments in history:

- Creation (Genesis 1–2)
- The burning bush (Exodus 3)
- The parting of the Red Sea (Exodus 14:21-31)
- Balaam's donkey speaks (Numbers 22:21-35)
- Daniel saved in the lion's den (Daniel 6:16-23)
- Jesus heals a man with leprosy (Matthew 8:1-4)
- Jesus feeds 5,000 (Matthew 14:15-21)
- Jesus calms a storm (Mark 4:37-41)
- Jesus walks on water (John 6:19-21)
- Lazarus returns to life (John 11:1-44)
- The Resurrection (John 21:1-14)

There are hundreds more miracles from the Bible that must have astonished those present—and that should astonish us today.

Or have we become complacent? Do we believe that God is still performing miracles? Or do we simply believe that those listed above, and hundreds more, are biblical miracles, and life today is controlled by the laws of nature, science, and man?

The probability is slim to none that we will ever notice God's miracles if we don't believe that God is still in the "miracle business." But He is.

When was the last time you held a newborn baby and noticed the fingers and toes, the formation of his or her legs and arms, and imagined the synchronization of internal organs working to sustain and advance life?

Do you remember a time when you weren't sure where your next job would come from—and then it came? Do you remember how sick your child was, and then she was well? How about the time you lost a loved one—and family and friends were there to carry you into tomorrow?

They're all around us—God's miracles—both large and small. His blessings, specifically for us, demonstrate His faithfulness and activity in our lives and within the world around us. How many did you notice last week?

Perhaps last week set the record for the number of miracles that occurred in our lives. But if you're anything like me—you missed many of them.

Let's not let that happen this week. I have word, from a reliable source, that the week unfolding before us is destined to be another record-setting week for the number of God's miracles that will take place in our lives.

IMPACT APPLICATION: As you go about your day, expect a miracle—and then get ready.

JANUARY 22

HANNAH'S WORLD

God looked over all he had made, and he saw that it was very good!
Genesis 1:31

GOD'S DECISIONS. God's way. God's world. Not ours.

It's an always-present tension in a never-ending learning process. We must choose to live in God's world or ours, to follow God's way or ours, and to choose God's plan or ours.

A few years ago Lynda and I attended an annual event at our granddaughter Hannah's school called Spring Fling. Part of Spring Fling included a gallery of students' paintings and other forms of art displayed on the walls throughout the school building. One of Hannah's paintings depicted the famous London Bridge spanning majestically across the Thames River. And there, breaking through the surface of the river in front of one of the bridge's support towers, swam a dolphin at play. In the river. In London, England . . . in Hannah's World.

It's a wonderful place to live, Hannah's World. There are a myriad of other examples to support that assertion, not the least of which are the hugs, kisses, laughter, and smiles always readily available for her Gran and Mimi.

Yet early the next morning, I saw another world through an outreach for mothers that our Kiwanis Club sponsors each year. As my eyes followed the moms and hundreds of little boys and girls who attended that morning, I couldn't help but think that their worlds might be difficult worlds. They might experience worlds that would not seem to be part of God's original plan for their lives and that certainly would not be depicted in the world Hannah imagines. But here's the good news. The God who painted all of creation keeps reaching down and reaching out, knocking on our doors and slipping little love notes to us, calling to us—to do life His way. And maybe He calls us to help those who live in what might be some of those difficult worlds.

"God looked over all he had made, and he saw that it was very good!"

There are many mornings when I think God's world must be a lot like Hannah's World—a wonderful place for us to live. A world of dolphins swimming in rivers, of children of all ages—you, me, Hannah, and those little boys and girls—dreaming and reaching for all they were meant to be as we help lift their precious lives to all they can be.

IMPACT APPLICATION: God's world is depicted in a painting of lives touching lives, of lives lifting lives. That's His way. It's about doing all you can do, with all He has given you, to impact the world for Him and His children through the platform you have been given. It's a world where we embrace all that He intended for us to be and help others to do the same, settling for no less until our last breath.

A BIGGER PICTURE

God is our refuge and strength, always ready to help in times of trouble. So we will not fear when earthquakes come and the mountains crumble into the sea. Let the oceans roar and foam. Let the mountains tremble as the waters surge! . . . Be still, and know that I am God! I will be honored by every nation. I will be honored throughout the world. **Psalm 46:1-3, 10**

THE TEMPORAL SIDE of my spirit—the side that feels better when I think I have control over the world around me—suspects that the psalmist was sitting in a setting similar to the calm, blue sky pictured outside my window. Even I could write the words of Psalm 46 in that setting. Or could I?

I wonder what he was really going through when he was inspired to write those words. I wonder if he had just heard the oft-used phrase of today from the local news pundits and prophets of his day, as they looked at the picture before them: "Conditions are beginning to deteriorate."

Amidst the helplessness and frustration that build inside me as I realize I am powerless to do anything to stop a storm or fix a condition—having absolutely no control—the psalmist suggests that I should stop and take a deep breath and a long, loving look at the God who is above everything. That I should focus on seeing a bigger picture.

Really.

In our better moments, we know that the eternal picture—which our relationship with Christ assures us of—is the picture we will eventually see. It's that big picture of our lives in the scheme of eternity. What we don't often take away from the psalmist's words is the truth: that the big picture is now, in the center of every one of our storms that can be characterized by, "Conditions are beginning to deteriorate."

One moment all seems under control, and the next, the collection agency calls. After a hard day at the office, you go home to what you hope is some relief and hear your wife say she can't live like this anymore. The phone rings; there's been an accident. The doctor does her best to wrap cotton around the words that someone you can't live without isn't going to make it.

Yet through it all the psalmist reminds us that God remains a safe place to hide, ready to help when we need Him. That's the big picture. God remains that safe place, that place of refuge and strength—forever.

 IMPACT APPLICATION: In the big picture of eternity, the psalmist reminds us that conditions are fine. God is there not only to comfort us but to help us, to guide us, to lift and encourage us to a better way and a better day. It's all part of His bigger picture.

JANUARY 24

"PRESS ON" FAITH

Faith shows the reality of what we hope for; it is the evidence of things we cannot see. **Hebrews 11:1**

THE WINDS GUSTED through a bright and cloudless day as I awoke. My grand-daughter was still asleep on the trundle bed next to her normal bed, where I had been sleeping. That simple morning scene seemed like another of the many godly reminders of the transforming winds of hope that blow away the worries of our lives.

Paul's description of his life in Christ always seems an appropriate follow-up to the verse from the writer of Hebrews above. Paul, a man who had endured much for the hope in his heart, shares this for the start of all of our mornings:

"Forgetting what is behind and straining toward what is ahead, I press on toward the goal to win the prize for which God has called me heavenward in Christ Jesus" (Philippians 3:13-14, NIV).

Do we have that kind of faith—even though we can't see what is coming around the bend of our tomorrows? Do we have a faith that causes us to "press on" in the face of disappointments, setbacks, and heartaches by continuing to embrace what we hope for? A faith that causes us to focus on the goal God has called us to with a certainty that says, "Thy will be done"?

Do we have a faith that causes us to press on in the face of doubt and doubters, a bare-bones budget, and the hope that the vision God laid before us was really His and not ours?

Do we have the kind of faith that causes us to press on, as one of our Impact for Living speakers does, to find a cure for the debilitating disease of cystic fibrosis?

Do we have the kind of faith that causes a father and mother entrusted with two precious sons with autism to press on by beginning an outreach to families in similar situations, sharing God's hope with those families?

I don't know what you're facing as the day unfolds before you. Perhaps you've lost a job, or a family member is seriously ill, or a relationship has taken an unexpected detour, or you just don't seem to know what the rest of your days should look like. Embrace the faith the writer of Hebrews calls us to.

It's a faith that causes us to press on in the face of all that is before us, all that tries to throw us off course, the distractions of doubt and criticism, and the heartaches, failures, and disappointments that will surely litter the path along our way.

It's a faith that will carry us through all of our days and into the hope of all our tomorrows.

IMPACT APPLICATION: It's faith that blows through our lives with the fresh winds of hope when we least expect it, reminding us that God is still in charge, has never left us, and still has much for us to do—for Him and for others.

ALIVE AND LIVING

"I know the plans I have for you," says the LORD. "They are plans for good and not for disaster, to give you a future and a hope."
Jeremiah 29:11

I DON'T KNOW THEM ALL—the faces. They are the images of face after face, some seen, some imagined through the years, and some still yet to be seen, racing through the windows of my mind.

Even though they are now beginning to fade, I can still see them—the faces of those who are alive but have stopped living.

I've seen those faces before when a loved one is lost or a relationship has ended. In their grief, those who remained stopped living. I've seen them when a career was thought to be thrown off track or became less than it was hoped to be during the climb up the ladder. You've seen it too. You and I have both seen it in the faces of too many "retired" folks—deciding simply to grow older, sink into their memories, and wait for that first step into eternity.

Still alive but not living.

And then I remember my granddaughter's words: "Tell me a story."

The story I would tell her was often about a little girl from Florida who grew up to be whatever and whoever she wanted to be. This was a wonderfully created child who was encouraged to imagine and strive for whatever her heart desired—whether a blank paper to be filled with brushstrokes of watercolors, an empty floor surrounded by building blocks, a dark night full of fireflies, a bedroom of stuffed furry friends, or a future full of promises.

The girl in the story was a beloved, gifted, passionate, and significant child—not just of parents of flesh and blood, but a precious child of the living God. She was someone just like you and like me. Someone who was encouraged and loved by a God who created her for a higher purpose—for significant, passionate living every day of her life with every breath she took.

More than about the girl, this story is about God—the God who created us not just to be alive, but to *live*.

The same God who created us for hope and a future. The same God whose heart aches when He sees those same faces I did. Faces that have stopped short in living the life they were meant to live. Lives that were created by God with the intention for them to soar with Him into all that life has to offer, not just to waddle through their day-to-day routines or disappointments, accepting less than He created them to be.

Still alive but not living? No more!

IMPACT APPLICATION: Abide in Him, rest in Him, follow Him, and live in and with the God who created you full of potential for impact and hope. And while you're at it, embrace and claim His promises for your life for the rest of your life.

JANUARY 26

BEST DAY OF MY LIFE

Tell your children about it in the years to come, and let your children tell their children. Pass the story down from generation to generation.
Joel 1:3

"YOU'RE SOMETHING, KID."

The words spewed forth in a choking torrent of tears. He had rushed the eighteenth green after the final putt to celebrate the moment with his son. But the best Kenny McDowell could do to describe how he was feeling was to bear-hug his son's neck while they sobbed on each other's shoulders.

It was enough. His son got it.

Kenny's son, Graeme McDowell, a thirty-year-old professional golfer from Northern Ireland, had just become the first golfer from the United Kingdom in forty years to win the United States Open. He scaled the mountain of the 110th U.S. Open on the famed Pebble Beach Golf Links with an even par effort over four days and seventy-two holes and by holding off some of the world's best golfers lurking just behind. He did it while a proud dad watched from the gallery on Father's Day during his first visit to Pebble Beach.

Between individuals, it's the most powerful molding influence in life—that of the relationship between a father and his child. And sadly, today it's absent in too many homes. Men often allow personal painful memories to color and overshadow those memories of joy and affirmation lying just beneath the surface.

I am reminded of a story I read in *Guideposts* more than thirty years ago. My son, Nathan, was nine at the time, and after dropping him off at school, I found myself still unable to penetrate the clouds that covered my attitude that morning—for no reason that I could identify. As I was about to drive from his school, the pages opened on the seat next to me to reveal the story of a successful businessman who finally found time from his busy schedule to take his twelve-year-old son fishing. An overachiever, this man considered leisure an extravagance. After a long day spent catching nothing, the pair returned home.

"Waste of time," the man grumbled to his wife that night as they got ready for bed. "Didn't catch a thing all day—waste of time." His wife handed him a small book, which his son had showed her earlier when she was putting him to bed, and said, "Maybe you should look at this." It was his son's diary, and in it his son had written, "Best day of my life. Went fishing with my dad."

It changed more than the man's mind. It changed the man.

And for me that day, it cleared the clouds and pointed me once again toward the important things in life.

IMPACT APPLICATION: All father-child relationships are different. Many are full of joy, nurturing, and wonderful memories; others have experienced heartache, neglect, and disappointment. Starting today, make yours the way God intended it to be.

WHAT MORE DO WE NEED?

Give all your worries and cares to God, for he cares about you.
1 Peter 5:7

IT'S NEARLY SUPER BOWL TIME again, and I'm sure anxiety is building for the owners, players, fans, and coaches. Anxiety occurs every day, with everyone, but it seems magnified for us all to see at certain times and in certain settings, especially in the world of sports. Worry, anxiety, living up to expectations, feeling at times that it is all about you and that God is nowhere to be found. We really do want to believe the promises of today's Scripture, but then all too often we feel that we still have to win.

When we win, we tend to believe that promise of Scripture a bit more. And if we don't win, then too often in our own eyes—and perhaps in the eyes of others—we see ourselves as less valuable and less important. And it happens every day in the midst of our struggles, uncertainty, failures, and losses, feeling that we are all alone and that no one cares—not our family, not our friends, not even God.

But God does care. And He is there to help us, to comfort us, to pick us up and strengthen us, and to send us out again—with Him. In our wins, our successes and joys, our losses, our failures, our uncertainty and heartaches, He is there; and He does care.

It reminds me of a story I heard of a man who lived by a river. One day it began to rain, and the rain continued day after day. After a number of days of steady rain, the man heard a radio report that the river was going to rise higher than ever and flood the town. The report went on to say that all the residents of the town should evacuate their homes.

But the man said to himself, *God loves me. God will save me.* And he stayed in his home.

Later, a rowboat and then a helicopter came along offering to rescue the man.

But the man shouted back each time, "God loves me! God will save me!" And both times he stayed.

The town flooded, and the man drowned. When he stood at the gates of heaven, he saw Peter and demanded an audience with God—which was granted.

"Lord," he said, "I thought you loved me. Why did you let this happen to me?"

God said, "I sent you a radio report, a guy in a rowboat, and a helicopter. What in the world are you doing here?"

God consistently cares for you—look for Him; He's all around you.

 IMPACT APPLICATION: In all the circumstances of our lives, God has continually been there—sending and providing help in our times of trouble and concern. Just look around, and you'll find Him—everywhere.

A HEALING RESPONSE

He heals the brokenhearted and bandages their wounds. **Psalm 147:3**

HER DADDY WAS AWAY, so Ellie Kate talked to him by phone.

"What's the matter, sweetie?" Nathan's words were gentle and comforting.

"Ellie is crying," she sobbed through the obvious.

"I'm sorry." His words gently spread relief over her soul, calming her pain. He didn't criticize or suggest that crying wouldn't help. He didn't label her with negative words or nick her self-esteem with a careless word.

And on the phone, Nathan recognized Ellie Kate as a wonderful creation of God. Nathan is that way with both of his girls. He looks in the short term into their hearts and in the long term into their futures that God has planned for them. He is always looking to brush a positive countenance on their faces with understanding and love, rather than covering them with criticism, defeat, or judgment.

As he and Ellie Kate continued to speak, he didn't suggest that she shouldn't feel this way. He simply listened and tried to paint a brighter picture for her day. But whether or not she saw it at the time, he accepted where she was and held her heart tenderly with his carefully chosen words. And after a while, her sadness thawed. That's good parenting, which results in healing. It takes more time and energy to heal than to criticize the way we may have been taught, and in the absence of a commitment to change or a strike of divine intervention, we will pass those critical traits on to our children and others.

While the long-term impact of a healer's approach is much more rewarding, positive, and productive—both for the one needing healing and for the healer—the interesting thing is that a healer's approach is also the example of our heavenly Father.

We've all needed gentle relief and a healing and understanding heart. And we've all had opportunities to be the ones dispensing healing or messing it up as we tried. The times of pain in our own lives have been many—the disappointments, falling short as a parent or a child, failures, or loss of a loved one. Our clothes don't fit, the food doesn't taste right, we've run short of funds, loneliness is never ending, real friends are absent, and addictions can become all too consuming.

The moments needing a healing response for all of us have been all too real and too regular in the journey of our lives—at any age. But surrendered to Him, each and every one of us will be held in His strong, gentle, healing, and everlasting arms and bathed in His words of grace—to help to heal us and carry us to a better day.

 IMPACT APPLICATION: In the pain of our lives, what we will find is that when we surrender, God is always there to lift us up.

A GENTLE WHISPER

After the earthquake there was a fire, but the LORD was not in the fire. And after the fire there was the sound of a gentle whisper. **1 Kings 19:12**

THE LORD SPOKE to Elijah in a still, small voice. How did He do that?

You walk through the woods or around the neighborhood and realize suddenly that you have been standing in the same spot for a while—waiting for direction, waiting for a clear call beckoning you to one way or the other. And you don't remember anything along the way; you were so wrapped up in worry, trying to figure out the next steps in life.

In his book *Quiet Strength*, Tony Dungy expresses this too-common occurrence in all of our lives:

> It would have been helpful to have a clear sign as to the direction the Lord wanted me to go—maybe something plastered on a billboard on the side of the road or flashed on a scoreboard at a stadium or written clearly in the clouds with a divine finger. I have to admit that I looked in all those places, just in case.
>
> At that moment, even a powerful wind, earthquake, or fire similar to what Elijah had experienced would have been helpful—although, as it turned out, the Lord didn't appear to Elijah in any of those. Instead, it was a gentle whisper—a still, small voice—in which Elijah heard the Lord speaking.

We've all been there. We may be there now. Trying to make a decision we can't seem to make. Trying to choose door one, two, or three, not realizing that God would probably honor any one of those choices because it's our heart He really cares about as we try to decide the right thing for us to do. If our choice is not the door He intended us to take, well, He'll eventually grind us around to where He intended somewhere down the road.

So go ahead and decide. For while we're standing at another one of those intersections in life, stuck, stymied, and at a standstill, the rest of the opportunities in front of us just keep rolling along, often passing us by, never to come again.

I wonder sometimes if the best approach, as we struggle with those decisions at the intersections in our lives, is to just keep on doing what is before us—nurturing family, checking our tongues, spending time with longtime friends, being sensitive to new ones God brings into our lives, and allowing our hearts to continue to draw closer to Him by spending time through those quiet moments in His presence.

IMPACT APPLICATION: Are you standing at an intersection waiting for divine inspiration for the next direction in your life? While you wait, keep living the life around you, because it's there that God may gently whisper the help you seek for the decision you face.

JANUARY 30

YOUR CHOICE—ALWAYS

After washing their feet, he put on his robe again and sat down and asked, "Do you understand what I was doing? . . . I have given you an example to follow. Do as I have done to you." **John 13:12, 15**

OUR DEPARTURE THAT MORNING from a glorious, although brief, sunshine-filled visit with our children and granddaughter was marked by yet another passing Tampa Bay–area rainstorm. Our previously unscheduled day now was scheduled to include an afternoon funeral service in the quiet Florida hamlet of Graham. Life, at times, seems to be a lot like that—moving from sunshine to rain.

Lynda and I had never met the deceased, but we knew her through her daughters. Her story is not without precedent. You'll find story after story of a life well lived, like hers, were you to wander amid the headstones of cemetery after cemetery across the communities of this land—stories of lives of impact and meaning, lives that made a difference. People who never made the headlines yet whose résumés are etched in the hearts, minds, and lives of those they have loved, led, and lifted.

In her commencement speech delivered before an excited gathering of soon-to-be graduates from Villanova University, Pulitzer Prize–winning author Anna Quindlen laid these poignant words before those gathered:

> There will be hundreds of people out there with your same degree; there will be thousands of people doing what you want to do for a living. . . . So here is what I wanted to tell you today: Get a life. A real life, not just the manic pursuit of the next promotion, the bigger paycheck, the larger house. . . . Get a life in which you are generous. . . . All of you want to do well. But if you do not do good too, then doing well will never be enough. It is so easy to waste our lives: our days, our hours, our minutes. . . . It is so easy to exist instead of live. I learned to love the journey, not the destination. I learned that it is not a dress rehearsal, and that today is the only guarantee you get.

Yesterday is over, tomorrow is not promised, and today is ours to live—for ourselves and those around us. It's our choice how we will live it. Let's follow Jesus in his example of love and service, investing in and lifting others as we live our life. The positive impact we have in the world and in the lives around us may surprise us—but not Him.

 IMPACT APPLICATION: You will have an impact—for good or not—every day. What will it be? It's always, always your choice.

FOLLOW HIM

Follow me. **Matthew 4:19**

IT WAS ONE OF THOSE MOMENTS when there was no light penetrating the darkness of doubt, second thoughts, and an internal struggle wondering if the path was really as clear as I thought it to be. Was it my idea or was it God's idea to follow this path?

Driving to meet some friends to discuss what I believed God had called me to, I realized halfway there that I might be the only one among family, friends, and others who believed in what I passionately felt God had called me to follow Him into.

And then He reached down through my doubt with a song on the car CD player, which I at first had skipped over because I didn't recognize the title. Michael W. Smith shares that he wrote the song "I'll Lead You Home" as a "very serious heart-cry out to God written from being in the valley longer than [he] imagined." And what Michael W. Smith couldn't have realized was that he had also written it for me.

The music swirled through my head, over, around, and through the crud of doubt, distraction, and road and traffic noise as the words began to break through the darkness: "Wandering the road of desperate life, aimlessly beneath the barren sky. Leave it to Me, I'll lead you home."

I realized that God knows what I'm going through. I may be headed in the right direction or not, but no matter, because He knows. Doubters, cynics, and others abound, and He knows. What He cares about is my heart's desire to follow Him the best I can. From there, He will lead me home.

Where are you in your journey? In the valley or standing on the precipice of a decision? Are you in doubt or despair? Maybe not today, but do you remember the day not too long ago when you were? Or maybe you will be tomorrow, when you least expect it.

If you are there or if you ever find yourself there, do yourself a favor and stand in front of the mirror. What do you see? Look deep, past any doubts you may have in your ability to be able to do anything whatsoever. Look past all the regrets for things you wish you had done.

Look deeper still, and this time do it with the eyes and heart of the God who created you. Look deeper, until you see the person Christ sees, loves, and is calling to follow Him, just as He called Peter in the first and last words He spoke to him.

In His first words, before He saw what Peter would do. And in His last words, after Peter had denied Him three times as He was going to the cross.

No matter what you face or feel, no matter the doubt or doubters or what the result may be—follow Him.

IMPACT APPLICATION: Go. Follow Him!

FEBRUARY 1

SO VERY SIMPLE

I don't have a sense of needing anything personally. I've learned by now to be quite content whatever my circumstances. **Philippians 4:11-13, MSG**

HERE'S THE PICTURE: thirty-six degrees outside under a morning covering of clear blue skies and a precious five-year-old sound asleep not ten feet away from me in the living room of what our two granddaughters call the "Mountain House" in North Carolina. It is peaceful, and we are content.

The best parts of life are so very simple with so very few needs and seem to come with an overwhelming sense of fulfillment and satisfaction—no matter how big or small our bank accounts, our accumulations, or the lists of our accomplishments are.

And yet for most of us, the worries and obstacles of today will try their best to contradict and steal from us what we know to be true—that it is in the simple pleasures of life, and ultimately in our relationship with Jesus Christ, that we find fulfillment and contentment. I don't know what worries and obstacles will try to steal the joy contained in that truth from you today or knock you off the path you should be on—maybe things similar to what I face. But it probably won't be anything near what the apostle Paul faced and was subjected to: whippings, ship-wrecks, hunger and thirst, imprisonment, and so much more.

But even though what Paul faced was much more intense than what we will face today, there is no doubt that what we face will be real for us. The question is whether we will allow what we face and the decisions we have before us to distract us or to knock us off our journey toward real fulfillment, satisfaction, and content-ment in life.

And the truth is, we're the only ones who can allow that to happen. We have control over whether we will allow worries or fruitless pursuits to distract us from what is truly important. Will we choose what the world tells us we should follow and be about? Or will we choose the path that leads to eternal contentment?

In our best moments we know what we should do. It's really that simple.

The best parts of life *are* so very simple. And really are the best!

 IMPACT APPLICATION: No matter what things we encounter that will try to knock us off the path toward fulfillment and contentment, they can never keep us from an intimate relationship with Jesus Christ. And He is the only One who is the source of real contentment, satisfaction, and fulfillment.

HIS POWER AND POTENTIAL

I can do everything through Christ, who gives me strength.
Philippians 4:13

I REMEMBER THE MORNING when I couldn't bring myself to go outside to check the weather. I had previously experienced a case of self-inflicted frostbite on the pinky finger of my left hand and was bound and determined not to do it again.

It was, by my best guess, which I determined from the warmth and comfort of my hotel room, about five degrees above zero just outside my window, not including any windchill factor, in Halifax, Nova Scotia, Canada. I was struggling through some final notes to share at a breakfast for pastors and community leaders gathering later that morning as they prepared for the East Coast/Maritimes Festival with Franklin Graham later that year. And in the warmth of that hotel room, the warmth of God's wisdom finally broke through my struggle to find the right words.

I had been looking within my own ability for the right answer, the right thing to say. I had been looking within my own potential. But it was not about my potential but the potential I have with Him within me that helps me to be the best I can be, to be all that He wants me to be, and to share what He wants me to share. In the deepest recesses of our journeys, the potential—the gifts, abilities, talents—that God has placed within us begins to bloom when we realize that it is about His wisdom and His plan for using them, not ours.

That's when things become clearer, when pathways are cleared and hope rises within our lives. Not just where others can see it, but in our ups and downs, our joys and heartaches. When we begin to align all of that with the plan God has for this moment, this day, this year, and this life, the journey becomes His.

It's in Christ and His potential for us, which He has poured into our lives, where we begin to find all the hope, strength, and enthusiasm we will ever need for the living of these days. The word *enthusiasm* itself is derived from the Greek word *entheos*—"in God"—and it's through that faith in God and His eternal plan for our lives, through His Son Jesus Christ, that we are provided with all the warmth, hope, strength, and peace to face whatever life throws our way.

It may be a little cold outside, but with Him in our lives, His warmth overcomes.

 IMPACT APPLICATION: It's all about Him and His power and potential within us. Trust Him today with the journey of your life. You won't be disappointed.

FEBRUARY 3

SPLASHING SUNSHINE

You're here to be light, bringing out the God-colors in the world.
Matthew 5:14, MSG

AS OUR TWO BASSET HOUNDS made their usual early-morning trip outdoors, I noticed as I looked up that the sun had come up over the horizon just enough to light the tops of the leafless trees lining our side yard.

It was another cold morning, and the now-golden glow shining off their branches reminded me of a similar wintry moment my son, Nathan, and I had experienced years ago as we stood on a ski slope in Colorado—as together we watched the advancing rays of the sun illuminating the barren tops of aspen trees lining the slope to the bottom of our next run.

In both instances, the sunshine painted a majestic picture now indelibly etched in my mind. Shining intensely across otherwise normal-looking moments, it had created breathtaking memories that would otherwise have passed by—I hesitate to admit it—as just another stand of trees.

Without the warm light from the morning sun, in either setting, the reflections in the mirror of my mind's eye would have been left with an image of gray, leafless, lifeless-looking trees standing against a barren landscape of winter.

Against that backdrop of simple recollections, I realized that it was a new day, and I couldn't help but wonder if I would shine—or not—on all that I would meet that day.

Will my approach to the day bring out the "God-colors" to be seen in the people and things of today, or will I simply reflect what the world sets before me? How will I respond to criticism today or to someone passing along gossip—something they wouldn't say to the person they're talking about?

How will I respond to the frustration of my child, granddaughters, spouse, perhaps someone I coach or mentor, or anyone else I encounter? Will my words mirror their words, or will my words splash sunshine on their day? Will I reflect their frustration for the situation of the moment—as they see it—or will I use gentle brushstrokes with "God-colors" to paint a different and better picture for them in that moment and for their day?

Will I simply reflect—as a mirror would—what I see before me today? Or will I respond by shining the light I am called to shine on the lives and moments before me? And will I begin in each of those moments to change the world for the better with and for the One who shines on all of us?

IMPACT APPLICATION: Each day the sun rises, offering us a new chance to splash sunshine on those around us. So embrace today, and splash sunshine on everything you see. At the end of the day, take stock of how you feel. Then do it again tomorrow and the next day and the next.

UNTAPPED POTENTIAL

One of the men lying there had been sick for thirty-eight years. When Jesus saw him and knew he had been ill for a long time, he asked him, "Would you like to get well?" "I can't, sir," the sick man said, "for I have no one to put me into the pool when the water bubbles up. Someone else always gets there ahead of me." **John 5:5-7**

DURING ONE OF THE JEWISH HOLY DAYS, Jesus arrived in Jerusalem and found His way to the pool of Bethesda. Beneath the pool were underground springs, which every now and then bubbled up and disturbed the surface of the waters. The people believed that the waters had curative powers, because they thought an angel caused the disturbance and that the first person to get into the pool after the water's movement would be healed from his or her illness.

By the pool lay a man who had been an invalid for thirty-eight years. His future was bleak. Sympathy, it seemed, was the only prescription the community could dispense, and he probably dispensed enough of it himself in the pity parties he threw after he missed yet another opportunity to get into the bubbling waters. In his illness he had become a prisoner of his own despair.

Jesus asked the man an interesting question: "Would you like to get well?" The question seems unnecessary. Why wouldn't he?

Why didn't Jesus just say, "Hey, sit tight and let me heal you"? But Jesus not only saw a person who couldn't move, he also saw a person full of excuses and defenses.

This man had lived in a rut, setting his own limits and never dreaming beyond them. And so the man responded, "I can't, sir. . . . I have no one to put me into the pool when the water bubbles up. Someone else always gets there ahead of me."

The Healer of healers stood before him, and instead of recognizing his renewing power, the man whined, "It's not my fault that I'm still this way. My friends have let me down!" Instead of answering with a resounding yes, his response was to offer an excuse.

When was the last time you asked God for something bigger than you could possibly do in your own ability and power? Why not step out in faith and ask God to help you?

I would venture to say that there are vast untapped areas of your life that have never been turned loose. I'll bet it's possible that no one knows who you really are or what you're really capable of, except the God who created you—and who stands ready to go with you when you are ready.

 IMPACT APPLICATION: What big thing have you been afraid to ask God to do for you or to help you with? Ask God to make it happen, and then be ready. And with Him keep moving into a brand-new season of your life.

FEBRUARY 5

A BETTER
SPIRIT—HOPE

In that day the wolf and the lamb will live together; the leopard will lie down with the baby goat. The calf and the yearling will be safe with the lion, and a little child will lead them all. **Isaiah 11:6**

THEY WOULD BE THE LAST to run the course. During the 2010 Winter Olympics, the American four-man bobsled team found itself facing its final of four runs to try to capture the gold medal for the first time in sixty-two years. The German team had just finished and waited anxiously at the bottom of the course; they stood in gold-medal position should the American team slip at all. The Americans didn't. They ran the course in a four-run time of 3 minutes, 24.46 seconds—just 38/100 of a second faster than the German team's cumulative four-run time. And with that, the Germans would settle for second place and the silver medal.

The television cameras captured the American four-man bobsled team jubilantly jumping out of their sled at the end of the course, then the cameras shifted to show the German team clapping and cheering their winning effort as well. It exemplified a spirit that permeated the games. It was a spirit that rose above winning and losing—to paint a picture of the very best that they (and we) can be.

The Olympics held an enlightening, uplifting, and hope-filled spirit that didn't have to end with the closing ceremony—despite no longer being in the center of our collective international attention. It was a spirit that reminded us that we don't always win or get it right—that not even the big guys get it right—yet we can celebrate and live peaceably with one another. That same spirit needs to linger for a while in our lives.

For too many around us, hope is not a reality. Perhaps in the uncertainty of each of our days, clinging to that spirit will point us toward a better place to begin each day.

Together we will begin to see and believe the power of hope for our lives, for the lives of our children and grandchildren, and for others. Together we can begin to reach across our differences to raise one another up to the top of the mountain.

Hope! Believe it!

 IMPACT APPLICATION: Hope is what leads us to a place where we begin to believe that we truly can become more than we ever thought we could be—for ourselves and for others.

LIVING IN THE TRYING

I'm not saying that I have this all together, that I have it made. But I am well on my way, reaching out for Christ, who has so wondrously reached out for me. Friends, don't get me wrong: By no means do I count myself an expert in all of this, but I've got my eye on the goal, where God is beckoning us onward—to Jesus. I'm off and running, and I'm not turning back. **Philippians 3:13-14, MSG**

WHILE SPENDING TIME with Lynda and me, our granddaughter asked us to build a fire in the fireplace so we could make s'mores together. Perfect for a wintry day.

Watching her snuggle around the warmth of the crackling fire, with our tiny rescue dog, Tulip, and eating her graham cracker, marshmallow, and chocolate treat reminded me, once again, what life is about and what it's not about.

It's not about doing. It's about trying.

It's not about winning. It's about how you play.

It's not about how much money you make. It's about how you made it and what you do with it afterward.

It's not about how many ladders you've climbed. It's about which ladders you climbed and how you climbed them.

It's not about the image you present to others in the world. It's about your influence and impact and how you treat others in the world.

It's not just about an end result. It's about the journey and relationships along the way.

The message of the world is that life is all about us, what we do, and what we should do next to be successful. It's about external things, about doing and achieving. But it's hard to find any short- or long-term warmth, comfort, stability, assurance, or, more important, direction in those worldly messages.

The message missed in all of that is this: God is at work in our lives—in the trying. God is at work in our lives in the journey. He is always within us, always at work internally—if we allow Him to be. He is always at work helping us to become all that He intended for us to be—helping us to decide which "ladders to climb" and which goals to reach for, encouraging us and applauding us in our trying and strivings, and smiling down on us when we do everything to honor and glorify Him.

That's the message and the journey that will provide warmth, comfort, eternal assurance, and clear direction for here and hereafter. It's what will leave the legacy of changed lives we were created to leave.

 IMPACT APPLICATION: Paul realized life was about reaching out for Christ. All the other stuff was rubbish. He realized it was about keeping his eyes on the goal God was calling him to—Christ. It was a calling for him to become more like Christ in every way and during every day.

SPACES IN A MOTHER'S HEART

Mary kept all these things in her heart and thought about them often.
Luke 2:19

OUR GRANDDAUGHTER HANNAH was sobbing uncontrollably as she walked out of her bedroom into the family room. She was beyond consolation.

Mother's Day was coming to an end, and in the busyness of the day, Hannah had forgotten to give her Mimi (my wife, Lynda) the card she had worked so hard to prepare.

When she finally gave it to her Mimi, Lynda took and treasured the one-of-a-kind card—"I [heart shape] U Mimi" with a picture below of a hugging Mimi and Hannah.

My thoughts turned to memories of Lynda and our then two-year-old son Nathan sitting together on the floor reading book after book, of them "chitchatting" together on the bed during one of his breaks from college, of their walking through the yard smelling flower after flower, of Lynda comforting him when he climbed out of his crib simply needing to be nearer to our voices, and of thousands of other moments.

Moments that Lynda still treasures in her heart.

Here's what I realized while watching her and loving her through the years: the relationship my precious bride has with her son, her granddaughters, godchildren, and many more is unique and something that I, as her husband, need to make sure I not only respect but also encourage and nurture. The impact she has and will have on those precious lives is immeasurable. It comes naturally to her, having seen her own mom do the same with her and with others.

There is a space in her heart—and in the heart of every mother—that is filled with time spent with her children, with talks, touches, tears, and accomplishments. The space empties a bit when the child grows and journeys out or is not as available as before or forgets to call home. And those spaces in a mother's heart empty a bit through the heartache they feel when a child is lost, loses their way, or forgets how wonderfully made they are.

Mothers have a space that causes them to sacrifice every personal advantage, every self-centered moment, and every longed-for opportunity for the sake of their child, grandchild, and—in the case of Lynda's mom—great-grandchild.

Mothers have a space that causes them to defer taking new roads to personal advancement, pleasure, and comfort—all for the sake of their children.

And those spaces always remain the exact size and shape of each child entrusted to their care, forever.

Only in a mother's heart.

Thank God.

IMPACT APPLICATION: Mothers like Mary, Lynda, Lynda's mom, and our daughter-in-law individually and together exemplify God's design for mothers. Make sure those women in your life have opportunities and time to have the impact God intended for them to have.

ALWAYS THERE

The LORD is my shepherd; I have all that I need. He lets me rest in green meadows; he leads me beside peaceful streams. He renews my strength. He guides me along right paths, bringing honor to his name.
Psalm 23:1-3

MY GRANDDAUGHTER and I were in the garage cleaning the windows on her Mimi's car. I was on the other side of the car and noticed that she had walked out of the garage and crossed the driveway, walking about twenty feet to the edge of the grass bordering the woods that run along the length of our side yard. Then I saw and heard her begin to cry.

As I quickly made my way to her, I could see that she wasn't hurt in any way to evoke what was now a steady sob of concern.

"What's the matter, sweetie?" I asked as I embraced her.

"Granddaddy," she choked out, tears falling down her soft cheeks. "You left me."

"But precious, I didn't," I reassured her. "I was here all the while."

Ah, that we would start every morning hearing God remind us that He is with us all the while. If we believed those words of comfort and assurance, I am certain the days would go smoother. With the fresh recollection that God was and will be with us always, our nightmares would seem less real and frightening, our problems more manageable, our distances shorter, and our heartaches shared.

Yet those words, and those of David in the twenty-third psalm, are really only a reminder of what He knows and we too often forget—that in the midst of this life and all the hurdles we face, God hasn't gone anywhere. Perhaps we have taken a detour that has led us away from Him, but He hasn't gone anywhere.

What grassy strip are you standing on, looking into woods that seem dark, scary, and impenetrable? He stands there with you. What dream do you chase, which you feel He has placed in your heart with the purpose of glorifying Him and which now you are beginning to doubt? He is chasing it with you. What illness has overcome a member of your family for which you realize, as you sit there, that all treatment options have been exhausted? He sits there with you. Whom have you lost in your life and weep silently over each night as you fall asleep, and who can never be replaced? He weeps with you. Where can you turn when you're searching for a glimmer of hope in a marriage that seems finally to have lost its purpose? He is there with you. Turn to Him. He hasn't gone anywhere.

"The Lord is my shepherd . . ."

These are words of truth, comfort, and assurance for today and every day for the rest of our lives.

IMPACT APPLICATION: He was and will be with you all the while. No matter what you face today or may face in the future, take comfort and courage knowing that He will be with you.

FEBRUARY 9

PARENT PLATFORM

Fathers, do not aggravate your children, or they will become discouraged. **Colossians 3:21**

IT WAS A LONG NIGHT, going over last-minute things for the upcoming Impact for Living conference. Nathan and I wrestled with many things, trying to figure out what would work best and trying to anticipate areas of concern that might never arise. But we created contingencies anyway, just in case.

Then I realized something big that I had overlooked. Never happened before.

I am blessed with a son who is smarter than me, has a gentle spirit, is unselfish and sacrificial even to the point of being taken advantage of, and who has a desire to have others come out ahead of him. He strives to be the husband Paul writes about in Ephesians 5 ("Love your wives, just as Christ loved the church") and the son and father Paul paints in chapter 6 ("Honor your father and mother. . . . [And] bring [your children] up with the discipline and instruction that comes from the Lord").

He is not always appreciated as he should be, and all too often he never hears words of affirmation for what he does. Those who know of his gentle nature may take advantage of him, yet he continues on. He continues to do good things anyway.

Sadly, I had fallen into the category of not appreciating him for that one moment. Of course, I didn't mean to. However, in the busyness of planning and preparing for the conference, it seemed I never stopped long enough to recognize that our final scheduled planning day was also Nathan's birthday. Instead of it being about him, it was all about something else: professional interests, conference agendas, and not near enough about him. Not enough at all.

That's too bad, because I will never get another chance to do that birthday of his over again. I know there's a part of him that missed something from the absence of all-out appreciation for his day. But I know Nathan, and he is looking for the next thing he can do to lift up someone else.

Do you have one of those children? Do you know one you can encourage—one created special, precious, and unique, one whom God sent into the world to be a light, His light?

Hard to imagine life without them, isn't it? Take the time to appreciate them today. Tell them how much they mean to you. Pour into your children's lives today, because today's chance probably won't come around again.

 IMPACT APPLICATION: Today spend some time using your platform as a parent to build up and encourage your child, or another child, into becoming the person God intended for them to become. Do it by loving them. And watch how quickly they'll love you right back.

A PIECE OF ME GOES WITH YOU

Every time you go away you take a piece of me with you. **Paul Young**

ELLIE KATE had spent a few days with us and was headed back home.

I watched, braved a smile, and returned her wave as the car carrying my family slowly pulled away and made its way down the street until it turned the distant curve and was out of sight. That was Lynda's and my cue to kick off the next stage of our tradition, started years earlier with our older granddaughter. We ran through the garage into the kitchen, called to our basset hound, Lily, who bounded out of her chair and followed us out the back door and across the side yard to the fence bordering the golf course.

In just a moment the car taking them away would appear on the roadway on the other side of the fairway with horn honking and a little voice yelling as loud as she could through the open window, "I love you!" while we waved, I whistled, and Lily barked. When the little shrieks of "I love you" no longer reached our ears, we returned to the house, leaving a little piece of our hearts somewhere between that fence and the car driving off. They always take a little piece of us with them.

Lynda and I never want them to leave—our granddaughters, their mommy and daddy, or even our "granddog," Jackson. It took me many years to get there, coming from a place where family didn't matter that much. But Lynda and her family modeled for me the true importance and meaning of real family—which goes beyond simply blood—and the joy family brings, along with the pain that is always felt when any separation occurs.

It's a part of the abundant life God envisioned and planned for each of us.

Family.

It is a matter of the priorities we choose for our lives. It's a part of the legacy God intended for each of us to have—which has nothing to do with things or accomplishments or what part of the country we were raised in or whether that's the way we were raised as a child or not.

Family.

It's sad, really, that too many spend their whole lives either not caring or not getting over what was done to them or looking for the abundant life somewhere else. It's sad, really, that they set aside the most important of all relationships, after a relationship with Him—family. And as a result, they too often will never fully realize the abundant life God intended for them to have. Never.

If that's been your life, draw a line, and don't let that define you for one more day.

 IMPACT APPLICATION: Let your life be defined by a relationship with Him, which moves you to a relationship with family, where you can honestly say to them, "Every time you go away you take a piece of me with you."

FEBRUARY 11

STAY CALM

The LORD himself will fight for you. Just stay calm. **Exodus 14:14**

AMID PREPARATIONS for a number of projects that all came to bloom simultaneously, I found myself worried, tense, and unsure, yet wanting to believe God would provide the resources, wisdom, and energy I needed.

A dear friend pointed me to Moses as an example of what it means to have faith amid tense circumstances.

In his better moments, Moses knew God would sustain the Israelites. Moses trusted that the Lord's plan would prevail and that it would be better than if Moses had tried to engineer it all by himself. Reaching the end of his own wisdom, ability, and expertise, Moses believed the Lord would always fight for him—and he needed to keep going in quiet trust of that eternal truth. Moses understood in the midst of whatever he faced that quitting was never an option. He had to follow the Lord as he led the Israelites through the desert.

But then the Israelites reached the shore of the Red Sea with Pharaoh's army nipping at their heels. With nowhere to go, the Israelites did what they usually did in desperate circumstances: they cried out in defeat and terror, wishing they could return to captivity in Egypt rather than die in the desert. They worried, whined, and wailed. And I can identify with them.

Moses answered their worrying, whining, and wailing by telling them to be quiet and to not be afraid, because "the LORD himself will fight for you. Just stay calm."

And then, as God directed him to do, Moses stretched out his hand and staff over the Red Sea, and the waters divided. The Israelites passed through the sea on dry ground.

I wonder if you find yourself standing on the shore of a Red Sea with the rest of the world and all its concerns closing in all around you. I wonder if you find yourself facing some seemingly insurmountable obstacles and challenges and—realizing you have come to the end of your own wisdom, ability, and expertise—know you can't deal with them alone.

History demonstrates that at some time or another we will all find ourselves on the shores of our own Red Seas—facing obstacles we won't know how to get around, over, or through, surrounded by a world closing in fast around us.

In those moments, I pray we will remember that through it all, the Lord our God is with us. I pray that we will also remember—as Moses knew—that the Lord will continue to fight for us. We just need to trust and be calm, knowing that God can part the seas before us.

It's just one of God's many promises to us.

Believe it. Embrace it. Claim it as your own.

IMPACT APPLICATION: No matter what you face, remember that through it all the Lord is still on the throne and the Lord will continue to fight for you.

DREAMS AND VALUES

Children are a gift from the LORD. **Psalm 127:3**

COULD IT BE TRUE, or am I just imagining that Barbie is losing her appeal? Could it really be that she's been flirting with Ken and going about skimpily clad for nearly sixty years? Barbie has been part of a discussion concerning basic societal values since she first showed up on the scene in 1959.

My son has declared the tantalizing temptress of tots off-limits for his daughters. He doesn't want them to buy into the idea that Barbie's proportions are the ideal. After all, the dreams of so many little girls everywhere of wanting to be just like Barbie can turn into potential teenage problems when they realize they will always be a little shorter and perhaps a little stockier, or a bit taller and perhaps—Ken, please don't look—a little plainer and ganglier than Barbie, their peers, and the way the world says they should be.

"Just a toy," you may say. Think again. Think about the children, girls *and* boys, whose self-image, desire for acceptance, and dreams are driven by a value-deficient society and media juggernaut. They watch strip shows that society calls Super Bowl halftimes. They see half-dressed men, women, boys, and girls parade across television screens, advocating a lifestyle that celebrates being skinny and "pretty." These celebrities send the message that kissing anyone, or allowing anyone to kiss them just to be part of the "in" group, is acceptable; that sex outside marriage is okay and should be without consequences; and that there are no moral absolutes.

It would seem to be time to reclaim the sacredly held dreams for ourselves and our children that once moved us to care, sacrifice, and believe that we, and they, were created for something greater than today's cultural standards. These dreams once aligned with a life of absolute values, rather than the incessant need to keep up with the Joneses, and were dreams that once moved us to reach for the unreachable.

We need to reclaim the dreams that moved us to protect our children from the whims of our own convenience and the valueless and frightening winds of a world that will not protect them.

 IMPACT APPLICATION: Is it time to reclaim the value-based dreams of your family so your children can become all they were created to be, one precious life at a time?

FEBRUARY 13

THE SHELTERING TREE OF FRIENDSHIP

Friendship is a sheltering tree; / O! the joys, that came down shower-like, / Of Friendship, Love, and Liberty, / Ere I was old!"
Samuel Taylor Coleridge

JONATHAN WAS ENDOWED with great mental ability and morality. He was handsome. He possessed a heart as big as all outdoors. And as the elder son of Saul, the current king of Israel, he was also next in line for that most prestigious position. Everyone knew this and also that the day for his advancement was imminent.

But Jonathan's best friend, David, received the promotion that all the world knew was his. And what was Jonathan's response to this news? Probably not what was expected or what we would expect today. It may not even be how we would respond.

Jonathan's response was to affirm his covenant of friendship with David by stripping himself of all the symbols of his position.

> Jonathan made a covenant with David because he loved him as himself.
> Jonathan took off the robe he was wearing and gave it to David, along with
> his tunic, and even his sword, his bow and his belt. (1 Samuel 18:34, NIV)

As if that weren't enough, he interceded on David's behalf before Saul to prevent him from killing David. Jonathan continued to come alongside his beloved friend "and helped him find strength in God" (1 Samuel 23:16, NIV).

Do you have a friend like Jonathan, a friend (as Coleridge put it) like "a sheltering tree"? A friend who takes second place without jealousy, and cheers loudly and sincerely as you stand above him on the podium? A friend who affirms and encourages, who stands by you loyally even when passed over? A friend who lovingly, yet boldly, confronts you when needed and points you to God? A friend who forgives you when you come up short, then forgives you again, and who every day embraces all of you—even the ugly parts? I hope you do.

During the journey of your life, you may experience disappointments when some you thought to be "friends" abandon you along the way. To be a "sheltering tree" friend, you may need to remember that friends can't replace what you never got years earlier. It may mean remembering that healthy relationships must stand on their own. And it may mean remembering that if you try to relive a relationship that you lost years ago in a new one found today, the new one may be lost also.

But the journey to meaningful, selfless, affirming, encouraging, lifelong friendships is a journey worth pursuing nonetheless—and for the rest of your days.

IMPACT APPLICATION: If you have a friend like "a sheltering tree," hold tightly to that person. And consider being that kind of friend to others. Beginning today, be the friend that lasts—always.

CAN'T HELP FALLING IN LOVE

Charm is deceptive, and beauty does not last; but a woman who fears the LORD will be greatly praised. Reward her for all she has done. Let her deeds publicly declare her praise. **Proverbs 31:30-31**

IT'S NOT HER BIRTHDAY, Mother's Day, or our anniversary. It is simply the first day of the rest of our lives together. And since I don't know what tomorrow may bring, I find myself moved to take this opportunity today to reflect on her life.

She's still asleep in our bedroom directly below me as I write this reflection, while the lyrics and music of Andrea Bocelli's remake of Elvis Presley's classic "Can't Help Falling in Love" float through my office. Lynda's doctors have consistently prescribed a full night's sleep for her to lessen the effects of some of her aches and pains, which have gradually become more prevalent through the years. Maybe today the aches she will feel will be a little less than yesterday.

I'll have to prod her a bit when she awakens to get her to tell me how she feels, since she won't acknowledge that anything is amiss or hurting. Instead, she will just begin to go on about the usual activities of the day and make our house a home and sustain and lift my life with a warmth and security I've done little to deserve. And each day, despite the insensitive signals I may send at times, everything about her makes me fall a bit more in love with her. It can't be helped, thank God.

She's never given herself much credit for success as the world prescribes it to be. Humility marks her every waking moment. She's never seen a budget she likes or a dog she doesn't. She's never met a child who shouldn't be held and kissed, or a friend or new acquaintance who shouldn't be helped. Her outreach of love to others is not always returned in equal measure—that, at least, must be my personal confession—but she still reaches out anyway.

She has always known better than anyone else the directions my life should take, the people I should trust, and the answers to questions I have confronted and decisions with which I have wrestled. She has taught me, by her example, how to love without qualification or reservation.

Maybe you know someone like that in your life. Proverbs 31:10 says that "a virtuous and capable wife" is "more precious than rubies." She's beyond rubies. You and I don't need a special occasion to honor a wife like that.

 IMPACT APPLICATION: Honor your bride or that other special person in your life today, and tell her how much you appreciate who she is and what she does. Better yet, maybe put a handwritten note in a special place where she will be sure to find it.

FEBRUARY 15

ETERNAL ABUNDANCE

I am the gate. Those who come in through me will be saved. They will come and go freely and will find good pastures. The thief's purpose is to steal and kill and destroy. My purpose is to give them a rich and satisfying life. **John 10:9-10**

WHEN HE RETIRED after a successful engineering career, he could have chosen to do almost anything he wanted. He chose to be homeless.

Richard Leroy Walters served in the United States Marine Corps during the Korean War. He went on to become an honors graduate from Purdue University in mechanical engineering and then earned a master's degree in education from Ball State University. He never married, fathered no children, and had no family with whom he stayed in touch.

When he retired from his career, he gave up his home, car, and everything else he owned in exchange for sleeping on the floor of the Mission of Mercy homeless shelter in Phoenix, Arizona. When he died of a stroke at age seventy-six, he left an estate, valued at four million dollars, to various charities, including the Mission of Mercy shelter.

He decided he didn't need material things to live each day. We can't help but speculate whether he ever asked the question, "How much is enough?" It's a question that no doubt has crossed our minds at times in the midst of our world's indulgence and affluence.

Walters was also in life a self-described atheist. Did he see places of abundance adjacent to so many places of want and need? Was that what moved him to abandon not only the world and its ways but also God and the "abundant life" He promises? But by abandoning God, he abandoned the only One who offers the lasting answer and hope.

We might learn something from Richard Walters. In some ways he reminds us that happiness in life—an abundant life—does not come from material and transient things. It is not derived from what the world marks as important—money, résumés, position, power, awards, degrees. Because if an abundant life is defined by those things, we will never be satisfied.

But there's a second lesson we might learn. An abundant life is defined by the divine gift of eternal life, a gift that becomes the possession of everyone who believes in Jesus Christ. That's the abundant life—the gift from God—that Christ talks about in John 10. And there is good evidence that Richard Walters learned this lesson on his deathbed.

Think about that: the gift that guarantees life with Him for eternity. Why would we choose any other option? Why would we not do what we need to do—today—to obtain that gift of the assurance of an abundant eternal life with God?

IMPACT APPLICATION: An abundant life is not found in the things of the world. An abundant life is found in a relationship with God through Jesus Christ.

SUPPORTING OUR CHILDREN'S DREAMS

But I, being poor, have only my dreams; / I have spread my dreams under your feet; / Tread softly because you tread on my dreams.
William Butler Yeats

IN THE PAST FEW WEEKS, Lynda has spent much of her spare time scanning photographs onto her computer. She often calls me to come look at one of the photos, and we share a moment as we reminisce over the memories the picture brings to mind.

A recent spate of pictures she scanned was of our son, Nathan, when he was between two and four years old. Many of them showed him and me playing and doing various projects together. As I looked at them—and in particular at his angelic, happy, expectant smile radiating in the midst of whatever we were doing together—I tried to remember what Lynda and I had dreamed of back then for our son and for his future.

I don't recall dreaming that he should be a professional baseball or football player, famous or worldly and well known. I was pretty sure we didn't dream that he would be a *New York Times* bestselling author (although we did encourage him to write regularly) or work in the NFL. I'm sure we dreamed of a number of things he might do one day.

But as I looked at photo after photo, I clearly remembered that in those years and all the years since, the overriding dream his mother and I quietly held in our hearts was that he would always be safe and healthy and happy and that he would love God and always remember how much God loved him. We realized that no matter what was going on in our lives, if Nathan was safe, good, healthy, and happy, then our lives were good. Those same feelings now fill our lives and cover our daughter-in-law, Amy, and our two granddaughters as well.

I also realized that our dreams for Nathan were wrapped within his dreams for himself, as he grew and expressed them in his own wonderfully innocent way. Our dreams were a safety net, supporting his dreams, and were woven out of our love and responsibility for him, understanding how fragile his dreams (and all dreams in general) were as they took root in the words and thoughts of such a fragile and impressionable gift of God.

Our dreams for our children should take shape in enabling and supporting theirs as they develop, so we must be careful not to dampen or trample—or impose our own dreams—on the dreams of those so young and impressionable around us, who are growing into all God created them to be.

IMPACT APPLICATION: What dreams do you hold for those closest to you? Tread lightly on their dreams. Embrace, support, and give wings to their dreams.

FEBRUARY 17

DOING OUR BEST—
TOGETHER

There is no greater love than to lay down one's life for one's friends.
John 15:13

"I REALLY WANT the United States to win, but I don't really care who wins. I just like their stories. I like everyone trying to do their best together," my granddaughter Hannah said as we watched an American swimmer edge out her competition for the gold medal in the Women's 100 Freestyle final. It was another perspective similar to the one that remained stuck in my memory from the Olympics' opening ceremonies a few days earlier.

It was a scripted mismatch, designed to soften the borders of our lives.

It worked, at least for mine.

They entered the stadium together. NBA star of the Houston Rockets and Chinese citizen Yao Ming, standing at 7'6", carried the Chinese flag before his country's delegation of 639 athletes. Walking alongside Yao Ming was a nine-year-old boy, Lin Hao, a student at Yuzixi Primary School in Wenchuan County—the epicenter of the May 12, 2008, earthquake in China, which killed 69,000 people.

While the pair made their way around the stadium, Lin Hao's story unfolded for the audience: Lin Hao, a second grader and hall monitor at his school, pulled himself out of the rubble of the earthquake in which twenty of his thirty classmates had died. Then he did what we all would like to believe we would do. He returned to rescue two other classmates. Why? Because as a hall monitor he was one of their leaders; it was his duty.

Wouldn't it be nice if stories like that, which inspire us to reach beyond ourselves, would last beyond the few weeks of any Olympiad?

Wouldn't it be nice if moments like that would turn people from selfish to selfless?

Wouldn't it be nice if evil didn't exist in the world? But since it does, wouldn't it be nice if people decided to stand together against it to make a real difference?

Wouldn't it be nice if people around the world, seeing the vast opportunities for change if unified, would mobilize their collective energies to expand freedom, prosperity, and hope for all the world? To let the best of who they are shine?

IMPACT APPLICATION: How are you using your God-given passions to influence those around you and make the world a better place for all to experience? Doing your best—it just may be your duty.

GOD'S VISION

When people do not accept divine guidance, they run wild. But whoever obeys the law is joyful. **Proverbs 29:18**

SOLOMON, the writer of most of Proverbs and of the passage above, understood that without a vision or purpose, people will run wild, each to their own direction. They will often look to anything and anyone to ease their sense of lostness, settling for any direction that momentarily numbs their anxiety or pain. They will be influenced by the popular winds of change, the newest fashions and fads, the latest celebrity, the latest oracle from on high—whatever those are for each of them.

Nations and their people throughout the history of recorded time have tended to look to leaders, to judges, to rules and legislation for a sense of vision. Children with an absolute trust in their parents and an idealism planted within them by the God who created them look to their parents and others they trust to guide them—to find a sense of vision for their lives. In the absence of that, children and the rest of us—although we may find it hard to admit—will look anywhere for that sense of vision. And that vision is usually where acceptance and relief for the moment can be found, even though all too often it is not aligned with the vision God would have for our lives.

Today is no different from any other time in history. "When people do not accept divine guidance, they run wild." History should tell us that a vision and direction coming from the leaders or legislatures of nations will not be made clear nor necessarily right. Neither will values be established, pain and anxiety numbed, nor light be found from those leaders or legislatures of nations.

History should tell us, though, that with the kind of vision of which Solomon spoke—God's vision, and His divine guidance—hearts will be changed, the direction will become clear, values will be laid before us, pain and anxiety will be relieved, and a light will be found, regardless of what is going on in the world around us.

And the end result of those who follow that vision for today, and throughout eternity, is joy.

IMPACT APPLICATION: Purpose—the kind God wants for our lives and of which Solomon wrote—isn't found in legislation, in judicial decisions, or in the elections of leaders held here or around the world. It isn't found in the totality of our things or in the values of a society or its institutions. It is found only in seeking the will of the Father and living in alignment with His vision for our lives.

TODAY'S IMPORTANT MOMENTS

Enjoy the little things, for one day you may look back and realize they were the big things. **Robert Brault**

I WAS REMINDED TODAY of Reba McEntire's haunting song "If I Had Only Known." You may remember the line: "If I had only known it was the last walk in the rain. . ."

Other songs have been written about that message. Books have been written and shared from generation to generation to remind us. Jesus' half-brother James tells us: "How do you know what your life will be like tomorrow? Your life is like the morning fog—it's here a little while, then it's gone" (James 4:14).

The simple lesson from the words of that Scripture, that song, and so many other sources is profound: you are not promised tomorrow, so don't miss the most important moments and people of your todays.

And we try to live that message. But then we are usually off to the races again in search of something we believe we should be after. Something better must be at the top of the ladder we are climbing. And then something happens; and looking back with regret, we hear again, "If I had only known it was the last walk in the rain. . . ."

With regret we ponder those moments with the most precious of people whom we let slip through our fingers and our lives. We don't really mean to let it happen. It's just that we have to deal with all the urgent stuff in the seemingly never-ending scramble of careers to advance, games and trophies to win, résumés to improve, status to seek, money to make, and things to acquire. For those are the big and important things.

Or are they?

A dear friend of mine, a successful sports figure, shared in a quiet moment one day that he wished he could tell others that pursuing worldly goals, believing they will lead them to satisfaction and fulfillment in life, will only lead to disappointment once they achieve them.

What if it really *was* our last walk in the rain? What if tomorrow never came? What if when we said good-bye to our family that one fateful morning as we headed out on a business trip, it turned out to be our last good-bye? If we allow the urgent scramble to continue, won't we always find something else to strive for, while all the most important and truly big things and moments—the most satisfying and fulfilling things of our lives—are missed and lost?

The conclusion should be obvious: Why not make a change today?

IMPACT APPLICATION: Why not commit today and every day to make each day count with those important people and moments in your life—those truly big things—as if there will be no tomorrow?

GRANDPA

The righteous who walks in his integrity—blessed are his children after him! **Proverbs 20:7,** ESV

THERE WAS A TIME when we celebrated the individual birthdays of presidents Abraham Lincoln, born February 12, 1809, and George Washington, born February 22, 1732. Today, we designate a federal holiday called Presidents' Day, honored by few, recognized most by commercial sales extravaganzas, with little known by the populace about the namesakes for the day.

My elementary school teachers fashioned a celebration around their birthdays throughout the entire month of February, even to the point of requiring us to memorize a song.

My Grandpa Regula, born in the early 1900s in Poland, knew the names of the first and sixteenth presidents before he could speak English. He wasn't educated but was far from illiterate. When he finally learned to read, he read about the lives of those two great men and of other men and women like them, for he knew that their footprints had helped to mark the pathway of his journey to the day of his arrival on these shores in the early part of the twentieth century. He loved this quote from Abraham Lincoln: "I leave you, hoping that the lamp of liberty will burn in your bosoms until there shall no longer be a doubt that all men are created free and equal."

I suppose he was the first best friend in my life, a man of faith and integrity, a confidant and comforter to a seven-year-old boy, whom both he and Grandma sheltered, cared for, and blessed when he was left all alone. Funny how Grandpa seemed to know that baseball and fishing were more important to that seven-year-old boy than catching the bus for school, but I caught the bus, because he wanted me to have the educational opportunities of his new country that he'd never had.

If he were alive, he would still be celebrating days that recognize our nation and its leaders, closing shop and hanging the stars and stripes. He would have wanted his great-great grandchildren to know all about these two presidents, their faults, their strengths, and their never-ending passion for this great land.

The story of America is written in the hearts and woven by the actions of these three noble men whom God created and set apart—George Washington, Abraham Lincoln, and Grandpa Regula, and others like them, in a remarkable tale of the triumph of the human spirit under the watchful eye of God.

We learn from them and are blessed by their lives. And the legacy they left for us under the watchful eye of God is the legacy we need to leave for others who will follow us.

IMPACT APPLICATION: Together may we pass on our torch of liberty with honesty, honor, integrity, pride, and gratitude to God for those who have gone before us and for this land which these three men loved—America.

FEBRUARY 21

DAYS OF HOPE

Fix your thoughts on what is true, and honorable, and right, and pure, and lovely, and admirable. Think about things that are excellent and worthy of praise. **Philippians 4:8**

WHEN WAS THE LAST TIME we gave today, or any day of the week, a fair shake? We tend to label days with feelings—Monday we're back at the grind; Tuesday we're still trying to get going; Wednesday is "hump day," halfway to the weekend; Thursday and Friday, we're almost there, and so we miss those two days entirely by looking ahead; and then it's the weekend, and we remember the lawn and yardwork and cleaning the house.

All too often we allow our days to be defined by problems, uncertainty, and what is coming next. We know things will happen that we wish wouldn't; we see things happen that are tough, and we allow those things to sour our perspective. But take a look at Paul's perspective.

I don't know on what day Paul was writing when he penned the words above to the church at Philippi, but it could have been any day, because all days are filled with life's up-and-down moments. But while others around him were allowing their minds to be filled with all the troubles of the day, Paul encouraged the church to fix their thoughts on "what is true, and honorable, and right, and pure, and lovely, and admirable" and to "think about things that are excellent and worthy of praise."

There's a story of a ship that sailed from the Orient on a long voyage around South America in an area unfamiliar to the captain and crew. As a result, they misjudged their needed water supply and so somewhere off the coast of South America, they ran out.

When they spotted a passing ship, the captain signaled to it: "Can you share your water?" The response came back: "Dip where you are." The distressed captain became irritated and repeated his request, but the response was the same.

So they rigged together a bucket and rope, and the crew lowered it into the salty ocean. When they lifted the bucket, the captain found to his amazement, that the water was sweet and fresh. What he hadn't known was they were in the center of a mile-wide current where the Amazon River was rushing into the sea.

What is your perspective for today? It may depend on what you put in your mind, into that reserve you draw on when you don't know what the rest of the week has in store. What do you draw on when you need the strength and hope to get through whatever you're facing?

Let me suggest that you fix your mind, as Paul suggested, on the hope that is present now and in the future, no matter the day—Jesus Christ.

IMPACT APPLICATION: No matter what you're facing, there is renewing potential bubbling around, under, and within you in the One who is always there.

LIVING YOUR LEGACY

Jesus replied, "'You must love the LORD your God with all your heart, all your soul, and all your mind.' This is the first and greatest commandment. A second is equally important: 'Love your neighbor as yourself.' The entire law and all the demands of the prophets are based on these two commandments." **Matthew 22:37-40**

MANY YEARS AGO, Lynda's dad, who was visiting us, arose early and walked a few blocks from our apartment to the hallowed grounds of a centuries-old cemetery in Dover, Delaware, which Lynda and I had mentioned to him the night before.

Lynda's dad did that a lot when he and Lynda's mom visited us. I had always supposed it was because he had developed and cared for memorial parks back home. I learned many years later that I was only partly right.

On a number of occasions I have done the same. You, too, perhaps. A peaceful tranquility overcomes me as I walk under the protective shade of stately oaks and magnolias guarding the memories of loved ones. During one visit to a cemetery, my eyes fell on a gravestone with a name that reminded me of a professor I had been privileged to study with in law school. That professor once told me, "A teacher affects eternity; he can never tell where his influence stops."

There it is. That's why Dad visited those earthly resting places in town after town. That's why he read markers and tombstones from the east coast to the west and at all points in between. It gave him a sense of the influence and legacy of the lives who had gone before him. In those moments of reflection, he was reminded that through his own thoughts, words, and deeds he would have influence, for good or not, and would leave a legacy that would impact the lives of so many others. (To be clear, his influence was for good.)

In Dad's heart it had nothing to do with things, money, possessions, or worldly accomplishments. Those things may come, as they did for him, through hard work, discipline, and sacrifice but never by sacrificing the legacy that was most important to him, which was to glorify God by adding value to the lives of everyone he met.

He knew that we have:

- One time around to leave a legacy that will add value and help everyone we meet to become all they were meant to be;
- One time around to support, love, and care for our families and others;
- One time around to leave a legacy of fingerprints on the hearts of those who are less because you're gone but more because you were here;
- One time around to leave a legacy of significance—simply that at least one life is better because we were here.

IMPACT APPLICATION: What will your legacy be—today, tomorrow, and forever? You will leave a legacy—so live the legacy you want to leave.

FEBRUARY 23

HEY, GRAN! IT'S ME!

Always be full of joy in the Lord. I say it again—rejoice! **Philippians 4:4**

A HOCKEY COACH had been watching one of his players squandering his potential, making mistake after mistake and just going through the motions with no enthusiasm or apparent desire to improve. One day after the coach had seen enough, he called the player into his office, looked him in the eyes, and asked, "Are you ignorant or just apathetic?"

The player lifted his head and mumbled, "I don't know, and I don't care!"

Compare that attitude to that of my younger granddaughter, Ellie Kate, as reflected in a message she left on my phone not too long ago. She was calling to tell me what she was doing with her mommy and unfortunately—for me—got my voice mail.

"Hey, Gran! It's me, Ellie Kate!" She continued to talk animatedly about all they were doing.

Her excited tone reflected all the sunshine in her day. Her voice was filled with all the enthusiasm she knew I would feel from just simply hearing her voice once again. She was right.

It's the kind of call we all need at times. Calls with a tone and words of excitement that point us back to an attitude of enthusiasm toward the life which we were created to live. An infusion of joy that instantly changes our perspective from one of apathy, self-pity, despair, or defeat to one of enthusiasm.

The word *enthusiasm* itself is derived from the Greek words *en theos*—"in God"—and it's through that faith in God, through His Son Jesus Christ, that we are provided with a hope to face whatever life throws us. Having an attitude of enthusiasm and hope sustains us through whatever adversity we face and allows the light of Jesus Christ to shine through us into a world in desperate need of His life-changing power and love.

"Hey, Gran! It's me, Ellie Kate!"

Thanks, I needed that. How about you? Need to infuse your attitude with enthusiasm? Look up—God is always there!

 IMPACT APPLICATION: Use your platform today to spread a little enthusiasm that reflects the love of God for each one of us—a love that will never disappoint, never desert, and provides us with all the strength and encouragement we will ever need to face whatever life throws our way.

HOPE IN THE MORNING

Because of our faith, Christ has brought us into this place of unde-served privilege where we now stand, and we confidently and joyfully look forward to sharing God's glory. . . . And this hope will not lead to disappointment. For we know how dearly God loves us, because he has given us the Holy Spirit to fill our hearts with his love. **Romans 5:2, 5**

IT'S THAT FEELING you had the instant your eyes opened to let in the sunshine of a new morning. It's the same feeling you have in that instant before your mind starts down the list of all the busyness or concern for the day.

Hope!

It's true. It's there!

It's in that moment when you sense the burst of excitement and anticipation. That feeling that sees the day as one full of possibilities. That moment when you believe that all you want to happen actually *will* happen.

Hope!

And it lies within us. It's too often covered with all the day's concerns or some insecurity formed within us by people from the past who didn't understand their role as nurturer and didn't see the potential God created within our lives. It may be covered by all the times in which we've fallen short in achieving what we set out to accomplish. Or maybe it's hidden because temptation or bad advice got us off track.

But it's still there: the hope of the risen Christ for all who believe. The hope of the Holy Spirit—the Helper Christ sent for us—standing ready within us to guide and see us through whatever obstacles have lined up within the hours of our day.

It's what gets us through those days we can't get through. Hope!

It's what fights the illnesses we can't fight. Hope!

It's what causes us to get up one more time when we fall. Hope!

It's knowing the sun will shine after the rain. Hope!

It's what I saw in the smile of a dear friend as she sported a baseball cap that covered the hair loss from a new round of chemotherapy. Hope!

It's what I felt in the grip of a warrior of God while visiting and praying with her and her husband in the hospital as she marched relentlessly onward into yet another day of a ten-year battle with multiple myeloma—continuing to believe in the love and power of her living Christ. Hope!

We are lifted with it by God's hand, loved with it by God's heart, warmed with it by God's breath, guided by it through God's gentle whisper, and encouraged with it by God's constant presence.

Hope!

IMPACT APPLICATION: The hope we have in Christ is a reminder that no matter what we go through—no matter the heartache, illness, or disappointment we experience—nothing of significant, eternal importance has changed or will ever change. Hope!

FEBRUARY 25

LET IT BE!

The angel answered her, "The Holy Spirit will come upon you, and the power of the Most High will overshadow you; therefore the child to be born will be called holy—the Son of God." . . . And Mary said, "Behold, I am the servant of the Lord; let it be to me according to your word."
Luke 1:35, 38, ESV

I CAN ONLY SHAKE MY HEAD as I try to understand it all: the plan to have the Son of the Most High God be born to a virgin in Bethlehem, in a stable, behind an inn, with only a few barnyard animals there to celebrate the occasion.

It is simply not the way any of us would have introduced the Savior into the world.

Think about it: Mary was a young girl, perhaps fourteen to sixteen years of age. No doubt she came from a poor family. And she was chosen by God for perhaps the most important act of obedience in history.

Strange.

Mary was probably not too sophisticated with the ways of the world when she asked Gabriel a quick, "How will this be?" to make sure he knew that she was virgin. But when the angel answered her, she was all in!

"I am the servant of the Lord; let it be to me according to your word."

She didn't question. She had to be overwhelmed, but she didn't seek to control the situation. She didn't have any idea how she would explain it to her family, to Joseph, to his family, or to the community when they observed her walking around unmarried and pregnant.

Instead, Mary gave up control of all of that—and said, "Let it be!" And in that moment, she got control of her life—God's control.

"Let it be!"

Mary's story is a lot like mine, maybe even like yours. We find ourselves in the middle of life—overwhelmed at times—not knowing which way to turn or what we should do with the decisions and difficulties we face.

At times, we've all reached a point where we're not sure how we can hold it all together much longer and don't know what to do or where to go for help and guidance. We look for answers and listen for God's direction—in whatever form it may come—and then hope we recognize it when it comes. Sometimes we even look in the wrong places for direction or relief. Does that sound like you, too?

Maybe it's simply time to give God control.

You can trust Him. Let it be!

 IMPACT APPLICATION: For God's purposes to be fully realized in your life, you must give God control of everything. So the next time you're holding on too tight, think of Mary! Let it be!

FIVE MINUTES

Wherever your treasure is, there the desires of your heart will also be.
Luke 12:34

THE MORNING'S COFFEE was fairly ordinary—Maxwell House original, I think. Not the flavored kind Lynda or I often prepare the night before, which fills the kitchen each morning with the aroma of vanilla, hazelnut, or southern pecan fragrances as we awake. "Fu-Fu" coffee, my nephew calls it. But this morning the coffee was fairly ordinary.

But there was nothing ordinary about the mug the coffee was poured into.

It was one of many mugs I have been given reminding me of the people I love—with their picture emblazoned on the side. I have mugs with my elder granddaughter, Hannah; some with a family picture; mugs with pictures of our two granddaughters together; and then mugs with a picture of each of those precious girls captured during one of our times together.

Yesterday's mug selection featured a picture of Hannah, smiling wistfully during one of her recent visits. Today's mug boasts a picture of our younger granddaughter, Ellie Kate, laughing heartily at dinner one evening during a recent family trip to Sea Island, Georgia. Looking at her picture on the mug, I can't help but laugh out loud myself and want to grab her up in my arms to hold forever.

Sadly, the times pictured don't last forever, but happily, their memories remain. Memories made during times with those we love and for whom we would move heaven and earth to help, to protect, and to encourage. Memories made that fill page after page of the scrapbooks of our lives. Memories made that make an eternal difference in our lives and the lives of the ones we love.

Today is a new day—the only one like it we will be given. I wonder what we will decide to do with it. I wonder how many pictures we will record of times with those we love—while we still have the time to make them. I wonder whether the pages of this year will reflect the eternal significance of the times with those we love or the temporal successes of a society bent on achievement and the accumulation of things, so often at the expense of moments we could have spent with those we love.

Christopher Morley once shared that "if we discovered that we had only five minutes left to say all we wanted to say, every telephone would be occupied by people calling other people to stammer that they loved them."

Just something for each of us to think about as we fill the pages of this year.

I wonder which mug I'll select tomorrow—perhaps the one with the picture of Hannah reading to Ellie Kate on her second birthday.

 IMPACT APPLICATION: The key to how we choose to fill our days is in our hands. I wonder what the memories will look like that we make and record in the pages of memory books.

DIXIELAND DELIGHT

The eternal God is your refuge, and his everlasting arms are under you.
Deuteronomy 33:27

FOR SOME REASON my beloved band of thirteen- and fourteen-year-old misfits, who had been selected by the coaches in the league to carry the banner of the Gainesville Pony League All-Star Baseball team into district and state championship tournament play, had selected "Dixieland Delight" as their theme song.

My nephew and I had been selected as their coaches. Talented individually, the players initially fell a wee bit short of their impression that they were the best team to ever grace a baseball diamond. And so in that first hour of our first practice, we began the process of unifying them as a selfless, competent, and focused unit as they moved closer to accepting their shared purpose.

The defining moment for them came in the last inning of an elimination-bracket game in the district tournament. One team was down by six runs, and tournament officials had already brought the trophies out to give to the other team. The outcome seemed inevitable to everyone except our players. One of them, Mike, a young man who never saw a pitch he shouldn't swing at, managed a moment of discipline and earned a walk. Then another managed a single, an error helped the cause, and another one of our guys coaxed out another walk, then a double, a home run, and before the dust cleared in that inning, we had tied the game.

An inning later, Brian—a quiet, determined young man—stepped to the plate as a pinch-hitter and hit a solo home run to win the game, allowing us to become one of only four teams to move on to Tampa to play in the Florida State Pony League Championships. The sounds of "Dixieland Delight" soared from the boom box in the dugout, lifting the hopes of everyone present.

How has this last week been for you? Have you had a moment or two when you felt like you were six runs down with an inning left to go in the game? Maybe things have happened that make you want to throw in the towel. Or maybe people are relying on you for direction, and you're not sure which way to go. Perhaps we all need a reminder of the presence, as well as the unbridled love and commitment to us in those kind of moments we may be going through, of the God who created us.

I don't know what you're facing today or tomorrow. But what I do know is that the One who loved you first loves you most and stands with you still, and He calls you to step out into all you can be with Him.

Misfits, hardly! Beloved, always! Loved by the God who is always with us.

 IMPACT APPLICATION: Six runs down with an inning to go—God is there to play it out with you until the end and into eternity.

MAXIMIZE
THE MOMENTS

When I was a child / . . . I heard a song in the breeze / It was there, singing out my name. **Susan Boyle, "Who I Was Born to Be"**

A FEW YEARS AGO my son shared with me that he believed God had called him to write. As I listened, I told Nathan what I have told countless others through the years: "Minimize the moments in life where you will look back and say, 'I wish I had done that.'"

With the blessing and support of his bride and daughters, he has stepped onto the path he felt God was calling him to, and the journey has led him to write nine children's books and seven books primarily for adults, one of which, *Quiet Strength* (with Tony Dungy), has become the all-time bestselling sports autobiography.

Somebody must have told Susan Boyle the same thing I told Nathan. On April 11, 2009, this plain and unassuming woman in her forties took the stage on *Britain's Got Talent* and announced to a mildly mocking audience and three unimpressed judges that she wanted to be a singer like England's great Elaine Paige. And then Susan Boyle sang. Her notoriety and career took wing, and shortly thereafter she released her first album, which sold more than two million copies in four weeks.

In the process of being who God made him, Nathan has blessed the lives of millions through his books. In the process of following her dream, which others initially mocked, Susan Boyle has blessed millions with her voice. They both have inspired others to do the same.

That was what caused me to listen to God's leading and start Impact for Living—through a dream I had one night. The dream encouraged me to step out and inspire people to allow God to transform them into the people He created them to be.

It is a dream now turned into reality through God's grace, guidance, and the belief and support of so many others. It is a reality that is helping people to understand that the bigger picture of our lives is painted by the God who has created each of us to leave a legacy that only we can leave, day by day. It is a call to embrace a journey of incredible impact that changes not only our lives but the lives of others around us and in the process forever expands His Kingdom.

So what is it that God has laid on your heart and is calling you to do? Sing? Write? Start a ministry? Mentor a child? Be a better husband? Spend more time with your children? Be a friend to someone who has none?

When you draw that last breath, make sure you have only a short list of those things that you wish you had done.

IMPACT APPLICATION: You have so much potential waiting to be released. Like Nathan and Susan, take the risk, release the dream, and watch as God uses you to change the world!

MARCH 1

RIGHT NEXT TO YOU!

I am convinced that nothing can ever separate us from God's love. Neither death nor life, neither angels nor demons, neither our fears for today nor our worries about tomorrow—not even the powers of hell can separate us from God's love. No power in the sky above or in the earth below—indeed, nothing in all creation will ever be able to separate us from the love of God that is revealed in Christ Jesus our Lord.
Romans 8:38-39

THOSE SCRIPTURE VERSES from Paul are one of the greatest passages of hope, assurance, and comfort anywhere in God's Word. For me this passage has been a continual comfort and source of strength through all the years of challenge, difficulty, disappointment, and opportunity.

We've probably all read or heard this passage before. And when we encounter it, we are comforted and strengthened again by the promise contained there. But Satan always does his very best to help us to forget that promise—that nothing can ever separate us from the love of God that was revealed to us in Christ and in what He did for us.

Nothing can separate us from Him and His love. He is closer to you than anyone else is, was, or ever will be, and He never leaves your side. He is within you, beside you, in front of you, and behind you—everywhere you are.

When our granddaughter Ellie Kate was three, we kept her and her sister, Hannah, for a few days while her parents were on a trip. Their dad called to talk to the girls, and while he was talking to Ellie, Ellie asked if she could speak to her mommy.

"Is she right beside you?" Ellie asked.

Actually, she wasn't. But that's how Ellie Kate saw her mom and dad—always next to each other, never separated.

That's how Paul wants us to see our relationship with Christ—never separated. That's what will give our lives the impact God intended them to have in the world around us.

So what have you allowed to creep on your list today that might try to separate you from the love and power of Christ? Doubt, fear, low self-esteem, having to prove yourself to someone or the world, some storm in your family you didn't expect, some guilt you can't get over, a mistake you've made, a habit you need to break, a tragedy that hit?

Give them to Christ. He is right there next to you, and He will help you. And remember—nothing can separate you from God through Christ. Nothing!

IMPACT APPLICATION: It's one of the great comforting truths and promises in all of Scripture. Don't just read it or listen to it—claim it for every day of your life. Nothing can separate you from the love of God in Christ Jesus!

NO ONE LIKE YOU

The LORD will work out his plans for my life—for your faithful love,
O LORD, endures forever. Don't abandon me, for you made me.
Psalm 138:8

RIGHT WHERE YOU ARE NOW, take a look at your fingertips—not just the
chapped skin or chipped nails from the cold weather—but look closely at the
whorls and lines on the inner surface of the last joint of your finger. We learned
the truth in grade school that our fingerprints are unique to each of us; no one else
has the same pattern of whorls or lines. Now work your way down to the palms
of your hands, looking closely at the configuration of lines and markings you see
there. Think about this truth: what you just saw is unique; no one else in the world
has ever had or will ever have what you just saw.

It doesn't stop with our fingerprints. Everything about you and me is uniquely
crafted and designed. Yet the world doesn't view us that way. If it did, the world
would cherish each of us the way the God who created us does. But instead we too
often forget our uniqueness and allow ourselves to listen to the lies the world tells
us about ourselves. And God's voice that whispers into our hearts, *special . . . best
. . . perfect . . . child of God*, is lost in the chorus of boos, criticisms, and put-downs
we hear from the world around us.

As the running back for the Green Bay Packers, Ryan Grant started a division
play-off game with two fumbles that led to two touchdowns for the opposing team,
the Seattle Seahawks. Ryan could tell that the home crowd that had gathered in
Lambeau Field in Green Bay for the game wasn't happy with him. His coach kept
him in, though; and the quarterback, Brett Favre, kept handing him the ball to
run with; and he ended the game with more than two hundred yards rushing and
was an instrumental part of his team's victory. Ryan experienced a God thing—not
in the victory, but in his refusal to let the crowd's put-downs or his past failures
dampen his gifts, talents, and the desires of his heart.

Several thousand years ago, David, anointed by God as a shepherd boy to
become the king of Israel, committed adultery and murder. The psalms he wrote
afterward reflected those past deeds and the guilt, anguish, and undeserving feelings he had for the position he continued to occupy. Yet, confronted, corrected,
and sent out by God, David moved on to lead the people of Israel.

IMPACT APPLICATION: No one has the same
potential, gifts, abilities, passions, desires, talents,
platforms, or intended purposes that you have. No
one. God made you unique. Keep going.

MARCH 3

NO REGRETS

My life has already been poured out as an offering to God. The time of my death is near. I have fought the good fight, I have finished the race, and I have remained faithful. **2 Timothy 4:6-7**

OUR GRANDDAUGHTER Hannah must have been disappointed when we didn't attend her piano recital. She knew that her Mimi and granddaddy always try to come to everything she is involved in. The problem was that we didn't know about it. I was crushed.

We're running out of moments. No regrets.

That's the undercurrent in those words the apostle Paul wrote to the younger Timothy. Paul knew he was running out of time. He wrote those words during his imprisonment in Rome, while the evil emperor Nero planned his execution. With death impending, Paul was making certain once again that Timothy understood what was really important in life.

We're running out of time. No regrets.

It's why a few years ago many of my Saturday mornings were devoted to a round-trip drive to Tampa to watch my two granddaughters play softball. That's it, and then it was back home to Gainesville. They knew I was there, but more than that, *I* knew I was there. And the memories of one Saturday would never have happened if I had stayed home.

The game for four-year-old Ellie Kate was first. I had just fist-bumped her during her game, while she was standing on first base after a clean base hit. Three outs later, her team was on defense, and she was playing second base—with her own style and flair—by standing *on* second base. I whistled to her.

Both Ellie Kate and Hannah know my whistle. Ellie looked my way and began to wrap her arms around herself while she was saying something I couldn't make out. The next time she yelled it louder across the ball field as she continued to wrap her arms around herself: "Gran, I love you!"

I returned the blessing with my own comparable display of hugs: "Ellie, I love you, too!"

She smiled her warm *I know!* smile back and then held up the "I love you" hand signal—thumb, index, and little finger raised high. I returned that blessing too.

Later, after holding Ellie a number of times and watching Hannah play her game, I kissed the girls—and "Marjorie," Hannah's doll—good-bye and drove home. I wouldn't have missed it.

We're running out of opportunities. No regrets.

 IMPACT APPLICATION: What haven't you done that you should have done? Who haven't you called that you should have called? Who haven't you taken to lunch that you should have—long ago? Who haven't you shared the eternal love of God with? We're running out of years. Live life with no regrets.

LIVE LIKE YOU
ARE DYING

The end of the world is coming soon. Therefore, be earnest and disciplined in your prayers. Most important of all, continue to show deep love for each other, for love covers a multitude of sins. **1 Peter 4:7-8**

MY LATEST VISIT to the doctor gave no indication of any problem or concern. The usual blood tests were on the good side of the normal range. Though my doctor couldn't put his professionally trained finger on any particular problem, it hit me once again that I am dying.

It was unnerving, to say the least.

I may have six months or less to live. I may have a year or more. But whatever time is left, I know it's not forever. Lynda and I don't talk about it, but I know we have both thought about it, especially in the forty-ninth year of our marriage. I suspect some of you—if you're honest with yourselves—have been in the same place.

So here's how we should pray today.

In the words of a song by country singer Tim McGraw, pray that in the time we have left on this earth, we would "live like [we are] dying." McGraw sang these words reflecting on his dad. His dad was a Major League Baseball pitcher, Tug McGraw, and Tim never really got to know him until very late in life when they discovered Tug had less than a year to live.

Nothing forces us to consider our life, our legacy, and our purpose like the prospect of dying. We know we don't have forever in this life, and the moments we let pass us by won't usually circle back for a second chance. But sadly, we still live like we have forever left here on this earth. Despite our good intentions, our best efforts, and our accomplishments to this point, there will still be things we've always wanted to do and many more we should have done long ago—still waiting to be done.

Peter writes that because the end of the world is coming, rather than retreating and focusing on comfort, followers of Christ should be even more bold, serious, and disciplined in our actions toward each other. He tells us specifically "to show deep love for each other," which is the example our Savior showed us and left for us to follow.

What does it mean to "live like we are dying"? To hold those close to us a little nearer and a little longer, to ensure they know we love them. To not waste the time given to us on things that don't really matter.

So today, pray that we will live like we are dying. Then it won't matter at all what the doctor might say.

 IMPACT APPLICATION: Live like today is your last day on this earth, and you will be amazed at the sense of purpose that fills every thought you have and every action you take.

MARCH 5

WHERE DID IT ALL GO?

Each man's life touches so many other lives. When he isn't around he leaves an awful hole, doesn't he? **Clarence the angel, from** *It's a Wonderful Life*

DO YOU EVER STOP TO WONDER, *Where did it all go?*

I was trying to articulate that feeling to a friend the other night. Although I struggled looking for the right words, it didn't matter because he knew anyway. He has an innate wisdom about such things.

Are so many years gone and seemingly empty of impact? Are the big dreams of our hearts, which were so full of promise, unfulfilled? Are the great plans we had mapped out still rolled up in their original blueprints? What happened to our memories of world-conquering idealism as we erupted out of our youth and headed toward eternity? Too many *if only*s strewn along the side of the road. And we wonder, *Where did it all go?* Perhaps we're looking in the wrong places.

A few years ago in a tiny fishing village, the villagers decided they needed one more big catch to get them through the winter. They determined that the next day they'd go out to sea one more time. As the men were out at sea, a storm materialized. The wind howled, the sea rolled, and darkness fell. Frightened wives and children huddled at the pier to hope, pray, and wait. But there was no sign of the boats.

Suddenly, back up on the hill, a fire started. Annie, the youngest of the wives, had forgotten to put out her house's candles. The women watched helplessly as the fire raged through her little cottage. Then, amid the seeming disaster on land and out of the darkness of the sea, they heard a shout. The boats were safely back.

There was celebration all around—except for Annie, whose home the fire had destroyed. That is, until her husband took her into his big fisherman's arms and said, "Don't worry, Annie. We were lost in the storm until we saw that light." The light of the flames had guided them home.

Take time to recognize the importance of the moments in your life. They may seem insignificant, but they may look different with some perspective.

Look into the faces of those you love. Look into the lives of family and friends whom you have touched through the years. Reflect on the hands and hearts of those who have helped to shape who you are. Smile with gratitude as you think of those who walk with you today and who need you to walk with them.

May you be able to point to the lives of the people around you as "where it all went."

 IMPACT APPLICATION: You will find that the answer to "Where did it all go?" is right there, in the rivers of recollection of the faces and lives that flood over you during your quietest moments, remembering how your life has touched and been touched by so many others.

THE EVERGREEN TREE

"I know the plans I have for you," says the LORD. "They are plans for good and not for disaster, to give you a future and a hope."
Jeremiah 29:11

IT WAS A MAJESTIC TREE, standing tall and pointing straight upward. The view from the top of that evergreen tree was spectacular.

Despite having nearly fallen out of my perch at the top on a couple of occasions, the view, and so much more, made it worth the climb. Because for a seven-year-old, the "more" was that it was a safe place, a place of hope. Up there, no one could hurt you. Up there, the world looked better. Up there, you could sense the presence of something or someone safe. Something almost sacred.

At the top, fifty feet in the air, I could see for miles, across the rooftops stretching beyond my aunt and uncle's two-story house where I stayed. I'd spend hours in that tree, just lying across a friendly branch. Way up high in the evergreen tree, I planned great things for my future—and dreamed how one day my family would be reunited, and I would be a great baseball player, and everyone would love me. In the top of that tree, I found the strength to withstand the world I would have to face again when my feet inevitably hit the ground—because I would eventually have to come down. My mother was gone, institutionalized in the dead of one night. I wouldn't see her again for fourteen years, assuming after a while that she was dead. My dad was too busy to come by and was living somewhere else.

But I always had that evergreen tree.

Those retreats high in the air sustained me through difficult times. The rejection and fear on the ground was still real and ever present. But the view from on high, with all its possibilities and hope, remained etched in my mind.

As things grew worse, my thoughts carried me back to the top of that tree. I always felt safer and stronger, just from remembering those moments. I still climb up there every now and then, at least in my mind and spirit. It's a nice reminder of God's presence today in the midst of whatever I may face.

Perhaps you need an evergreen tree to climb to the top of today. And at the top, you may just discover the potential and future He has planned for you—because He *does* have a future planned for you.

Go ahead. Enjoy the view.

IMPACT APPLICATION: The climb to the top of your evergreen tree may not always change the reality on the ground. But when you get to the top, you will find renewal, restoration, and the strength to regroup for those moments when your feet hit the ground again.

MARCH 7

NO DILL PICKLE ZONE

[Jesus] said, "I tell you the truth, unless you turn from your sins and become like little children, you will never get into the Kingdom of Heaven. So anyone who becomes as humble as this little child is the greatest in the Kingdom of Heaven." **Matthew 18:3-4**

RECENTLY OUR GRANDDAUGHTERS, Hannah and Ellie Kate, were playing with their American Girl dolls at their home. Their Mimi had ordered some new doll clothes, which had just arrived, and they were trying the outfits on their "children."

In that time together they were switching outfits between their dolls, fixing their dolls' hair, remaking the dolls' sleeping locations in the corners of their rooms, and generally playing make-believe—or was it real?

In the context of that setting, they started talking about jobs and asked each other, "What is your dream job?"

Hannah reflected for a moment and then said, "Veterinarian!"

Ellie Kate smiled—she loves animals too—and without skipping a beat said, "Good. Or an angel!"

What do we do to our little children to dampen such fertile imaginations, fervent wonder, kindness, and unbridled enthusiasm? Seriously, if we heard such comments from adults, we would call them crazy.

Maybe we're too serious around God's little children and don't smile enough. Or worse, maybe we take *ourselves* too seriously, thinking we're being wise and mature, when maybe we're just being too downcast or practical.

We should make a rule that no adult (or person of any age who reminds us of an adult) whose smile looks like it was formed from sucking on a dill pickle can get anywhere near any "happiness zone" that children create. And such a rule would apply until the person gains the Christlike maturity, humility, and enthusiasm of children, which Christ depicted in the passage from Matthew 18.

It's no wonder my heart jumps for joy when I know that our granddaughters are coming to visit. It's no wonder Mimi gets the cookie-making stuff ready, I pull out the paints and easel in our upstairs office, and even our little rescue dog, Tulip, senses the pending excitement of their approach.

Those precious little girls return us to where God wants us to be every day: to His land of wonder, joy, and excitement that He specifically created for all of us!

Listen to it again: "Unless you turn from your sins and become like little children, you will never get into the Kingdom of Heaven." Count me in, please!

IMPACT APPLICATION: Approach and embrace every moment of your life with an attitude of unbridled, childlike enthusiasm.

BLESSINGS RESTORED AND PASSED ON

One day when Isaac was old and turning blind, he called for Esau, his older son, and said, "My son." "Yes, Father?" Esau replied. "I am an old man now," Isaac said, "and I don't know when I may die. Take your bow and a quiver full of arrows, and go out into the open country to hunt some wild game for me. Prepare my favorite dish, and bring it here for me to eat. Then I will pronounce the blessing that belongs to you, my firstborn son, before I die." **Genesis 27:1-4**

IN HIS EXCEPTIONAL BOOK *The Blessing*, Gary Smalley points out that when we bless others, it includes daily affirmations of meaningful touch, a spoken message, attaching high value to their lives, picturing a special future for them, and a devotion to an active commitment to fulfill that blessing in their lives.

The blessing he refers to, which is described in Genesis 27, happens in our lives in many ways. Usually it is the moment-by-moment commitment we show through positive words, tone, and facial expressions and through nurturing children and raising them with love, security, and gentle touching. It occurs when we continually paint a picture of all they can be as wonderful children of God.

Many of you probably remember receiving the blessing of your parents and other loved ones. Sadly, too many of us don't, having never received such a day-by-day blessing. And we have a hard time accepting that we may never receive it from those who didn't give it.

And yet despite this, we are called to bless others. Often we don't—or can't—because we don't know how. We struggle, and thus too often others miss out—another generation loses the blessing. We can make the blessing too much about ourselves and what we never got, when it should be all about God and what He has called us to give to others. The person we need to bless may be our child, our spouse, our friend, our coworker, or our student. And the blessing for their lives lies in our hands, whether we ever received one or not.

Let God do it through you for others. And in the process you may be blessed as well through the sense of fulfillment you get as God looks down upon you while you bless others—others, who like you, are His children. It's not about you. It's not about us. It's not about seeking what we never got or what we should get. Instead, it's all about Him and what He calls us to do for others. To bless them.

And the miraculous thing is that when you do—not thinking of yourself—you will sense His hand of blessing on your shoulder.

His Blessing! It doesn't get any better than that!

IMPACT APPLICATION: Whether you received a blessing or not, bless others with and for Him. Every day extend a blessing to those around you who you love and who you are entrusted by Him to love.

MARCH 9

MAGIC CARPET RIDES

A four-year-old girl was overheard whispering into her newborn baby brother's ear. "Baby," she whispers, "tell me what God sounds like. I am starting to forget." **Robert Benson**

THE NEWEST OPPORTUNITY for Granddaddy to play with and serve his grand-daughters is with the "Magic Carpet Ride." A small couch pillow serves as the "magic carpet," with either Hannah or Ellie Kate kneeling in a scrunched-up position on the pillow in the family room.

Then the engine—Granddaddy—takes a firm hold of both sides of the pillow and slowly begins the liftoff. The magic carpet gains speed as it flies high into the heavens, high above cities and countryside, and over bridges and around sky-scrapers. As the fuel gets low—often sooner than expected—the "magic carpet" begins a high-speed whirly-bird-like circling descent with a couple of upside-down loops thrown in to elicit shrieks from the passenger, until it lands safely.

"Again, Gran, again!"

There's a reason Christ gathered little children around Him. There's a reason He said, "The Kingdom of Heaven belongs to those who are like these children" (Matthew 19:14). They were humble and unconcerned with social status. And they were fun to be around. They were probably always making up games to play.

Part of the reason Christ gathered the children around Him may have been because the adults around Him were no longer smiling; life had become too serious. They were no fun to be around anymore.

Christ knew that what He saw on the outside of folks reflected what was on the inside. I can't help but think it made Him sad when he looked into the faces of the adults who came to see Him. I also can't help but believe that He wanted them to change—to start hearing His voice again, to spend time with Him, to reclaim His joy in their lives. I know too many people who are in desperate need of a magic carpet ride. You do too. Years ago I was one of them too.

A. W. Tozer wrote, "Culture is putting out the light in men and women's souls." I think he was right. Too many people—men, women, mothers, fathers, pastors, coaches, business folks, young, and old—walk around with emptiness written all over their faces. They awake each morning with frowns. And the saddest thing— the thing that must give Christ a fit—is that they pass it on to loved ones around them, who pass it on to their children as the cycle repeats itself.

You want to catch a glimpse of the life Christ intended for you? Watch the heart of a little child. Then go for a magic carpet ride.

 IMPACT APPLICATION: Watch children and learn from them. Don't throw cold water on them, but instead, change and become like them, no matter your age. It will be a ride you, and those around you, will never forget.

MARCH MADNESS

I can do everything through Christ, who gives me strength.
Philippians 4:13

"DO THEY DO THIS EVERY YEAR?" my then brand-new, wide-eyed daughter-in-law, Amy, asked as she caught her first glimpse, through Nathan, of the NCAA basketball championship's March Madness.

March Madness is so special because it is the annual spring pilgrimage where college basketball players—talented kids from every walk of life—reach for that one magical moment they have dreamed of in all the pickup games they have ever played on all the basketball courts, driveways, and backyards they could find as they were growing up.

Wouldn't it be wonderful if you and I, and every child everywhere, could have such moments that cause us to reach beyond where we thought we could reach—out into the darkness of uncertainty—for all we were meant to be?

Ever wonder why there are some kids living in poverty who are abused, disenfranchised, and disconnected from opportunities available to the rest of the world? Ever wonder why there are so many homeless families and so few soup kitchens and medical clinics for the needy? Ever wonder why some kids do poorly in school and are forever labeled as underachievers, developmentally disabled, or slow?

That was not God's intention when He created them and entrusted them to parents, family, friends, and—dare I say—to the rest of us.

Reflect with me for a moment on the "children of all ages" whose dreams are often snuffed out at an early age through no fault of their own, on the man or woman in the middle of life for whom the wind has seemed to have gone out of their sails, or on the elderly who sit alone with only their memories to get them through the day. They are all dreamers—like you and me—who may need a lift up to encourage them to rekindle that desire to reach again for that one shining star in the darkness—and perhaps that one shining moment where a dream is finally fulfilled. And in that moment when they reach for their dream, whether they're successful or not, they will come closer to becoming the person God created them to be.

Yes, Amy, as you now know, they do this every year. NCAA's March Madness. Sixty-eight teams, one national champion, and an incalculable number of magical moments that will last a lifetime for those who participate and for those of us who cheer them on.

And perhaps there will be moments that will inspire each of us to reach, and keep reaching, for all He intended for us to be—for ourselves and for dreamers of all ages everywhere.

 IMPACT APPLICATION: What potential has God already gifted you with? Answer that question, and reach for it, and you will experience the excitement of March Madness every day.

MARCH 11

ELLIE'S TIGHTLY WRAPPED HUG

I pray for you constantly . . . that you will understand the incredible greatness of God's power for us who believe him. This is the same mighty power that raised Christ from the dead and seated him in the place of honor at God's right hand in the heavenly realms.
Ephesians 1:16, 19-20

I WASN'T SURE I could get loose from her grip. I knew I didn't want to, although I knew deep inside that eventually I would have to. Yet in that moment I realized it was something more than just a hug.

As I leaned close to pray with Ellie Kate, interrupting the bedtime reading with her Mimi, Ellie Kate wrapped both arms tightly around my neck and whispered in my ear, "I love you, Gran." It was a playful, affirming, and powerfully sacred reminder.

It was almost as if she knew I needed to hear that right then.

Moments like these are sacred moments in which you almost feel you are touching the face of God. Moments like these are short and too infrequent, it seems. And afterward everything seems to return to the way it was.

Things will seem overwhelming again. Life will throw us fastballs that we'll swing right through. We'll strike out. Relationships will become strained again. Fear will grab us, and our dreams will begin to fade into simply wishful notions. Our perspective will betray what we don't want to believe—that God doesn't care and that the emptiness and helplessness we feel at times have replaced the hope we long for and desperately need just to be able to put one foot in front of another. But then we remember moments like this one, and a measure of perspective returns, and we sense the presence of God in the middle of our difficulties.

This moment with Ellie Kate was a simple reminder that the God who blessed our weekend with a visit from our granddaughter is the same God who created her and the ends of the universe, the same God who hung the stars in the heavens and raised our Savior from the grave. The same God who will be with us when moments like that end and everyday life continues.

This moment was an eternal moment, cast in a tightly wrapped hug and a gentle whisper. It was a warm and sacred reminder that no matter what we face or what the day may throw at us or where or how the world around us may be spinning, that same eternal power that hung the stars is there and available for you and for me to help us to deal with whatever the days before us hold.

 IMPACT APPLICATION: Now with that power alongside, with that love wrapped tightly around your neck, and with that quiet message whispering in your ear, you can begin. Live your day having the impact God intended you to have.

THE SECOND MAILBOX

To all who believed him and accepted him, he gave the right to become children of God. **John 1:12**

I DON'T REMEMBER what caused our young son, Nathan, to decide to strike out on his own. To him it must have been significant. But there he stood before us with a traveling bag in hand—packed with some clothes and an ample supply of books—and announced he was running away from home. It was the polite thing to do, to at least let us know, so we wouldn't worry later. He was always thoughtful that way. The ensuing, albeit brief, discussion failed to dissuade him from his commitment.

And so as his mother and I watched from the living room window, he began his journey onto the sidewalk, into the cul-de-sac, and down the street leading away from all he knew into a brand-new life. The wind blew through his hair while his brisk gait signaled a clear conscience, focused thoughts, and little worry as his plan unfolded before him, step by step.

Until he reached the second mailbox from the house.

We watched with a smile as his steps halted. We could tell from a distance, as he stood there, that he remembered. He wasn't allowed to go past the second mailbox on the street. Whether playing or riding his bike, it was always clear: he could go no farther than the second mailbox.

We watched him take a seat on the curb just short of that mailbox to ponder his dilemma. He needed a sign, a signal, and a direction. He would eventually, we learned, take stock of things and find that on balance the very best alternative was what he was running away from.

We are in the midst of what the organized church recognizes as the Lenten season heading to Easter Sunday. It's a period of reflection, penance, and preparation for Christ's resurrection Sunday. Yet in the midst of this season, our world seems to be spinning out of control. And personally, many of us have come to a point where we feel we've reached rock bottom, finding ourselves in the depths of despair or having compromised the values we should live by. We have reached the "second mailbox from the house" and find ourselves sitting on the curb by the side of the road.

It's then we need to remember who we are, from where we came, and whose we are. It's then we need to remember that we are beloved children of God. That no matter what we have done or where we have gone, He will wait for us to return to His waiting arms.

 IMPACT APPLICATION: I don't know where you are in your life, and I don't know what you face. But I do know that when you reach the second mailbox and don't know which way to go, the very best you can do is to turn—and return—to Him.

MARCH 13

NOW

Teach us to realize the brevity of life, so that we may grow in wisdom.
Psalm 90:12

NOW. In this world, *now* is about all the time we have for certain.

Consider this: During our time in this world, will we have tomorrow? Maybe. Maybe not.

Will we have at least one more hour? Maybe. Maybe not.

One more minute? You get the point.

Can we go back and redo yesterday? Oh, if only wishing made it so!

None of us is promised one moment beyond *now.* Yet we spend an awful lot of time wishing we could do some things from yesterday differently or worrying about tomorrow when *now* is really all we ever have. So what we do with the *now* we are given is important. *Now* is the one point in time we are given to make an impact.

A dear friend recently told me a story about a friend of his. That friend was driving home from the office when he got caught in an unexpected traffic jam. Soon he realized that he would be late for the plans he and his bride had made for the evening.

Always one to see something positive in every situation, that man viewed the traffic jam not as a burden but as a chance to catch up with family and friends. So for an hour, while stuck in traffic, he spoke with his bride, his two married daughters, and his son at college. He spoke with a friend he hadn't connected with in some time and with his pastor, who needed a bit of encouragement.

A few minutes after his last phone call, while still in traffic, he suffered a fatal heart attack.

In the last hour of his life, he left unforgettable memories in the lives of those he loved, thanks to a traffic jam most would have viewed as a forgettable inconvenience.

What will you and I do with our *now?* Will we spend too much time thinking about how we can change the things of yesterday? Wonder and worry about what may happen tomorrow? Complain about the "traffic jams" of our lives? None of that would be anything but a waste of the time we have left today and of any time we may receive in the rest of our tomorrows.

Now is what we've been given, whether spending it with family or friends, at the office or at home. *Now* is ours, whether at a ball game or in a traffic jam. What will be the memories we leave?

In the midst of the "traffic jams" in which you may find yourself, look for the opportunities they present to impact the lives of others around you.

IMPACT APPLICATION: Imagine the legacy you will leave if you live today as if it were the only day you had left. Imagine the impact you can have today—*now.*

STOPPING TO HELP

The first question that the Levite asked was, "If I stop to help this man, what will happen to me?" But then the Good Samaritan came by. And he reversed the question: "If I do not stop to help this man, what will happen to him?" **Martin Luther King Jr.**

I SUPPOSE WHERE I first noticed Him was in the steadfastness and love of Lynda's parents.

Then I began to notice that He was always apparent in Lynda's steady, daily, accepting, and uncompromising example.

Then I saw Him in the powerful, challenging, and joy-filled teachings uttered by David Scoates, pastor of a local church and a dear friend until his untimely death a number of years later. David always talked about an empowering and loving Jesus I had not heard of as a child.

After David, I saw Him through a conference speaker who said something that caused my heart to warm to His approach. That speaker's words, coupled with an "unexpected" meeting at two in the morning with a dear friend, Bob Wood, who had invited Lynda and me to attend the conference, finally drew me into a life-saving and eternally changing relationship with Him.

At some earlier time, all of those people who touched my life had given their hearts to the Lord—and it changed their lives. And they continued along their journey in their relationship with the Lord, no longer thinking of themselves but instead all the while giving Him their time, talents, and treasures to touch the world with and for Him.

As a result of those relationships and the path of their lives crossing over mine, my life was forever changed. At every juncture on their journeys, they were never concerned about themselves but instead were concerned about the people God placed before them. If you listened closely to their lives, you would never have heard them asking, "What will happen to me?" when confronted with someone in need, but instead you would have heard them asking, "What will happen to this person if I don't stop and help?"

And just think—they could have passed me by.

But they didn't. Instead they stopped to help. Thank God!

And when we do that, moment by moment, one life after another, just like mine, is changed for all eternity as He uses so many to draw yet so many others to Himself.

Thank You, Lord.

IMPACT APPLICATION: How can you use the platform God has given you today to extend a hand and lift somebody else up above the clouds, perhaps even into a relationship with the living God?

MARCH 15

THE FOCUS
OF OUR LIVES

We do this by keeping our eyes on Jesus, the champion who initiates and perfects our faith. Because of the joy awaiting him, he endured the cross, disregarding its shame. Now he is seated in the place of honor beside God's throne. **Hebrews 12:2**

THE AUTHOR OF HEBREWS makes it clear that there is a focus that helps us steadfastly run the race we face in so many different arenas. A focus that will energize and empower us to do our best in all we undertake and that will carry us through and beyond the games we play, the problems we face, and the temptations and failures we experience.

That focus is Jesus.

Look, I don't know what you're facing—illness, broken dreams, career struggles, a lost relationship. You may feel as though the wind always seems to be blowing in your face and your legs are always wobbling. But the writer of Hebrews reminds us that we are never alone. The One who loved us first has already run the race and crossed the finish line. He sits watching, waiting, cheering, and encouraging us on through the valleys, over the mountains, and through the storms that seem to test, challenge, buffet, and bounce us, sometimes temporarily causing us to lose our focus.

In the 1994 Winter Olympic games in Lillehammer, Norway, an American speed skater, Dan Jansen, was about to skate in the final speed skating event—the 1,000-meter race. He was an American and world record holder, but in this and previous Olympics, he had never won the ultimate goal—the gold medal. In the 500-meter race, which he skated four days earlier and in which he was favored to win gold, he fell. This would probably be his last Olympics. So the pressure was on for the 1,000-meter race. His family—including his little daughter, Jane—waited and watched from their seats in the stands.

And he won! During his victory laps around the track, he held his daughter in his arms and waved to the thousands of cheering witnesses. And if you watched the face and eyes of his daughter throughout those laps, you would catch a glimpse of the kind of focus the writer calls us to in the passage of Hebrews. Her eyes were fixed, focused on her daddy. She didn't turn away, despite all the celebration, noise, and distraction that was going on around her.

That's the kind of focus we must have on Jesus Christ. The kind that looks away from all else—and focuses directly on Him.

IMPACT APPLICATION: Facing the toughest game or moment of your day or life? Keep your eyes on Jesus, the Lord of all there is, remembering that He has already finished the race and is with you wherever you go.

PATHWAY TO
FULFILLMENT

I observed everything going on under the sun, and really, it is all meaningless—like chasing the wind. **Ecclesiastes 1:14**

QUIETLY NOW, I let her sleep. She was up late with the adrenaline of anticipation of this day coursing through heavy, flickering eyelids.

This is the day she turns thirteen. Where have the years gone?

Quietly now, I must check my own enthusiasm as I sit remembering the day our precious granddaughter Hannah was born.

You remember those special days in your life and the life of your family, don't you? I certainly do. Those days are indelibly etched with fondness as I remember the expression on our son's face, as well as where he was standing as he found us in the waiting room, and exactly what he said to introduce his new gift to us moments after her birth.

Every moment since then has been woven into a collage of memories. Some of those moments her Mimi and I witnessed. Others, her parents or she herself reported to us: growth spurts, softly falling tears from a sensitive heart, heart-melting smiles from her trusting soul, tiny steps toward a relationship with the loving God who created her, and excited shrieks as a new revelation of God's creation wrapped around her sense of wonder.

We have given Solomon a lot of credit for being wise, wealthy, and intelligent, for building the Temple, and for ruling Israel well during forty years of peace, but it wasn't until the end of his life that he realized that all he had been seeking after was meaningless—like chasing the wind. It wasn't until the end of his life that he really understood the priorities God had placed on his life. It wasn't until the end of his life that he realized life wasn't about priorities rooted in stuff and things. It was about those moments with God and with those He placed in Solomon's life to love—family and friends. On our last day on earth, which pathway will have brought us more satisfaction and a sense of fulfillment? Follow that pathway—beginning today and every day thereafter.

The memories of the journey of those thirteen years with our precious grand-daughter Hannah are vivid—as are the occasional gaps. I pray the next thirteen years, and the thirteen after that, and so on, will be flooded with even more memories—and fewer and fewer gaps—in our journey with her precious life.

I pray the same for you in the midst of all those important priorities and people in your life.

IMPACT APPLICATION: Which will be the path of your life? Will you choose to take a pathway on which you seek things, accolades, acknowledgments, and awards? Or will you choose a pathway that will reflect a life lived striving after God and embracing the precious lives and sacred moments all around you?

MARCH 17

BEING LIGHT

You are the light of the world—like a city on a hilltop that cannot be hidden. No one lights a lamp and then puts it under a basket. Instead, a lamp is placed on a stand, where it gives light to everyone in the house. In the same way, let your good deeds shine out for all to see, so that everyone will praise your heavenly Father. **Matthew 5:14-16**

AS I READ and re-read Jesus' words from Matthew 5, I want to believe the message those words convey, and I want to do it.

I want to be a light to the world.

Being a light to others. Helping others. Giving them a lift up.

But here's the truth: it seems too much to do and way too often to do it. It's too hard. Most days I am exhausted even before I get out of bed and stay that way right up to the time when I pass out on my pillow at night.

How about you? Can you connect with that?

But there it is in Jesus' own words: "You are the light." Probably means me, too; I don't suppose he was just talking to you.

We are light.

We are to be light to others.

We are to be light to the world.

But how? Seriously, how can we do it?

Let me suggest that we don't need to do anything special, other than to let the light of Christ shine through us in our everyday moments. For example, let the light of Christ shine

- through our bright "hello" and soft "good-bye";
- through our warm smiles and our inclusive laughter;
- through an unexpected kindness or a thoughtful, encouraging word;
- through a gentle hug;
- through a genuine, heartfelt apology without explanation or qualification; or
- through an arm on their shoulder, a kiss on their cheek, an affirming "good try" with a readiness to help your children do better.

How can we be the light we are called to be? Simple. Let it be Christ who is the light shining through us. Then others who see us will see Christ, because we are letting Him shine, talk, and act through us.

That's how. It's never too hard for Him, and He'll help us when it seems too hard for us to be the light He says we are to be.

Not too hard at all. Not with Him. Not ever.

IMPACT APPLICATION: In the moments when we are hard pressed to be the light He calls us to be, let Him be the light shining through us. Let Him be the sparkle in our eyes, the soft, encouraging tone in our voices, the gentle touches, the spring in our steps, and the fire in our hearts—for others.

WORRY OR TRUST GOD

I tell you not to worry about everyday life. . . . Your heavenly Father already knows all your needs. Seek the Kingdom of God above all else, and live righteously, and he will give you everything you need.
Matthew 6:25, 32-33

HIS CARICATURE BEGAN to grace the cover of *MAD* magazine years ago, and even though I seldom picked one up, I couldn't help but see the image of Alfred E. Neuman everywhere I looked and hear the echo of one of his most famous quotes: "What, me worry?"

There you have it. In the words of the "reverend" Alfred E. Neuman we find full-blown and accurate biblical exposition. Because, unstated in that phrase is the choice we face every day: to worry or to trust God.

I suspect if we are honest with ourselves, we find that we usually end up consumed more by worry than by trusting God, since trusting God often seems too vaporous to wrap our limited minds around other than in halfhearted attempts to demonstrate a faith we are forever striving to understand and live out. In our most spiritual moments—in times like worship services, Bible studies, prayer times, or when we don't know where else to turn—we try to embrace trusting God. But the decisions of day-to-day living seem too overwhelming, too regular, and all too important to trust someone else with them. And so we take charge and worry. And worry almost always paralyzes our potential.

Trusting God is not an attitude of "what will be will be" or of lying in the corner in a fetal position, whimpering and waiting for the hand of God to pluck us up by our collar. Trusting God is an attitude of seeking Him, His way, and His purposes for what is going on in the full spectacle of our days. Trusting God begins with the belief that God loves us. Trusting God begins with God.

It begins with an attitude that recognizes that we may need to reset our priorities and release things that should no longer be important to us. God will guide our steps and cause the gifts He has planted in us to bloom. He will place us where He wants us to be—or He just may more firmly plant us and use us right where we are.

Here's the key: trusting God is about Him. It's not about us. It's not about what we are going through. It's not about where we are or want to be or what we want to do. While those things may in fact align with His desires for us, it all starts with Him. It is all about Him.

All together now: "What, me worry?" No—choose instead to trust God!

 IMPACT APPLICATION: Trusting God is believing that He knows what is best for us and is the One who always wants what is best for us, no matter what we are facing or feeling.

MARCH 19

THE TEMPORAL OR THE ETERNAL?

What do you benefit if you gain the whole world but lose your own soul? Is anything worth more than your soul? **Matthew 16:26**

THE PLAYERS OF THE FOOTBALL TEAM from Penn State University walked onto the football field, arm in arm in a display of solidarity and support. A display for one another, perhaps, because at that moment it would have been hard to find something or someone to support, other than one another, as the allegations regarding the horrific, unbelievable, and sad events of abuse by a trusted individual in the football program in years past continued to unfold.

An alumnus was heard to say, "How did it happen here?"

This was a place referred to as Happy Valley, held in high esteem for so many years. A place where doing things the right way had always been the way, or so it had seemed. A place where "Success with Honor" was the motto adopted and believed.

It was a tragic and sad period in the life of an otherwise great institution of higher learning. How did it happen there?

How does it happen *anywhere*?

Whatever the circumstances, how does it happen that we move from doing that which is right in every setting to doing that which is wrong? We are always surprised when those we least expect to fall, fall. We have seen it happen in our homes, schools, corporations, churches, and political systems.

How does it happen here or there?

It seems to happen when the temporal or the transient things of the world become our "gods." When things like success, money, image, power, trophies, and résumés—all highly honored by society—become the things against which we measure our worth and value. So we embrace them—the temporal, the worldly— because that is what those around us pay homage to and award us for achieving, accomplishing, or acquiring.

When we fall short, we don't fall into the arms of God, but sadly, too often, we fall into the lure of things that temporarily take away the sting of falling short— things and habits that cause further destruction to the life God intended for us to live.

We've seen it before. We've seen it too many times.

How does it happen here, there, anywhere?

In Matthew, Jesus reminds us that the real profit we should seek is the profit we find in the eternal, the profit that safeguards our souls. The profit that begins in a relationship with Jesus Christ and grows as we align our hearts and priorities—and all those things of true, lasting, and eternal value—within that relationship with Christ and the eternal values to which He calls us to live and follow.

The temporal or the eternal?

Choose wisely—today and every day—for the sake of your soul.

 IMPACT APPLICATION: Steward every platform that God has given you with the eternal in mind. People's lives depend on it.

MARCH MADNESS
OR BUST

This is the day the LORD has made. We will rejoice and be glad in it.
Psalm 118:24

A NEW SEASON was in full bloom. A line had been drawn from winter, and spring had sprung. And time was ushering in the annual saga of NCAA March Madness.

For Lynda's mother this was always a special time of year, not necessarily for the basketball, but because it was one more time she could root for one of her grandchildren. Even though she could no longer see the television screen that clearly, it didn't diminish her passion to watch her Duke Blue Devils—the alma mater of her grandson, our son, Nathan.

Annual events like March Madness or the changing of the seasons remind us that it's a brand-new day to draw a line in the journey of our lives, leaving the past where it belongs and starting afresh and anew. It's a time for stepping out into a new day, new experiences, and, yes, some uncertainties. It's a new day to reach again for the unreachable, for following dreams, all the way perhaps to that one shining moment. And it's an opportunity to experience many shining moments.

I wonder if you're at all like me. Not from the standpoint of scheduling my calendar to watch this once-a-year event of basketball madness. Maybe that, too. But I wonder if you're like me in finding that every now and then you need a chance at a fresh start.

Perhaps you find yourself standing on the edge of a valley that looks daunting, afraid to step out. Or you're facing a mountaintop that seems beyond your ability to climb. We've all been there. Perhaps you're coming out of a period of illness, or a family member has left you and you are empty and groping for a light in the darkness. Perhaps all that you have dreamed you would be is still out in front of you, seemingly out of reach.

We may not get as far as we had hoped, and we may not even get out of the first round of the tournament. But we certainly won't get anywhere by staying where we are now.

We've all been there. The question is, where will we be tomorrow?

IMPACT APPLICATION: No matter our situation, we all have choices. We can stay where we are, perhaps not recognizing that tomorrow will soon become the past, or we can realize that the past is the past and that today is what matters. We can stay on the edge of that valley and never move. We can look up at that mountain and never take the first step upward. We can stay in the darkness and never find the light. We can just keep dreaming about what we might have been. Or we can move on toward our purpose.

MARCH 21

COMING HOME

The only thing you ever had to do to make me happy was come home at the end of the day. **President Bartlet, from** *The West Wing*

"I JUST GOT OFF I-10 at Baldwin. I should be home in an hour or so." Our son's voice seemed energized and enthusiastic. Nathan had called as he was driving home from Duke University for the Christmas break to update us on the progress of his journey.

The excitement anticipating his safe arrival had both his mom and me running around finishing up a few last things for his return home. Nathan's basset hound, Amos, could sense that something special was going on, beyond the Christmas tree and decorations, and despite his aching, older joints, he happily followed us around the house overseeing the final preparations.

Five minutes later the front doorbell chimes interrupted our efforts.

The door swung open to reveal our son in all his exhausted glory after a ten-hour drive, sporting a mile-wide smile.

His phone call had come from just a few blocks away. He wanted to surprise us. It was evident that he was as excited to be home as we were to have him there. No one, though, was more excited than Amos, who locked onto Nathan's side for the duration of his holiday stay.

"The only thing you ever had to do to make me happy was come home at the end of the day." Such a great line spoken from a father to a child.

I wonder what the world would be like if more people were made to feel that way as children. I suspect it would be a better place. Much better. I wonder what your life and mine would be like if we had been made to feel that way from day one. If we had lives in which we were affirmed just because we were there. Lives in which we always felt welcome just because we came home at the end of the day. A home where we never felt we had to do anything to earn love or respect or even to keep a parent's, or someone else's, presence in our lives.

Well, I don't know what it was like for you growing up. I don't know how you were made to feel as a child or are made to feel even now. Some things change. Some things don't. "The only thing you ever had to do to make me happy was come home at the end of the day."

Start to make that affirmation true today in the lives of all of those around you who need it to be true.

 IMPACT APPLICATION: How do those who are close around you—your spouse, children, others—feel when they come home to you at the end of the day? In one moment, one beautiful moment, you really can change the world for the better—one life at a time.

REACHING

I don't mean to say that I have already achieved these things or that I have already reached perfection. But I press on to possess that perfection for which Christ Jesus first possessed me. . . . I have not achieved it, but I focus on this one thing: Forgetting the past and looking forward to what lies ahead, I press on to reach the end of the race and receive the heavenly prize for which God, through Christ Jesus, is calling us. **Philippians 3:12-14**

MARCH MADNESS IS UPON US, and it reminds me of a unique situation that occurred a few years ago. When all the teams had played it out weekend after weekend for a chance to get to the Final Four, all of the #1 and #2 seeded teams had lost and been eliminated. And it was the first time in the history of the championship that there were no #1 or #2 seeded teams in the Final Four.

Sixty-eight teams had begun the journey three weeks before, and only four remained. And after the Final Four games, only one team would be crowned the NCAA Men's Division I Basketball Champion.

And as a result, sixty-seven teams fell short of their original goal and dream. Sixty-seven teams reached for a "perfect 10" and landed lower than their beginning goal.

And this year as well, sixty-seven teams will come up short.

Sixty-seven teams will be characterized by some as failures.

But when they began, all the teams knew they would never win the national championship if they didn't try. And so they reached, and in that reaching they became more than they were before. In each step, dribble, bounce, rebound, and shot they attempted along the way, they became more than they were before. And in that effort they moved beyond any characterization of "failure" the world might impose and reached a new place in the journey we are all on.

Don't get me wrong—it would be great to be crowned the national champion in college basketball. It's always a great moment to stand victorious after striving for anything worthy of our reach. But along the way, whether in exhilarating victory or agonizing defeat, something happens in the effort—something that grows us and builds a platform for good for us to use to touch the world—while moving us closer and closer to all we were meant to be as individuals and together. We become better people when we reach to become all we can be.

Failures? Absolutely not! Far from it.

Reach for all the potential within you—you won't reach it by going back or standing still.

 IMPACT APPLICATION: Your potential is vast, untapped, and will at times seem elusive, but don't give up. Keep reaching for all God intended for you to be.

GOD, ARE YOU THERE?

O LORD, I have so many enemies; so many are against me. So many are saying, "God will never rescue him!" But you, O LORD, are a shield around me; you are my glory, the one who holds my head high.
Psalm 3:1-3

"GOD, ARE YOU THERE?" I got my answer—my reminder of what I already knew—last night during an anthem sung at an evening worship service I almost didn't attend. I needed to be there.

It's a natural enough question to ponder, I suppose, when you look around at the decisions being made in our families, communities, nation, and world. Natural enough also when facing a slowing economy, families disconnected and distant, divorce rates hovering between forty and fifty percent, child abuse soaring, churches focused on getting more to come on any given Sunday rather than on preaching the gospel, poverty and genocide still getting the world's blind eye, and political correctness supplanting truth as the guiding light in any dialogue or decision-making process.

It seems natural enough that such a question would infiltrate our thoughts amid a society in a moral free fall that faces so many issues.

Abortion is not a doctor/patient privilege issue or a privacy issue—it's a values issue. It's a symptom of a culture in moral decline. Sub-prime mortgage problems, bailouts, and spreading the wealth around are not economic issues—they're issues of greed, dependence, and "free lunches"; of borrowers and others wanting something for nothing; lenders looking to make it rich quick; and politicians—our elected leaders—encouraging it all by turning their heads to assure their reelection coffers are filled. Political correctness, tolerance, and appeasement—and their attendant failure to recognize right and wrong, good and evil—are values issues.

They are all values issues—every one of the issues we face as a people and a nation. They are issues related to values that God would ascribe to our lives—yet which are too often ignored, misplaced, or lost today.

And yes, God is there—always—watching and waiting. "The Lord isn't really being slow about his promise, as some people think. No, he is being patient for your sake. He does not want anyone to be destroyed, but wants everyone to repent" (2 Peter 3:9).

"God, are you there?" Yes, He is there—our shield, our glory, and the One lifting our heads. God is there. The question is, Will we be faithful to the values God has called us to?

IMPACT APPLICATION: God is there—always. He is "a shield around me . . . my glory, the one who holds my head high."

GROWING IN WISDOM AND STATURE

[Jesus] returned to Nazareth with them and was obedient to them. And his mother stored all these things in her heart. Jesus grew in wisdom and in stature and in favor with God and all the people.
Luke 2:51-52

IT WAS A MORNING I'll never forget. As it did almost every day in the Tampa Bay area, the sun that morning over forty years ago filled every nook and cranny of the sky as we waited for the word.

We prayed for Lynda, as we knew these would be some difficult and painful hours for her, but ones she would gladly and proudly give for her son. We fought off increasingly intense hunger pangs that beckoned us to the cafeteria for breakfast. We talked and waited instead. I silently hoped I would have enough money from savings while in the US Air Force to pay for the hospital bills.

And then the word we anxiously awaited came. And as the nurse introduced me to our son, I noticed that his new armband memorialized his birth at 10:54 a.m. on what was now an even more glorious Sunday morning. After telling me, his grandma, his granddaddy, and his godparents not to touch him just yet, the nurse announced that the precious little boy in her arms weighed a very conservative 7 pounds, 5.5 ounces and measured 20.5 inches long. The perfect stature.

It was a number of years later when Nathan's call came late at night as he and Amy were preparing to board a plane returning from the National Prayer Breakfast in Washington, DC. They were both tired but filled to overflowing with stories of how God had used speaker after speaker to lift and encourage others throughout the world. His voice broke and his heart filled as he told the story of a four-year-old girl who is alive today because of the courage and fortitude of one US senator standing all alone, speaking words of encouragement and hope in the chambers of our nation's capital. Nathan couldn't help but wonder how God would use him in the days ahead as he continued to grow in wisdom and stature—*time will tell*, he thought.

We're all there, wondering how God will use us—from the time of our birth through the last breath we take on earth. And the neat thing is that He will use us as we continue to grow closer to Him—in wisdom and in stature.

His call came much later the other night announcing their safe return home. His mother heard the phone and took the call, and she continued to treasure him in her heart, as he grows in wisdom and stature and in favor with God and men.

 IMPACT APPLICATION: Thank the Lord for your life and for His plans for your future. May He bless you as you grow closer to Him in wisdom and in stature.

MARCH 25

BELIEVE

Just believe that I am in the Father and the Father is in me. Or at least believe because of the work you have seen me do. **John 14:11**

THE MORNING SUNSHINE is coming an hour later now that Daylight Savings Time has turned our clocks ahead an hour, so as I sit here I can see only darkness outside my windows. Experience tells me I can believe the morning light is about to break over the horizon. Experience also tells me that no matter what happens, God's eternal light will always break over the horizon.

Do you believe that?

I didn't see a lot of that belief happening the other day as I ran some errands. It became eerily apparent that I saw fewer smiles and heard less laughter than I remembered from times in the recent past.

It was like sitting in the darkness.

Perhaps it was because the folks I saw were having a hard time believing things would get better with the economy anytime soon. Many of them were without work. Soon-to-be college graduates realized the jobs that used to be there were no longer readily available. Folks once settling in for retirement were scaling back or, in some cases, postponing their retirement while they tried to earn back some of what was lost from their savings accounts.

I don't know what you're going through. Maybe it's some of the things those folks are going through. Maybe that feeling of hope you have had in the past is waning.

If that's the case, think about this for a moment. In the midst of all the storms we're going through, it has never been clearer that whether or not we believe in something is not really what's important, but rather *what* we believe in is of paramount importance. Do we believe in the things that are subject to the winds and whims of whatever is going on around us, or do we believe in something more long lasting? Do we believe in the things of the world or the things of a more eternal nature? Does our hope reside in the wild swings of the stock market or whether we'll get the next promotion or start a successful business, or does it reside in something constant and never changing?

What do you believe in? Where do you put your hope?

Believe in the God who created you and cares for you. Put your hope in the God who is always there, has never left you, and never will.

Believe that God's eternal light really will come over the horizon—today, tomorrow, and for all eternity.

Why? Because with Him, it will!

 IMPACT APPLICATION: We all experience a dampening of our passion from time to time, and it often happens when we place our hope in the wrong people or things. Rekindle your passion by shifting your hope to Christ and His purposes.

TWENTY-SIX THOUSAND CHILDREN A DAY

[Jesus] said to the crowd, "If any of you wants to be my follower, you must give up your own way, take up your cross daily, and follow me. If you try to hang on to your life, you will lose it. But if you give up your life for my sake, you will save it." **Luke 9:23-24**

TWENTY-SIX THOUSAND children a day.

That was the number the speaker mentioned to all of us who were gathered for a missions conference.

That number, he said, is the number of children around the world who starve to death or die from preventable diseases each day. Every day. I don't know how he got that number or how accurate it is—some sources say the number is closer to seventeen thousand children. But either way, the number is way too high.

But the conference is over now, and Easter is coming soon. Right now we're in the middle of the season recognized by the Christian church as Lent, a season of preparation and reflection, heading toward Easter Sunday—that glorious day when we celebrate again the resurrection of Christ.

We'll color a few Easter eggs, have Easter egg hunts, talk about what the Easter bunny left in our Easter baskets, put on our finest Easter attire, and have Easter dinner. And someone will talk about the risen Christ, as once again, on that Sunday, I suspect that more people will attend Easter sunrise services and other Christian services around the world than at any other time during the year.

And on the way toward Easter we'll pass right through Good Friday again. The day that Christ hung on the cross for those back then and for you and for me today—His day of ultimate sacrifice for us all. He was pointing toward that cross with His words in the Scripture above as He was speaking to His disciples.

Those words weren't pleasant for His disciples to hear—especially the part about taking up their own cross if they wanted to follow Him. They wanted to follow Him, but they had hoped He would establish His Kingdom there and stay awhile and rule and that they would be given places of honor and comfort with lots of perks. But Jesus was persistent in pointing them to the Cross and talking about sacrifice and things like "giv[ing] up your life for my sake." It's not what they had hoped for.

Sacrifice for them would mean death; for us today it may not mean death but rather denial of self, turning from the things of the world, and denying ourselves excess material possessions and comfort.

Maybe for the sake of the twenty-six thousand children a day.

 IMPACT APPLICATION: As we remember the sacrifice of Christ on our behalf this Easter season, ask what we might sacrifice for others on His behalf.

MARCH 27

HERMIT CRAB MOMENTS

If you cause one of these little ones who trusts in me to fall into sin, it would be better for you to have a large millstone tied around your neck and be drowned in the depths of the sea. **Matthew 18:6**

HANNAH NARROWED her selection down to the five shells she wanted to take home—each of the shells with a hermit crab inside. She knew her daddy had a pet hermit crab when he was her age, and she adores her daddy. As to the shells she wasn't keeping, she showed me how to carefully set each hermit crab at the water's edge to allow it to return to whatever the day had in store for it.

One of the five shells—the smallest, less than one inch in length—had within it, according to Hannah, a hermit crab baby that had taken up residence inside. She watched it carefully, hoping it would live until she could get what it needed at the pet store.

The beautiful, caring, innocent heart of a child.

In a world where parents are pressured to conform their children to the harmful influences of the world, I pray for the protection of our children. In a world where children are allowed to be exposed—by default, negligence, or intent—to things that destroy their innocence, I pray for their protection.

In a world where we tend to try to relive our lives through our children, I pray for our own maturing and healing. In a world where children are hurt, are abused, and go to bed hungry, I pray for our children. And in all of that, I pray for the strength and wisdom that others and I will do more than just pray.

I spoke to Hannah again last night. Her words were quiet—sad, in a way—as she eulogized the baby hermit crab who had died. "We didn't do enough for him," she pined. "He was little and wasn't strong enough to make it until we could get some more stuff for him." She fell silent, except for her gentle sobs.

I shared with her that I thought she did a good job trying to care for him the best that she could. "Thank you," she sighed. A weight seemingly lifted, and we talked about other things.

Lewis Wickes Hine has said, "Let children be children." When we set aside all the burdens of our own lives—all regrets and wishes of our pasts; all the pressures of peer acceptance; all the influences of a society unhealthily directed by media, commercialization, and conformity, all of which disrupt and interfere with the unique plans God has for each of His children—why wouldn't we want children to be children?

"Let children be children."

IMPACT APPLICATION: Children are sacred trusts given to us by God to nurture, protect, and mold into all that He desires them to be. Honor them as God created them—sacred.

FINISHED

Most of the crowd spread their garments on the road ahead of him, and others cut branches from the trees and spread them on the road. Jesus was in the center of the procession, and the people all around him were shouting, "Praise God for the Son of David! Blessings on the one who comes in the name of the Lord! Praise God in highest heaven!" **Matthew 21:8-9**

WE ALL HAVE THOSE DAYS, and I was having a bit of one yesterday. I almost didn't go to the kids' house last night but decided to stop in quickly to say hello to their guests. Good thing I did. When I arrived, I quietly ascended the staircase to the upstairs area where sounds of tiny voices could be heard.

As I peered over the upstairs railing trying to surprise my two granddaughters and their friends, Hannah's friend Sydney saw me first and, with a huge smile, she bounded over to hug me. Then Hannah saw me; and with a melody in her voice that touches the souls of grandparents like nothing else, she greeted me, jumped to her feet, and wrapped her arms around my waist and reminded me again of the gift she is.

On that day over two thousand years ago, which we acknowledge as Palm Sunday, people gathered on the streets and peered around corners and out of windows to see the triumphal entry of Jesus Christ into Jerusalem. They too had been having one of those days—they'd had a lot of them the last four hundred years, waiting for the coming of the promised Messiah. This was He. They were sure of it. He had been with them for a while, particularly in the last three years—teaching, healing, performing some miracles, and wandering the countryside with His disciples. He had given them hope that He would take over the government and make their lives better, here and now.

And now He was heading to Jerusalem. This had to be the moment, they thought, when He would finish the job and rule their land and their lives. It was, but it would not happen the way they had long expected.

As they peered at Him while He hung on the cross, they didn't get it. They wouldn't fully understand until three days later. But He was finished. The mission was accomplished.

And He did it for them, for you, for me, and for all those times and days we struggle through—today, tomorrow, and all the way into eternity.

Now that's a melody that will cause an eternal lift in our hearts.

IMPACT APPLICATION: With the words "It is finished," Jesus breathed His last and did what He came to do. He took all our misgivings, mistakes, and sins upon Himself onto that cross so that we might have an eternal relationship with Him and a relationship through Him with the Father.

MARCH 29

ENDURING SPIRITS

Once you were full of darkness, but now you have light from the Lord. So live as people of light! For this light within you produces only what is good and right and true. **Ephesians 5:8-9**

GEORGE KENNAN, ambassador to the former USSR and Medal of Freedom recipient, inspires us with his words: "Heroism is endurance for one moment more."

In the continuing account of our nation across the centuries, we have had our share of long, hard weeks, where the time usually measured in days, hours, and minutes has been recorded in tears, fears, darkness, and uncertainty.

Yet as a people, we have walked in darkness before. As our heads rise to survey our surroundings, we have always stepped forward, one day at a time, embracing encouragement like that from the apostle Paul to walk as children of light, knowing that when we do, the darkness cannot and will not prevail. We draw strength from a collective ancestry of those who came to this great land looking for a better life. Many didn't make it, but those who did wanted a better life for themselves and their families and through the centuries have made us all, and America, a better and more cherished place, reflecting the very best of who we were meant to be.

Together we make up the fabric of the American spirit, proudly American and rooted in a myriad of cultures, nationalities, races, and stories of courage and determination. A collage of hopes, pain, dreams, faith, determination, and individual journeys—the face of America, past, present, and future. Today, with our collective compassion, resilience, and resolve, we add to the storehouse containing the innumerable sacrifices of those generations who have gone before us, and we continue to build on the foundation of a nation established under God, which is at its greatest when lifting those who need us.

At one poignant moment of despair in the musical version of Victor Hugo's *Les Misérables*, the people in the streets of Paris, with their backs to the wall yet refusing to succumb to the unspeakable desperation and oppression all around them, issue a stirring challenge of encouragement to others to claim for their days and lives what they believe their God means for them to live: "Tomorrow we'll discover / What our God in heaven has in store! / One more dawn / One more day / One day more!"

Together, as a nation and in our individual lives, we have had our share of hard weeks, months, and years. We have endured together, as Americans, in difficult moments after difficult moments. And we find heroes within each of us, with spirits that continue to endure for one moment and one day more.

IMPACT APPLICATION: One day at a time, one dawn at a time, one day more of raising our heads and our hopes, let's continue to walk as children of light and continue to endure.

I LOVE YOU TOO

Dear friends, let us continue to love one another, for love comes from God. Anyone who loves is a child of God and knows God. But anyone who does not love does not know God, for God is love. **1 John 4:7-8**

"I LOVE YOU TOO!" That's how she said it. Not "I love you!" but "I love you *too*!"

The dismal discussions from the prior day's *Meet the Press* and then *Face the Nation* began to form front and center in my thoughts. And then her words began to dominate my thinking: "I love you too!"

It's how our granddaughter Ellie Kate proclaimed her affection. And it was around that time of her life when we joyously celebrated another birthday. Actually, we would be celebrating it for a couple of days—her mom had seen to that by arranging a princess birthday party for the one who proclaims she is a princess. She is still, of course, a princess, as is her older sister. And she has come a long way under the divine hand of her Creator since those days spent in the hospital's neonatal intensive care unit after she was born.

Whenever she saw me for the first time in a few days or entered a room where I happened to be or as thanks after doing something for her, she would lift my spirits higher with her usual, "Gran. I love you too!"

Even though I hadn't prefaced her affectionate offering yet with "Ellie Kate, I love you," which in a normal interchange would elicit a response like "I love you too," she just offered it to begin with. I suppose one could say she's probably heard us say it to her so often after she's said "I love you" that she has simply adopted it as her way of expressing that term of endearment.

More likely, though, is that she feels so bathed and secure in love and assumes that the words "Ellie, I love you" and corresponding feelings for her held by her mommy, daddy, her Mimi, me, and others are an absolute truth she can count on, even when they are not spoken first at a particular moment.

Maybe it would have been a different conversation on *Meet the Press* or *Face the Nation* if more in the world felt as Ellie Kate does. Princesses or princes. Maybe there would be no more need for *Meet the Press* or *Face the Nation* and the like—or at least need for the conversations I heard that day—if we all felt the consistent, loving embrace of our God and of those around us.

 IMPACT APPLICATION: Maybe that's the first step on the pathway to resolution of world issues. Maybe the person across the room from you and me needs to feel "I love you" so deep within their soul that they too can say, "I love you too!"

MARCH 31

CELEBRATING—BURNT KNEES AND ALL

Mary was standing outside the tomb crying, and as she wept, she stooped and looked in. She saw two white-robed angels, one sitting at the head and the other at the foot of the place where the body of Jesus had been lying. "Dear woman, why are you crying?" the angels asked her. "Because they have taken away my Lord," she replied, "and I don't know where they have put him." She turned to leave and saw someone standing there. It was Jesus, but she didn't recognize him. "Dear woman, why are you crying?" Jesus asked her. "Who are you looking for?" **John 20:11-15**

BOTH KNEES ENDED UP BURNED—through my jeans—by the heat from the roof shingles. And so, even though I would like to say that I felt hope when I awoke, I really didn't. Hope would have been appropriate in this season, which will eventually lead to and surround the celebration of my risen Christ on Easter Sunday.

But the truth is it wasn't only my knees that I was feeling but also my shoulders and lower back. It was from something I decided I just had to do up on our roof. Couldn't wait for help—I had to do it right then.

It reminds me of a scene at a tomb many years ago—the last place you would expect a celebration to occur. It's recorded in the passage of Scripture above. Mary was at the tomb early on Sunday morning, looking for her Lord. She wanted to anoint His body with spices. All she could remember was the Cross.

The image of three days earlier was seared in her memory. She could still hear the religious leaders screaming for His blood. She could see the Roman whip in the air landing to shred even more of His already bloody back. She winced, remembering the thorns cutting His forehead, and she cried, remembering His lifeless body hanging on the cross.

And on this day, as we approach Easter Sunday once again and remember all that Mary felt and experienced, I know that many of you might be a bit like Mary did. Worn down, worn out, overcome, and a bit defeated. Times are difficult, and there doesn't seem to be much sunshine breaking through.

"Mary, why are you crying?" came the voice from behind her. She thought it was the gardener—so she couldn't have imagined the joy about to be hers—but then she realized it was her Lord. You can almost hear Him saying to her, "Hi, Mary. Don't cry. I'm here. I'm alive. Let's celebrate."

And that is exactly what He is saying to us today, tomorrow, and every day. "I'm alive. Let's celebrate."

 IMPACT APPLICATION: Put your hope in the risen Christ, and let your sorrow, difficulty, or disappointment be turned into celebration.

ALL ALONE—NEVER

Because Jesus was raised from the dead, we've been given a brand-new life and have everything to live for, including a future in heaven—and the future starts now! **1 Peter 1:3-4,** MSG

HE WAS ALL ALONE.

There were people all around Him—lining the streets as He slowly dragged the cross toward the hill at Calvary—but He was all alone. There were some watching this spectacle who were supportive of Him, but most of those you would have thought He could count on had taken off when the heat got turned up.

He was all alone—all the way to the cross, nailed to the cross, and lying in the tomb.

We know the feeling of being all alone. We've all been there—at any and every age in life. Too many times we have found ourselves facing something we hadn't planned on and couldn't get beyond, hoping a ray of wisdom would fall down upon us from heaven. Instead the clouds continued to gather, the sky darkened, and the lights went down.

Too many times we have found ourselves walking through life all alone, not sure which way to turn for help, not knowing who to trust, let alone who could possibly help. Too many times we've looked down a long, dark, and winding road stretched out before us, uncertain where it would lead but knowing we had to go. All alone—or so it seemed.

And then the stone was rolled away, and the tomb was empty! He is risen! And we are reminded that we are not alone. In the midst of all the stuff of life that overwhelms us at times, we are not alone. And knowing we are not alone provides us with the energy, even though faint at times, to continue to press on, to punch our heads through the gathering clouds, knowing that He will provide a way through into the sunshine of every brand-new day.

He is risen! For you and for me. We are never alone.

That's the message of hope, which millions around the world gather to celebrate each Easter. But Easter is not about millions, thousands, or hundreds gathering to celebrate and worship. Easter is about Christ—the risen Christ—breaking the chains of sin and death and connecting with that one person in need. That one person struggling to take just one more step.

We've been there, feeling all alone with hopelessness circling around and around for the final descent. But the message of Easter is that today and all the way to the end of our lives and into eternity—hope reigns. Hopelessness has been defeated.

We are not alone. Christ is risen! Christ is alive!

That's the message of Easter—that's the message of the risen Christ—that's the message of today, tomorrow, and forever. We are not alone!

IMPACT APPLICATION: Feeling all alone? Look again—it's just not so.

APRIL 2

BE THE CHANGE

If any of you wants to be my follower, you must give up your own way, take up your cross daily, and follow me. **Luke 9:23**

DID YOU MAKE ANY RESOLUTIONS this year that are still intact? Did you make any that are hanging on by the slimmest of threads? Did you make any resolutions that have since fallen along the side of the road of best intentions?

What personal habits or behaviors in your life—which you needed to change—have you changed? What needs in your family and community—which needed to be addressed—have you addressed? What problems, turmoil, heartaches, or injustices in the world—which needed to be fixed—have you fixed or attempted to fix?

You know, I'm not sure it is fair to impose any of those questions on any of us. I mean, we all know that life itself is tough enough, finishing each day by sliding into bed exhausted. Just the daily living of life and trying to keep up is always full and fast paced enough. And then to attempt to add anything else in the way of time-consuming personal adjustments, additional family responsibilities, or concerns within the community, nation, or world—well, it's just too much to even think about, let alone do anything about.

At the end of it all, our lives will have left an imprint, in some form or fashion, on the world and on the lives around us. In some cases, it will be barely noticeable—those lives that could have been changed for the better or could have been lifted by us to the sunshine of a brighter day will remain unchanged because we didn't reach out to them.

Even though we may have planned to.

In some cases our imprint may be remembered as perhaps having made the slightest of differences if one looks closely enough. And, in some cases, the imprint we leave will have God smiling brightly upon all we have done and the lives who are better because we have lived.

Jesus said, "If any of you wants to be my follower, you must give up your own way, take up your cross daily, and follow me."

I wonder what imprint our lives will leave?

What is it we need to change in our lives and in the world?

 IMPACT APPLICATION: Looking from this point forward, if you could change anything in your personal life (or within your personal sphere of influence)—what would it be? It will make a difference in the imprint you leave on the lives around you.

A PLACE OF INFLUENCE

Don't be misled—you cannot mock the justice of God. You will always harvest what you plant. **Galatians 6:7**

THEIR JET GOT INTO THE AIR quickly, and my friends were on their way to watch a practice round of the Masters Golf Tournament in Augusta, Georgia. Their invitation to join them was tempting, but I opted for a rain check. I took comfort knowing that it was a responsible decision.

As I walked to the kitchen in the morning darkness, I prayed for a dear friend and his continuing recovery. Then I checked outside the laundry room door to see how our tiny boarder and her new family were doing that morning.

It was still dark outside, but from the back porch light, I was able to see her head poking from the edge of the nest she had spent many days constructing in one of the flower pots fastened to one wall of the porch. Lynda believed her to be a Carolina wren, now sitting on six eggs. And despite the cooler-than-normal temperatures for springtime, you could still hear the chorus from her awakening friends through the trees in our backyard.

My thoughts drifted again, this time to a twelve-year-old standing in the back-yard of his home in upstate New York. The air was also cool that spring morning as he stood there with his BB gun, looking for another target on which to hone his less-than-perfect marksmanship skills. He shot into the distant tree, and to his shock a beautiful Baltimore oriole perched on a limb fell to the ground. It was a decision and consequence the little boy wasn't ready for and which lingers to this day.

Decisions, actions, and consequences are inextricably woven together to shape who we and the world around us become. There are big ones and seemingly little ones, but all our decisions and actions have consequences for someone. We are given platforms as men, husbands, and fathers, and each platform comes with the opportunity to influence lives for good or not. Our decisions affect us and others, and consequently have an impact on the world around us. They are made and shaped by our past experiences with family, friends, and the world and often set the initial direction of the decisions for our journey into the future.

I wonder what you will do today with the platforms on which you stand and with the life-shaping decisions and actions you will make today. I wonder what opportunities to positively or negatively shape your child's life and future you will have today. I wonder what opportunities you will have to make a difference in someone's life.

Actually, now that I think about it, the answer is that every decision you make will impact someone's life. Make that impact for the better.

IMPACT APPLICATION: Each and every one of us stands in a place of influence and makes decisions affecting the lives of those around us. Make those decisions well.

APRIL 4

IMPACT OUTREACH

Now, dear brothers and sisters, one final thing. Fix your thoughts on what is true, and honorable, and right, and pure, and lovely, and admirable. Think about things that are excellent and worthy of praise. Keep putting into practice all you learned and received from me—everything you heard from me and saw me doing. Then the God of peace will be with you. **Philippians 4:8-9**

I SUPPOSE if every morning were like today, we would eventually appreciate the peace and beauty of such a morning a little bit less. It seems to be winter's farewell breath rustling the leaves and cooling the air. With spring just around the corner and spring training for baseball in full swing, hope springs eternal in the hearts of all fans that this is the year their favorite team will claim a World Series Championship. This surely will be the year.

And preparing for the upcoming season, I looked closely inside the front cover of the *Illustrated History of Baseball* by Alex Chadwick and found these words about me, written by a younger friend who gave me the book years ago:

Friend, counselor . . . spiritual advisor, role model, parent, husband, community leader, Christian, athlete. For me to express in words the feelings I have for you and your family is tough, even with a degree in Journalism. Giving, committed, unselfish, providing . . . you have gone beyond the boundaries of friendship (if indeed there are any) so many times for me, and oh, how I appreciated it you'll never know. In patterning one's life after someone, I'd choose to strive to uphold the standards you have set. You are the most giving person I have ever met. God blessed me when you walked into my life. It is an honor and a privilege to be your friend.

On a cool morning like today, my friend's words to me would warm anyone's heart, as they did mine. I wonder if he was aware when he penned his thoughts that they would forever provide a source of renewal for me in the years following.

When was the last time you reached out to someone to share a word of encouragement or thanks? I wonder if there is anyone you know who could use a lift today. "Yes," you say, and tomorrow you believe you will have time to reach out to them. Are you sure you will have that chance tomorrow? Are you sure they don't need to hear words of encouragement today to help them find their way through a valley or over a mountain they may be facing?

Reach out to them today. The impact for good could be beyond anything you imagine.

IMPACT APPLICATION: Somebody you know needs to hear a word of encouragement or thanks from you—today. Don't miss the chance to impact their life.

CHANCES AT THE EMPTY TOMB

Go and tell his disciples, including Peter, that Jesus is going ahead of you to Galilee. You will see him there, just as he told you before he died. **Mark 16:7**

THE THREE WOMEN came to the tomb that Easter morning, looking for Jesus' body. However, He was not there. An angel told the women to "go and tell the disciples," and then specifically said, "including Peter." The same Peter who had on three separate occasions denied that he knew Christ the night before Jesus was crucified. That same Peter was given a divine second chance: "Go and tell his disciples, including Peter." How about that!

Do you need a second chance today? Perhaps something's off track in your career plans? Something you should have said, or shouldn't have said, to your spouse?

Maybe you made a big mistake and can't forgive yourself and move on. Maybe you need to turn some area of weakness, or a habit you can't get beyond, over to God and ask Him to help you with it and give you strength to overcome. Or maybe you need a second chance to be a meaningful part of your child's life. With the same God who gave Peter a second chance, you have a God willing to give you another chance to change the way things are, to lift yourself after you fall, to touch and change another life for the better, and most important, to turn to Him for love and forgiveness, even if with your last breath here on this planet.

The God of the second chance. And more.

The God of the empty tomb—the God of Peter—stands ready to give you a second chance and a third and a fourth, whether you believe you deserve it or not. Because if the truth be known, we don't deserve it, but that's what God's grace for us is all about—His unmerited love, undeserved second chances, and more, when we come back to Him.

You guessed it, God is always there—no matter the gray or the sunshine of the day, the heartaches or the disappointments of your life—with yet another chance for you to leap into all the potential He planned for you.

Reach for it—that second chance—to become all that God has always intended for you to be.

Reach for it—that life of shining moments, which He created for you to live with Him—today and every day for the rest of your life.

IMPACT APPLICATION: Need a second chance? Today is the day. Before you run out of time, look up, reach out, and step forward into the arms of the God of the empty tomb.

APRIL 6

WHITNEY

No power in the sky above or in the earth below—indeed, nothing in all creation will ever be able to separate us from the love of God that is revealed in Christ Jesus our Lord. **Romans 8:39**

GOD CLEARLY GIFTED Whitney Houston with a voice like none other, a voice that lifted and inspired those of us who were blessed to hear it to dream, to reach, and to hope in our own lives. Despite that reality, at some point, Whitney seemed to lose sight of those promises set out by the apostle Paul in Romans 8.

Maintaining status, celebrity, and image is a path filled with peril. We can find that pressure almost anywhere—in politics, entertainment, sports, business, and even within our families. In sports it's all about victories, championships, money, and stardom. Seldom do we hear someone say, "Nice job," or at least we don't hear it for long. Instead it always seems to be about something *more*.

Sadly, Whitney Houston's life is over. I suspect that she fell prey to some of those pressures and expectations, hearing whispers of "more" as she sought to find relief in the margins of her life, looking for a place where she didn't have to always live up to the expectations of others. But it seems instead that her relief, which was temporary at best, came through the dark alleys of escape into drugs and alcohol.

She lived a life that positively contributed to the world through the gifts God gave her through her music and acting talents. Yet in that, and despite her death, her legacy wasn't finished.

One of her most famous songs was "I Will Always Love You." As I read and reread the title of that song, I can't help but wonder what might have been if she had ever heard those words as if spoken to her by the God who created her and loved her.

With a belief in God's love filling our hearts, what will we see each morning when we look in the mirror? A "celebrity" as one of God's precious children? Isn't that celebrity enough for us? To have the God of the universe cheering us on, filling us up, always loving us, never separated from us, and never leaving us?

Wow! Think about that for a moment. With that belief to fill us, what else will we need? Certainly not fame, fortune, adoration, championships, drugs, celebrity, alcohol, victories, or material things.

We are already all the celebrity we will ever need to be in God's eyes.

IMPACT APPLICATION: How different our lives can be when we believe that the God who created us will always love us and that no matter what happens, no matter what others say, think, or expect—no matter even if we ignore all that He promises us—He will always love us.

"GOD IS *SO* NICE"

I knew you before I formed you in your mother's womb. Before you were born I set you apart and appointed you as my prophet to the nations. **Jeremiah 1:5**

DURING A WEEKEND sleepover with our youngest granddaughter, Ellie Kate, we watched a DVD of animated Bible stories, one in particular where God called Joshua to lead the Israelites across the Jordan River and into the Promised Land. As the Ark of the Covenant (the "Holy Box" full of God-stuff) was carried into the Jordan River, God parted the waters so Joshua and all of God's children could pass safely through.

As that scene unfolded before us on the television screen, I was moved to remark, "God is really something, isn't He?" To which Ellie Kate quietly and matter-of-factly added, "Gran, God is *so* nice."

I was reminded to thank her daddy for being a strong example of a "nice" father whom she can draw from and extrapolate into a Heavenly Father.

What was the message you received about God as a Father when you were a child?

Too many of us walk around still wounded from the example of fathers who were much less than what they should have been, or of mothers who forgot—if they ever knew at all—how precious the children that they carried for nine months are. Too many of us remember only expectations rather than encouragement, demands rather than mutual accomplishments. Too many of us remember no one being there at all—physically or emotionally. Too many of us never really remember a sense of sacrificial caring or concern for us. And those experiences shape how we view God.

But stop for a moment and look around. What happened or didn't happen to you is real. But no matter the example we had, there are so many others who count on you and who are looking for you to be the parent, mentor, and encourager you never had. So why not make their lives better? Unless you recognize, admit, break, get over, and move past the destructive cycle from childhood, it will be repeated in the lives of those around you—especially those who are most vulnerable around you. Break the cycle—make a difference from this point on in the lives of those who count on you.

"Gran, God is *so* nice." He is. You can be too. And through your actions you can show others how nice God is.

IMPACT APPLICATION: Children will often become what you are, what you showed them, told them, and demonstrated to them by the allocation of your time, the tone of your voice, the encouragement of your expression, and the protective tenderness of your touch. And through you, they will catch a glimpse of what their Heavenly Father is like.

APRIL 8

BEYOND THE WALLS

He gives power to the weak and strength to the powerless. Even youths will become weak and tired, and young men will fall in exhaustion. But those who trust in the LORD will find new strength. They will soar high on wings like eagles. They will run and not grow weary. They will walk and not faint. **Isaiah 40:29-31**

HE LIVED BEHIND a stone wall. I can still see him there.

The hand-laid stone wall was four feet high and encircled the entire two acres that his beautiful, colonial-style, historic house sat on in central Connecticut. He didn't venture out much past that stone wall, other than to attend school a few blocks away or church on an occasional Sunday or to caddy for golfers at a nearby country club.

The little boy used to look out at the stone wall from his upstairs bedroom windows and wonder what dreams and hopes lay beyond it for him. In those moments, sometimes he thought about God and wondered whether He was real. He wondered if God knew him at all or if He knew any of the boy's dreams.

At times that stone wall felt like a barrier to fulfilling those dreams.

What are your walls made of? Stone walls of isolation, rejection, or maybe guilt. Walls of a childhood that wasn't all it should have been. Walls of a career that has come up short of your dreams. Walls of sorrow, self-doubt, disappointments, and tragedies. Walls of your own brokenness. Walls you put up for the benefit of others—to pretend you weren't or aren't broken. Walls of unmet expectations.

When times are difficult, when the wall is too high or too hard or too wide, I wonder if we remember what that little boy eventually discovered: that God is there to help us scale those walls, waiting to help us, as Isaiah reminds us, to mount up with wings like eagles, to run when we are weary, and to continue when we falter or tire.

All too often we find ourselves caught up in striving to scale those walls with the help of false gods like money, power, stuff, and prestige. Those won't ever get us beyond our walls, and they won't leave us fulfilled or satisfied. What we eventually realize is we need a fresh, new experience with the God who's already on the other side of the wall and knows the way.

He knows who we are, what we've been through, and what we face—and He is there on *both* sides of our walls to help us to not only scale those walls but to become all He intended for us to be.

IMPACT APPLICATION: Not only is God already on the other side of whatever wall we're trying to climb, He's also on this side standing with us, ready to help us over whatever wall is keeping us from becoming all we were created to be.

DECISIONS AND CONSEQUENCES

Generous in love—God, give grace! Huge in mercy—wipe out my bad record. . . . I know how bad I've been; my sins are staring me down. . . . God, make a fresh start in me . . . don't throw me out with the trash . . . put a fresh wind in my sails! **Psalm 51:1-3, 10-12; MSG**

FOLLOWING HIS DEATH, while the people of Massachusetts and much of our nation were looking on, Senator Ted Kennedy's family participated in many public activities surrounding his memorial services. As night fell, those services concluded at Arlington National Cemetery with the committal service at the gravesite, which is shared with his brothers John and Robert.

A commentator who disagreed with almost every political position the senator took praised Kennedy for the passion he displayed in always standing for what he believed. Whether one agrees with any position of his, Kennedy's passion for standing up for what he believed in is a trait we should consider embracing for our own lives and future.

Known as the "liberal lion," Senator Ted Kennedy was the voice for the voiceless. Using his power through a life of politics, he said, "For all those whose cares have been our concern, the work goes on, the cause endures, the hope still lives, and the dream shall never die."

Yet despite his work on behalf of the helpless, Senator Kennedy's life was marked by personal and professional decisions and failures that seemed to color his legacy, something David realized was the case for his own life when he penned Psalm 51. In David's case, he wrote the psalm after he was discovered to be both an adulterer and a murderer.

But if we look in the mirror, we will see that it's not just David and Senator Kennedy who lived lives marked by missteps, mistakes, and wrongs. Thank God for forgiveness and mercy—for each and every one of us. David pleaded for God to give grace, to wipe out his bad record, to not throw him out with the trash, to make a fresh start in him, and to put a fresh wind in his sails—and God did. God equipped David to continue serving as a king of Israel and to do many great things.

Yet decisions have consequences, and the consequences of David's wrongdoings—even though forgiven by God—forever marked him in the eyes of those around him. It is a lesson repeated in the lives of many throughout history since the time of David, and a lesson we may all be well-advised to learn.

IMPACT APPLICATION: Each day adds another piece to our legacy that we will someday leave for others to follow. Live a legacy that seeks to honor and glorify God every day, and know that God's grace is present to help us get back on the right path on those days when we stumble and fall.

APRIL 10

WHAT NOW?

When you pray, go away by yourself, shut the door behind you, and pray to your Father in private. Then your Father, who sees everything, will reward you. **Matthew 6:6**

THE CORRIDORS at Coors Field will never be the same.

And the lives that Keli Scott McGregor touched will also never be the same. Keli was the president of the Colorado Rockies baseball club—but that was simply a role from which he did so much more.

At Keli's memorial service Clint Hurdle, former manager of the Rockies and then the hitting coach with the Texas Rangers, shared that he heard of Keli's passing while he was in the visitor's clubhouse at Boston's Fenway Park. He immediately walked out to the Green Monster—the nickname of the left field wall at Fenway—sat on the left field grass, and sobbed. Keli was his friend and had helped Clint turn his life around, to embrace his roles as a husband and father.

Keli's sudden and unexpected passing left many wondering "Why?" At forty-eight years old and in great physical condition, he was a beloved husband, a father to four precious children, a friend to many, a community leader, and a figure respected, admired, and appreciated throughout baseball. Keli was an encourager to everyone he knew and met. I'm not sure we will ever be able to understand or answer the "Why?" on this side of heaven.

But as Clint Hurdle pointed out, maybe the question is not "Why?" but instead, "What now?" What can we learn from Keli's life now that will make our lives and the lives of others better? In whatever time we are given, what is the impact we are meant to have now in the lives of the people around us? What do we need to be about now in the time we have left?

Keli's seventeen-year-old daughter, Taylor, closed Keli's memorial service by reading a quote by Muhammad Ali. Her dad had framed and hung it, among others, on the wall of the training facility within the stadium. It read, "The fight is won or lost far away from witnesses—behind the lines, in the gym, and out there on the road, long before I dance under those lights."

Keli had a great influence on the world because of his character, the things he did when no one was watching. We may be tempted to build our platforms by focusing only on the things that others see, but our own influence depends on our preparation far outside the spotlight—our influence in our families, in serving those in need, in our places of employment, in sports and education, and behind closed doors.

What now?

 IMPACT APPLICATION: For Keli Scott McGregor, the victory began in a relationship with Jesus Christ. Keli built his character through small acts that weren't related to his position and used his platforms to touch so many lives in so many areas. We should do the same.

REACH THE UNREACHABLE

We don't look at the troubles we can see now; rather, we fix our gaze on things that cannot be seen. For the things we see now will soon be gone, but the things we cannot see will last forever. **2 Corinthians 4:18**

IT'S A FEELING THAT ENTERS MORE than my thoughts as I wake most mornings. It seems to come from something deep within me. A feeling that always seems intensified as I wander through God's early morning creation to retrieve the morning paper.

This morning the feeling took on the form of words I heard yesterday during a worship service: *Sense the possibility of this world.*

On occasion I suppose we've all had that feeling wander across our perspective of tomorrow, when all the dreams we have for our lives and the lives of those we love seem within our reach.

In the midst of all that we face every day, however, I suspect that it doesn't stay there as long as we'd like it to. Yet for the rest of our lives, a sense of longing for all the possibilities will continue to interrupt our days and cause us to look beyond where we are to where we dream to be.

It's the way God intended it.

The hero of the musical *Man of La Mancha*, Don Quixote, was thought to be a bit insane as he followed his "quest" with his faithful sidekick, Sancho Panza, crusading against injustice, hopelessness, sorrow, and other foes which he saw that held people back from becoming all they should be.

And at one poignant moment, Dulcinea asks Don Quixote, "What is this quest?" He answers her with a song—"The Impossible Dream." In other words, Don Quixote pursues this quest because he believes in the possibilities of life. He believes that he reaches nothing he was created to reach unless he dreams big and then pursues that dream with fervor, never backing down, never giving up.

Cervantes, the author of *Don Quixote*, notes that "too much sanity may be madness and, the maddest of all, to see life as it is and not as it should be." But we know for sure that focusing only on what is seen is not what God intended for our lives when He created us.

To sense the possibility of this world, to dream the impossible dream, to reach the unreachable star—that's what God intended for our lives when He created us.

IMPACT APPLICATION: Follow your quest—sense, dream, and reach—with God. Strive with your last ounce of courage to reach the unreachable star. It's what God created you to do.

INTEGRITY

Daniel soon proved himself more capable than all the other administrators and high officers. Because of Daniel's great ability, the king made plans to place him over the entire empire. Then the other administrators and high officers began searching for some fault in the way Daniel was handling government affairs, but they couldn't find anything to criticize or condemn. He was faithful, always responsible, and completely trustworthy. **Daniel 6:3-4**

I HAVE A CHALLENGE FOR US, beginning today and for the rest of this week: Always keep your word, "even when it hurts" (Psalm 15:4). What do you think?

Do you think there's a good chance you'll succeed? I mean, will you succeed in every second of every moment of every hour of every day this week? How about when you make that oft-made comment, "I'll be right there"? Or when you assure someone else, "I promise I won't say anything"? Or how about when people are relying on you to put the team or the organization first? Can you be counted on to keep their trust as a part of the team rather than pushing your own agenda for your own advantage?

In his book *Inspiring Quotations*, Albert Wells Sr. shares this sobering quote:

> Honesty was always rare. . . . Blaise Pascal said he didn't expect to meet three honest men in a century. The Institute of Behavior Motivation has found that ninety-seven out of one hundred people tell lies—and they do it about one thousand times a year.

And against that backdrop I offer the challenge to always keep your word, "even when it hurts."

Three men built that core value (and many others) into my life. One is Lynda's dad, who went on to his heavenly reward years ago yet to this day positively influences the decisions and direction of my days. And the other two are federal judges I was privileged to clerk for following graduation from law school: Judge William Terrell Hodges and Judge William Stafford.

All three men taught me, through their words and examples, the virtue of keeping my word and living with absolute integrity.

They lived lives that others could count on. They lived lives marked by always doing the right thing, even when they were alone. They lived lives of keeping their word and standing up for others. As a result, others came to count on the fact that these men could be trusted and that their word could be relied on.

Always keep your word, "even when it hurts."

How are you doing so far?

IMPACT APPLICATION: When integrity is present, it touches every area of our lives and the lives and world around us for good. It builds lives. It builds solid foundations within institutions, churches, and other organizations. It honors God. The world is a better place.

CROSSING OVER— WITHOUT A DOUBT

This is my command—be strong and courageous! Do not be afraid or discouraged. For the LORD your God is with you wherever you go.
Joshua 1:9

MOSES HAD JUST DIED, and God had selected Joshua to lead the Israelites into the Promised Land.

"Me?" Joshua might have uttered. "But Lord, I'm too inadequate; surely there is someone more capable of crossing the Jordan River—and with all these people following me! And what's on the other side, anyway?"

I can identify with Joshua. I sometimes face something I have the ability to do—or something I should do—and I begin to wonder whether I *can* do it. I know I *can* do it; I know it's time. But then the subtle enemy of my faith slips in—doubt.

Its timing is always the same—right at that moment when I need to move forward in faith. We have all been where Joshua was that day. And his story of that moment three thousand years ago is as relevant for us today as it was true for him then. Facing a river with currents stronger than our shaking legs can manage, we know we have to cross in order to become all God created us to be.

But here's a promise to remember: God will go with us and ahead of us. Will it be easy? Maybe not. Will it require staying close to Him and following His direction? Yes. Will the currents take us to a place on the other side we didn't intend to go? Maybe. But will He be with us wherever we end up? You can bet your life on it!

What Jordan River are you facing?

Perhaps you're facing a family illness or a career change or challenge. Perhaps you made a mistake, a bad decision, and now you have to walk it back to a new place where God can continue to mold you. Perhaps you need to change something God has been tugging at you for a while to change.

Perhaps you need to forgive someone or ask God to forgive you for something you've done. Or maybe there's something you know you should have done or tried to do long ago, and instead you've been sitting on the bank of the Jordan for too long, dangling your feet in the rushing waters, afraid you may fail if you try. It may be time to jump in and make a mad dash for the other side.

So what Jordan River are you facing today?

Whatever it is, remember this promise from the One who created you: "Be strong and courageous! Do not be afraid or discouraged. For the Lord your God is with you wherever you go."

IMPACT APPLICATION: Without a doubt, God will go with you and ahead of you as you cross into all He has planned for your tomorrow.

APRIL 14

GO AHEAD—STEP OUT

What shall we say about such wonderful things as these? If God is for us, who can ever be against us? **Romans 8:31**

IN CASE YOU HAVEN'T NOTICED, today is not yesterday. It is a brand-new day. Ready?

Maybe a day of uncertainty, maybe some doubt. But for sure a day of brand-new beginnings.

A number of years ago, after I graduated from the University of Florida School of Law and passed the Florida bar exam, I had the privilege to be sworn in to the Florida bar at the Supreme Court of Florida in Tallahassee. Lynda and Nathan were with me as I was sworn in with two hundred other soon-to-be lawyers.

After the chief justice asked the standard questions of us and then administered the oath for entry into the Florida bar, he shared some brief remarks. One thing he said, we had all heard before, but it hit me that day with a new reality.

We had worked hard to get where we were that day, he noted, and now we were starting again, at the threshold of a brand-new career, a brand-new day, with a fresh, new door opening before us. To put it bluntly, he said, we were starting once again at the bottom rung of the ladder. It was a brand-new day, and I realized I was once again at the very beginning of something—starting all over again.

Then later that day, I was reminded of another point I needed to add to what the chief justice had shared, a point that provided the assurance, passion, and strength I would need as I stepped out and started anew: God was there. God was for me. And God would go with me.

And in those assurances, I would find the passion and the peace I would need as I started out on that new day and new adventure, stepping through that new door.

That's what we need to remember every day of our lives. Each new day is God opening a new door for us. And He is not only with us and alongside us, but even more than that, He is waiting for each of us where we are headed. How about that!

He is there with you. He is rooting for you. And He is waiting for you in all your tomorrows.

That's the picture of a God who is always for us. A God who is always with us. A God who always has us in His embrace. A God who calls us to follow Him into being the best He created us to be as we step out into each new day, into each new adventure and new opportunity He opens up for us.

IMPACT APPLICATION: He opens the doors and walks through them with us. That's enough. So go ahead: step out. God's got you.

NO BARRIERS BETWEEN US

Christ himself has brought peace to us. He united Jews and Gentiles into one people when, in his own body on the cross, he broke down the wall of hostility that separated us. **Ephesians 2:14**

IN 1947 JACKIE ROBINSON became the first African-American to play baseball in the major leagues. He played for the Brooklyn Dodgers. He was named Rookie of the Year, and two years later he won the National League batting championship with a .342 average and was selected as the National League's most valuable player. He ended his career with a lifetime .311 batting average and was elected to the Major League Baseball Hall of Fame.

But Jackie Robinson's life was not all glory and awards. On the contrary, he constantly faced painful racial slurs and deep-seated prejudice.

As the story goes, once when Robinson's team was playing in Cincinnati against the Reds, angry racial taunts had reached a deafening crescendo.

A white teammate, Pee Wee Reese, called time out in the middle of an inning. As the crowd quieted, wondering what was happening, Reese left his shortstop position and walked over to Robinson, put his arm around his shoulder, and stood there. It was a wordless but powerful message that said to the now-hushed crowd, "This man is my friend; this man is my brother."

This reminder surfaced for me again that cold January day in Atlanta as I took a break from daylong meetings. I walked to the lobby and stood at the hotel entrance to watch the parade march by, honoring the birthday, life, and ministry of Martin Luther King Jr. After a while, I noticed a young boy standing a few feet from me. We silently watched together as one of the many marching bands rolled by. Jackie Robinson and Dr. King had toiled for him, I thought. Our eyes met and he returned my smile, and I knew in that moment we had no barriers between us. I prayed then and I prayed later that he would never learn differently.

I prayed that I would continue to learn. I remembered that God created us all unique and in His image and with incredible potential. I remembered Dr. King's words: "I have a dream that my four little children will one day live in a nation where they will not be judged by the color of their skin but by the content of their character . . . that one day . . . little black boys and black girls will be able to join hands with little white boys and white girls as sisters and brothers."

They're not my words, but they are my dreams. Yours too, I'm sure. Together we've got some work to do, but we know that dreams do come true.

IMPACT APPLICATION: Reach your full potential, and live your legacy by helping each and every person God puts in your path to reach theirs!

APRIL 16

MAKING MEMORIES

Teach those who are rich in this world not to be proud and not to trust in their money, which is so unreliable. Their trust should be in God, who richly gives us all we need for our enjoyment. **1 Timothy 6:17**

IT'S A MOMENT forever etched in my memory.

As I watched our two granddaughters swimming in our pool, I decided I would surprise them again. I had done the same thing a year earlier. And so I began to empty my pockets of keys, my wallet, and other valuables. I removed my watch, cell phone, shoes, socks, and belt and stood at the edge of the pool ready to jump in fully dressed.

"Wait, Granddaddy!" Hannah said as she climbed from the pool. "Wait! I remember. I'll show you what you did before!"

She had remembered everything about that moment from the year before, when I had shocked the family and left her in wide-eyed disbelief, when I had jumped—fully clothed—into the pool feet first. And she was now demonstrating it for me. It was a positive moment indelibly etched in her memory.

Making memories.

I suppose that's why I did it. That's probably why on occasion I drove two and a half hours early in the morning to pick her up and take her to school with a stop on the way for potato crispers. It's why my bride and I try never to miss a birthday or other special occasion in our granddaughters' lives (or our son's or our daughter-in-law's, for that matter).

Making memories gives us a warm, safe, and affirming place of acceptance to return to when we need a boost to help carry us through our days.

So let me ask you a few questions: When was the last time you went to see someone who needed a visit? When was the last time you made a call or wrote a letter to someone who could use a lift with a special and unforgettable moment? When was the last time you had a date with your spouse or a "date night" with your little girl who adores you? When was the last time you played catch or did whatever else your son or daughter wanted to do? When was the last time you did something that caused others to question your sanity—such as jumping into a pool with your clothes on?

Because when you look back on your life, you will discover that life's finest moments were just simply those which left indelible memories, like jumping into the pool with your clothes on!

Make some memories today.

 IMPACT APPLICATION: No matter where you are on your life's journey and no matter how many moments you've lost or let slip through your fingers, beginning today, leave a trail of positive benchmarks—warm memories—in the lives of those around you.

DIPSTICK CHECK— FAITH LEVEL

Faith shows the reality of what we hope for; it is the evidence of things we cannot see. **Hebrews 11:1**

IT WAS ONE of those mornings to get the dipstick out and check the level of my faith.

Looking outside, it seemed a bit overcast, cloudy, and gray without much of a breeze. It wasn't what I had hoped for. The walk to retrieve the morning paper and set the trash out confirmed that analysis—and managed to add muggy to the list. Not really what I needed for a little pick-me-up to start the day. And a pick-me-up was what I needed.

The dipstick was not reading empty, but it was definitely indicating very *low*. Have you ever been there?

Days that seem to be without the sunshine you had hoped for—inside of you, that is—no matter what it looked like outside. You, or someone you know, may be having a bit of one today, whether it's cloudy outside or not. It may be one of those days where it seems all you have to hold on to is, in fact, faith. This plaintive prayer seems relevant to a low faith dipstick reading, a pick-me-up kind of situation:

Lord, I'm tired, the burdens that are mine are heavy indeed.
And constant. And depressing.
They may seem small to someone else,
but someone else isn't carrying them. . . .
Sometimes I get so tangled up in my problems,
I let whole days go by . . . unnoticed, unenjoyed, unlived.

We've all had them. Days where every turn seems to present an insurmountable problem, where the issues from yesterday seem to be front and center again today. Doubt prevails and faith is hard to come by. It can feel like a too-regular occurrence in the midst of too many days.

But no matter what condition you find yourself in, no matter how burdened you are, no matter what you're facing, no matter what you've just been through, no matter whether the day is cloudy or gray, there is always renewing hope bubbling all around you in the person of the God who is always there.

What do you want to change? What do you want to happen? Claim it in faith—with the confident assurance that it will actually happen. And remember that the God we can always rely on is always with us.

With that assurance, when we check the levels again, trust me, they will show *full*!

IMPACT APPLICATION: We can stay on empty, letting day after day go by, as many do; or we can embrace a faith within us that is undergirded by hope. Hope in things not yet seen but that our past experiences with the living God assure us we can claim. Hope in Him.

APRIL 18

LOVE AT THE PIGPEN

"This son of mine was dead and has now returned to life. He was lost, but now he is found." So the party began. **Luke 15:24**

I SUSPECT THAT Jesus was smiling as He told it—knowing the punch line that was coming. You have to admit He really had a way with parables, our Jesus.

The central moment of this parable is a theme woven throughout the Old and New Testaments—from Genesis 1:1 to Revelation 22:21. It is simply and clearly a poignant reminder of God's continual presence in our lives and His never-ending love for us—no matter what pigpens we find ourselves wallowing in.

The father of the younger son never gave him a chance to ask to be a hired servant. Instead he picked him up out of his pigpen and restored him to all the fullness of life.

Maybe you can't identify with that young son. Maybe you've never been there. Maybe you've never felt as low as that young man, with the filth caked on his clothes and pig slop staining the edges of his lips, betraying where he had been. Maybe you can't identify with that story.

Maybe you've never failed at something in life, felt ashamed at something you've done, or disappointed or hurt someone close. Maybe you've never stood with your knees shaking—afraid to move—facing something you were sure you couldn't do. Maybe that bag of names and stereotypes that others have labeled you with hasn't gotten too heavy to carry another step yet. Maybe you've never been at a place where it wasn't worth waking up to another day. Maybe you've never been where that young man was.

I suspect, though, that you're breathing rarified air if you haven't. The truth is that we've all felt the pain and sting from the roadblocks, detours, ruts, and fallen trees along the road of our lives.

But the message of that story and the message to us woven throughout God's Word is that through all of that, God is there to love us unconditionally and lift us out of the pigpens in which we find ourselves into all the potential He has placed in our lives.

 IMPACT APPLICATION: The Father's love is always there to embrace and redeem us from our fallings, failures, and disappointments. It comes with a smile. And more than that, He is our example to do the same for others who are often standing nearby. Move toward the God who loves you—it's hard to make an impact from the pigpen!

GETTING TO SOLID GROUND—NOW

A strong wind was blowing and the waters grew rough. When [the disciples] had rowed about three or four miles, they saw Jesus approaching the boat, walking on the water; and they were frightened. But he said to them, "It is I; don't be afraid." Then they were willing to take him into the boat, and immediately the boat reached the shore where they were heading. **John 6:18-21,** NIV

PEACE ROLLS IN as I watch the sparkling drops of sunshine dance around the room. More peace is now present than through the storms of the last four or five days, storms that occurred because of things I did or forgot to do. I was adrift and felt like I was being thrown up the side of one wave and down another.

There I was, feeling like those disciples in the boat on a storm-tossed sea. Knowing better, knowing Jesus, and yet confused, unsettled, disoriented, and anxious. And then I heard again His words through a friend—words I knew but had forgotten in the midst of the moment's storms. It's almost embarrassing to have to admit that I forgot who was in control. But the reminder came through that friend from the words in the Gospel of John: "They were willing to take him into the boat, and immediately the boat reached the shore where they were heading."

Any storms in your life at the moment? Or perhaps you're just coming out of some. We know that at times we will face them. They will come our way. The issue for us is how we will choose to go through them and also whom will we choose to go through them with us.

Perhaps we will try to convince ourselves that we can avoid them. Yet careers are thrown off track, finances run short, loved ones are lost, unexpected illnesses occur. Maybe we would do well to remember that no matter how we live our lives, the rains will fall on "the just and the unjust alike" (Matthew 5:45).

We can stay in the boat hanging on to the flailing rudder all by ourselves, hoping to make it through. We've all done that before—just open your hands and look at the calluses that linger there.

Or we can let Jesus into the boat—turn over control of the rudder to Him—and find ourselves immediately at the shore. The wind may still be blowing and the rain falling in torrents, but now it's with our feet next to His on solid ground.

 IMPACT APPLICATION: No matter where we are in life, no matter what storms we face or find ourselves in the middle of—no matter the losses, the challenges, the valleys, the obstacles, and the heartaches we are in the midst of or find ominously looming out in front of us—we will all decide how and with whom we will choose to go through them. Choose Christ.

APRIL 20

FOLLOWED BY GOODNESS AND MERCY

Surely your goodness and unfailing love will pursue me all the days of my life, and I will live in the house of the LORD forever. **Psalm 23:6**

AN EVERYDAY, TYPICAL DAD had been listening patiently as his three children—ages ten, seven, and four—complained about how bad they had it in their home. None of their friends had chores like they did, and their friends' parents always bought them what they wanted.

The ordinary, everyday Dad finally had heard enough and launched into a diatribe of how good his kids had it, telling them that when he was their age, he didn't have the nice clothes they had to wear or any of the toys they had to play with. He had to walk to school, sunshine or rain.

When the Dad had finished telling his children how bad he'd had it as a child, his four-year-old shared, "Boy, Dad, I'll bet you're glad you live with us now!"

Have you walked up any hills lately that seemed to go on and on and on? Without shoes? Uphill in both directions? Have you had to travel through snowstorms or rainstorms that seemed to wash out your plans? Or searing heat or freezing temperatures that never allowed you to get comfortable and find your stride?

I hope not, but I suspect you have. And if life is anything like we've experienced, we will probably face a few more of those hills and rough patches that we will feel ill-equipped to handle. And in our own power and with our own wisdom, we probably can't handle them. But as David reminds us in Psalm 23, we don't have to handle them alone.

Here's the point David found to be true: no matter where we find ourselves, no matter what we face, no matter how many others tell us we can't, no matter how many times we fall and fail, God's goodness and mercy continue to follow us and are with us always.

Surely there is God's "goodness" to supply our every need, and His mercy to forgive our every sin. That's what it says! Then, as if that weren't enough, He follows us! He pursues us, chases us, and tracks us down. In His love for us, God seeks after us—time and time again—until we enter into a saving relationship with Him.

Aren't you glad that's the God and the family you are with now? If you're not there yet, why not? Why not have the God of the universe in your court today and forever?

Surely that is a life worth living—no matter what we face.

 IMPACT APPLICATION: Through whatever we face, wherever we are, through our fears and doubts, through our failures and fallings—through to the very end of it all—surely God's goodness and mercy will follow us all the days of our lives, and we shall dwell in the house of the Lord forever.

REFRESHINGLY DIFFERENT AND MAK- ING A DIFFERENCE

Dear children, keep away from anything that might take God's place in your hearts. **1 John 5:21**

WOW! There it was on the front page of the A-section of the Sunday edition of the *Gainesville Sun*. The headline of the article, set just below-the-fold, read, "Poll: Tebow 3rd Most Influential Athlete in U.S." Such a result is admirable and remarkable.

But it's not admirable and remarkable because of his finish close behind the likes of Lance Armstrong and LeBron James. Instead, it's because in the world of professional football, where Tim was the twenty-fifth pick by the Denver Broncos in the first round of the NFL Draft, Tim Tebow hadn't played a down. Tim Tebow hadn't yet gathered a huddle in the NFL, called a play, thrown a pass, or run over a linebacker for a first down. He hadn't even showcased his classic fake-the-run-jump-pass-for-a-touchdown yet.

So from where does his influence come—landing him in third place among the most influential athletes in the nation at that time? What causes those polled to mention his name so often?

Is it the eye black we remember pasted under his eyes before every college game he played citing John 3:16 or some other Scripture verse? Maybe. Was it stating in public that he was a virgin? Maybe. Praying before, during, and after games by himself and with his teammates and coaches? Maybe. Unashamedly expressing his faith in Jesus Christ? Maybe. Missionary work overseas? Maybe. Answering every question asked of him—even though it was the tenth time? Maybe. Hugging his mother in public? No doubt about it!

In our world of sports with idols and platforms and winning and money, it's refreshing to see something different. With a culture of sports centered around "me" instead of "we" and around more money, yearly expectancies of championships, building luxury boxes on the sides of stadiums until they blot out the sun, expanding trophy cases with championship hardware, and other idols which our society looks up to and aspires to be a part of, it is life-giving to see someone different. Much different. Even if he didn't make number one on the list.

But it's refreshing to see someone we can look up to cry on the sidelines, hug his mother, unashamedly pray with teammates, share Scripture for ninety million people to read, and spend time in the poorest parts of the world with some precious children the world may have forgotten but whom God—and Tim—hasn't.

Third most influential. What can you do to make an impact?

IMPACT APPLICATION: Platforms are sacred trusts. Honor God and others with yours to the best of your ability today and every day. With God, you will be making a difference.

APRIL 22

ROADS TO SOMEWHERE

This is what the LORD says: "Stop at the crossroads and look around. Ask for the old, godly way, and walk in it. Travel its path, and you will find rest for your souls." **Jeremiah 6:16**

THE WORDS OF A DEAR FRIEND, James Dodson, from his book *The Road to Somewhere,* were floating through my thoughts as I sat waiting for another day to stretch out before me. In his book, he describes the experiences from a once-in-a-lifetime odyssey which he and his young son took together through some of the great cities and small towns of Europe.

At one bend in the road, with the pair having just finished exploring Great Britain and planning to head toward Holland, Jim penned these poignant words: "I was just pleased to keep on keeping on, wherever the good road took us."

The road may be a familiar one, like the road to see your grandchildren or them to see you, or the roads might be both old and new, taken as families gather to celebrate at holidays. It may be a road like the Emmaus road, traveled by two downcast men running away from the tragedy they saw of Christ's death, which took place in Jerusalem days before. Or like the happier road that, upon hearing the good news of His resurrection, they took to tell the world that Christ is risen.

"I was just pleased to keep on keeping on, wherever the good road took us."

They're all before us. Roads of every shape and size, bend and adventure.

Some old, familiar, and comfortable. Some monotonous—beginning to look a lot like ruts. Some new ones, full of breathtaking scenery we've never seen before yet with a bit of the unknown lurking around each bend, raising our blood pressure just a bit. Roads with twists and turns, detours, forks, and side streets—leaving us confused about which way to go. And some roads with valleys and hills or—as my younger granddaughter called them from her safety seat in our car—roller coasters.

Upon reflection, we can recall roads with memories both fond and sad. Roads leaving scars as well as ones leaving brightly colored ribbons. Roads which led to success and to failure. Roads which evoked fear and roads which demanded courage. Roads to places which may be destined to be our greatest achievements and roads to what may be our greatest disappointments. And even roads that led to dead ends.

We've been on them all. And with the sunrise of each new day, we will have a choice and a chance to journey on some of them again. Each new day is positioned on the threshold of one of the roads that stretches before us. Upon which ones will we choose to journey?

IMPACT APPLICATION: Facing a fork in the road? Seek the road that will follow God—wherever He is leading you.

MEMORABLE MEMORIZATION

Taste and see that the LORD is good. Oh, the joys of those who take refuge in him! Fear the LORD, you his godly people, for those who fear him will have all they need. Even strong young lions sometimes go hungry, but those who trust in the LORD will lack no good thing. Come, my children, and listen to me, and I will teach you to fear the LORD.
Psalm 34:8-11

I WAS IN THE EIGHTH GRADE in a junior high school in a small town in upstate New York. Our history teacher threw out an extra credit challenge and opportunity to the class, which reintroduced me—for life—to an inspiring moment in American history. Our task: to memorize the entirety of Henry Wadsworth Longfellow's classic poem "Paul Revere's Ride." That memorization, and the memorable and lyrical depiction of history in Longfellow's account of Paul Revere's midnight ride, has stayed with me since that day when I stood before the class to recite it in all its patriotic splendor.

> *Listen, my children, and you shall hear*
> *Of the midnight ride of Paul Revere . . .*
> *On the eighteenth of April, in Seventy-five;*
> *Hardly a man is now alive*
> *Who remembers that famous day and year.*

Today, even after the passing of all those years and even though I am a little rusty, I can still recite those lines that paint the picture of what that historic moment must have been like.

That's what happens with things we put in our hearts and minds as opposed to our bodies. They remain. And that's something we need to remember in our lives and in the lives of those we love. What we allow in, what we dwell upon today, is what we will probably remember tomorrow and for a long time to come.

Perhaps, as we consider that, we would all do well to remember the words of the apostle Paul: "Dear brothers and sisters, one final thing. Fix your thoughts on what is true, and honorable, and right, and pure, and lovely, and admirable. Think about things that are excellent and worthy of praise" (Philippians 4:8).

Right there in God's Word.

You never know when someone might want to know about a magnificent moment in our history or about something even more splendid—like an encounter with the living God.

IMPACT APPLICATION: What we allow in our hearts and minds today is what we will probably remember tomorrow and for a long time to come. So "fix your thoughts" on things that are "worthy of praise."

APRIL 24

GOD-SIZED RISK

Look here, you who say, "Today or tomorrow we are going to a certain town and will stay there a year. We will do business there and make a profit." How do you know what your life will be like tomorrow? Your life is like the morning fog—it's here a little while, then it's gone."
James 4:13-14

RISK.

I've witnessed a number of its many faces in my life. And I'll bet you have had your own experiences with it also. A step toward "risk" is not the usual choice to start a day full of decisions. As a matter of fact, it's often something most of us try our best to avoid altogether—unless we're not thinking or are just showing off or we find ourselves in a corner of expectancy or are trying to prove something to someone we hope will finally take notice of us.

Risk.

Every moment of our lives is lived a bit on this side of unpredictable, and so risk is part of the tapestry of our lives. Truth be told, everywhere we turn there is uncertainty and unpredictability. We don't know what tomorrow will bring—or what the next moment will bring, for that matter. And so we often move into the next moment hand in hand with risk.

But God knows. And He never takes risks because He knows. Do you suppose God knows what the result of our taking a certain risk will be? I suppose the answer is yes. And do you suppose that there are those risks He might want us to take that would honor Him and be consistent with His plan for our lives and the lives of others? I suppose the answer is also yes.

Clearly, too, there are risks inconsistent with His will—risks that God would not want us to take. For example, taking a risk that violates a sacred trust God gives us in caring for ourselves or others, risks that put us or others foolishly in danger, risks that go against God's Word and risk the sanctity of God-given relationships, or anything else inconsistent with the priorities of God.

Instead, the kind of risk that will honor God is that which is consistent with His will and His Word—like following a call to a career that no one expected, maybe writing, teaching, coaching, or answering a call to serve your country through military service. Like reaching out to an underprivileged neighborhood with an educational initiative that will give children hope.

Risk—it's a part of the fabric of our lives. And it's God's pathway for significant living.

IMPACT APPLICATION: God-honoring risk is the kind that requires stepping into the unknown with the possibility of doing something that we believe will ultimately honor God by providing good to others— and maybe even good to ourselves.

GOOD-BYE, BUT FOR ONLY A MOMENT

"He will wipe every tear from their eyes, and there will be no more death or sorrow or crying or pain. All these things are gone forever." And the one sitting on the throne said, "Look, I am making everything new!" **Revelation 21:4-5**

THERE IS NO SUNSHINE anywhere as I sit here in the very early hours of this morning. It's about two-thirty, and I have taken a moment from my resting place next to her. Ten feet away from where she lies, I can see her chest slowly and weakly rising and falling.

It is the second night in a row that I have stayed with our precious little Lily downstairs in the kitchen area on a pallet of pillows on the floor next to her bed so she does not feel alone in what the doctors say is her last season with us. Lily, who won our hearts at first glance nine years ago, is the last, for now at least, in a long line of basset hounds who have blessed our lives. Together we catch an occasional moment of sleep, and I am there to pet and calm her when she stirs and raises her head, trying to understand where she is and what is happening.

Our granddaughters were feeling the impending loss deeply a few hours ago before they headed to bed. Our elder granddaughter, Hannah, was unable to calm herself for a moment tonight as tears flowed from her eyes while she held Lily.

In my transparency and tears, as I held Hannah in my arms for a time, I talked to her about a word in Korean which comes close to capturing what we were feeling: *han*. The translation into English escapes complete accuracy, but as closely as we dare, *han* means a deep sorrow and sadness, so deep and numb that often tears don't even come, encompassing a sense of incompleteness and emptiness—yet in the midst of all of that, a glimmer of hope shines through.

The hope of Scripture is that there is coming a day when God will wipe every tear from our eyes. And in the midst of that day, God says, "Look, I am making everything new!"

Just before His death, Jesus told His disciples, "Here on earth you will have many trials and sorrows." Today I see this part of the verse clearly. But He went on to say, "Take heart, because I have overcome the world" (John 16:33).

It may soon be time to say good-bye—but not yet and then only for a moment. Look! God is making everything new.

 IMPACT APPLICATION: In the midst of our deepest sorrow, we can take heart. There is a coming day—in heaven—when God will wipe every tear from our eyes and make everything new. Cling to that promise of hope today.

APRIL 26

STANDING IN THE GAP FOR GOD

Watch what God does, and then you do it, like children who learn proper behavior from their parents. Mostly what God does is love you. Keep company with him and learn a life of love. Observe how Christ loved us. His love was not cautious but extravagant. He didn't love in order to get something from us but to give everything of himself to us. Love like that. **Ephesians 5:1-2, MSG**

DICK ENBERG, legendary and respected sportscaster, said it well: "His greatness was exceeded only by his goodness."

Coach John Wooden was born October 14, 1910, on a farm that didn't have electricity or indoor plumbing near Martinsville, Indiana. From that humble beginning, he became a three-time all-American basketball player at Purdue University and a member of the 1932 Purdue Boilermakers national championship team. Thereafter, as head coach at UCLA, he led his teams to seven consecutive national championships while notching ten in all. The greatest of the great basketball coaches consider him to be the greatest basketball coach of all time.

But not just for his accomplishments on the court. It was also for the impact he made in the lives of his family, players, coaches, students, teachers, and administrators. His day-to-day life was a reflection of the words he shared with his players and all who would listen:

- "People who win at life know God intimately, and they know He only wants a few things from them . . . to do everything to His glory by being efficient with all that He's given to us."
- "Don't let what you cannot do interfere with what you can do."
- "Be more concerned with your character than with your reputation, because your character is what you really are, while your reputation is merely what others think you are."
- "Material possessions, winning scores, and great reputations are meaningless in the eyes of the Lord, because He knows what we really are . . . and that is all that really matters."
- "You cannot live a perfect day without doing something for someone who will never be able to repay you."

A. W. Tozer once wrote that "nothing of God dies when a man of God dies." Of course, we all know that to be true. But we can't help but wonder—who will stand in the gap to touch and lift lives for God in the world of sports and elsewhere as Coach John Wooden once did?

IMPACT APPLICATION: Who will stand in the gap as Coach Wooden, and so many others like him, have done throughout the years? Will you?

A LEGACY WORTH LEAVING

Hold firmly to the word of life. And then I will be able to boast on the day of Christ that I did not run or labor in vain. **Philippians 2:16**, NIV

I WONDERED WHAT he was thinking as the television cameras captured him descending from their charter aircraft, which had just brought him and his Seattle Seahawks team to Detroit for Super Bowl XL. Given a chance to continue as head coach for his seventh season despite less than stellar results, Michael George Holmgren, the Seahawks' head coach, had led his team through a Cinderella season and now stood at the precipice of his third Super Bowl appearance and second Lombardi trophy, emblematic of the best in professional football.

I'm pretty sure he never met Jesse Wilder Johnson, my father-in-law. Dad hardly even watched the Super Bowl before he left us on October 1, 1985. But I'm pretty sure they would have liked each other. By worldly standards they shared some similarities. They had large families that were a priority to them. And they were both well off; their work ethic saw to that. They both had dreams that, at times, were painful to pursue. And they knew that somewhere along the way someone gave them a chance, and so throughout their lives they did the same for others.

Their success in life came not from winning football games or building commercial centers, plant nurseries, or memorial parks. Their real success came instead from a courageous and caring style of leadership that was more concerned about leaving a legacy in the lives of others than adding another trophy or award to the case. Those came, but not because they pursued them for their sake only. Their success in life came because they realized:

- They didn't get where they were solely by their own initiative. People along the way saw their potential and, risking their own credibility, gave them a chance;
- Each and every person is a creation of unlimited potential, which they were willing to mentor and mold;
- They would die. And looking ahead at when their life would end, they realized that they would not be remembered because of the size of their house, bank account, or number of cars or trophies gathering dust on the mantel, but by the legacy of the lives they changed because they courageously gave people a chance when no one else would.

Each of them held in their hands the power to change the world for the better by embracing a forward-looking leadership style.

When you die, what will the legacy you leave behind look like? Make your legacy one that's worth reading about.

IMPACT APPLICATION: Want to make a lasting impact and leave a legacy of changed lives? Help as many people as you can, as many times as you can, remembering that what we do for others lives on.

APRIL 28

I'VE BEEN WATCHING YOU

Direct your children onto the right path, and when they are older, they will not leave it. **Proverbs 22:6**

LOOKING BACK NOW, Rodney Atkins' song "Watching You" has it right—"I've been watching you, Dad. Ain't that cool? . . . I wanna be like you." That's, at least, how I remember it at age ten.

In everything. Sitting next to him at dinner. Picking the same dessert as my dad when there was a choice. Singing in the church choir with him. Learning to play his favorite card game—Casino. Watching his favorite television show with him. Walking outside with him wherever he was going. Watching and waving good-bye as he drove off to work and waiting at the curb for him to return. Looking for him in the stands time after time during my Little League baseball games.

I cared deeply about being like my dad and gaining his approval. I suppose that's how God has set it up with our children, grandchildren, and others who watch us for an example and need us to know which way to grow in life. And then He watches from heaven, hoping the sacred trust of the lives which He has placed in our hands is nurtured by us.

It was the time my dad gave me—his presence, his looks of affirmation, his touch, his gentle words of encouragement—that mattered. Circumstances and decisions he made during the years that followed caused the pedestal I had placed him on to crumble. And in its place I harbored a knotted heart—until it was loosened years later by forgiveness and understanding.

There are children in our homes, extended families, neighborhoods, on the ball fields and courts, in our schools, on the streets where we walk, who are all watching us, looking up to us, often longing to be like us. They may even be grown. They probably think that we can do just about anything. They may want to do what they see us do. Or be like us.

Do we notice them, or even see them at all?

Or do we walk by them, rationalizing that they are someone else's concern, or perhaps acknowledging them as our concern but just not now because we don't have time—we'll definitely make up for it when we have more time?

By our example, we will show them the path they should walk. By the example we set for them, they step out into their own lives. I wonder where their footsteps will lead them.

"I've been watching you, Dad. . . . I wanna be like you."

They're watching us. Do we see them?

 IMPACT APPLICATION: By our example, we will show our children, and others who look up to us, the path they should walk. I wonder where their footsteps will lead them?

ALWAYS GOOD NEWS

How beautiful on the mountains are the feet of the messenger who brings good news, the good news of peace and salvation, the news that the God of Israel reigns! **Isaiah 52:7**

THE PHONE CALL from my daughter-in-law interrupted one of many morning meetings and stopped us in our tracks.

With tears in her voice, she choked out that our son was being taken by ambulance to the hospital with chest pains. Not knowing what to expect when we arrived, and coming from different locations, his mom and I arrived at the hospital a few hours later.

The preliminary news was good. Further tests that day continued to provide good news. Follow-up tests later continued to pierce the darkness of this moment and provide more good news.

I should have known that no matter what our son faced—even if the tests showed that there was a problem—good news would be the end result. Good news should be what I always claim, because that's the way God has it all planned out for us. I wish I could say I always did. My granddaughter Hannah reminded me of that not too long ago.

It seems that a few weeks before that moment, she learned that some of her friends were coming to play. Hannah bubbled with excitement, and coupled with the earlier promise of playtime with some other friends, she stopped in her tracks and in a wise, reflective little voice exclaimed, "Wow, I've really been getting a lot of good news lately!"

Why, of course! And if we stop for a moment to think about the moments of uncertainty in the darkness and in the valleys of disappointment and loss, at the end of it all we have all also gotten a lot of good news.

I don't know what today will reveal to you. I don't know what expectations are on your horizons. I don't know what difficulties you're going through, what losses still numb your reality, or what concerns may be occupying your minds. I don't know if you're in a hole so deep you won't be able to see the sunshine even when it does arrive. I don't know if you'll get a phone call interrupting your day that knocks you to your knees.

But for as long as I can remember, the sunshine eventually arrives. That's the way it has always worked, and I'm counting on it today and every day for the rest of my life.

I may even take a page out of Hannah's playbook and exclaim over and over today, "Wow! I'm really expecting a lot of good news today!"

IMPACT APPLICATION: At the end of it all, I know there is always the One who came with the Good News of peace and salvation. At the end of it all stands the One who is always good news no matter what we face.

THE PLATES CAN WAIT

For everything there is a season, a time for every activity under heaven. **Ecclesiastes 3:1**

I HAD SEEN THAT faraway, pensive look in her eyes before. Sometimes she would tell me what she was thinking, sometimes not. She would usually tell her Mimi what was on her mind, and for that I was always thankful.

"What are you thinking about, Hannah?"

I leaned back in the chair, hoping to reel her focus back from somewhere beyond our setting. We had just finished eating grilled hot dogs around the pool when I had suggested that she and Mimi swim again before her bedtime while I cleared the table and put everything away.

"I was thinking of something, Granddaddy, but wasn't going to say it because I didn't want to hurt your feelings." Her face was soft and radiant with gentle concern.

"That's okay, Hannah. What were you thinking?"

"Well, Gran," she began, "you could clean up while Mimi and I are swimming, or I was thinking that you could do it after I went to bed so you could swim with us too."

A mixture of tears and laughter bubbled from someplace deep within as I looked at Lynda, whose countenance betrayed what might be a recurring thought of why she had decided to marry such a slow learner. Even though through the years I had gotten so much better at recognizing those once-in-a-lifetime moments, I still had trouble recognizing that they usually come without fanfare. Precious moments—like swimming with my granddaughter while the dishes stood until later—were all around me, perhaps never to come again.

I pray that you know better. I pray that you know that the dishes, lawn, and housework will keep. I pray that you begin to see that all the work from the office, which you have earmarked as so important, pales against those once-in-a-lifetime moments with your spouse, children, grandchildren, students, teammates, players you coach, coworkers, and friends—moments that will never come again.

I pray that long-ingrained behaviors that delay, postpone, and preempt memory-making moments with the meaningless—in comparison—other things have now been put in their proper place in your life. And I pray that expressions like "We'll save it for a rainy day," "Let's save it to use on a special occasion," "We can do it tomorrow," "I'll call her another day," "Someday we'll . . . ," or "One of these days, I'll . . ." begin to fade from your vocabulary.

I didn't even notice the plates and food still standing in the places we had left them as I carefully tossed my granddaughter into the pool for the fourth time and waited for her to say when her head bobbed to the surface of the water, "One more time, Granddaddy. Just one more time."

 IMPACT APPLICATION: Dirty dishes or loved ones? Isn't it obvious?

GOD ALONE IS ENOUGH

Man's despair is not despair of God at all, but despair of all that is not God. Beyond that despair lies Christian hope, the certainty that God alone is enough for man. **William McNamara**

SO HOW IS THIS MORNING going for you?

From my perspective, the sun is shining. My bride is in the yard trimming bushes and planting flowers and aggravating her arthritis, which she will feel tomorrow. Our son is working hard on his next book. Our daughter-in-law and granddaughters are well and as precious and silly as ever, despite trying to figure out what to do about two raccoons who have taken up residence in a tree in their backyard. And Lily, our basset hound, is curled up sleeping downstairs in the kitchen without a care in the world.

In the midst of it all and from all I can tell around me—despite evidences to the contrary in various pockets of our society and world—God is still on the throne.

So what's your perspective on things this day? Is it rooted in a view God wants you to have, or is it rooted in one you are prone to slip into when things around you seem to be caving in?

In his book *The Light and the Glory*, Peter Marshall writes, "This nation was founded by God with a special calling. The people who first came here knew that they were being led here by the Lord Jesus Christ, to found a nation where men, women, and children were to live in obedience to him."

Marshall goes on to quote from Christopher Columbus's journal, *Book of Prophecies*. Columbus writes: "It was the Lord who put into my mind (I could feel His hand upon me) the fact that it would be possible to sail from here to the Indies. All who heard of my project rejected it with laughter, ridiculing me. There is no question that the inspiration was from the Holy Spirit, because He comforted me with rays of marvelous inspiration from the Holy Scriptures."

In the midst of what must have been a difficult and, at times, despairing journey, in which he ended up in the Americas rather than the Indies, Columbus maintained a perspective rooted in a belief that God alone was enough.

If you're anything like me, I suspect that in the middle of your challenging circumstances, you haven't always felt that God alone is enough. But as you face them, the only thing that is enough, the only thing that will last, is the only thing that is the best: God and God alone.

 IMPACT APPLICATION: In the midst of whatever you are going through, find hope and purpose for yourself and those around you in the truth that God alone is enough.

MAY 2

FRIENDS BEYOND THE ICE CREAM

"Lord," the man said, "if you are willing, you can heal me and make me clean." Jesus reached out and touched him. "I am willing," he said. "Be healed!" And instantly the leprosy disappeared. **Matthew 8:2-3**

WHEN I WAS TWELVE, as predictable as the sunrise, before the school bus arrived each morning, a neatly stacked supply of the *Hartford Courant* newspapers was deposited on my front porch for delivery to the neighborhood. I then made sure the folded papers were loaded into the front basket of my refurbished bicycle, as well as into the sack over my shoulder, and faithfully delivered them each morning.

Friday evening was collection time for my paper route, and it was then—on my very first round of collections—that I learned a poignant lesson about finances and friends: when collecting on your paper route, avoid the area where your friends and the Good Humor ice-cream truck are located—at least until you can count how much money you *really* have to spend on ice cream for all gathered.

With that lesson in finances learned and the newspaper budget now consistently balanced, I also watched as another phenomenon unfolded: a lot of my "friends" fell away. It was a sad moment.

But we know also that not all friendships are determined by who buys the ice cream, and the pains and disappointments of friendships are almost always outnumbered by the joys.

There are those friends you seem to pick right up with after a long absence, as if you were never apart. Those friends who remain and walk alongside you—even when they see the worst in you. Friends who sacrifice for you when they really can't afford to. Friends who heal the broken places in your life. You may even be married to one, as I am.

A leper came to Jesus one day and asked to be made clean. Lepers in those days suffered not only from physical, visible scars but also from the emotional scars they held inside from years of rejection and isolation.

Yet there he stood before his would-be friend, asking to be healed. Jesus could have said, "Sure, but don't get too close," and zapped him from a distance. But instead, Jesus reached out and touched him.

It was no doubt the first touch by anyone other than another leper. Jesus knew that and knew that the man needed emotional healing as well. And in that moment, that friend—that God—healed not only the external, physical scars of leprosy but also the internal scars he experienced from years of rejection and hatred.

Who will stay with you like that, even when the ice cream is gone?

 IMPACT APPLICATION: Stay close to those friends who embody the hands and feet of Jesus. Cherish them. Walk with them. Let them pick you up when you are down. And then do the same for them when they need a touch from above.

THROW OFF THE BOWLINES

The thief's purpose is to steal and kill and destroy. My purpose is to give them a rich and satisfying life. **John 10:10**

BY THE TIME he called early this morning, he himself had probably been up for a couple of hours. For more than thirty-five years he has been an encourager to me and many others and an example of what God calls us to do with the life He gave us.

At age seventy-seven, and after having doctors tend to some heart issues he was having not too long ago, he is back to his old life—using the tractor, checking up on friends, following family, and putting in very full days living the life God calls him to live. He just returned with his bride from a weekend trip to watch his grandson play in a Southeastern Conference football game. He wouldn't miss it, or anything else his family is involved in, and he already has his reservations for his grandson's remaining games. He likes football, but it's his grandson that causes him to pick himself up and go.

At any age, we always have a choice—to embrace, set the direction of, dream about, reach for, and live the lives God has given us or not. At any age—despite our health, our economic situation, our opportunities, or our disappointments—we have a choice to accept the abundant life Christ offers to us or not. An abundant life that is not only life as good as it can be, but when walking with Him, life beyond what we could ever imagine.

A number of years ago, the iconic American humorist Mark Twain wrote this for us to think about today:

> Twenty years from now, you will be more disappointed by the things that you didn't do than by the ones you did do. So throw off the bowlines. Sail away from the safe harbor. Catch the trade winds in your sails. Explore. Dream. Discover.

I don't know what's going on in your life right now. I don't know what season of life you are in right now or where you are on your list of things you had hoped to achieve in your life.

I do know that whether seven, thirty-seven, seventy-seven, ninety-seven, or beyond, God's desire for us for each day is to live an abundant and purpose-filled life with Him. One day we will kneel before Him, either worn out from living life to the fullest or with plenty of tread still left on the soles of our shoes. I know which I will choose. What about you?

Let me suggest that you choose abundance. Choose fullness. Choose reaching and dreaming and becoming all you were meant to be.

 IMPACT APPLICATION: Right now, wherever you are, throw off the bowlines, sail away from the safe harbor, catch the trade winds in your sails, and explore, dream, and discover all that God still has in store for you.

SOMEONE YOU SHOULD KNOW

Dear friends, do you think you'll get anywhere in this if you learn all the right words but never do anything? Does merely talking about faith indicate that a person really has it? . . . Isn't it obvious that God-talk without God-acts is outrageous nonsense? . . . Faith and works, works and faith, fit together hand in glove. **James 2:14-18,** MSG

THE SETTING WAS BEAUTIFUL as we gathered at the white-capped Gulf of Mexico to pay our last respects to someone you probably don't know.

But Mr. Rayment was someone you would never forget if you had ever met him.

You know folks like that. People who are in your life for a moment or more, and as a result your life is forever better. Those who offer an encouraging smile, a gleam of approval in their eyes, or a caring act of kindness, who are there to help you face whatever you confront in life, or who simply offer a timely word of affirmation.

Mr. Rayment wasn't particularly famous by the world's standards, although he supervised the development of the first condominium project (and others) built in modern times. And even as he approached his ninety-second birthday and a marriage of seventy-two years, he retained the childlike wonder of his youth, allowing him to always see the good, the positive, and the possible in whatever he faced.

Death is a real and difficult part of life for us who remain. But for those of us who believe in Jesus Christ as Savior and Lord, as Mr. Rayment did, we know that death is simply the end of one moment in our eternal relationship with God and the beginning of another—even more glorious.

The sadness remained for many days after. It will always be there at some level or another. But with it also remains joy in the assurance of knowing he sits within that great cloud of witnesses in the presence of his God. And with that assurance, those of us who remain are provided hope, comfort, and strength for today and tomorrow. And his legacy—both of faith in Christ and his consistent acts of love and kindness—is deeply embedded into the lives of all the family, friends, coworkers, and church and community members that were part of his life.

What will we remember from his life? What will we do with ours because of the lessons of those like him?

IMPACT APPLICATION: What do we need to examine in our own lives? Perhaps we need to evaluate where we stand in our own decision to ask Jesus Christ into our lives. It's not about attending church or church membership. It's not about just doing good. It's about a personal decision—a defining moment—of asking Jesus Christ into our lives. And then, once assured of that eternal life through Christ, perhaps our lives of kindness will begin to look a bit like those whose examples we remember.

NO PROBLEM TOO BIG, POGO

There is no problem so huge, so widespread, and so difficult to solve, that it cannot be run away from. **Pogo (Walt Kelly)**

I DON'T KNOW if you've ever phrased it quite that way, but my hunch is that you've felt that way before. I don't have a clue whether Pogo's statement is true. I suppose it may be or may have been for someone at some time, but as a way of life—well, that may be another story altogether.

I've had times when something like that has crossed my mind. Busy times lend themselves to a feeling that you wish you could just get away and hide from it all.

But my sneaking suspicion is that at a number of other times in our lives we've come to moments we didn't want to face. Moments where we stood ready to throw our hands in the air and run away, refused to answer the phone or return a phone call, called in sick for the day, crawled under a bed, or hid in the nearest closet until enough days had passed so the problem had to be gone.

Maybe we've lost a loved one and don't know how to go on. We've lost a job with no prospects on the horizon. Or perhaps we've made yet another mess of a relationship and have no idea how to make amends. Maybe we've fallen into one "mud puddle" too many and have gotten to a place where we can't stand up again for fear of yet one more failure.

Maybe you've come to a place in whatever you're going through where the only options you seem to have left are to quit, to give up, to run, and to stop living the life you always thought you were meant to live.

Do yourself a favor—don't quit, don't give up, don't run, and don't stop reaching for the life you know God has always meant for you to live.

Instead, do something else—by rephrasing Pogo's comment, like this: "There is no problem so huge, so widespread, and so difficult to solve . . . that God can't handle!"

At those moments, which we all will face, take comfort in the words of Peter—the same Peter who denied Christ on three separate occasions and yet Christ was there for him afterward—when he said, "Give all your worries and cares to God, for he cares about you" (1 Peter 5:7). God can handle whatever busy times you're trying your best to juggle, whatever disappointments have come your way, and whatever heartaches you're walking through.

Now that is something I know to be true—and in your better moments, I suspect that you do too.

IMPACT APPLICATION: God can handle whatever it is that you're facing today. So trust God and face the day boldly, remembering that no problem is too big for Him.

MAY 6

TAKE ANOTHER
GOOD-BYE

Don't store up treasures here on earth, where moths eat them and rust destroys them, and where thieves break in and steal. Store your treasures in heaven, where moths and rust cannot destroy, and thieves do not break in and steal. Wherever your treasure is, there the desires of your heart will also be. **Matthew 6:19-21**

WHEN WAS THE LAST TIME you remember your children coming down from their rooms to breakfast? Did you ever think those moments would end? When was the last time you had your grandchildren come to stay with you and then, upon their return home, felt an empty place in your heart and home?

A few years ago Matt Bryant kicked three field goals and three extra points after touchdowns to help the Tampa Bay Buccaneers beat the Green Bay Packers at Raymond James Stadium in Tampa, Florida. I don't know how he could begin to perform—let alone perform well. But he had to—even if he felt as though he was just going through the motions. He had to follow his feeling that it would honor his baby boy. Because on Wednesday morning before the game, Matt and Melissa Bryant couldn't wake their three-month-old son, Matthew.

That morning, he was gone.

"We had a terrible tragedy this morning," Jon Gruden, the head coach of the Buccaneers began at a press conference. "We lost a key member of our family. Matt Bryant and Melissa lost their youngest son."

Three times this head coach asked that fans and others keep the Bryants in their prayers.

It gets our attention, but does it change our day? Sometimes, for a while it may. Too bad it doesn't linger forever. What do we do instead? Sadly, too often, we simply get back to building up treasures on earth. We go back to spending time on the things the world says are important and miss the moments that give us glimpses into what heaven will be like. Each of us has been given opportunities in so many ways, and we too often miss the important moments, instead being caught up in the less important things of the world.

But what could be more important than storing up treasures that will last—relationships, adding eternal value by lifting Christ among those entrusted to us with the influence we have, making memories and embracing times with those we love? We'll surely find all those treasures again in heaven, and they will live beyond our lives here on earth.

 IMPACT APPLICATION: So, here are two questions for you: What are you doing with the rest of your life? Do those things really matter compared to the platform that God has given you to make an eternal difference in the lives entrusted to you today? Think about your answers while you still have the time.

HOOP DREAMS

Even youths will become weak and tired, and young men will fall in exhaustion. But those who trust in the LORD will find new strength. They will soar high on wings like eagles. They will run and not grow weary. They will walk and not faint. **Isaiah 40:30-31**

BACK IN 2008, Davidson College's run for the stars had finally come to an end. And sadly for them, just a little bit sooner than they expected.

It was an amazing performance, though, for any team, let alone for a ten-seed out of the Mid-West Region in a field of sixty-four of the best teams in collegiate basketball. The Davidson College men's basketball team gave it all they had in the NCAA basketball championships and came up two points—and a missed three-point attempt at the buzzer—short of reaching their dream of a first-ever Final Four appearance and a chance to play for the national championship.

And they did it on their second wind—a place many of us never experience. Yet they did. All born out of their dream of achieving something more.

They ran hard enough, long enough, fast enough—past the abilities and capabilities others saw and assigned to them. They did it by replacing every doubt, second thought, hesitation, and fear with a deep and abiding trust in each other, their coaches, their preparation, their past experiences, and most important, their dreams. They did it with the energy born of their dreams, realizing somewhere along the way that if they couldn't imagine being national champions, they never would be.

It's why we and people all across the nation watched and cheered and rooted them on. It was a place we all aspire to be. Not necessarily playing for the national championship—although secretly we have seen ourselves throwing in the game winner at the buzzer—but a place where we find ourselves reaching beyond the reality of our days into the dreams we have for our lives, whatever those might be or whatever those were that we may have now set aside.

American writer William James once wrote: "Most people never run far enough on their first wind to find out they've got a second. Give your dreams all you've got and you'll be amazed at the energy that comes out of you."

Been a while since you've dreamed? Been a while since you've reached for your dreams? Been a while since you've given your dreams the second wind of your life? Been a while since you've been amazed at something you've accomplished? Remember the words in today's Scripture.

Davidson's run for the stars is over for now. But only for now.

 IMPACT APPLICATION: Let me suggest that beginning today you dream dreams for your life. Run far enough to catch your second wind as you pursue them, and then trust that God will help you soar high on wings like eagles as you do it again and again and again.

MAY 8

TWELVE WORDS

Never be afraid to trust an unknown future to a known God.
Corrie ten Boom

THERE IT IS. A mission statement for all our todays—in just twelve words.

Twelve words to embrace as the morning sunshine begins to illuminate all the unknowns that will rapidly unfold in the day before us.

Twelve words from a woman whose father died after the Nazis arrested her family for harboring and helping Dutch Jews escape to freedom.

Twelve words from a woman who watched as her sister Betsie ran out of breath in the horrible confines of Ravensbrück concentration camp just months before those imprisoned there were liberated by Allied forces in the defeat of Nazi Germany in World War II.

Twelve words to offer us hope in the face of the loss of a loved one, the reoccurrence of an illness we thought was long since cured, a relationship that has finally ended, or the loss of a job.

Twelve words to embrace in the face of a country whose moral and spiritual foundations seem to be eroding at every level. Twelve words to cling to as too many press on toward the threshold of a slippery slope in a culture where the echoes of voices pointing us to the absolute truths of God's Word and desire for us seem eerily faint.

Twelve timely words, which provide the spiritual and moral rudder still available to guide the decisions of our individual, corporate, religious, institutional, and national lives in the face of a sprint toward a moral and spiritual desert, a rudder still available to pass on to the next generation and the next.

Twelve words.

It's time to claim or reclaim them for today and tomorrow.

It's time to embrace them for the courage to be bold for what is right, to lift us in our lives to all God intends for us, to make decisions of eternal and godly consequence, both now and in the future.

As the life on earth faded from her in that horrific place, Corrie ten Boom's sister Betsie left her—and us—with this admonition:

> We must tell them [the world] what we have learned here. We must tell them that there is no pit so deep that He is not deeper still. They will listen to us, Corrie, because we have been there.

Never be afraid to trust an unknown future to a known God.

 IMPACT APPLICATION: Twelve words that remind us that the only object worthy of our trust and focus each day is the God who created us and created all that is around us everywhere and created His Son—Jesus Christ.

RARE AND SPECIAL
MOMENTS

Special and rare are those who can see the potential in the child standing before them without having to see its fulfillment—but those who do see the potential are the builders of the promise of the next generation. **Anonymous**

"WAIT, GRAN!"

As I turned, I saw my precious five-year-old granddaughter bounding down the stairs from the porch. And then I watched as she ran across a stretch of our driveway to jump into my arms, nestle her head on my shoulder, and hug me good-bye as if to never let me go. I didn't want her to let go either.

As I drove on, my thoughts drifted to that day years ago when Hannah was first introduced to us and the rest of the world.

I'm not sure why I felt the urging at that particular moment on the morning she was born to take the elevator down two floors to the labor and delivery area of the hospital—it may have had something to do with my energy level. But leaving the boring environment of the waiting room, minutes later I found myself standing outside the electric doors which prevented admittance to the delivery rooms by anyone other than medical personnel or parents.

Unbelievably, grandparents waiting to meet their first grandchild were not on the list of those who were welcome in that area. Unless, that is, someone just happened to be entering or leaving and thereby caused the doors to miraculously open and allow someone like me—a new grandparent—to step through into the sanctum sanctorum of the labor and delivery hallway just a few rooms down from where Hannah was making her way into the world those many years ago.

I had left the waiting room to be closer to where she was to be born and to pray specifically for her and for her mom and dad—so pray I did. Right there in that delivery room hallway, especially reserved for me. Maybe the proximity helped the divine connection. And as it turned out, I was praying in that off-limits hallway at the very moment our precious Hannah was being delivered.

You have them in your life—children, grandchildren, godchildren, nieces, nephews, those other children of family and friends. As you see them standing, running, or jumping before you or hear their voices at play or calling from the porch—what do you see and what do you hear?

A precious child of the living God! Cherish those children, and pray for God's protection and blessing over them.

IMPACT APPLICATION: Be one of those special and rare souls who sees and hears all the potential within children and those others God has entrusted to your care. Do you see the promise of a generation in each life before you? Do you hear the voice of someone whom God has created to make a difference in this world?

RETIREMENT IS NOT AN OPTION

I heard again what sounded like the shout of a vast crowd or the roar of mighty ocean waves or the crash of loud thunder: "Praise the LORD! For the Lord our God, the Almighty, reigns." **Revelation 19:6**

IT WAS AN UNBELIEVABLE MOMENT in golfing history, which served to point us outside of ourselves, remind us of things we want to do, and expand our vision of what is possible.

I imagine that tears formed, palms sweated, and pulses quickened as Tom Watson walked up the eighteenth fairway of the Turnberry golf course. He needed a par to complete his attempt to win The Open Championship and become the oldest man—at two months shy of sixty—to win one of the four major golf tournaments. Announcers who had known and respected him for years couldn't string words together to describe it.

The words "God Almighty" in the Scripture above are translated from the Greek word *pantokrator*, which means "the one who controls all things." The word is used ten times in the New Testament—once in 2 Corinthians and nine times in John's writing of Revelation. The interesting thing about John's use of that term is that at the time he wrote Revelation in approximately AD 90, never was there a time when the Christian church faced more violent persecution. Yet in the face of those difficult times, John kept writing to remind us that God Almighty—*pantokrator*—is still in control and still reigns.

Maybe it was a reminder to one who is a couple of years older than the man who nearly won The Open Championship that whatever your age, it's only a number. Maybe it reminded a lot of us of all the faces we have seen throughout the years of those who had stopped living. They were done. Retired from work. Retired from trying. Retired from having an impact and making a difference. Their legacy had flatlined.

We have all vowed at one point or another that we would never let that be our legacy.

So then, what are you going through today? Retired? Just graduated from school with no prospects for employment? Lost your job or have had an unexpected career stumble? Finances short and looking shorter a little farther down the fairway? Just reached another "number" on the calendar and others are suggesting that it may be time to stop, retire, and leave tomorrow to the next generation?

That day when Tom Watson almost did it again was simply another of those reminders from the God who controls all things that no matter where you are in life, it's not over.

Tee it up again—and again and again!

IMPACT APPLICATION: The God who created you and me still reigns and still calls us to tee it up one more time. He's in control, and as long as there is breath in our body, in His eyes we're not done.

THE IMAGE YOU PAINT
FOR THEM

Fathers, . . . bring [your children] up with the discipline and instruction that comes from the Lord. **Ephesians 6:4**

MY SON, NATHAN, knew that his elder daughter, Hannah, loved to look in the mirror. As Hannah gazed into the glass, the reflection of her smile affirmed for her what she had heard from those who love her—wonderful. I just wasn't sure how easy it was for her to see past the collage of paper that had been stuck to the mirror.

Hannah's daddy had taken the time to tape crisply typed messages, both direct and subliminal, sticking them onto the mirror he knew she visited regularly. Each word carried a message of affirmation, hope, and inspiration for her—"Kind," "Outgoing," "Bright," "Amazing," "Lovely," "Friendly," "Athletic," "Honest," "Artistic," "Musical," "Generous," "Clever," "Relaxed," "Hilarious," "Articulate."

I suspect those words served to influence in large measure the image our precious granddaughter saw in the mirror. I suspect also that she heard and still hears those words circling around in her thoughts as she scurries about the halls and rooms of her home. I suspect she feels a sense of encouragement from them in the touch, tone, manner, and attention given her by those around her who love her.

She's lucky to have a father who takes her on "date nights" to Pizza Hut or Steak & Shake. She's lucky to have a father who recognizes that one of her strongest needs is to feel her father's protection, love, and encouragement every moment of every day. She needs to feel his positive presence and outlook on her future, his uplifting whispers, and his gentle correction in her life every day.

Yet too often we simply turn our children over to television sets, nannies, schools, and other caregivers to watch and care for them while we attend to other, "more important" things.

About 30 percent of our children go to bed without a father in the home or without one who cares or is regularly there. Seventy percent of children who get into legal trouble have no father in the home or at least not one who cares. Almost every presentence investigation report a judge sees paints a picture of a home with a physically or emotionally absent or abusive father.

And here's the rub—the boys in those homes become fathers, and the girls become mothers, and without some intervention, they are destined to continue the cycle. Yet all along the way, all they really wanted and needed was to believe there was something to hope for in life, something they could believe in, and someone they could trust, who was always painting a picture for them of all they can be.

Remember the words of George Herbert: "One father is more than a hundred schoolmasters." A father's role is indispensable.

 IMPACT APPLICATION: What picture do you paint of those God has entrusted to your care? Paint the picture for them that God would paint.

PASSIONS—GODLY DIRECTION

Work willingly at whatever you do, as though you were working for the Lord rather than for people. **Colossians 3:23**

WOULD YOU have done it?

Would you have followed the passion of your heart, as she apparently did, which ultimately led to that moment? Or would you have turned away?

Several years ago, the world watched the performance of Susan Boyle on *Britain's Got Talent* as she sang "I Dreamed a Dream" from *Les Misérables*.

She was a plain-spoken and plain-looking woman, and her manner and appearance set a tone of low expectation within the audience and judges. As Boyle moved from the introductions to her song, the show's three judges, along with the theater and television audiences, were moved quickly from cynicism, snide glances, and raised eyebrows to inspiration, warmed hearts, and smiles of joy as the lyrics and music floated from her angelic yet powerful voice.

When she had finished, one of the judges, Piers Morgan, said, "Without a doubt, that is the biggest surprise I have had in three years on this show."

Would you have followed the passion God poured into your heart, like Susan Boyle did, to follow those "want to" feelings that He placed in your life?

As I sit here this morning, I can reflect on so many moments in my life when I failed to follow the passion of my heart like she did. Instead, I let fear of being laughed at, fear of failure, the limits others or my parents imposed on me, uncertainty of the unknown, and forgetting that God was going with me and before me prevent me from following those passions He placed in my heart.

But many years ago, after accumulating a growing list of regrets, I committed to follow those passions God has placed on my heart. And I committed to change all the foolishness and failures that *might* occur when I stepped out into all the moments of significance, life change, and impact for God, others, myself, and God's Kingdom that *could* and probably *would* occur when I did.

Try it. Better yet, *do it*. The flames of passion God has placed within you and me will begin to burn brightly for not just each of us but for all the world to see.

And when you begin to follow those passions God placed within you, you will begin to live the life God intended for you to live—rather than to leave it standing quietly in the wings, wasted.

 IMPACT APPLICATION: Maybe this is the moment to commit to follow those God-breathed passions that lie beneath the "almost actions" of our hearts. Together with God we can commit and recommit to follow the passions He has placed within us—those "want-to" feelings gnawing at our hearts—and follow them into all the godly impact that will follow.

RESTORING JOY— BLESSED ARE THE MEEK

God blesses those who are humble, for they will inherit the whole earth. **Matthew 5:5**

LYNDA AND I were in North Carolina. I was in the midst of dealing with many issues from home, including some business issues involving our larger family circle.

I would have described my manner and countenance as "focused," "stoic," "resolute," and "determined." Lynda hit the nail on the head, though, when she stood before me after a particularly stressful day and said, "You don't seem to have any joy in your face anymore."

I realized, without discussion or rebuttal, that she was right.

What I thought was an otherwise impregnable exterior betrayed—to someone who knew me best—an inner world full of worry, trembling with fear in the face of the uncertainty before me and wondering moment by moment whether I could handle what I had to handle.

How many people do you know who seem to have an exterior air of impregnability only to discover they tremble inside with fear? How many times have you faced anxieties and fears with the outward appearance of strength, only to fall asleep at night gently pulsing with worry? Or perhaps you try to shore up the insecurities of life by gathering wealth or things or status around you.

But in the end, those things prove wanting in delivering us from our fears and helping us to move into each new day. If strength could deliver us, the dictators of the past would have carried the day. But they didn't. If possessions could, well, the list would be endless with people who seemed to have it all—and in the end had nothing. If fame or status could, then pick a celebrity from the list of those whose fears were conquered simply because their face made the front cover of *People* magazine.

Blessed are the meek. Blessed are those who are available to and submissive to God for their direction in life. Blessed are those who trust God for the fullness of their day, who realize that at the sunset of the day, God has been and remains in control. Blessed are those who walk in meekness—trusting in God—rather than trying to walk on their own and in their own power, eventually falling prey to the fear of something—fear of death, fear of failure, fear of tomorrow.

Blessed are the meek, those willing to follow God's direction for their lives, for they will live with a courage that overcomes the concerns of the day, a courage that recognizes that in the end, God wins, and those who trust in Him win also.

They will have joy in their faces.

IMPACT APPLICATION: Nothing paralyzes our potential like fear and anxiety. These emotions keep us from living a joy-filled life. Give your fear to God, acknowledging you can no longer carry the burden. You will be blessed!

MAY 14

THE EXAMPLE WE SET

Be imitators of God, as beloved children. And walk in love, as Christ loved us and gave himself up for us, a fragrant offering and sacrifice to God. **Ephesians 5:1-2,** ESV

HE WAS PRETTY CLEAR with his words. Pretty calm and matter of fact about it.

"I never curse at the players or coaches—or anywhere, for that matter," he said. "I might be a bit sarcastic at times, but even then I realize I need to go back, apologize, and ask forgiveness for that. My job is to teach them, set the example for the behavior I personally want them to display, and be able to walk away from every situation, every day, every season and look back and see that God was glorified."

Those were the words, in essence, spoken during a conversation not too long ago with a highly successful Division I college football coach.

Another very successful long-term Division I college baseball coach always asks me to pray that in the midst of the "battle" on the baseball diamond, players, coaches, and people who see him from the stands and on their television screens would always see God glorified by his words and actions.

And yet another former Division I basketball coach asks for prayers daily that those he coaches and leads, as well as those who watch him, would see something different than the world expects and advocates.

Something different. Something that looks like God at work.

Very encouraging to hear and know, but unfortunately their example is not the norm in the high-profile world of sports. Too bad. Because there is no bigger platform than in the world of sports, which society holds in such high esteem, very often undeservedly so. And beyond that, looking toward eternity, there is no bigger platform from which to glorify God and encourage others to follow that path.

The apostle Paul tells us in the passage above to be imitators of Christ and to walk in love. And not just in the high-profile world of sports, where our example is magnified and followed for good or not. How about also in our numerous other platforms and roles? What legacy are we leaving?

For instance, how about your example as a husband? How about as a dad? Are you setting a good example in your conversations, actions, instruction, and encouragement? How about as an employer or coworker or brother? How about as a friend or neighbor? Is God glorified in your life? I hope so.

IMPACT APPLICATION: "Be imitators of God." How are you doing where you are?

SAVING HANNAH

You are my refuge and my shield; your word is my source of hope.
Psalm 119:114

WAKING UP IS A WONDERFUL EXPERIENCE! Have you noticed it before? I mean really noticed how wonderful it is? As the cobwebs of sleepiness fall away, if you notice, your senses begin flooding with all the fullness of a brand-new day.

The grass you had always simply seen as wet you now notice is a safe resting place for millions of crystal-clear droplets dispersing the morning sun into rainbows. Daylilies of yellow, lavender, and purple trumpet the arrival of the new day. The sun pours through the branches in a neighbor's yard, forming a column of radiant glory reminding you of the Author of all that is before you.

Waking to a new morning is a wonderful experience. And you hope it's a wonderful experience for everyone everywhere.

As she often does, my granddaughter Hannah clarified some things for me not too long ago in a moment her daddy later shared with me. They had been reading a book about great white sharks after dinner and learned that the longest great white that was ever caught and recorded was twenty-one feet long. My son demonstrated its length for Hannah by laying down almost four of his body lengths on the floor as they both marveled at its size.

Sitting down with her again to continue their reading, he posed a hypothetical to demonstrate he would always protect her: "Hannah, do you know who would win a fight between me and a shark that big, if we were both in the water?"

"Granddaddy!" She didn't even blink.

"Who?" he asked, feeling his point slip away.

"Granddaddy. Because he's your dad, and he has to take care of you."

Of course! She gets the point and makes an even better one. And of course I would take care of her daddy, as I always have. Granddaddy's little girl got it right, yet in that exchange she issued a prophetic reminder to me and her daddy, and all of us, just in case we should ever forget.

There are people all around us who need to know there is someone always watching out for them, someone who will always be there to protect them from great white sharks—or other, similar things from which they need protection. They need those protective arms to wrap around them in the midst of whatever uncertainty they face. They need a place of security and peace.

Waking up is a wonderful experience! But it's not that way for everyone and not always for those near and dear to us. For some around us, who need and depend on us, the wonder of their waking experience depends a lot upon us.

IMPACT APPLICATION: We all need a place where we can feel at home and safe, even from twenty-one-foot sharks. What can you do about assuring that for others around you?

WHAT WILL THEY REMEMBER?

You have proudly defied the Lord of heaven and have had these cups from his Temple brought before you. You and your nobles and your wives and concubines have been drinking wine from them while praising gods of silver, gold, bronze, iron, wood, and stone—gods that neither see nor hear nor know anything at all. But you have not honored the God who gives you the breath of life and controls your destiny!
Daniel 5:23

NOT FAR FROM where most of us live, we can find luxury communities where opulence is the word of the day. Places where self-defined worth is determined by the very best that money can buy—houses, cars, country clubs, shopping malls, restaurants—and where, if one looked long enough, one might even see or brush elbows with a celebrity or catch a glimpse into the lifestyle of someone who is rich or famous.

Every form of media today glamorizes it, and we allow it into our homes through magazines, television, movies, and the things we acquire. And then we wonder why our children soon hand us lists of things they want or "need" instead of things they see that others need.

Daniel was summoned before King Belshazzar, the son of King Nebuchadnezzar, and extolled as one who could explain the enigmas of the day. Daniel was promised that if he could explain the strange writing on the wall of the king's palace, he would be clothed in purple and gold and be made the third ruler of the kingdom.

Any interpretation probably would have sufficed.

But Daniel had the unmitigated gall and temerity to stand before one of those who—like so many today—defined his worth by the number of things he had and by the power he wielded and let fly with what the Scripture above records. And further, he went on to add that God had numbered the days of the kingdom of Belshazzar and determined how the kingdom would be divided up among others. That very night Belshazzar was slain, and the kingdom was turned over to Darius.

At the end of it all, what will you have left? What will you have built into the lives of your children? Will your life be characterized by your desire to keep up with others—or in serving the Lord?

Will those who love you remember the stuff you left behind or didn't leave behind, or will they remember that with every breath, you honored the God who gave you the breath of life and controlled your destiny?

IMPACT APPLICATION: Will your life reflect a never-ending marathon of having to do more, acquire more, or achieve more in order to have worth? Or will your life reflect a realization that the only affirmation, approval, and love that matters has already been given to you on the cross by Christ?

PRESSED ALWAYS
IN CHRIST

We are pressed on every side by troubles, but we are not crushed. We are perplexed, but not driven to despair. We are hunted down, but never abandoned by God. We get knocked down, but we are not destroyed. **2 Corinthians 4:8-9**

AS I REFLECT on those words inspired by God and penned by the apostle Paul, I can't help but wonder if Paul wrote them with the world of sports in mind. Never was there a verse more fitting for all the ups and downs or highs and lows experienced within the world of sports.

My son and I are blessed with associations and a lifelong journey within the world of sports as players, coaches, spectators, and fans and through walking with others in their professional, personal, and spiritual journey within that setting. At any given moment we have dear friends within major college and professional venues who experience heartbreaking disappointments, while others embrace major celebrations of joy. And to a society that has elevated the world of sports to a level of interest impossible to imagine or fathom, it seems that the highs and lows are felt even more deeply.

But the reason sports are such a passion in the hearts of most is that in the microcosm of a game we can often see the span of our lives with all its joys and heartaches, successes and failures. In the course of a dropped touchdown pass to win a game—now lost—we relive many moments of falling short and experiencing failure in the struggles of our own lives. Or while watching a basketball player, who missed his or her previous seven shots, shoot one more time and watch as the ball falls straight through the hoop to win the game, we remember those moments where we refused to quit, believing that the next best moment of our lives was just around the corner.

There it is. That's the key. That's what became so clear to Paul after he devoted his life to Christ, no matter what he went through. That key to dealing with whatever was before him was the reality of the living Christ within him, and within us, who keeps us safe and strengthens us to press on.

In the ups and downs and pressures of all our days, why not go to that person we can always count on—Christ—who will pick us up and send us back into all we face? And when He does send us back, we go knowing that we will never go alone!

IMPACT APPLICATION: There is one place where we will find steady and consistent energy, the right direction, and an eternal reason for getting up when we get knocked down. It's that safe place of the living Christ where we will always—and for all eternity—be secure.

MAY 18

ROOTED

"Everything is meaningless," says the Teacher, "completely mean-
ingless!" What do people get for all their hard work under the sun?
Generations come and generations go, but the earth never changes.
Ecclesiastes 1:2-4

WE HAVE GIVEN Solomon a lot of credit for being wise, wealthy, and intelligent.
He built the Temple and ruled Israel well during forty years of peace. But it wasn't
until the end of his life that he really understood the priorities God had placed
on his life—priorities not rooted in "things" but in moments with God and with
those He placed in his life to love.

Near the end of a life, which the world viewed as successful, Solomon put it
this way:

> I have seen all the works which have been done under the sun, and
> behold, all is vanity and striving after wind (Ecclesiastes 1:14, NASB).
> For what does a man get in all his labor and in his striving with which
> he labors under the sun? (Ecclesiastes 2:22, NASB) What advantage does
> man have in all his work which he does under the sun? (Ecclesiastes 1:3,
> NASB) Vanity of vanities! All is vanity (Ecclesiastes 1:2, NASB).

Solomon said it was all "striving after wind" to live life "under the sun." He
clearly tells us, from his own experience, that a life rooted solely in worldly values
and riches is vanity. It is empty—there is nothing to it. A life like that will not
satisfy. And Solomon should know.

Yet as Solomon's life on earth neared its end—not too late and not wishing for
more "things"—he shares this for children of all ages to follow: "Remember also
your Creator . . . before the sun and the light, the moon and the stars are darkened,
and clouds return after the rain. . . . Fear God and keep His commandments"
(Ecclesiastes 12:1-2, 13, NASB).

It took Solomon getting to the end of his life to learn that lesson. What about
us? Which will be the paths of your life and mine? Will ours be pathways on
which we seek things, accolades, comfort, gratification, and awards? Or will they
be pathways that reflect lives striving after God and striving to add value to the
others around us?

On our last day, which pathway do we believe will give us more satisfaction
and a sense of fulfillment? Follow that path—today and every day.

IMPACT APPLICATION: Solomon's answer to a
meaningful, fulfilling life is God and to seek a life that
is rooted in a relationship with the God who created
us and with those whom God has placed in our lives.

THE SEVEN DWARFS

Jesus said, "Come to me, all of you who are weary and carry heavy burdens, and I will give you rest." **Matthew 11:28**

ANOTHER MORNING, and their cheery tune unexpectedly rises from the recesses of my memory.

Heigh-ho, heigh-ho, it's off to work we go.

The dwarfs in Walt Disney's *Snow White and the Seven Dwarfs* happily sang and whistled their way to and from their work in the diamond mines. By society's standards you wouldn't expect a cheerful disposition in that particular work, but there they were, singing and whistling along.

We were attending the annual Campbell reunion banquet, a gathering of Lynda's family. The oldest lit the room with every one of his 102 years, and the youngest, at three months, stayed at home as he bravely readied for yet another surgery to remedy a problem following him from birth. We were an eclectic assemblage of uniquely created lives, and all of us had, or will, struggle at some point or another with the ultimate question as to our impact and purpose on this journey from dust to dust. Where do we find our purpose? What makes us whistle and sing?

As you look around your own life, you'll notice that you will not find that purpose intended by God in the wearying and coma-inducing pursuit of power, prestige, awards, or money, as those things will eventually all fade into insignificance.

But you will find the answer to the question about our purpose in the circle of loved ones and friends, as Lynda's family reunion reminded us. You will find it and feel it in the warmth of the hand holding yours, in the person who cares that you are there. You will find it when you sit at the knee of wisdom and experience, asking those who have gone before you questions about the important things in life. You will find it where you find your joy each day—in that which puts a song in your heart and a whistle on your lips every day of your life.

And by Jesus' example and through His love, power, and peace, you will find your answer for the purpose and impact of your life when you can find satisfaction in each moment of your day, no matter the outcome of what you're doing. And when you reach out to light up someone else's day, to spend time with others, encouraging them and being encouraged yourself, you will remember how much you are loved, by so many and by Him.

 IMPACT APPLICATION: The answer to the question of the purpose of your life may be closer than you think. Enjoy those whom God has placed in your life, and pour your life into them.

MAY 20

LIFE WITH A GOD WHO SEES

Thereafter, Hagar used another name to refer to the LORD, who had spoken to her. She said, "You are the God who sees me." **Genesis 16:13**

M'LYNN'S ANGER was palpable. Her daughter Shelby's death through childbirth had always been a possibility—which is why she had advised her daughter against a pregnancy in the first place. Her daughter died from complications of delivering her son, Jack Jr., into the world.

And as we watched *Steel Magnolias*, we screamed silently along with her. Good acting? Sure. Sally Field is a great actress. But more likely we felt what she felt because we remembered having been there before and through our own tears screaming silently, *Why?*

And the answer never came for that mother in that movie. It seldom does in life. And the anger remains, and the pain lingers, and we wonder if the God we believe in knows—or even cares—how we feel.

And then a reminder comes. From somewhere. Sometimes it's a memory that creases a smile across our face or forms a tear in our eye. A reminder that—as hard as it gets at times and as much as we'd like to scream and hit something—life still goes on. God still sees us and cares for us.

For Hagar, Sarah's Egyptian maidservant, life seemed bitter indeed. Compelled by Sarah to bear the child Sarah never could, Hagar was an object of scorn when she was found to be pregnant. Sarah, envious of her servant's ability to do what she couldn't, treated Hagar harshly, and Hagar's only recourse was to run away.

Alone in the wilderness, Hagar had few prospects, and life seemed at its lowest ebb. And that's where the angel of the Lord found her.

The angel told her to return to Sarah and submit to her authority. He didn't say that Sarah would treat her well now. He didn't promise immediate security or well-being. But he did promise "more descendants than you can count" (Genesis 16:10).

And Hagar's response to this encounter? Hagar returned home with a promise and an understanding of God, whom she called "the God who sees me."

Sometimes we are reminded that God still sees us when we encounter something miraculous. Other times it's a call from a granddaughter or another loved one.

It helps us get through the inexplicable and gut-wrenching "whys" of life.

And, in time, we remember that the God we believe in really does know and really does care how we feel. And so, in time a smile comes, a tear falls, and we can call Him "the God who sees me."

And life goes on, all for the better for all our tomorrows and all the way on through to eternity.

 IMPACT APPLICATION: "Why?" The question is not always easy, and not necessarily fair, and the answer seldom comes. But in this midst of our "whys," we are helped, shaped, and reminded that life does go on with "the God who sees."

ON THE TOP OF THE MOUNTAIN

Those who live in the shelter of the Most High will find rest in the shadow of the Almighty. This I declare about the LORD: He alone is my refuge, my place of safety; he is my God, and I trust him. **Psalm 91:1-2**

LYNDA AND I had watched the closing ceremonies of a recent Winter Olympics when I realized that I ached from having to say good-bye to them. It was more than just the games being over; it was as if the spirit of the best of what they stood for would be gone with them.

Perhaps it's because all around us our world is at war. Perhaps it's because in too many lives around us hope is not real. Perhaps it's because of the paucity of strong, selfless voices of calm, peace, or hope calling and lifting us to the top of the mountain for a view of all we were meant to be. Perhaps it's because the hope-filled philosophy of unity espoused by the Olympic movement would be forgotten.

And even the few examples of behavior that fell well short of the spirit of the Olympic Games could not dampen the indelible images of hope and unity, of athlete after athlete who, in the true Olympic spirit, used the platform they were given in this Olympic moment in their lives. They reached for a connection with each other beyond their differences, refusing to recognize those differences as impregnable walls of separation.

None did that any better than Shizuka Arakawa, who with her smile and elegance rekindled for me the flame of Olympic hope our world desperately needs to embrace Cheered as Japan's only medal recipient and that country's first-ever gold medal–winner in women's Olympic figure skating, she radiated the Olympic spirit as she floated, jumped, and spun on the ice to the music and lyrics of Celtic Woman's "You Raise Me Up."

In the recollection of the music and the power and elegance of her performance, I am reminded that even in my darkest moments each day, God is my source of refuge and hope, who will draw me to Him to the top of the mountain. And in those moments, standing on the top of the mountain with Him, I know that hope is real and that we are all raised to use the platform we each have to help one another to be more than we ever thought we and our world could be.

 IMPACT APPLICATION: In the uncertainty of each day in a world of uncertainty, we may not know where to begin. But let me suggest this: begin by believing that with the Lord on high as our place of rest, refuge, and safety, our hope is real, and together with Him we will be raised to the top of the mountain.

MEMORY BOX

Since we are surrounded by such a huge crowd of witnesses to the life of faith, let us strip off every weight that slows us down, especially the sin that so easily trips us up. And let us run with endurance the race God has set before us. We do this by keeping our eyes on Jesus, the champion who initiates and perfects our faith. Because of the joy awaiting him, he endured the cross, disregarding its shame. Now he is seated in the place of honor beside God's throne. **Hebrews 12:1-2**

MEMORIES. Some good, some not. No matter which, they inform and influence who we are. And they carry us from where we were into today and to where God wants us to be tomorrow.

On my dresser sits a little wooden box full of memories. An average brown in color, it stands about twelve inches wide, ten inches deep, and eight inches high, with four small drawers and a swing-open panel. It was a wedding gift from a dear friend, and for some reason Lynda has allowed it to adorn my dresser all these years. She has learned that I am a bit of a memory collector, and she has graciously accepted that quirk. The word *eclectic* comes to mind, as the little box matches nothing in the room.

On a number of occasions, a brief review of its contents has caused a refocusing of my thoughts as to what is important. It brings to life once again the passion of those who have gone before me and on whose shoulders I now stand as a great cloud of witnesses encourages my steps. Notwithstanding its limited storage capability, it contains a collection of homemade cards with "I love you" neatly scrawled inside from my then much younger son.

There are a couple of cards and letters from my three godchildren, demonstrating a grasp of the English language divinely and appropriately reserved only for a child; a prayer in my father-in-law's own handwriting, which he had given at a Kiwanis Club meeting; an article in the *Durham Morning Herald* about our son, Nathan, as he embarked on his football-playing days at Duke; a few pictures of him; a four-leaf clover; an old knife; some foreign coins; and a beautiful card Lynda's mom gave me just before we were married.

Every now and then I revisit the items and the stories they bring to mind, realizing that they also mark those moments of God's faithfulness and passionate encouragement through the ups and downs of my journey. Even in the note tucked neatly away in the bottom of that little wooden box, containing the words of a song from the musical *Annie*: "The sun'll come out tomorrow."

 IMPACT APPLICATION: The memories of yesterday fuel the passions we need for today and remind us of God's faithfulness, which is always there to carry us through the daily struggles and joys.

TURN THE TV OFF

We don't look at the troubles we can see now; rather, we fix our gaze on things that cannot be seen. For the things we see now will soon be gone, but the things we cannot see will last forever. **2 Corinthians 4:18**

I SHOULD KNOW BETTER by now—you should too—not to turn the television news on in the morning. It's enough to make you forget how beautiful it was outside when you walked out a moment earlier.

Between news of the stock market's continuing wobble that is causing investments, savings, and retirement accounts to be reduced in value and some polls I've seen showing that 59 percent of Americans believe we should throw the entire Congress—all 535 members—out of office, to financial rescue plans and campaign ads with spoken and printed words occasionally sprinkled with the truth, it's enough to cause you to want to assume the fetal position under the bedcovers until it all goes away.

But step back for a minute and look at it again. I wonder if it all seems to depend on your perspective. In the midst of all the junk of the day, what is important to us, and where are you and I placing value? On the things and events I've mentioned, or on something else?

Consider this—

While you watch the Dow Industrial Average go down, how is your wife doing? Is she healthy? Awake? Still tolerating your mood swings? Does she still love you?

While you watch politicians twist the truth, how are your children? Happy, cheerful, mischievous, and still not wanting to eat their vegetables? Did they get a good report from their last doctor's visit? If not, did they still get a chance to find comfort in your arms?

While you try to figure out from where your next paycheck will come, have you lost sight of all the things you can do? In the midst of all the stuff of the day, have you forgotten all the people who still look to you for comfort, guidance, and help?

As you sit and wonder about the future effects of the outcome of campaigns, how are your grandchildren doing? Do they still think you hung the moon? Do they still take your breath away when you hear their precious little voices? Do their heads still fit perfectly on your shoulder?

Where are you placing value? Where is your focus? What do you really see as having value in your life?

Turn the television sets and radios off—and turn instead to the things of real and lasting value all around you. You'll be surprised at how beautiful the day becomes.

IMPACT APPLICATION: True value is found in what is eternal—especially relationships with other people. Spend your mornings tuned to that station!

MAY 24

STOPPING YOUR WORLD

Be still in the presence of the LORD, and wait patiently for him to act. Don't worry about evil people who prosper or fret about their wicked schemes. **Psalm 37:7**

A SMILE BROKE across my face as I listened to Nathan recount our younger granddaughter's case for staying one more night with Mimi and Gran.

"Daddy, I have three reasons that I want to tell you to stay another night with Mimi and Gran. One, because I can help Mimi around the house while I'm here; two, Mimi will be able to have me for company in the morning when we wake up in case Gran has to go to somewhere; and three, well, because I want to." Ellie Kate always has a way of getting to the essence of the issue.

Quite a day—being a part of the lives and activities of two precious grand-daughters. I find myself reminded of Lynda's comment when she held our elder granddaughter, Hannah, in her arms for the very first time, just hours after she was born—"She took my breath away!"

Simply put—they stop our world.

We all have people like that in our lives, whom God has placed there to add a bit of the eternal into what are at times overwhelming moments of the everyday. God has given us moments when we stop—or are stopped—and catch a glimpse into a quieter place, a holier place, where the transient activities, problems, and uncertainties of the day are replaced with the eternal and with a glimpse into what heaven will be like.

And when we are privileged to catch a glimpse of moments like those, something wonderful happens. They stop our world. All of the busyness and preoccupation with the unimportant things that keep us way too busy fall aside, as today replaces someday and the blessings of now replace all of my planning for tomorrow.

In her book *Gift from the Sea*, Anne Morrow Lindbergh suggests "an end toward which we could strive—to be the still axis within the revolving wheel of relationships, obligations and activities." That still axis is that quiet center of our lives where we begin to focus on the eternal moments of today, as our world continues to spin all around us, presumably heading toward tomorrow. It's that quiet center where stillness replaces busyness and priorities align in a God-ordained order.

For Lynda and me there are many—but our granddaughters do it every time. They simply stop our world.

 IMPACT APPLICATION: Embrace those people and moments around you where your life is marked by sacred memories, where your world is stopped to reflect upon the eternal, the important, and the God who is over it all.

ROPE BRIDGES AND THE FATHER'S TOUCH

Jabez cried out to the God of Israel, "Oh, that you would bless me and enlarge my territory! Let your hand be with me, and keep me from harm so that I will be free from pain." And God granted his request.
1 Chronicles 4:10, NIV

DURING A TRIP to Busch Gardens, we came upon one of those playgrounds with ladders, slides, rope walkways, and hiding places, all of which towered above the walkway below. By the excited utterances of our granddaughter Hannah, I knew we were going to be there for a while.

Hannah, under her own power, climbed one of the ladders that led to a landing and then made her way up the wooden platforms and stairs to the very top. You could tell she was pleased with herself. Of course, I followed her up all the way, close at hand just in case.

But when she reached the top, she stopped. In front of her was a rope bridge that spanned the walkway below. Her mom and dad and Mimi stood below, urging her to cross. She stood there—frozen—afraid to move forward and afraid to move back.

I suspect all of us have been at a similar point in our lives, standing in front of an intimidating rope bridge we know we need to cross. And if our fear of the height—with seemingly no safety net below—isn't enough to stall our journey, we often find that the winds are too strong, the rain too intense, or the thunder and lightning in the gathering storm too great for us to even consider taking another step. Whatever it is, we just can't seem to find the power or assurance we need to try to make it across.

And if we attempt it only under our own power, we may be right—we just may not make it across.

But then there's the example of Jabez. Jabez knew he lacked the power to accomplish great things on his own, so he prayed to the Lord for help. And God answered his prayer. And with God's hand upon him, Jabez moved forward in his life, blessed by the power of God.

And so there Hannah and I stood, me just behind her as she looked across the length of that intimidating expanse. In a moment, she looked back at me with a knowing glance and then reached back toward me.

She did something she'd never done before. With my touch and dependent on my power, which she trusted because of her past experiences with me, together we enlarged her territory and crossed the bridge together.

That's what God stands ready to do for you and me, if only we will trust His power and remember that His hand is upon us.

IMPACT APPLICATION: What rope bridges are you standing before today? God is there to help you across. Just reach and take His hand.

MAY 26

LOOK DEEPER

Jesus found a young donkey and rode on it, fulfilling the prophecy that said: "Don't be afraid, people of Jerusalem. Look, your King is coming, riding on a donkey's colt." **John 12:14-15**

NOT TOO LONG AGO, our younger granddaughter had piqued my interest in a movie she had recently seen. And so while traveling with Lynda, I watched Ellie Kate's recommended movie *Bolt*. It is the animated tale of an endearing dog who plays the role of a superhero dog on a TV show.

At some point in all of his adventures, he discovers that—in his real life—he really isn't the superhero dog he portrays for the television cameras each week. But he also learns that the little girl who is on the show with him loves him just as he is.

Things aren't always what they appear to be.

We spend a lot of time on the surface of life. We experience promotions in our careers, build our résumés, or are handed diplomas signifying graduation from high schools and colleges. We build new homes, buy new cars, and increase our wealth. We embark on new ventures and establish new relationships. We rise and fall, win and lose, sometimes come up more, and too often come up less, as we try to make our way through what we see as the path before us.

We're so busy that we don't get beyond our surface impressions—of others or of ourselves. But life wasn't meant to be lived on the surface. Life was meant to be lived much deeper than that.

At the end of Jesus' ministry, He rode into Jerusalem on a donkey. The people of the time were expecting Jesus to be a military messiah who would lead Israel into a new golden age of prosperity. Their expectation was that Jesus would ride on a warhorse, ready to subdue His enemies. But instead, Jesus made His long-awaited entrance riding an animal that was a symbol for peace. Jesus defied the people's expectations, and by the end of the week, the triumphal entry became the Via Dolorosa, the "way of grief," with Jesus on the way to the Cross. The people had looked at the surface and had missed the Savior. Rather than delivering the people from the oppression of their temporal enemies, He came to deliver them into eternal life.

We were created to look beyond the things that appear on the surface. To look deeper into what is before us. When we do, we find a dog who realizes that life isn't about fanfare and fans but about his relationship with a little girl who loves him. And we find a Savior riding on a donkey.

Things aren't always what they appear to be.

 IMPACT APPLICATION: Look deeper into the way things really are and, more importantly, at the way they ought to be. Start by looking into a relationship with the long-awaited Messiah, and then deepen that relationship for the rest of your life.

IT'S GREAT BEING YOU

I live in this earthly body by trusting in the Son of God, who loved me and gave himself for me. **Galatians 2:20**

THEY HAD MANY A WONDERFUL MOMENT together before Hannah's dear friend Lauren moved west with her family, like this exchange I overheard between them when they were just five as they played a game they called "pretend we are adults and change names."

Hannah started the "pretending game" by announcing that her name would be "Lauren," and then asked Lauren, "What name will you be?" "Hannah" was Lauren's reply, which prompted Hannah to say, "Isn't it great being me?"

It wasn't proud or arrogant, but simply a reflection from her heart. I suspect that Lauren would say the same thing and feel the same way. It was a very telling and poignant comment, though, warranting a grateful thank-you to her parents who have deposited well more than they have withdrawn into the bank account of self-image of those most precious of God's creations.

I wonder how many of us could honestly say that happened to us. Or do we secretly harbor feelings of low self-image and worth, and in our most intimate places we wish we could look like so-and-so or be this-and-that or have such-and-such, and even as adults we wish we could be someone else. Only then would we be able to say that "it's great being me."

It happens gradually through the years of childhood and as adults. No one is immune. A hurtful comment by a peer, and then another and another. A parent's insensitive remark or act ignoring the fragile nature of an impressionable soul and tiny body. An endless bombardment by a materialistic world through television, movies, and print media that it would be better to be or look like somebody else because we don't quite measure up. All internalized again and again until the thought *Isn't it great being me?* slowly disappears and then, sadly, never comes to mind again.

In his book *Seeds of Greatness*, Dennis Waitley says, "If there is no deep, internalized feeling of value inside of us [and love for ourselves], then we have nothing to give or to share with others." And think of the potential impact of that, one way or the other, in a world in desperate need of a kind word, a gentle touch, or a helping hand.

The next time you look into a mirror, look deeply at the image you see and repeat this line: "Isn't it great being me?"

And then listen closely for the whisper that descends softly from above—"Yes."

 IMPACT APPLICATION: Take a moment to look in the mirror, and keep looking until you see what the God who loves you and made you sees: a wondrous, beautiful creation, unique and gifted in ways that only He can create.

MAY 28

NEVER LEFT BEHIND

If a man has a hundred sheep and one of them wanders away, what will he do? Won't he leave the ninety-nine others on the hills and go out to search for the one that is lost? And if he finds it, I tell you the truth, he will rejoice over it more than over the ninety-nine that didn't wander away! **Matthew 18:12-13**

THE BEST I CAN REMEMBER is that I heard a retired military officer on the television news one day remark that "the hallmark of the United States military is that not one be left behind."

Of course, at that moment, he was referring to the US Marines' rescue of seven of our troops that had been captured in the conflict theater called Operation Iraqi Freedom. As I learned from his statement, he could have been referring to any number of successful rescue operations staged throughout the course of our history.

As I thought about his words and reflected on the faces flashing across the television screen of some of those recently rescued, I thought of the little child who had fallen in the Texas well a few years earlier, and the trapped horse and beached whales, of stranded tornado and hurricane victims, entombed coal miners, and those in icy waters off the 14th Street bridge as a result of a plane crash in our nation's capital. I thought of the Twin Towers, the Pentagon, and a field somewhere near Shanksville, Pennsylvania. And I remembered the heroic and self-sacrificial efforts of Americans, in every instance, to make sure that "not one be left behind."

The best of our military, the best of our communities, the best of our families, and the very best of America is demonstrated by the value we place on human life, exemplified by the never-ending commitment that not one be left behind. As I thought about the officer's words and the faces of all those who at one time or another were lost or in need around us, the words of Christ in today's Scripture came to mind.

That's what He is doing for each of us, reaching for us in our moment of need. It is what He is always doing in our lives, knocking on our door to let Him in, following us, walking with us, lifting us back to where we should be with Him.

I don't know what's going on in your life today, but you need to remember that no matter where you are, no matter how lost you may feel—perhaps like one of those soldiers who was rescued—the Christ who is always with you is following you and will never leave you behind. Believe it!

IMPACT APPLICATION: Jesus Christ is with you and will never leave you behind. Work today to ensure that others will not be left behind—in your family, in your workplace, in your community.

MEMORIAL DAY MEMORIES

If my people who are called by my name will humble themselves and pray and seek my face and turn from their wicked ways, I will hear from heaven and will forgive their sins and restore their land.
2 Chronicles 7:14

THE AIR WAS SURPRISINGLY COOL as I walked outside at dawn to post our American flag. It was another Memorial Day, and my gratitude was full to over-flowing, my heart awash in memories and hopes in harmony with the sacredness of the day.

A day where we pause to remember and accept anew the legacy of freedom now resting in our hands and the duty imposed on us to assure its safe passage into the hands of those generations who follow.

A day when we pause as a nation to honor the sacrifice of those who have stood in the gap for us and for this great land and to consider what it all should mean as we live the lives their courage has secured for us. And a day when we pause to remember the very roots of this nation for which those lives were given.

A day of remembrance that began in 1866 with placing some flowers on the graves of our Civil War veterans, Memorial Day has been highlighted since the dedication in 1921 of The Tomb of the Unknown Soldier in Arlington National Cemetery.

We recall on this day the words of President Abraham Lincoln delivered on November 19, 1863, at the dedication of the Soldiers' National Cemetery in Gettysburg, Pennsylvania: "The world will little note nor long remember what we say here, but it can never forget what they did here. It is for us, the living, rather, to be dedicated here to the unfinished work which they who fought here have thus far so nobly advanced . . . that we here highly resolve that these dead shall not have died in vain; that this nation, under God, shall have a new birth of freedom."

Their legacy of belief in something better—in a hope for a brighter tomor-row—must not end with them but must live on in us and in the purpose of each day of our lives. And it begins when we humbly turn back to the God who created this great land and entrusted it to our care.

May God continue to bless the United States of America, the lives and families of all those who have sacrificed for us and for this great nation, and all of us who remain and are yet to come as we pray and seek God's guidance and turn from our own ways.

IMPACT APPLICATION: Each passing generation has the responsibility to not only remember those who have sacrificed but to honor them by turning back to the God who created everything.

MAY 30

JOSEPH'S LIGHT

Send out your light and your truth; let them guide me. Let them lead me to your holy mountain, to the place where you live. **Psalm 43:3**

YOU MAY NOT KNOW HIM, but he understood the responsibility he had to be all he could be. You would have been blessed by his life, as so many were. You may yet be blessed by the imprint he left on the lives of others—whose lives may yet touch yours. His life embraced those words of the psalmist set out above. As the psalmist says of God, so Joseph's light always shined to light the path of others.

Joseph, only age 32—a son, brother, uncle, friend—was gone too soon from our midst. The season of his life passed quicker than those who knew him wanted. The seasons in the arms of his heavenly Father and God's Son, Joseph's Savior, will, of course, continue forever. And the legacy he left each day he was with us will serve as an inspiration for all of us on how to live each day with the uncertainty that is always there about the next and in the face of the adversity that always comes in life—often when we least expect it.

Through a progressively debilitating disease diagnosed at age six, Joseph weathered eight surgical procedures and the insidious, painful spread of the disease through the years with a courage that could only come from above and from the encouragement of those around him. He worked two jobs during sixty-hour weeks, trained for and ran in the New York City Marathon, lived each day with a grateful heart and a childlike expectancy toward the next, and loved the world around him without exception or expectation. And he did it all with a smile on his face, pain in his body, and a force of will and faith in God that refused to allow him to be defined by this disease.

He didn't choose this painful platform, but he made the most of where he stood on it throughout his life. And in that journey of courage, he shone a light on the path before each of us—reminding us that no matter the mountains we will have to climb or the valleys we will walk, the light of the God who loves us is there.

And it is a light that always grows brighter to penetrate the darkness. A light that always shines with the strength and person of Christ who walks with us and before us into all we face. A light that shines no matter what we face, no matter the crush of defeats, no matter the pain of life's journey. No matter.

 IMPACT APPLICATION: As God, through Christ, is the light of the world shining in our lives and the darkness around us, we are also to be a light to others in the midst of their days of darkness and difficulties. Shine today.

FREELY RECEIVED,
FREELY GIVEN

Heal the sick, raise the dead, cleanse those who have leprosy, drive out demons. Freely you have received; freely give. **Matthew 10:8,** NIV

A GENTLE, STEADY RAIN is falling now on Luke's gravesite. Our precious five-year-old basset hound had succumbed to cancer and other problems that for some reason were undetectable until it was too late.

As we were about to lower him into the grave we had prepared, our youngest granddaughter, Ellie Kate, looked into my eyes and shared one last hope, almost as an appeal to me to do something she was sure I could do: "Granddaddy, I want him to be alive."

We were all overcome once again, hearing her expression of our silent heartfelt hopes. We had fought for weeks for his life, but it wasn't enough. Not here, anyway; not on this side of heaven. A life so precious and full of grace and joy was gone much too soon.

"I do too, sweetie," I mumbled through tears.

Throughout our lives and in our society we are confronted with decisions regarding life, based on considerations of health, suffering, punishment, safety, and other factors. With each decision we try to do more to save, restore, and lift a life. And I suspect that we will always be left with the feeling that we wish we could have done more to save or restore a life.

I would suggest that these decisions should always be made in the context of the best example of grace, passion, and mercy who ever lived, Jesus Christ. He healed the sick, restored the disabled, and gave sight to the blind, hearing to the deaf, and even life to the dead. He drew prostitutes, tax collectors, the depraved, and the drunken into His circle of love and forgiveness. And He continued to do that throughout every day of His life, even to His death on the cross. Every life was valuable to Him and worth restoring to all the fullness of life He intended for us to live.

One day we'll stand before Christ—as I was before Ellie Kate the other day—weeping, mumbling, and saying, "I wish I could have done more. I wish I could have helped more, saved more, I wish . . ." And Christ will extend mercy to us in that moment and in our weakness. And His mercy to us will be so much more than we deserve.

A fresh rain is now falling on Luke's gravesite in the backyard. "Granddaddy, I want him to be alive." Me too, sweetie. Me too.

IMPACT APPLICATION: It's never easy—each day of our lives and each decision we face with every life entrusted to our care. God's mercy passionately reminds us and leads us to do more for each precious life in our care.

JUNE 1

YOU KNOW WHAT?

No power in the sky above or in the earth below—indeed, nothing in all creation will ever be able to separate us from the love of God that is revealed in Christ Jesus our Lord. **Romans 8:39**

"HANNAH, WHERE ARE YOU?" I called from the top of the staircase. From somewhere below, a little voice faintly answered back, "I'm in Mimi's bedroom."

A moment earlier I could hear her enchanted monologue from her upstairs bedroom adjacent to what she affectionately, and with the authority of full ownership, refers to as "Hannah and Granddaddy's office." At any given moment, whether the "office" door is open or not, she would blow through the doorway, billowing with some exciting dream couched in the usual words, "Granddaddy, you know what?" My history with her has demonstrated that it is always a "what" without which my life would have been much less. And it's the same with her younger sister, Ellie Kate.

Time after time, through dream after dream and "what" after "what," Hannah and Ellie Kate have lifted me above the frays of what I'm facing. And thankfully, mine are frays they are totally oblivious of for the moment. Will it always be that way? Sadly, I fear not. So how do we keep them that way? How do we protect our children and grandchildren from the creep of the frays of life into their innocent little lives? How do we reassure them when they begin to feel the painful pinch of the world around them?

We remember that God is there. We are never separated from Him.

How do we assure a continuing purity of heart in a world that is disintegrating through its glorification of sex, violence, drugs, selfishness, power, greed, and evil? How do we assure them that there is a purpose and point to their lives, above the fray? And just what is that purpose and point? We remember that God is there.

As I reflect on that, I am reminded of that morning's blessing that Hannah sang and shared with her Mimi and me and realize that perhaps I worry about her too much: "God our Father, God our Father, once again, once again, We will ask your blessing, we will ask your blessing. Amen. Amen."

I sometimes wonder if that will make a difference. But you know what? It will and it does.

God is there and will always be—for us, with us, and ahead of us.

I pray that you will know and embrace and remember that today and every day for the rest of your life.

IMPACT APPLICATION: Imagine the difference in our day if we started it by running into God's "office" and yelling, "What?" Then hearing God tell us the wonderful purpose He has planned for us. And through all of that, simply being reminded that He is there.

DOWNRIVER

Peter called to him, "Lord, if it's really you, tell me to come to you, walking on the water." "Yes, come," Jesus said. So Peter went over the side of the boat and walked on the water toward Jesus. But when he saw the strong wind and the waves, he was terrified and began to sink. **Matthew 14:28-30**

HE WASN'T SURE where to look, but the imprint of the brightly colored Easter eggs his mom and I had dyed with him the day before defined our son's journey that morning. And so off he went through the yard at five years old with a basket in hand.

A number of years after that Easter egg hunt, Nathan was asked to write his own question that would reveal more of who he was and then to answer it on one of his applications to college. He asked this question: "Why are you alive, and does your life have a purpose?"

And, in part, he answered it this way: "My life has a definite purpose. As a Christian, Jesus Christ is my Lord and Savior, and I have a responsibility to show God's love through my words and actions. I find waking up each morning exciting, and I would like to share that with others."

Along the way, he has tried to look in that direction to where he believed his life should go. It hasn't always been easy. He has questioned and doubted himself, endured the skepticism of others, and experienced setbacks.

A key principle of white-water rafting is "Don't look where you don't want to go."

We have all at times "looked where we didn't want to go"—at all the problems and pitfalls of "white-water living" that beset our paths. In today's Scripture passage, Peter takes his eyes off Christ, looks at the storm, and begins to sink.

Nathan was distracted at times, but he always looked toward where he wanted to go, that purpose and path he described in his college application. He maintained his focus on Christ. And as a result, through it all, he has remained a blessing to his family and others, a hero to me and his mom, and an inspiration and comfort to those grinding through difficult times in their lives.

We've all got backstories to what the world sees out front. The key to where those stories come out will most likely be determined by where we look in the white-water journeys of our lives. We'll all have plenty of opportunities to look at all the places we don't want to go—the distractions, temptations, worries, the comfortable escapes, and safe roadways—but where is it you want to go?

Look for Christ—go there.

 IMPACT APPLICATION: The key to getting down the river—the key to finding all the bright-colored Easter eggs—is to keep looking where you want to go and to where you know you should go. Follow Christ's lead today.

JUNE 3

OUR HIGHEST AND BEST USE

The LORD doesn't see things the way you see them. People judge by outward appearance, but the LORD looks at the heart. **1 Samuel 16:7**

"WHERE'S THE BEEF?" a gruff-voiced elderly woman asked in a fast-food TV ad a number of years ago. Where and what is the substance—or not—of those heroes our society reveres today? And what does that society look like?

If we judge our heroes to be those who wield the most wealth, power, and prestige, we are not faring very well. Hardly a day goes by without news of a new scandal, a new moral failure, or a new crime perpetrated by those society looks up to. And if we judge our society by those we choose as heroes, we're not faring very well either.

So, where's the beef?

Maybe we'll find it when we begin to look at the lives of those who are trying to address some of the issues of our day and the plight of some of those around the world who need a hand up. Maybe it's individuals who refuse to accept some of these statistics as inevitable:

- One child dies every three seconds
- One billion people live in extreme poverty (defined as less than $1 a day)
- One in five people throughout the world lives in extreme poverty
- One in seven people goes to bed hungry and one in ten has no access to clean water
- More than eighteen million children have lost one or both parents to AIDS (fifteen million in Africa alone)
- Thirty-eight million people are infected with HIV/AIDS (twenty-five million in Africa)
- One hundred and four million children will not even go to elementary school.

Many of the people who work to do something about these statistics are unnoticed. Are they heroes? I think so. I can begin to smell the beef.

When we are considering who to elevate, let's not look at others from a human or worldly perspective. Rather, let's try God's perspective. Instead of looking to money, power, or accomplishments as a determiner of hero status, let's use a different yardstick: love, mercy, and compassion.

Some heroes have big platforms and noteworthy accomplishments; others have small platforms and are largely unnoticed. Let's honor those who are doing truly heroic things and serve with them in their work. That just may be the way to produce a society with a lasting and eternal foundation.

IMPACT APPLICATION: Isn't it time you and I got our eyes off of the type of platform society worships and instead honor and work with those whose service God endorses?

THE POWER WITHIN

Very early on Sunday morning the women went to the tomb, taking the spices they had prepared. They found that the stone had been rolled away from the entrance. So they went in, but they didn't find the body of the Lord Jesus. **Luke 24:1-3**

IT WAS MANY YEARS AGO now that I traveled to Scotland for a week of golf on some of the historic courses there. What made the trip especially memorable was that I took it with my son, Nathan, as the two of us joined seven other father-son pairings.

While in St. Andrews, Nathan arranged a notable moment for both of us. We walked onto the beach nestled between the first fairway of the Old Course and the body of water called the Firth of Forth where—Nathan informed me after we were standing on the beach—some scenes from one of my favorite movies of all time, *Chariots of Fire*, were filmed.

There's one scene in that movie that takes place at the conclusion of a track-and-field event, where Eric Liddell, one of the central figures in the story, is speaking in the rain against a backdrop of umbrellas to a group of spectators who have gathered to hear him share. As the rain falls steadily on that gathering assembled on the now-quiet track, he compares faith to running in a race. He asks, "Where does the power come from, to see the race to its end?"

As he continues, the rain slows and then stops while one by one the umbrellas are folded away, and as everyone stands in the now-glorious sunshine, he answers his own question: "From within. Jesus said, 'Behold, the Kingdom of God is within you. If with all your hearts, you truly seek me, you shall ever surely find me.' If you commit yourself to the love of Christ, then that is how you run a straight race."

I wonder if we feel that sense of power within. That love of Christ.

On Easter morning, after seeing the empty tomb and learning that Jesus was raised from the dead, Mary and the other women went from tragedy to triumph. They remembered what Jesus had said about Himself. And they began to realize just what He had done for them—and for you and me—on the cross. In that realization they were lifted from the tragedy of Good Friday to the triumph of Easter Sunday—all through the love of Christ.

And they saw, and they remembered, and then they believed.

Christ has risen. Christ is alive. And, as Paul writes, "Christ lives in you" (Colossians 1:27).

And that's all the power that you and I will ever need.

 IMPACT APPLICATION: Remember—if you belong to Jesus, the power of the risen Christ is within you and will never leave you. His work on the cross for us is finished. No matter what we are going through, no matter what we face, Christ is risen and alive, and He will never leave us.

JUNE 5

VOICES

For the third time he demanded, "Why? What crime has he committed? I have found no reason to sentence him to death. So I will have him flogged, and then I will release him." But the mob shouted louder and louder, demanding that Jesus be crucified, and their voices prevailed.
Luke 23:22-23

MY BRIDE'S VOICE has always been a fresh, crisp morning breeze in my life. It has been a voice of encouragement, love, and godly wisdom throughout our many years together.

There have been other voices too—good ones as well as bad ones trying to beckon me to the ways of the world. But her voice has demonstrated an unwavering integrity of wanting what is best for me amid the lure and glamour of a world of voices attempting to detour me from the path that God has set before me. Her voice has been the one that has always offered the best path, the godly path, for me to travel.

Pilate gave in to the chorus of other voices and sentenced Jesus to die. He could have listened to the voice of his wife, who pleaded with him, "Leave that innocent man alone. I suffered through a terrible nightmare about him last night" (Matthew 27:19). While Jewish leaders were clamoring for His death, a Gentile woman, Pilate's wife, offered a voice of truth.

He could have listened to his own voice. Pilate knew that Christ was innocent. "I find nothing wrong with this man!" he proclaimed (Luke 23:4). Or he could have listened to the voice of Jesus, who revealed His identity to Pilate.

But the voices of the mob still prevailed over Pilate. Of course, it was all part of God's plan, but the lesson for us, of which voices we listen to in our lives, is critical for us today and in the days ahead. The voices tempting us away from Christ will never stop.

And the voice we would do well to listen to is the voice of the One who hung on the cross for us. That steady voice of hope and character, of courage and truth, which is always present, quietly directing us toward the path of that transforming power available to each of us because of what He did for us on the cross and then three days later when He rose from the tomb.

The voice of the risen Christ. Listen for it amid all the voices, the noise around us pointing us in different directions. Listen to His voice to point us to the way.

 IMPACT APPLICATION: What voices do you hear? What voices will you follow? The voices pointing to the ways of the world? Or will you follow the quiet, steady voices of encouragement, peace, power, and hope— those voices pointing to a better purpose for the rest of your life?

THREADS OF THE JOURNEY

A person standing alone can be attacked and defeated, but two can stand back-to-back and conquer. Three are even better, for a triple-braided cord is not easily broken. **Ecclesiastes 4:12**

THEY SEEM TO COME IN WAVES. They come crashing into our feelings with tides of emotions often impossible to explain. They come in a wash of tears mingled with smiles, reflections of heartaches inextricably entwined with joys. The recollections of life's littlest yet often greatest moments hit us when least expected. They are the threads of relationships, making up the tapestry of our lives.

I remember the morning she could barely wend her way down the stairs of the side porch as I ushered her outside. Our twelve-year-old basset hound, Pansy, was obviously having an off day in her fight against a cancer that seemed to be blowing in and out at the slightest whim lately. Threads.

The memory of the other four-legged friends through the years flashed through my thoughts—Echo, Amos, Abbey, Abigail, Luke, Jackson, and Lily—all always standing alongside us. Threads. Relationships.

And the return trip home a few years ago with my granddaughter, Hannah, as I regularly stole a glance at her through the rearview mirror while she gently fell asleep to the hum of the road and the melody of the voices on her praise CD. Reaching back to rub her tiny foot and then, when she awoke, she only wanted to be silly, laughing all the way home to return to an excited mom and dad. Threads.

And then there was Lynda, wondering how to explain the tears flowing from her eyes as she gave our giggling youngest granddaughter, Elise Katherine, her bedtime bath. Or as we changed her diaper a few hours later when she awoke talking and singing happily in her crib. And today, feeding the birds and finding golf balls in the backyard. Threads.

They seem to come in waves, those recollections from the deepest of daily experiences. The many moments with our son and daughter-in-law. The remembrances of times with other family and friends, those still here and those gone too soon, all part of the journey marked by a fabric of threads composed of the deepest experiences and relationships of our lives.

The waves seem to come more when we get older. They really should come when we are younger to assure we weave the most beautiful tapestries of the very deepest experiences of our hearts, from the very beginning of the moments with others that truly matter. Threads.

 IMPACT APPLICATION: I wonder what threads of relationships you are weaving today. Cherish those threads and the tapestry they will produce.

JUNE 7

THANK YOU, LORD, THANK YOU

Enter his gates with thanksgiving; go into his courts with praise. Give thanks to him and praise his name. **Psalm 100:4**

EVERY NOW AND THEN I stop and reflect on the things and people for which I need to be thankful. It happened today when I reflected that I have been married now for forty-nine years. Those who know Lynda and me know I am the blessed one in the relationship.

Lynda is clearly at the top of my list of things to be thankful for. Who and what are on your list?

A young boy was walking home from school late one day. It was cold—snow was on the ground, with more falling as he walked. It was dinnertime, and he needed to hurry home. But a light through the cracked glass of a little shack's window caught his eye. Forgetting about dinner for the moment, he cautiously made his way to the window, and what he saw stunned him.

What that little boy saw was a scene of abject poverty. He saw a cot with a wooden frame and tattered blanket, a small wooden table and one chair, and a small wooden bowl half filled with broth. On the wall was a picture of Jesus, and kneeling below that picture was a man in tattered clothes, with worn and wrinkled hands and the years of a difficult life written all over his face.

As the boy moved closer to the window, he could hear the words of that kneeling man—and he'd never forget those words. For amid all of that apparent poverty, all he heard were the repeated words of that kneeling man: "Thank You, Lord, thank You. . . ."

Upon first glance, it may seem that the man was walking in a desperate valley. And by the standards of our society, he was. But those standards are not what govern the days and abundant blessings of our lives.

That man walked to the beat of his Creator. His list of things to be thankful for was not written on a piece of paper but was written instead all over the walls of a humble heart. He was thankful for a God who walked with him and never left him and who would be with him throughout eternity.

Did you put that on your list of things you're thankful for? A relationship with the God who will never leave you? If you didn't, I would encourage you to think about that relationship and make it a part of your life—a life with Jesus Christ as your Savior and Lord. It is the most important relationship you will ever be blessed with—now and forever.

IMPACT APPLICATION: The list of things we are thankful for is long—you'll see as you make it. But first on the list is the God who created you and me and loves us like no one else can.

RELATIONSHIPS—
ON THE LINE

Use your worldly resources to benefit others and make friends. Then, when your possessions are gone, they will welcome you to an eternal home. **Luke 16:9**

MY EVALUATION as I sit here this morning is that life is hard sometimes.

I can even go so far as to say that at times life seems to stink. Money, careers, and health all seem to have their moments pegging the needle on the "life stinks" meter. But from a long-term view we should remember that when relationships are involved—relationships that we allow to sour or go south or that are unexpectedly lost—the meter often measures off the scale. Relationships matter.

It was one of my first baseball coaching opportunities. I was attending college, and our son, Nathan, age four, was our team mascot. Andy played center field and had good speed, a decent glove, and blond hair that flowed from beneath his baseball cap when he ran. His parents were supportive but not pushy. They were secure in their relationship and didn't see a need to relive any part of their child-hoods through Andy.

The game was on the line, with two outs in the last inning. We were up by one run. Our opponents had the tying and winning runs on base. On the pitch, their best hitter launched a line drive screaming toward the gap in right center field. Andy was off at the crack of the bat and running for what seemed like a lifetime, but only a few seconds later, the ball dropped into his glove for the last out of the game, securing our victory.

I can still see Andy's beaming smile, with the baseball held proudly aloft as he ran in to be mobbed by his teammates. He was only ten. I can still remember reflecting on that moment seven years later as I sat quietly in the pew waiting for the memorial service to begin. A car accident. A careless, stupid, and selfish decision had taken his winning smile and flowing blond hair from our presence. A relationship ended. *Gone at seventeen*, I reflected, as I sat at his memorial service with only his memory to hold onto. An accident, and his life was over.

There are some things in relationships over which we have control, some we don't. Some may end like Andy's in a tragic accident. Some, though, will tragically end or be affected because of our willful choices. They all lead to the saddest of moments.

Jesus reminds us that while wealth and possessions are temporary, relationships last forever.

Don't miss living them while you can. You may not get another chance.

IMPACT APPLICATION: No matter our age, the relationships through numerous platforms God has given us are fragile and fleeting. Care for and nurture them with love before it is too late and they are gone, leaving you sitting all alone with only your regrets.

WHICH WAY
DO I GO?

"Cheshire Puss," she began, rather timidly. . . . "Would you tell me, please, which way I ought to go from here?" "That depends a good deal on where you want to get to," said the Cat. "I don't much care where—" said Alice. "Then it doesn't matter which way you go," said the Cat. **Lewis Carroll, *Alice's Adventures in Wonderland***

IT WAS ANOTHER one of those endearing memory-making moments for me, as I listened unnoticed from my office not too long ago to Lynda's soft voice and our granddaughter Hannah's probing utterances for clarification as the story her Mimi was reading to her began to unfold.

And if we're honest with ourselves, as we read the passage above, we can all identify with Alice and the point at which she finds herself in the story. The reality, though, as we have come to discover all too often, is that we may find ourselves standing at that "fork in the road" at this very moment, or perhaps not too long ago, or maybe all signs seem to indicate we're heading there again, always to be confronted with that never-ending question—"which way I ought to go from here?" Which way do I go?

"'That depends a good deal on where you want to get to,' said the Cat."

"'I don't much care where—' said Alice."

Ah, but there's the rub, Alice. You need to care, because the answer to "which way" will be determined by those values that internally govern and direct your life.

Call them what you will—values, rules of the road, your own internal sense of decency, whatever. But whatever you call them, they will tell the world what you stand for, how you will treat others, how you will respond to others' treatment of you—now, in the past, and in the days to come.

How do we set the values for our days? Where do we look to find benchmarks of values that will help guide our steps, decisions, and directions in the days ahead? Start here with this simple reminder: "Whatever you do or say, do it as a representative of the Lord Jesus, giving thanks through him to God the Father" (Colossians 3:17).

Too simple? Try it. Apply it in any setting when faced with any situation, question, or issue.

Try it, Alice. You may not have to search out the Cheshire Cat the next time.

Try it, friends. It will make all the difference in your lives and in the lives of those around you—for the rest of all of your lives.

 IMPACT APPLICATION: Those values that govern your life will tell your loved ones and the rest of the world what you care most about. They'll hear what you say, but they'll believe how you live and the choices they see you make each day. Those values will define your standard of "success" and will affect everyone and everything around you, either for good or not.

THE JOURNEY

Look up into the heavens. Who created all the stars? He brings them out like an army, one after another, calling each by its name. Because of his great power and incomparable strength, not a single one is missing. **Isaiah 40:26**

THE MORNING BEGAN as any other. It was a beautiful, clear, cool, and crisp first day of February 2003, beginning as our three basset hounds made their usual early morning rounds in the side yard and then stood excitedly waiting at the back door, watching through the nose-smeared glass panels of the door as I prepared their breakfast.

I guess it was a little past nine when the quietness of my spiritual retreat was unexpectedly interrupted by an anxious call from Lynda, who was in the kitchen below, urging me to turn on the television. Reports were coming in about the space shuttle Columbia's reentry—something seemed terribly wrong. Announcers on station after station were attempting to piece together the bits of information as they came in, hoping there was some rational explanation that would stem the wave of another storm we would have to weather as a nation. Minutes became hours as the incoming information painted a picture we couldn't, and wouldn't, allow to be framed in our minds.

Early in the afternoon of what was becoming the longest day since September 11, 2001, President Bush addressed the nation, saying, "The Columbia is lost; there are no survivors."

Then, claiming the promises of Scripture from the book of Isaiah, he reminded us that "the same Creator Who names the stars also knows the names of the seven souls we mourn today. The crew of the shuttle Columbia did not return safely to Earth; yet we can pray that all are safely home."

Husband, McCool, Chawla, Anderson, Brown, Clark, and Ramon—we weren't ready for them to go; we weren't ready for their lives among us to end. As they reached for the stars, we reached with them.

Their journey was shorter than they or we anticipated, but it was full.

I wonder what the journey of this last year of your life looks like. Has your focus been too often on simply getting from one point to another, from morning to evening, from one beginning to one ending? Or have you noticed the blue of your skies and felt the breeze on your face along the journey of those days?

What should the next year of your life look like? The gifts and abilities within you are enormous. Don't let your life be colored by regret. Use all the potential God has placed within you on this journey He has set you on. Reach for all you can be.

IMPACT APPLICATION: How about this year? What will your journey look like? With God always close at hand, make sure it is full and all He and you have ever dreamed it could be.

JUNE 11

ON THE ALTAR

Abraham picked up the knife to kill his son as a sacrifice. At that moment the angel of the LORD called to him from heaven, "Abraham! Abraham!" "Yes," Abraham replied. "Here I am!" "Don't lay a hand on the boy!" the angel said. "Do not hurt him in any way, for now I know that you truly fear God. You have not withheld from me even your son, your only son." **Genesis 22:10-12**

IT'S A GREAT STORY if we could just leave it there—as a story about a father and a son, Abraham and Isaac. But God never seems to do that. He just keeps tapping us on the shoulder until He really gets our attention, until things become uncomfortable.

I don't know how you could do what Abraham did. I don't know where that kind of obedience to God exists today. To sacrifice something that precious—to, and at the request of, God. Your son. Your grandchildren. Whomever. I don't want to sell anyone out there short on this, but I'm not sure I've seen that kind of faith, obedience, and sacrifice in a while.

Maybe that's the problem. Or maybe I've seen it but have forgotten. Maybe I need a refresher course in obedience to God. Maybe we all do.

God calls us to complete obedience and sacrifice, and well, sometimes we come partway at least. Here I sit in my den in comfortable surroundings, looking out the window and reading the story of Abraham's faith, trust, obedience, and sacrifice—and seem to understand the lesson—but I wonder, if I were put to the test, would I do what he did?

Don't make me answer just yet.

And let's not forget Isaac's faith and trust as well. Isaac was a young man who was strong enough to carry the wood that would be stacked on the altar for his funeral fire. Abraham was an old man, and if Isaac didn't want to go through with this scheme God had hatched, certainly he could have run or at least have kept Abraham away from him. He had the youth and strength to prevent this plan from happening.

But his heart told him otherwise. He trusted God, and he trusted his dad. And he allowed his dad to bind him and place him on the altar. I'll bet Isaac even climbed upon the altar himself—that's the heart of obedience, faith, and sacrifice he had for God.

And the place where Abraham built the altar to sacrifice Isaac—Mount Moriah—later was unearthed and became known as Calvary.

What is God calling you to put on the altar today?

 IMPACT APPLICATION: The story of Abraham and Isaac is more than a story about a father and son. It is the story about God the Father and you and me. It is the reminder of the continual call on our lives to obedience, faith, trust, and sacrifice.

SPECIAL BY GOD

The LORD will work out his plans for my life—for your faithful love, O LORD, endures forever. Don't abandon me, for you made me.
Psalm 138:8

I WONDER IF you have had some of the same experiences that I have which seem to make it clear that the world doesn't see us the way God sees us. Because if they did, the world would cherish each of us the way the God who created us does. And then God's voice whispering, "Special, Best, Wonderful, Precious, Child of God" wouldn't be drowned out in the chorus of boos, criticism, and put-downs from the world around us.

It may all be unintended. Comments, facial expressions, tones of voice, ignoring one person over others. I've been guilty of all of those, and I have been on the receiving end of all of those. You have too.

Perhaps it's our circumstances that we allow to put us down. Others seem to be dressed better than we are; seem more in control than we are; seem more polished than we are; or have better jobs, more money, or nicer homes and cars. And people around them seem to be attracted to them, while we stand against the wall wishing this moment in public would end or that someone who loves us—anyone—would come to rescue and affirm us.

Perhaps it's our past track record that we allow to put us down. As our feet hit the floor each morning, all we can remember are the problems and mistakes of yesterday and others' criticisms. The failures and mistakes—you just can't seem to shake them from the present back into the past where they belong.

No one has the same potential or the same gifts, abilities, passions, desires, talents, platforms, or intended purposes that you have—no one. You were created, formed, and sent forth by the incredible God like no one else—to do what no one else can or is supposed to do.

Each of us is unique—on both the outside and the inside. Uniquely created by the God who knew what the world would be like when we lived and knew what the world would need when we lived. Not perfect, and as a result there will be times when we fall short—and when the grace of the God who created us will pick us back up and send us back out. The same God who is always busy creating and placing within each of us unique gifts, passions, abilities, talents, potential, desires, platforms, and purposes so that we might become all He intended for us to be.

Now go and be all He created you to be!

 IMPACT APPLICATION: Here's a final truth to embrace: with the God of all creation behind us and with all that He put within us, who or what do you think can put us down or keep us from having and using the platform God has given us?

JUNE 13

THROUGH EYES
OF LOVE

Her children stand and bless her. Her husband praises her: "There are many virtuous and capable women in the world, but you surpass them all!" **Proverbs 31:28-29**

I KNOW IT TRULY WARMED his heart when it happened, despite his incessant feigned whining about some things being "just not fair." The way our son, Nathan, described the scene, he was holding and playing with his youngest daughter, Ellie Kate. Contentment, coos, and cuddling were the order of the moment until her mother, Amy, walked onto the scene.

In an instant the atmosphere changed. It was as if Nathan had left the room, as Ellie Kate's eyes caught Amy's approach and her joy built into a crescendo of laughter. Her tiny arms reached as far as they could while her little body leaned heavily out of her daddy's protective embrace, until finally her tiny head was snuggled softly on the shoulder of the one she held so dear. Something for Amy to cherish when the message radiating from her daughter's eyes fades in her heart through the slog of day-to-day living.

The moment rekindled recollections of similar times during the earlier years of our oldest granddaughter, Hannah, and also of when Nathan, as a little boy, teenager, and young man returned home from college sat for hours and hours chitchatting with his mom about things only they would remember. As they spoke, the warm glow in his eyes told his mother the special place she occupied in his heart. Something for her to cherish when the message in his eyes fades at times in her heart.

I wonder how our hearts would feel if we had those moments like those two children had with their mothers. I wonder what our lives would be like if every day we saw ourselves as those two children saw their mothers. And how about the way their mothers saw them? I wonder: What would change about the decisions we make as we go about our days? I suspect our decisions may be different from some of the ones we make now.

Ponder this, though—I wonder how we would view ourselves and the decisions we would make if we knew how God sees us, with all the passion and love He has for us.

Let me suggest that we step back each day and look at ourselves and at those who love us, at those God has placed in our lives, through God's eyes. Through the eyes of love He has for you, for me, and for all the world.

IMPACT APPLICATION: Live with all the passion God intended for your life by seeing yourself and others through the loving eyes of God.

LONG MAY SHE WAVE

The harder the conflict, the more glorious the triumph. What we obtain too cheaply, we esteem too lightly; it is dearness only that gives everything its value. **Thomas Paine**

ALMOST AS SOON AS she was posted in her bracket on the front of our house, our American flag billowed in the breeze with a wave of assurance that all she has stood for still remains.

Each year since June 14, 1777, our country has continued the annual tribute to honor and remember that grand old flag, a flag that has become a symbol of freedom, courage, and sacrifice.

The flag's red, white, and blue colors are woven together to represent a nation bound by the courage and sacrifice of so many who have held a clear allegiance to duty, commitment to country, and hope in something better. That flag represents lives dedicated to a nation intended to be bound together from its beginnings by a faith in our God, who is able to lead and carry us to heights much greater than our individual or collective efforts could ever hope to accomplish.

Yet today, our foundations of faith, values, virtue, and economic stability seem to be under assault. In the midst of that, perhaps we need to remember how far we've come under the protection of the red, white, and blue. Perhaps a moment of personal sacrifice and patience—taken from the examples of those who have gone before us—would serve us well.

Perhaps we need a moment of remembrance that as a nation we have faced times like these before.

Perhaps we need to follow that with a moment of commitment to do all we can, individually and collectively, to set this "great experiment" back on a course that is aligned with the God who established our foundations. A course upon which we have traveled in all our best days—remembering that, as Thomas Paine reminded those during this nation's founding, "the harder the conflict, the more glorious the triumph."

Perhaps we need a moment where we are called to something outside of ourselves, as President John F. Kennedy encouraged us to do during his inaugural address on January 20, 1961:

My fellow Americans: ask not what your country can do for you—ask what you can do for your country. . . . With a good conscience our only sure reward, with history the final judge of our deeds, let us go forth to lead the land we love, asking His blessing and His help, but knowing that here on earth God's work must truly be our own.

Looking back, my friends, the best moments never seemed to arrive with ease, yet they always seemed so much dearer when they finally were achieved.

And so, in the journey ahead, long may our flag wave—over our nation, our lives, and the generations to follow—all under the leadership of God.

IMPACT APPLICATION: Together may we reclaim the God-honoring traditions of our lives—and long may they wave under the red, white, and blue.

YOUR CHOICE—
YOUR LIFE

Dear brothers and sisters, when troubles of any kind come your way, consider it an opportunity for great joy. **James 1:2**

I SOMETIMES WONDER what Wes is doing these days.

This is hard to admit to you, but I had a momentary lapse the other day and found I was viewing the glass as "half empty" and wondering "why me?" and thinking "if only." I had all the makings of a pity party going. I was struggling with perspective, and I had allowed worry to replace trust in God.

But that's when I remembered Wes.

It's been over twenty years since Wes and I met. I haven't seen him since. My dear friend Jake and I had just finished a long day planning an upcoming conference in southwest Florida, and we decided to play a late afternoon round of golf. I started off playing well. A good drive and a seven iron put me within ten feet of a birdie on the first green. And then, despite the blessings of beautiful surroundings, dear friendship, and good health, my pity party began—I missed the putt for the birdie. On the next hole, I ended up with a bogey. A double bogey followed on the next.

My attitude was in the tank and not even close to "half full" or even "half empty." While Jake began praying for a miracle to change my perspective, I saw to it that all friendly conversation ground to a halt as irritation now governed my focus.

And then he appeared out of nowhere. Wes.

Neither Jake nor I remember seeing him behind us on the course before this moment; but there he was, a golfer playing a round by himself and wanting to play through us on a par three, where my ball had found a way to bury itself deep within a cavernous greenside bunker.

We watched him approach from a distance as he hit his ball to within fifteen feet of the pin. As he drew closer, we noticed a marked limp in his stride—he had only one leg, the other having been replaced by a prosthesis.

Seeing Wes cheerful and active in the face of adversity not only changed my perspective and my day, it changed my heart. And although I've had lapses since, I vowed to never again allow the circumstances of my life to determine my attitude and the eternal perspective set before me by my risen Savior.

What I know is that amid the winds and storms of life, and the gnats and elephants that seem to bother and impede us, and the people around us who too often seem to see the disastrous, fearful, draining side of every circumstance in life, I choose to see life as Wes did.

IMPACT APPLICATION: Choose to see life not full of human shortcomings and human failings but full of God-ordained possibility. Choose to see life through the lenses of God's love and grace for us.

THE PROMISE OF TOMORROW

The LORD said to Samuel, "Don't judge by his appearance or height, for I have rejected him. The LORD doesn't see things the way you see them. People judge by outward appearance, but the LORD looks at the heart." **1 Samuel 16:7**

LOOKING OUTSIDE THIS MORNING, it's hard to see it in the darkness before the dawn, but I know there's a promise in the approaching light. It was hard to see when we heard our son's words announcing the glorious news of our newest granddaughter's birth woven with the solemnity that she had been taken to the neonatal intensive care unit because of fluid in her lungs. Yet his tone assured me there was promise in our littlest of flowers, our newest hero.

Webster's dictionary defines *hero* as "a legendary figure often of divine descent endowed with great strength, ability, or courage."

Ellie Kate's little body was just over eight pounds and not quite twenty inches long. Yet her tiny heart would need to be as defiant and heroic as it could, because for the next few days Ellie Kate lay all alone, watched by an attentive medical staff, in a warm oxygenated incubator fighting to clear her lungs, fighting for each breath. And with all due respect to the doctors' extensive medical acumen, they didn't know that God had already laid His hand upon this newest and tiniest of His heroes.

It is impossible to talk about my children and grandchildren, to see them or think about them, without being overcome with tears of joy at all the promises of tomorrow in the precious beats of their hearts today. God clearly is still in the miracle business.

And in that we find the eternal reminder and promise of the morning for them and for each of us, for the living of these days. For the same God that sent Samuel on a king-picking mission in the Scripture above and laid His mighty hand on David years ago, and then on Ellie Kate nine months before she was born when He first knit her together in the womb, is the same God who laid His hand on you and me and who can and will do anything for us. But when that same faithful and powerful God talks about, looks at, or thinks about you, He is overcome with emotion and filled to overflowing with tears of joy.

In you and me, in His tiny hero Ellie Kate, He has created all the promise of tomorrow. No matter what we face, believe it, embrace it.

It will make all the difference in your life.

IMPACT APPLICATION: God's hand is upon us, caring for us, lifting us, and protecting us.

JUNE 17

THAT'S OKAY, RIGHT?

"The day is coming," says the LORD, "when I will make a new covenant with the people of Israel and Judah." **Jeremiah 31:31**

IT'S EARLY YET, and despite an occasional coughing spell, my granddaughter Hannah continues to sleep.

Looking in the bedroom at her, I can see her surrounded by at least three of her precious baby dolls and some other friends who were her last playmates of the night before. She will awaken in a moment, fully equipped to teach this sometimes slow but always ready pupil of hers about the abundant blessings of God in every day of our lives.

"Isn't it a beautiful day?" she exclaimed from her vantage point on the couch the other day, looking out the window at a gray, drizzly, damp morning, which is what I had seen just moments before. She saw something different, and I learned yet another lesson from her. So, with lesson one in the books for that day, we began to arrange her toy friends around the room for what was described as a game of hide-and-seek. Carrying a small table from one room to another, to an area where I was informed it would magically become a boat, we accidentally bumped it against a half-opened door. While I suggested that she and I probably needed to be more careful, she softly chortled: "Well, sometimes things happen, but that's okay, right? Sometimes things get broken, but that's okay, right, Gran? Sometimes we make mistakes, but that's okay, right?"

Her tone was not disrespectful. It did not convey a disregard for our need to care for people or things. And although fashioned in the form of a question, it was so much more than that. It was a statement of the truth she had learned that sometimes things happen in life, and we learn to move on. Things happen to us. We do things we shouldn't. "But that's okay, right?" Yes, it's okay, because we've learned the lessons of forgiveness and grace from our gracious God.

A God who reaches down and helps us wipe up the "spilled milk" of our lives. A God who through the Old Testament prophet Jeremiah tells us, "I will make a new covenant. . . . I will put my instructions deep within them, and I will write them on their hearts. I will be their God, and they will be my people" (Jeremiah 31:31, 34). A God who says, "I know what has happened to you, I know what you have done," and yet stands ready to pick us up and offer us a second chance to move on. That's okay, right?

IMPACT APPLICATION: I don't know what burdens or problems you're carrying today. I don't know what doors you're bumping into, but God does. And with Him at your side, "that's okay, right?"

JUNE 18

FATHERS AND CHILDREN

Direct your children onto the right path, and when they are older, they will not leave it. **Proverbs 22:6**

WORDS WOULDN'T COME without a rush of tears, so the best he could do was to hug his dad before he prepared to navigate the historic Olympia Fields North Course for the final day of the US Open Championship. Jim Furyk's father's nurturing example helped to carry him to the winner's circle of the United States Open Golf Championship that day.

Later, after hugging his bride and mom and gently stroking his ten-month-old daughter's hair and as he accepted the trophy for his achievement, Jim was able to muster the words that couldn't be spoken earlier, although still through tears: "Happy Father's Day." It was a moment that transcended golf and all the lesser things in the lives of those gathered around that eighteenth green or watching on television sets around the world.

Between individuals, it's simply the most molding influence in life, the relationship between a father and his child. Sadly, today, it's absent in too many homes. Sadly, today, too many allow personal painful memories to color and over-shadow those memories of joy and affirmation lying just beneath the surface. But on Father's Day, amid newspaper and television stories everywhere highlighting fathers, many of us rightly pause to reflect, remember, and honor that relationship. As my good friend Jack Levine shared in his tribute to his dad, "Most men live up to what's expected of them; others stumble, yet few do not try to do their best for their family. I think of Father's Day as a chance to cherish the gifts he gave me that had no wrapping paper."

Despite the bumps along the path that many of us have experienced in moments with our fathers, a deeper, more honest inspection of our hearts will uncover the truth that many of the wonderful qualities others see in us are a reflection of the man who did the best he could to raise, nurture, and teach us. And if somehow we feel shortchanged in that relationship, perhaps our forgiveness of those shortcomings and thankfulness for others who came alongside us will help us to bridge the gap of our own longing for things that never were—a longing which tends to hold us back from becoming all we were meant to be.

Congratulations to you, Mike and Jim Furyk, for a reminder to us all of the important things in life. Thank you for the reminder of the importance of the father-child relationship. Thank you for helping us to be grateful for all there was and is of ours.

 IMPACT APPLICATION: It is never too late to be the father, son, or mentor to someone else who will have an impact and leave a legacy for the next generation to follow.

JUNE 19

SHEPHERDS AND
SHRIEKS

The LORD *is my shepherd; I have all that I need.* **Psalm 23:1**

IF PUSHED, we could probably roughly recite the six remaining verses of Psalm 23, one of the most familiar passages in all of Scripture. Yet those first five words—"The LORD is my shepherd"—offer a comforting, courage-building, exciting, and focusing promise for all the ages.

It was a couple of years ago that Lynda experienced yet another blessing from one of our granddaughters. She had driven to Tampa for a few days for her regular granddaughter fix, leaving me at home with our two pups. Hannah was not at home when she arrived, as she was in her last day at school. Ellie Kate was in the back of the house when she first heard Lynda's voice as she entered the house. That's all it took.

"Mimi, yeah!" she shrieked over and over as her little legs carried her as fast as they could toward the voice at the front door, and she kept shrieking once she saw her. She began spinning around and around, her little feet pumping up and down and her hands waving in the air, while she continued shrieking her Mimi's name. This was her Mimi, and her heart was happy, excited, and comforted because she remembered all her past experiences with Mimi.

We may not read Psalm 23 as a shrieking, jumping, dancing, and hand-waving psalm, but the truth it contains should be enough to make us want to do all those things Ellie Kate did when she heard her Mimi's voice.

Psalm 23 reveals that God is not a cruel taskmaster, putting us to work long hours to earn His favor, nor is He a stern judge, waiting to bring His gavel down at the first sign of disobedience. Rather, David, the author of the psalm, reveals that the God of the universe is a shepherd, someone who lovingly leads and tenderly cares for him.

As the rest of the psalm says, God "lets me rest," "renews my strength," "guides me along right paths," and "protect[s] and comfort[s] me." When God does all this for us, what more do we need? We don't have to worry about getting things done or about chasing things that won't last. Instead, we can simply enjoy being in God's presence because He has given us everything we need.

Based on our past experiences with God, we can rest in Him—or can dance and shout for joy, as Ellie Kate did when she saw Lynda. That we will "live in the house of the Lord forever" means that we won't have to get a God "fix" every once in a while. Instead, we will always be with Him, content and comforted in His presence. And that is cause for shrieking, jumping, dancing, and hand-waving for all eternity.

 IMPACT APPLICATION: Teach those you love that the Lord is their shepherd, and in that truth we and they will find all the security needed for this life and beyond.

WIPED CLEAN
WITH LOVE

If we confess our sins to him, he is faithful and just to forgive us our sins and to cleanse us from all wickedness. **1 John 1:9**

AS SO MANY OF HER QUESTIONS seem to, this one, too, came from out of the blue. "Mimi," my granddaughter Hannah asked Lynda one day, "why does grand-daddy love God so much?" The events of that particular morning and weekend of a few years ago raised the question and also may have helped to provide the answer.

During a trip to one of our favorite family getaway spots, I did what I usually do and took off early for a walk on the beach. The quiet sky was graced with clouds, which sheltered my steps as I walked on the beach, splashing through the surging and receding ankle-deep surf. As I walked, I watched as each billowy pass of the surf restored the sand to its natural beauty and cleared my path ahead while also erasing any account of my journey to that point. No debris, no footprints. Just smooth, glistening, wet sand canvases stretched behind me, before me, and beyond.

Stopping for a moment, I wrote in the sand the names of Lynda's parents, who passed on to their heavenly reward in 1985 and 1999. The surf washed my scrawling away but not their memory or influence. I wrote Lynda's name and our son, daughter-in-law, and granddaughter's names. I was grateful that the result was the same. The surf washed the sand clean of their names, but the best essence of who they are, and are to me, remained. Encouraged, I walked on.

Stopping again, I reached down to write in the sand the remembrance of a mistake I had made in years past that I couldn't seem to get beyond. Predictably, the surf cleansed the sand smooth and left me standing there free of the debris of the past yet still with all the gifts, abilities, and dreams God had given me.

Mimi, tell Hannah this: I love God so much because He forgives and forgets all the mistakes of my life and cleanses, restores, and reenergizes me for all that He has dreamed and planned for my life, with each day better than the one before. And tell her this: I love Him because He holds each of us and those we love, both those still here and those who have passed on before us, in the palm of His hand throughout all the sunrises and sunsets of our lives and for all eternity.

On second thought, just tell her that I love God so much because He loves *me* so much.

 IMPACT APPLICATION: Why do you love God so much? Answering and living in that full response will unleash your passion like nothing else will.

A RENEWED SENSE OF YOUTHFUL WONDER

This is the day the LORD has made. We will rejoice and be glad in it.
Psalm 118:24

HOW DID YOU WAKE UP this morning?

I mean beyond rubbing your eyes, rolling out of bed, and wobbling through your early morning rituals. I mean before your usual morning infusion of caffeine. Did you sense a twinge of excitement with each successive step toward the coffee pot? Was there a sense that something unexpected might occur today—and you found your gait quickening with anticipation, excited rather than apprehensive of what that might be?

Did you feel a surge of adrenaline coursing through your waking limbs? Did you notice the sunrise God sent to start your day? Were you still preoccupied by the baggage of yesterday and the restless dreams of the night before, or were you ready to go to the "playroom" to continue from yesterday or to throw open the front door and claim the day before you as a day of adventure?

In his book *The Diary of a Country Priest*, George Bernanos, writing of his youth, confesses regretfully in one candid admission, "I was never young because I never dared be young." I wonder if that resonates with you. Did you notice that as you got older, you seemed to act older at times?

Listen to me. That's not how God intended it to be.

But sadly, somewhere along the journey of our lives, too many of us lose our childlike sense of wonder and amazement—the sense of adventure that still exists in each day set before us. Somewhere along the roadway of our lives, the sunshine of the morning has become dimmed by the expected and routine rather than a bright, sacred moment of appreciation of God's creation, where our hearts are set ablaze once again with all the promise of the day. Somewhere along the path of our lives we learned to become "responsible" and were reprogrammed to march to an acceptable beat, conformed to the way life "should" be and domesticated to fit into bland templates of aging that outline appropriate and expected behaviors. Somewhere along the way, too many of us have learned to be careful and have lost that sense of wonder and abandonment that was planted in us for every day and eternity by the Creator.

It's not the way it was meant to be. We weren't created for a life predictably outlined by a world mindlessly spinning through sameness each day.

How did you wake up this morning? Did you remember that "this is the day the Lord has made"? Are you "glad in it"?

- -

 IMPACT APPLICATION: The good news is that no matter our age the child within us—knit by the hand of God—is still there, waiting to be let out.

WIRE-TO-WIRE

We now have this light shining in our hearts, but we ourselves are like fragile clay jars containing this great treasure. This makes it clear that our great power is from God, not from ourselves. We are pressed on every side by troubles, but we are not crushed. We are perplexed, but not driven to despair. We are hunted down, but never abandoned by God. We get knocked down, but we are not destroyed.
2 Corinthians 4:7-9

NOBODY PICKED him to win.

Nobody, that is, except his owners, jockey, trainer, some loyal family and friends, and one man who said if he could get out quickly he might be able to hold the lead from wire-to-wire and win the horse race.

At 20-1 odds, nobody was picking First Dude—the three-year-old big bay colt owned by dear and wonderful friends—to win the 135th Preakness Stakes at the famed Pimlico Racetrack in Baltimore, Maryland.

But wire-to-wire First Dude went, in the lead all the way, maintaining a powerful, long-reaching stride for most of the 1 3/16–mile journey totaling about one minute and fifty-five seconds around the Pimlico Racetrack—until the last few lengths.

It was more than just a race; it was an unexpected moment of inspiration for us to embrace for the race that is the rest of our lives. For in the midst of all sorts of obstacles pressing in on all sides from start to finish—as well as the low expectations of everyone except those of us who believed in him—First Dude ran all the way to the end.

He didn't win first place, but he led all the way until the very end, going wire-to-wire with all he had in him. From the twelve-horse start to the twelve-horse finish, he went wire-to-wire with every muscle, breath, and ounce of determination he could muster. And in that, he won.

What problems, issues, uncertainties, disappointments, and heartaches are you facing today? What does it all look like tomorrow? What have you just come through and feel completely wrung out from? What relationship is still bouncing from post to post with no apparent hope of ever settling down? Maybe an old addiction has entangled you again. What dream was just deflated by an unexpected turn of events? Perhaps the light you thought was shining on your pathway into tomorrow has just gone dim.

How about we face whatever is before us together by remembering and believing in the encouragement from the words of the apostle Paul above: "We are pressed on every side by troubles, but we are not crushed. We are perplexed, but not driven to despair. We are hunted down, but never abandoned by God. We get knocked down, but we are not destroyed."

Face troubles all the way into eternity, wire-to-wire.

 IMPACT APPLICATION: No matter what issues, problems, or uncertainties you might be facing, face them from now until whenever with all that you have and with the God who goes with you.

JUNE 23

CELEBRATE

The next day there was a wedding celebration in the village of Cana in Galilee. Jesus' mother was there, and Jesus and his disciples were also invited to the celebration. **John 2:1-2**

YOU'VE GOT to be kidding!

In the midst of His supposed mission to save the world, a mission still going on to this day, Jesus dropped by to be a part of a wedding celebration?

It's got to be a misprint in Scripture! Or the disciple John was hallucinating as he recorded the scene.

And then, Jesus' mother put Him to work. But not straightening crooked limbs or restoring sight to the blind or bringing someone back from the dead. No, she put Him to work making some wine so that the weeklong wedding celebration could continue and the host would not be embarrassed. After all, you just can't run out of wine at a wedding celebration.

Right at the start of His mission, Jesus finds a chance for celebration. Is it a detour? Is it a brief bend in the road from the thoroughfare of His Kingdom purposes? Or is it an integral part of His mission and a statement to us about how to live life? Celebration!

What are you going through? Have you "run out of wine" or just run out of energy and hope? Have you been hit full in the face with the betrayal of false friends? Do you find yourself standing right up against a dreaded disease or impending surgery? Have you gotten another year older and no longer feel young anymore? Or has your daughter just gotten married and everyone keeps telling you that you're not losing a daughter but gaining a son? Easy for them to say.

Yet Jesus' example is clear. John was not hallucinating when he recorded the scene in Cana of Galilee. Christ really was at a wedding, celebrating with the happy couple and all assembled, some of the very people He came to save. And His message is joyfully clear.

In the midst of the circumstances of life, celebrate! In the midst of the circumstances of life, take a long look at the eternal and important things of life. In the midst of the circumstances of life, take a long look through eyes of a joyful moment with Christ. Take a long look through the eyes of the celebrating Savior.

IMPACT APPLICATION: In the midst of all that you may be going through, remember this: we have a Savior who finds time to turn water into wine. How much more will He do for you?

SANDCASTLES

I waited patiently for the LORD to help me, and he turned to me and heard my cry. He lifted me out of the pit of despair, out of the mud and the mire. He set my feet on solid ground and steadied me as I walked along. **Psalm 40:1-2**

FROM THEIR VIEW on the top-floor balcony, our granddaughters had seen it in the distance just the day before. Their beautiful creation in the sand was still standing despite the odds being against it lasting even to the end of the day on which it was painstakingly built.

A day later, Lynda and I left our days at the beach with Hannah and Ellie Kate, but before we did, we decided to take one more walk on the beach with them. After packing the car for the return, checking out, and waving good-bye to friends, we made our way to the beach.

We entered the beach area, and there it stood—the sandcastle and moat our granddaughters made three days earlier—still a part of the glistening, smooth, sandy surface of the beach. It had been eroded just a bit from the ocean breezes that had whipped regularly across those sands during the past few days, but it still clearly stood out as the castle they had created—not having been washed away by the regularly rising and falling surf as other sand creations had been.

The reason it was still standing is that our girls had built their sandcastle and moat just outside the highest mark of the highest tide of the day. They had carefully gauged and then constructed their sand creations just beyond the farthest reaches of the crashing foam, waves, and surge of the sea.

What would you have done? I'm not sure I would have paid attention to the high-tide line as I built my sandcastle and moat. My life is sometimes like that— turning my head from the safety and security of a more solid foundation while taking off in one direction after another. A bit like many days of your life, perhaps, when you go off on your own without an appreciation of what you face or what might be the best course for you to take, making mighty good time but not being exactly sure where you're headed or why you were headed that way.

And yet, even as God watches us head off in our own directions—as the psalmist wrote in the psalm above—He is always there to lift us out of the surging sea, crashing surf, and howling winds and put our feet back on solid ground, above the high-tide watermarks of life.

IMPACT APPLICATION: We often find ourselves in the midst of the onrush of a surging sea, crashing waves, and blowing winds when all the while God stands ready, waiting patiently to place our feet upon solid rock, above the high-tide watermark of the oncoming problems, uncertainties, and obstacles that often await our next steps.

JUNE 25

WHEN A MIRACLE SMILES UP AT YOU

Jesus said, "Let the children come to me. Don't stop them! For the Kingdom of Heaven belongs to those who are like these children."
Matthew 19:14

I LOVE A LINE from the Heartland song "I Loved Her First": "Someday you might know what I'm going through / When a miracle smiles up at you / I loved her first."

Those words convey the feelings of a father watching his daughter dance at her wedding reception with her new husband. Those words convey my feelings toward my son from the time I met him until today and into all my tomorrows.

Although the words are inspirational in how they paint the possibility of a nurturing relationship through the years, they are only words too many times, in too many relationships with fathers and their daughters and sons.

Born in 1969, our son was about eight when his mom captured one of my favorite pictures of all time. We were walking through the woods, and she snapped it from behind us—of Nathan looking up at me and me looking at him—amid the changing colors on a cold fall afternoon in the mountains around Highlands, North Carolina.

That picture is now framed alongside another of the two of us—of him as groom and me as his best man—taken in August 1994. Part of the caption Nathan inserted in the matting of those pictures he framed together says, "Dad and Me, Friends Since 1969."

I see those same feelings in my son's glances and in his words for his two precious girls—our granddaughters. Everything they depend upon and trust is in him and is conveyed to them in his glances, in his affirming words and approving smiles, in his strong hand of protection and gentle touch of comfort. So much of what they feel about themselves and what Jesus wants them to know about how much He loves them comes from him.

So much of what other little girls or boys feel about themselves comes from their fathers, good or not.

"When a miracle smiles up at you . . ."

Maybe that's the view fathers need to have of their children—one that sees them as miracles, as Christ created them.

Maybe that's the view God intended for them to have. That when fathers look their child all over from the top of their heads to the tips of their toes—they realize that God's still in the miracle business. That's what that little boy or that little girl is—a miracle.

And as they look upon that little miracle, perhaps those fathers will begin to realize that's what they are too—God's miracles.

 IMPACT APPLICATION: There is only one opportunity to nurture and embrace that special relationship with a child God has placed in your life. Don't miss the moment. Don't miss the miracle looking up at you.

THE JOURNEY OF YOUR LIFE

I can do everything through Christ, who gives me strength.
Philippians 4:13

OUR YOUNGER GRANDDAUGHTER, Ellie Kate, has had worse moments in the journey of her young life. But even knowing that didn't serve to make what was happening any less scary for me or for her older sister, Hannah, at the time the events on that day were rapidly unfolding.

Ellie Kate was silently gasping for air—choking on a cracker that had lodged in her windpipe—after she thumped her head on the floor in an uninceremonious conclusion to a spontaneous attempt at a cartwheel off the footstool she had been sitting on.

She's fine now. But when it happened—for a brief moment that seemed much longer—Hannah and I were scrambling to make things right for her.

It had been five years since we waited anxiously throughout the early-morning hours in an empty lobby of St. Joseph's Hospital in Tampa for the news of Ellie Kate's birth. Instead, the news that came was of a labored delivery resulting in our younger granddaughter being confined for five days in the neonatal intensive care unit.

Maybe that's why today Ellie Kate scales the face of cabinets to sit on countertops, while a hard tile floor waits below to catch any slip or misstep. Maybe that's why she often refuses help, saying, "I got it, Gran." Maybe that's why she unexpectedly launches her precious little self into cartwheels off footstools.

Yet even though I worry about and wish she would not do some of the things that create anxious moments for us, I realize there is a bigger picture for all of us to embrace and understand. A desire to reach out, to become all you can be. That's what Ellie Kate does. She probably doesn't evaluate it from that perspective—but she does leave a trail for each of us to consider following in our own lives.

What about you? What have you always wanted to scale? What pathways have you always dreamed of following to some far-off place but your "better judgment" held you back from taking that first step? What footstools have you wanted to cartwheel from? What's holding you back? Of course, you may bump your head, fall from the climb, or hit a detour or ditch along the way, but surely there will be someone to pick you up, a bridge to cross, or something to encourage you and to set your feet back on the pathway toward all you were created to be.

The journey your life was meant to follow is before you. You are the only one who can travel it, the only one who can live it. That's the way God intended it. With Him.

 IMPACT APPLICATION: It's your life, your journey; and you have one time on each path, in each day, and in each experience. What will you make of it? What will you embrace each day to become all you can be?

JUNE 27

TEND TO THE
IMPORTANT

God said to him, "You fool! This very night your life will be demanded from you. Then who will get what you have prepared for yourself?" This is how it will be with whoever stores up things for themselves but is not rich toward God. **Luke 12:20-21**, NIV

THE RINGING TELEPHONE intruded into my quiet thoughts one morning several years ago. I recognized the caller and lifted the receiver to my ear.

The voice of a dear friend at the other end began to share about the recent loss of her mom and the illness and ache of loneliness her dad felt now. She wondered how much longer he would be with them. She and her husband had just returned home from time spent with her dad and the rest of the family in the hills of north Georgia.

Not too far, actually, from the site of the 2007 NCAA men's basketball Final Four championship in Atlanta, the site where four schools competed, each seeking to grasp the coveted National Championship trophy late into the night.

Jason, from nearby Concord and a senior at the University of North Carolina, Chapel Hill, was set to graduate in May with a 3.6 GPA in business administration, while spending his free time at UNC dressing for games as the team's mascot—Rameses.

On Friday, before UNC's win over the University of Southern California, Jason walked along a stretch of highway from his hotel toward a nearby 7-Eleven to get a burrito and a Coke and was gravely injured by an SUV traveling that roadway.

The UNC basketball team and their head coach, Roy Williams, were unaware of the accident until after their game on Friday night and—as one would expect—they were understandably and noticeably shaken by the report. Perspective began to set in again.

Millions watched the Final Four on TV, and millions of dollars were spent on advertising, tickets, travel, and food to attend the games in the Georgia Dome. Millions more were spent afterward on basketball coaches' contracts to get them to move to a new school or stay where they were.

Dozens of family members and friends attended Jason's bedside vigil. Even the Duke loyal were there for Jason and his family—bleeding, of all things, Carolina blue. Things like that tend to have a way of knocking down the artificial, meaningless walls we set up between ourselves.

And things like that—whether early-morning telephone calls, illnesses, accidents, or the loss of a loved one—that interrupt the often irrelevant pursuits of our lives tend to shine a bright light on the important things in life. They tend to put things into proper perspective for us, at least for a while anyway. And next time this perspective comes, for you and for me, I pray that it stays.

 IMPACT APPLICATION: Don't wait for something unexpected to change your perspective. Change it today by valuing what's important.

IMPACT IN ANY SIZE

God chose things despised by the world, things counted as nothing at all, and used them to bring to nothing what the world considers important. **1 Corinthians 1:28**

IT WAS A COMPLETELY innocent mistake. The *Finding Nemo* movie had not been released yet, but the shelves in the Disney Store were full of Nemo stuffed fish. Remembering my daughter-in-law's encouragement that a child cannot have too many stuffed animals, I selected one that seemed to be a perfect fit for the arms of my elder granddaughter, Hannah, after a careful inspection of its facial features and markings.

I didn't notice that one flipper was smaller than the other until I returned home. And so back to the store I went to return the defective stuffed animal.

I did my best to hide my embarrassment as the sales clerk explained that the Nemo toy was normal and that one flipper was supposed to be smaller than the other. She assured me that I would understand once I saw the movie. She was right, and I had fallen into the same cultural trap we all do at times.

I had given myself more credit than I deserved for being able to see past those artificial walls of meaningless differences we tend to erect that too often determine intrinsic value. Certainly the impact we have in the world is not determined by size or looks or any other external characteristics. You would have thought that some of the "not fitting in" experiences of childhood would have steeled me against that happening. Yet the power of a culture affirming perfection and beauty is more pervasive than I had realized. It had infected me, too.

I wonder if you have ever had someone notice that you had one flipper smaller than the other. I wonder if you allowed it to determine your own view of yourself.

Or perhaps with no help at all, you have felt as though you had one flipper smaller than the other and that somehow you didn't measure up. Perhaps you felt like you were on the outside looking in. Perhaps something or someone reminded you that you were born on the wrong side of the tracks. Perhaps it was family finances or clothes you didn't have that the "cool kids" were wearing.

Perhaps your smaller flipper has been defined by others in terms of color, size, or shape, by looks or gender, by wealth or things. Perhaps your child, or someone you know, has a flipper smaller than society thinks it should be. Perhaps you have accepted what society thinks.

Well, as it turned out, Nemo was pretty cool, despite his smaller flipper. Or was it because of it? Either way, my granddaughters think he is simply the best.

 IMPACT APPLICATION: The value God sees in us is not what the world sees. Embrace who you are to have the impact you were created to have.

JUNE 29

ALL THE WAY TO
THE FINISH

You take over. I'm about to die, my life an offering on God's altar. This is the only race worth running. I've run hard right to the finish, believed all the way. All that's left now is the shouting—God's applause! Depend on it, he's an honest judge. He'll do right not only by me, but by everyone eager for his coming.

2 Timothy 4:6-8, MSG

THAT PASSAGE in Paul's second letter to his beloved protégé Timothy is one of the great passages of encouragement contained in Scripture, where Paul begins to pass the mantle of responsibility to Timothy.

Did you notice the subtle challenge Paul sets forth to Timothy and to each of us? "I've run hard right to the finish," he says, "believed all the way."

There's the challenge for Timothy and for us—that no matter what we are going through, no matter what we face, no matter how many times we've fallen or how many missteps or detours we've suffered, we must run to the finish. Or as the New Living Translation says, "[fight] the good fight."

But that's easier said than done. Maybe you're facing a painful illness. Maybe the cancer has returned, or the heart problems are still there and the medical experts can't figure out a resolution. Maybe Alzheimer's is robbing you of the vibrancy of your loved one right before your very eyes. Maybe you're at a crossroads in your career and none of the turns seems to be just right.

Of course it's difficult. It's life. But the admonition of Paul is clear: keep running hard, all the way to the finish. Retirement is not an option in the Kingdom of God. The impact, memories, and legacy of your life is still being written.

I love what Hubert Humphrey had to say about that. Regardless of your politics, you've got to admire Hubert Humphrey and his view of the journey of the sixty-six years of life he was given. He served as a senator from Minnesota and then as the thirty-eighth vice president of the United States of America.

Near death, fighting against a cancer that would ultimately take his life, he whispered a truth for the ages: "In life it isn't what you've lost, it's what you've got left that counts."

No matter what we've been through, no matter what has happened, and no matter what we are facing—our lives aren't over.

The story of our lives is still being written—fight the good fight, run hard right to the finish.

 IMPACT APPLICATION: Every moment of our lives—to the very last breath we take on earth—we are to have an impact on the people all around us, living lives that are better because we have lived and run hard to the finish.

NUMBERS

Teach us to realize the brevity of life, so that we may grow in wisdom.
Psalm 90:12

I WONDER IF the morning sun knows the true significance of what it brings to us each and every day. I mean, beyond the potential for growth and the power of its golden rays for the flora, fauna, and our own energy consumption. I suppose not, but it's nice that it just keeps shining anyway.

And every day, among so many other things we receive with the morning sunshine, we are presented with another number. It can represent the date of that day, our age, or a special moment in our lives. Another occurred a few years ago as our son, Nathan, and his bride, Amy, spent the weekend with us to celebrate his twentieth high school class reunion. Twenty. Just a number, but one of many numbers representing a lifetime of the sun's gift of days and a reminder of our mortality.

Yet even in the face of our own mortality, the persistent passing of time brings clarity that in the overall scheme of eternity, the numbers representing the years of our lives—and the length of our mortality—are minuscule, indeed. They represent a mere dot on the long and eternal line which is our lives. Yet they are still lives colored with milestone after milestone of numbers, which serve to paint a portrait of our lives in moment after moment and memory after memory, all of which we treasure today. A collection of numbers in which we will have had an immeasurable opportunity to leave a legacy of lasting impact behind us and around us.

I wonder what the numbers that have made up our lives will look like when we are done. Can they be counted up in the lives in which we have made a difference in the world and for the world? Have our lives made a difference in the life of just one other person? Have they been lived self-centered or selflessly—for how many days in how many ways? Or will our lives be reflected solely by the numbers etched on trophies gathering dust on our mantels and bookshelves, on the lines on our résumés, or by the size of our bank accounts?

Our relationship with our heavenly Father through His Son Jesus Christ assures us of a life in eternity—part here, part forever. He has assured us of the forever part with our acceptance of His free gift of His Son.

He is watching to see what we do with the part of our lives which we live here.

 IMPACT APPLICATION: When we look back, I wonder if some of the numbers of our lives will signify the people whose lives are better because of how we lived ours. What will our legacies look like?

JULY 1

STARTING RIGHT

Humble yourselves under the mighty power of God, and at the right time he will lift you up in honor. Give all your worries and cares to God, for he cares about you.

1 Peter 5:6-7

HOW ARE YOU this morning? How did your day start out? It seems that the start to a lot of things in life is important. Just ask a one-hundred-meter-dash sprinter.

Through the years I have come to appreciate that the start to our day is pretty important. Nutritionists have been telling us for years that breakfast is the most important meal of the day. So did you eat breakfast today?

How about what you put in your mind this morning? Was it the morning newspaper, a book, or the local news?

When I graduated from the University of Florida Law School, I had the privilege of clerking for two years for a federal judge. I then returned to Gainesville, and after working with two good law firms in town, I opened my own law practice. Things were busy for a time as the practice built up. Lynda—who is gifted administratively and is bright and personable—helped me get started and then brought others on for some additional assistance.

Before I left the house each morning, I tried to make sure I read my Bible, maybe a devotion from another book, and then had some quiet time alone with God to pray. There were some mornings, though, when, for whatever reason, I didn't spend that quiet time at home before heading to the office.

One morning shortly after we had opened the law office, I must have been responding poorly to phone calls and reacting abruptly when Lynda asked me a question or reminded me of something. About eleven o'clock, Lynda walked into my office, quietly closed the door behind her, and said, "I just want you to know, I can always tell when you have had your quiet time with the Lord in the morning, and when you haven't. You're different. You behave, talk to others, and respond differently to things that happen. And the difference doesn't become you, or honor God."

I changed. I made sure I had time alone in the morning to read the Bible, maybe a devotion or two, and then talk to Him quietly for a while.

How do you start your day? Eating breakfast, I hope. Breakfast is good. But what else?

Let me suggest something even more important than breakfast. Take some time to focus on the One who cares for you. Read His Word and maybe some other wise words of encouragement. Spend time in prayer with Him. It will change your day.

 IMPACT APPLICATION: Cast all your worries on Him. He will set your feet on the right path—as you start out and go through your day. Trust me, I know!

FAITH FOR AROUND THE BEND

Faith shows the reality of what we hope for; it is the evidence of things we cannot see. **Hebrews 11:1**

I WONDER at times why I am surprised.

The unbelievable seemed to happen in Jacksonville, Florida, as the hearts of over 2,400 men who attended another Impact for Living men's conference were challenged to become more than they ever thought they could be. Through session after session, speaker after speaker, moment after moment, changes began to take place to move the attendees past what had already occurred in their lives toward the future God has in mind for each of them. It's the same future God has in mind for each of us.

Paul's encouragement to us in his letter to the Philippians always seems an appropriate follow-up to the verse from the writer of Hebrews above. The man who endured much for the hope he held in his heart shares this as a good place to start all the mornings of all our days: "Forgetting the past and looking forward to what lies ahead, I press on to reach the end of the race and receive the heavenly prize for which God, through Christ Jesus, is calling us" (Philippians 3:13-14).

So as our day begins, I wonder if we have that kind of faith that believes in pressing on even though we can't see what is coming around the bend. I wonder if we have that kind of God-inspired faith that causes us to press on in the face of disappointments, setbacks, and heartaches. I wonder if we have that faith—that certainty in God—that causes us to continue to embrace the future He has created for us.

I wonder if we have that kind of faith that causes us to press on in the face of doubt and doubters, waning resources, and tough times, believing that the vision God laid before us was really His and that He will continue to bring it all about. While all He asks us to do is to believe, we need faith to press on and at times to simply hang on to the hem of His robe for dear life as He leads us into the future He has set before us.

It's tenacious faith that causes us to press on in the face of all that is before us, all that happens to throw us off course, all the distractions of doubt and criticism, and all the heartaches, failures, and disappointments that will surely litter the path along our way. We need that kind of faith to press on today and every day.

IMPACT APPLICATION: With the God who created you, you can embrace for your life the faith God calls you to—being sure of what we hope for and certain of what we do not see. And press on.

JULY 3

A SENSE OF DUTY

That's the whole story. Here now is my final conclusion: Fear God and obey his commands, for this is everyone's duty. **Ecclesiastes 12:13**

THOMAS PAINE WROTE, "These are the times that try men's souls. The summer soldier and the sunshine patriot will, in this crisis, shrink from the service of their country; but he that stands by it now, deserves the love and thanks of man and woman." Paine penned those words after the loss of New York to the British. On December 23, 1776, his words were read to the troops by order of General George Washington.

It was all about duty, I thought, even in that moment as I sat there waiting to pick up one of our granddaughters after school. It is all about duty in everything and every moment of each of our lives. It is a responsibility before us each day that comes with the privilege we cherish.

And it is all about duty, as together as a nation we remember those who have stood in the gap for us throughout the centuries since that beginning in 1776. Those who have stood, in the face of uncertainty, and embraced the dream for us when we couldn't and even when the light flickered in our own hearts. Those who stood to lose it all—and often did—and had an impact on our lives as they stood, reminding us that the value of freedom and everything else we hold dear and often take for granted was not obtained cheaply, but at great cost.

And it is all about duty as we look within our lives and areas of responsibility—family, friends, work, church, community, and beyond—areas where we and we alone can have an impact. It is about a sense of obligation, responsibility, and regard for someone or something beyond ourselves.

The balance of Thomas Paine's words read on that morning so many years ago suggest that "what we obtain too cheap, we esteem too lightly: it is dearness only that gives every thing its value. Heaven knows how to put a proper price upon its goods; and it would be strange indeed if so celestial an article as freedom should not be highly rated."

I began to try to arrive for after-school pickup much earlier to assure that I was close to the front of the line so our girls didn't have to wait too long.

A sense of duty, without a doubt. And maybe coupled with a granddaddy just anxious to see his granddaughters?

 IMPACT APPLICATION: Life under God's banner is much about duty, and begins, as Solomon says in the Scripture above, with obedience to those things contained in His Word. Start there as you begin to understand the sense of duty in life and in all things to which we are each called.

THE STARS DANCED

When America was created, the stars must have danced in the sky.
Bernard DeVoto

FROM WHERE I STOOD, he seemed to be an ordinary fellow. *He must have done this a thousand times before,* I thought, yet the passion in his voice seemed fresh and new as he read from the original document before us: "We hold these truths to be self-evident, that all men are created equal, that they are endowed by their Creator with certain unalienable Rights, that among these are Life, Liberty, and the pursuit of Happiness. . . ."

I found myself standing taller while the tour guide's voice soared:

We, therefore, the Representatives of the united States of America . . .
appealing to the Supreme Judge of the world . . . do . . . solemnly
publish and declare, That these United Colonies are, and of Right ought
to be Free and Independent States . . .

And as he concluded this memorable moment for us, his countenance claimed the words as if they were his own: "And for the support of this Declaration, with a firm reliance on the protection of divine Providence, we mutually pledge to each other our Lives, our Fortunes and our sacred Honor."

Before me was a document representing the lifeblood of valiant and decent patriots.

In our journey as citizens of the United States of America, I wonder if we are up to the same sacrifice of the signers of the Declaration of Independence—farmers, planters, merchants, lawyers, and doctors who knew when they signed it that if they were captured by the British, they could die. But they still signed, because they had a dream for the future of this nation and because—no matter what you may hear to the contrary—they had a deep faith in God.

These men who loved liberty more than they valued their own lives paid the price for us. They paid the price beginning at Bunker Hill, and Lexington and Concord, and down through Valley Forge. These men—who with burlap wrapped around their feet and their muskets held under their tattered garments to keep them dry from the winter—paid the price for us. They made the first payment, and that payment has been kept up to date throughout our history.

As we celebrate this great nation, might we always remember with gratitude that the stars still dance in the sky and God still blesses America.

IMPACT APPLICATION: Legacy is built by sacrifice. We must embrace that truth as we build our legacy through the sacrifice of our lives, built upon the sacrifice of those who have gone before us.

JULY 5

AMERICAN BLESSING

Christ has truly set us free. Now make sure that you stay free, and don't get tied up again in slavery to the law. **Galatians 5:1**

THE BIRDS' EUPHONY gave proof that they were obviously still excited from the July 4th celebrations, almost as if they knew they were a part of something special. Hearing their chorus of praise for yet another beautiful day, the memory of those words of our Declaration of Independence burn brightly, just as surely as they did when the fifty-six men signed that noble document, knowing full well that if they were captured by the British, it would mean the death penalty. But they signed it anyway, setting in motion a God-inspired vision and dream for the future of this nation.

Leaning into history over that document, they penned their names to embrace the dream:

> We hold these truths to be self-evident, that all men are created equal, that they are endowed by their Creator with certain unalienable Rights, that among these are Life, Liberty and the pursuit of Happiness. . . .
>   And for the support of this Declaration, with a firm reliance on the protection of divine Providence, we mutually pledge to each other our Lives, our Fortunes and our sacred Honor.

And the fragile, noble dream of one nation under God began—a dream that has lit the torch of liberty throughout our history and that will continue to shine brightly as long as courageous men, women, and children awaken each day to stand against the ill winds that seek to blow her out.

I wonder what you say about a country where children can laugh together without concern under the security of the folds of a red, white, and blue banner while the lights from fireworks displays twinkle in their eyes. God bless America.

What do you say about a country that does all it can do to protect the rights of everyone, even those who would seek to undermine it? God bless America.

What do you say about a nation where ordinary people within our midst rise from towns both large and small and from sea to shining sea to meet any need, anywhere around the world, without expectation of thanks? God bless America.

What do you say about a country where the advance of human freedom and hope for a better day draws millions to our shores, sensing a glimpse of the dream of so long ago? God bless America.

May He continue to do so as we trust in Him.

 IMPACT APPLICATION: America, a fragile, noble vision with a dream of liberty, justice, freedom, and opportunity for all. What will we do with it?

TOMORROW—DREAMS FULFILLED

All these people died still believing what God had promised them. They did not receive what was promised, but they saw it all from a distance and welcomed it. . . . They were looking for a better place, a heavenly homeland. **Hebrews 11:13, 16**

TOMORROW IS A DAY for you and for me. Tomorrow is a day for children of all ages everywhere who have stood on a playground somewhere and dreamed dreams for their lives and longed for the opportunity to be whatever they held in their hearts. Tomorrow is where our dreams are fulfilled.

But there is something we need to do for that to happen—dream.

There are dreams we hold that God has placed in our hearts that have yet to be realized. Dreams for our own lives and for our family and our nation. There are things we have thought of doing for years, and other things have taken their place. There are dreams we have held for our children, and just a twist in the economy can put a damper on them.

As Christians, we dream many dreams for this world. We have much to do to restore a sense of respect and civility in our daily discourse. We have a long way to go toward embracing personal responsibility—not handing it off to our government—to lift those who need to see the sunshine that follows the rain. We have much to do to reclaim a culture that respects the sanctity of life for all—the born and unborn, the young and old. We have a long way to go toward making God welcome again in our schools and public buildings, in the decisions of our leaders, and in the quiet direction of our homes.

Dreams held dear but, in many cases, unfulfilled.

Through the ages some have dreamed of a day they hoped to see fulfilled but ran out of time to see their dreams become reality. But they pursued them anyway. Some of us hold dreams that God has planted in our hearts, which we may never see fulfilled in our lifetime. But we pursue them anyway. And even though we may not be here to see them fulfilled, those dreams are still worth pursuing and handing off to those who come after us—because God will still remain.

Tomorrow is always a day for us all to look toward. Tomorrow is a great day for you and your family and perhaps for our nation and our world. But there is still a long way for us to go to reach the dreams we hold in our hearts, individually and collectively.

Pursue those dreams God has placed in your heart. One day they will all come true—either with Him here or with Him in eternity.

Maybe even tomorrow.

 IMPACT APPLICATION: What are your dreams for tomorrow? Not only for yourself, but those you call friends and family. Dream them. Pursue them.

JULY 7

A GLANCE BACK INTO
THE FUTURE

No eye has seen, no ear has heard, and no mind has imagined what God has prepared for those who love him. **1 Corinthians 2:9**

IT LOOKS AS THOUGH it will be another day for the scrapbook. Memories made in the mountains with blue skies, a sixty-degree start to the morning, and a fire crackling in the fireplace nearby while our granddaughters continue to sleep in the other room with their Mimi. It will be easy to look back in the years ahead at those pictures that will adorn the pages of the ever-growing family scrapbook.

If only all days were like that, filled with soft, fond memories and easy quiet times of gentle breathing and sleeping loved ones in safe places with secure futures. But looking back we know that some of the pages of our scrapbooks were never filled. The disappointment, pain, and heartache of some of those moments would have been too palpable to include. Yet the memories from those pages that were left out—like the ones chosen—also remain woven into our hearts.

Time softens their edges; distance dulls their pain; but they remain etched on the pages of our hearts, there to remain to direct our today and control our tomorrow because we can't move on. Or those memories remain so we can move forward by facing them, learning from them, forgiving the causes of them, and releasing them to the pages of the past, firming the foundations for our future. The choice will be ours.

But the choices are not ours alone. And together, we should look back and reflect on the pages from the scrapbook of our individual lives and of our nation. We may notice that there are many pages that have been left out—representing some darker days where we needed to do better together. We have faced many of those as a people and learned from them, and there are others we still must face—to do better. The foundation of the future of our communities and country depends upon that.

Yet there are still many pages that stir pride in our hearts and that contain pictures of the lives and sacrifices of those who have gone before us—who looked forward with a bold vision into today and set a course that wrote the history of their lives and of this great nation, which is now ours to write.

Looking back should move us to always ask God to continue to help us as we add to the pages of our scrapbooks and boldly look forward into the futures God has set before us.

 IMPACT APPLICATION: Look back and reflect on the pages of the scrapbooks of your life and of our nation but with an eye toward asking God to help you to write the pages to come.

ALL IS WELL

The LORD is God, and he created the heavens and earth and put everything in place. He made the world to be lived in, not to be a place of empty chaos. "I am the LORD," he says, "and there is no other."
Isaiah 45:18

IT'S HAPPENING AGAIN this morning. I am once again being reminded of the truth of that Scripture. It seems to happen in the rising fullness of each new day.

Because no matter the clouds which cover the day, the storms which gather and threaten or which ultimately come, or the darkness of the world around me, each new morning always seems to come with a fresh reminder of the promise, which in our better moments we know to be true. The promise that all is well. All is well.

Really, though, you have to wonder when you're confronted with today's news accounts describing numerous acts of violence, the negative state of the economy, and the severity of about a dozen other social ills.

All is well. All is well.

"I am the LORD, and there is no other." All is well.

Yet how can that be? To even say that—all is well—seems incredible and naive when in your lives the burdens of the day are too heavy for you to carry and the future seems to hold only uncertainty, despair, and failure.

Maybe you are sitting there having just lost a job with no new prospects in sight. Or maybe you watch as the vibrancy of a beloved family member dissipates before your very eyes with the onset of Alzheimer's. Perhaps you stand at the side of a child struggling to find their way in life in a world that is unforgiving and harsh and seeks to strip them of their innocence and values. You try your best to step out into each new day but remain full of uncertainty as you try to figure out what God intends for this next season of your life.

All is well, my friends. All is well. Because the Lord is still on the throne. All is well.

Read those words from Isaiah again, this time with a firmness and conviction which claims the promise of His presence through all the stuff of life.

All is well. All is well.

He who created you and me and the heavens and the earth proclaims today as He did then, "I am the LORD, and there is no other."

Trust Him. In the midst of the storms, and when they end, trust Him.

All is well.

 IMPACT APPLICATION: No matter what storms we are going through, this we know to be true: the storms will end, and God is Lord in them and after them. And as we face and endure whatever storms may come our way, He will always be with us through them and with us after them. All is well.

JULY 9

BIGGIE FRIES

He was the one who prayed to the God of Israel, "Oh, that you would bless me and expand my territory! Please be with me in all that I do, and keep me from all trouble and pain!" And God granted him his request. **1 Chronicles 4:10**

AFTER I HAD PICKED UP my granddaughter, Hannah, from a long day at school, we stopped to order her a snack in the drive-through at a nearby fast-food restaurant. "Let's see, Hannah," I summarized, "you would like a small Frosty, a small drink, and small fries?"

"Yes, Granddaddy," she said, "except I would like Biggie fries." Wow! Imagine that. Nothing small or ordinary about that. And she ate them all.

Jabez cried out to the God of Israel, "Oh, that you would bless me and expand my territory." Here was a man whose future had been cast for him to be "ordinary." His name—"he will cause pain"—took care of that. Yet he would not be denied, and he imagined something more for himself. He reasoned that the God of miracles who had created him would surely want more than "ordinary" for his life. And he was right.

What do you imagine for your life? What big, special, remarkable future do you imagine God has for you? What dreams still flicker within your heart? What relationship do you want restored? What child needs their life lifted enough to see the sunshine just beyond the rainbow?

Or perhaps you're seeing the picture others have painted for you of "ordinary." Perhaps you've heard too many times that "you're not a good test-taker" or "that's just too big to try" or "you can never do that" or "you probably won't like that" or "what if you try and fail?" Perhaps you remind yourself that you'll never reach who God created you to be because you've failed so many times before. Better just order the small fries.

Here's the generational tragedy in that kind of thinking. We pass that same kind of thinking on to our children. The same messages we received as a child we pass on to our children. The same defeatist messages we have finally resigned ourselves to embrace, we pass to our children, either through negligence, resignation, envy, or spite. And in the process we jeopardize the future God created for them.

Today is the first day of the rest of our lives. And we need to remember that God's history is replete with examples of people who have sought to overcome ordinary expectations and imagined something special for their lives—something as big as God.

Jabez dared to ask God, "Oh, that you would bless me and expand my territory." Imagine that.

Yes, imagine that, and order the Biggie fries.

 IMPACT APPLICATION: What do you want to do in your life? Ever think that God may want to help you with it? God wants to bless you—order the Biggie fries!

HOTEL RWANDAS

The King will say, "I tell you the truth, when you did it to one of the least of these my brothers and sisters, you were doing it to me!"
Matthew 25:40

AS I SIT HERE in the fading darkness, I know that the sunlight of the morning will soon reveal the cracks, crevices, and other imperfections in the world around me. And it will no doubt shine on mine and remind me of my personal responsibility to those close and far, of moments when I could have done something to change things—and didn't.

It is a harsh reminder to me of those times I fell short in reaching out to make a difference. And I suspect the sunlight will do little to assuage the regret and sadness I feel as I reflect on why the world did little to nothing to help the people of Rwanda during the hundred days of genocide in 1994. If you don't want to be reminded of "the least of these" and our responsibility to them, I might suggest that you see something other than the movie *Hotel Rwanda*.

And, at minimum, be afraid to see the movie because you don't know if you can stand to see the inhumanity of it all. Maybe it didn't happen if I don't see it. Maybe it won't happen again if I turn my head again. That's the safe place that distance seems to allow us. But I wonder if by our inaction, it has already affected us and watered down the significant lives we were meant to live.

As so many turned a blind eye toward the Nazi onslaught, the world continues to prove itself ineffective, a far cry from what it should be.

We have been here before, and we will be here again—faced with things that we should stand up to stop. It may be part of the impact God intended that your life and mine have, not just in our families, our work, and our communities, but in those other places we often choose to turn from. Maybe they're too big and we don't believe we can have an impact. But maybe one step will lead to another, and someone else will join in our steps. The question for us becomes—what must I do?

Enjoy the sunshine of the day. But in the context of figuring out the impact we are meant to have in this life we live, we cannot turn away from those who need us.

Begin embracing a life of truly significant living—which God is waiting for us to do—by actually beginning to take that first sacrificial step of trust toward making a real difference in the lives of the "least of these."

 IMPACT APPLICATION: God has given us unique opportunities to have an impact on the "least of these." Isn't it time we start using them?

JULY 11

CAPTURED

"In those days when you pray, I will listen. If you look for me whole-heartedly, you will find me. I will be found by you," says the LORD. "I will end your captivity and restore your fortunes." **Jeremiah 29:12-14**

HER WORDS still pierce me today as they did that night nearly thirty-seven years ago. I was in my second year at the University of Florida Law School; and despite having some personal say over my comings and goings, the truth was that my classes, studies, law review responsibilities, and employment at the Center for Governmental Responsibility had begun to demand my presence at the school from very early in the morning until nearly midnight every day. Finances were tight as the GI bill educational assistance, earned from my service in the US Air Force, was nearing an end.

My values seemed clear and my responsibilities many—surely she understood as others seemed to. What I didn't realize was that I was being held captive to values of the world.

Her words slammed hard as I walked out of my five-year-old son's room that night, having just kissed him on the forehead while he lay sleeping. "You know," Lynda said, "you haven't seen Nathan awake for the last three days." Her words hung between us, as my first impulse—anger—was replaced with tears. Tears flowed as regret grew and as I stood there thinking about that little boy who thought I hung the moon.

I changed—right then.

I wish I could say the change was complete, perfect, and obvious. It was not, but it was steady, gradual, and lasting. It was a change that began from within. I was brought back from the captivity of worldly things toward the start of my journey to freedom.

Webster's dictionary defines transient as "passing away with time; not permanent; temporary; fleeting; passing quickly or soon." It defines eternal as "existing through all time; everlasting; forever the same; always true or valid; unchanging; timeless."

I wonder which category defines the values that capture your life. Which category guides the decisions and choices you make, the truths you hold as "sacred," the relationships with which you've been entrusted, the priorities of your day, and the faith and passion with which you live out God's call and purpose on your life? Because the truth is, a battle rages between the worldly and sacred values in life, between the transient and eternal, to capture our hearts.

By the way, Lynda's lesson of years ago was learned well—almost every day I have a chance to see or talk to Nathan and tell him I love him.

What captures your heart? The transient or the eternal?

IMPACT APPLICATION: The good news of each brand-new day is this: no matter the mistakes, lost moments and memories, and missed opportunities behind you, God has laid the future before you. Make it one that lasts for all eternity and honors Him as you love others.

BUG-LOOKERS

If you give even a cup of cold water to one of the least of my followers, you will surely be rewarded. **Matthew 10:42**

I REMEMBERED her face as I recalled watching her in the waiting room of the doctor's office. She seemed to be my granddaughter Hannah's age. She was turning the pages of a magazine but with some difficulty because her hands and fingers were deformed from what appeared to be a birth defect. I tried not to stare.

Her hair was deep, dark, and shining beautifully from the ceiling light; but her face was placid, belying what I felt, by her presence in the doctor's office, must be a cry from deep within. Of course, I couldn't know; but I wanted to brush her pain away just the same. Yet as she got up to go into the doctor's office, I knew I would never see her again. And I wondered what her future might hold.

"Hannah, what do you want to be when you grow up?" a family friend once asked. Hannah paused for a moment from the next bite of her hot dog, looked trustingly into the distance, and responded that she wanted to be a "bug-looker." Made sense to me, since my precious young granddaughter never saw a bug that shouldn't be picked up, examined, housed, and fed for a while.

The people of our nation have been called by various names through the years—explorers, pioneers, settlers, achievers, sailors, mountain climbers, adventurers, colonists, astronauts, entrepreneurs, and last but not least, naive, idealistic, and crazy dreamers. I don't know which characterization I prefer, but you probably won't be surprised to hear that I'm leaning toward "bug-looker" as my favorite. Granddaddies are that way.

What will be the next thing that makes us go farther and work harder? What will be the next great achievement of our times? Perhaps it's right in front of us.

Perhaps each of us will commit to lift the lives of the most helpless and desperate in our midst until they are able to reach for all they were intended to be. We have done great things, yet sadly what we may be most remembered for are the generations of would-be "bug-lookers" with enormous potential who we held briefly in our hands before we let them slip forever through our fingers. I pray that won't be the case.

I think often of the girl in the doctor's office. I don't know her story, but her face reminds me that I must constantly help life others so they don't fall short of becoming all that God created them to be.

IMPACT APPLICATION: We all have enormous opportunities in the world around us to help those "bug-lookers," little girls and boys waiting to be lifted up through us to God! Don't miss them.

JULY 13

A DISNEY WORLD KIND OF TOMORROW

God has made everything beautiful for its own time. He has planted eternity in the human heart, but even so, people cannot see the whole scope of God's work from beginning to end. **Ecclesiastes 3:11**

HAD YOU WALKED into my office a few years ago, you would have found eighteen pictures of my granddaughter Hannah positioned in various places of honor around the room. I can assure you that as she and my younger granddaughter grow, that number will continue to grow too.

A reminder of that came not too long ago after arrangements were finalized for our family trip to Disney World a few weeks from then. It occurred while my son, Nathan, was overseeing the completion of Hannah's nightly bedtime rituals, which included brushing her teeth, when he exclaimed to her, "Hannah, I'm so excited about our trip to Disney World!"

As she emptied her mouth with her usual flair, spitting out the residue of her bubble gum–flavored toothpaste, she reflected on her daddy's words for a moment and then matter-of-factly responded, "Daddy, I'm so excited about tomorrow!"

Nathan assured me there was nothing planned for the following day. There was nothing "Disney World–like" to look forward to, just another tomorrow.

Well, here's the true and sad reality. I don't know about you, but it took me the better part of half a lifetime to come to that optimistic view of life and to embrace with excitement the promise of tomorrow. Half a lifetime of excitement and joy about all my tomorrows being governed not simply by the promise of a brand-new day but instead being dictated by the troubles of the day and whether something exciting was planned or expected for my tomorrow.

And with many of my todays filled with the gnats and elephants we all have to deal with, and many of the tomorrows containing nothing to "look forward to," the result was that too many days of my life lacked the joy that life should have held for me.

The remedy though is found in a relationship with the living God through His Son, Jesus Christ. That's what an encounter with the living God will do for us—provide a daily joy, an expected joy, built upon a relationship with Him and not dependent upon the ups and downs of today or tomorrow.

Life for me was lived for too long in the peaks and valleys and the problems and events of the days, instead of in a childlike expectation and appreciation of the gift of today and the never-ending promise of tomorrow, provided through an encounter with the living God.

"Daddy, I'm so excited about tomorrow!" Me too, Hannah. Me too!

How about you? Me too!

IMPACT APPLICATION: Let me assure you that a fresh encounter with the living God will remind you of the precious gift of today and all the glorious promises of tomorrow.

GOD LOVES ME — THIS I KNOW

We know that God causes everything to work together for the good of those who love God and are called according to his purpose for them. **Romans 8:28**

THE STORMS IN MY AREA had been pretty intense. But the sun eventually broke through. It always does, and it always will.

And as I watched the winds from the passing storm remind the trees in our yard to wave good-bye, I want you to know that in the midst of whatever storm you may be going through right now, if you'll look closely, you will see that the sun is about to break through.

It always does, and it always will.

A few years ago my dear stepmother reminded me of that, when she called to see if we were all set in our preparations to deal with what looked like another hurricane heading our way. In the course of our conversation, she wondered aloud, "What is God trying to tell us?" Shortly thereafter, as I watched the weather team track the progress of the hurricane, the news anchor's words marked that truth again as they also betrayed an uncertainty in his heart. "What have we done to deserve this?"

I'll leave it to the pundits and theological scholars to share what I'm sure would be far more profound theological answers to those two questions. I'll leave it to them to wrestle with those and other lofty issues such as pre- and post-millennium, whether that storm was a sign of Christ's return, judgment, and other related issues they might be thinking about.

The only response I had to my stepmother's question was this—"All I can say is that through it all, I know God loves me." Through it all, I know that God doesn't make cars crash, cause drive-by shootings where the innocent are killed, cause children to go to bed hungry, or cause people to lose their jobs. Through it all, I know that God doesn't swirl His finger in the heavens to create storms and havoc to destroy His children and creation.

The God who created me and walked with me through the sometimes lonely and desperate days of childhood, career changes, peaks and valleys of relationships, and the fears, failures, and triumphs of my life's journey intimately walks and leads me this very day into all the fullness of life He intends for me, working it all out for my good.

I don't know why it all happens. You'll have to ask others for the answers. The truth is I know that one day God will explain it all to me. All I need to know today is that He loves me, and He loves you.

Reporting from storm central, that's all I know. And that's enough.

 IMPACT APPLICATION: Trust God through every situation. Leave the "why" behind, and rest in the knowledge that in the end all things work together for the good of those who love Him.

JULY 15

IT'S ALL IN OUR ATTITUDE

We can rejoice, too, when we run into problems and trials, for we know that they help us develop endurance. And endurance develops strength of character, and character strengthens our confident hope of salvation. And this hope will not lead to disappointment. For we know how dearly God loves us, because he has given us the Holy Spirit to fill our hearts with his love. **Romans 5:3-5**

AS I WALKED into the kitchen, I could hear our basset hound, Lily, still asleep and breathing softly in her crate. I opened the cabinet door to the coffee cups standing ready for that first pour of the day. The sight of them evoked memories that flooded my thoughts—cups engraved, painted, and marked with remembrances of travels and family, of friendships and challenges.

Myriad memories returned as I read the words inscribed on some of the curved sides—Kapalua, Beaver Creek, Super Bowl XXXVII, Gators, Augusta National, Duke Dad, Harvard Mom. There were others, too, that had been specially prepared for me with a picture of Hannah and with a picture of Ellie Kate and still others of them both and ones with pictures of our precious godchildren. Wonderful moments and memories indelibly etched in my heart filled me with joy as my gaze surveyed the even now slightly faded pictures and inscriptions.

But there was one there that seemed as bright and beautiful as the day it first graced our collection many years ago. It reminded me as I was about to start my day that a lot of how my day would turn out depended upon me.

It read, "Attitude—Is Everything."

In his book *Man's Search for Meaning*, Viktor Frankl recounts the unspeakable horrors of his longtime imprisonment in Nazi concentration camps like Auschwitz and Dachau, in which he was stripped of everything down to his naked existence. His father, mother, brother, and wife died in similar prison camps.

And yet he found that despite his circumstances, he was never stripped of one of our "last human freedoms—the ability to choose our attitude despite our given set of circumstances."

Frankl's experiences should remind us that even though we can't always choose our circumstances, we can always choose our attitude; and with God's hand on our backs, we can choose to rise above those circumstances.

How is your attitude today? Do your circumstances seem a bit overwhelming and, as a result, are they getting you down? Or are you choosing, like the apostle Paul, to "rejoice . . . when we run into problems and trials"? Rejoice, with your gaze focused on Jesus Christ, the hope of all the world.

IMPACT APPLICATION: The circumstances of our day are often difficult. They try our souls, strain our relationships, and test our resolve. Yet we have been called to make an impact on others and on this world. With God, we can choose our attitudes despite our circumstances and press on.

DEPTH BEFORE
HEIGHT

Anyone who listens to my teaching and follows it is wise, like a person who builds a house on solid rock. Though the rain comes in torrents and the floodwaters rise and the winds beat against that house, it won't collapse because it is built on bedrock. **Matthew 7:24-25**

WHAT CAN WE LEARN from the joys and sorrows, the ups and downs of the past? What will we learn from the example of others—whose lives are played out for all the world to see and who seem to wrestle with the same things we do? What should we take from this past year—perhaps even just one thing that will make a difference in the next and may help us to reach potential we have never reached before?

Perhaps we will see that the foundation of our lives will set the stage for everything else.

Or, as James Brown puts it in his book *Role of a Lifetime*, "Depth before height."

He explains what he means this way: "'Depth,' of course refers to the foundation we build or need to build that will undergird everything in our lives . . . [and] includes our faith, our character, integrity, and honesty. . . . The depth in our lives . . . is marked by courage." It is the courage it takes to change our behavior. And that foundation determines the height we attain in and with our lives. But Brown goes on to explain what he means by "height": "Height has nothing to do with trophies, résumés and awards [or] with the amount of money you make, the number of cars you have, the house you live in, or the size of your investment portfolio. . . . 'Height' is very simply striving to become all you were created to be."

Here we stand every day, peering into all the expectations, uncertainties, and opportunities of a brand-new day. And we have no idea how it will all play out or end up or whether we'll even finish the year out.

What we see when we look back will depend on the foundations we've established for our lives—those we dig today. Foundations that are not aligned with the world's values or that give only a passing nod toward God. The foundation we need to build, embrace, and establish in our lives is the one set on the rock of Jesus Christ.

And when we do that, we might be pleasantly surprised with the heights we achieve.

IMPACT APPLICATION: "Height" involves maximizing your God-given gifts and abilities, finding those things you are passionate about, and pursuing them, recognizing the opportunities you have each day to add value to the lives around you and to make a difference in your world. Why not start today?

JULY 17

ETERNAL MOMENTS

They said to each other, "Didn't our hearts burn within us as he talked with us on the road and explained the Scriptures to us?" **Luke 24:32**

ETERNAL MOMENTS.

They happen more often than we realize—penetrating the darkness and disappointments of some of our days—and are always designed for our enjoyment, growth, and good. Yet we miss them—too often, too many, too bad. Those eternal moments in our journey where we meet Christ in the seemingly ordinary moments of every day that is before us.

We had one of those moments a few years ago—and for a change I recognized it when God unfolded it before us. Lynda and I had our two granddaughters with us as we were driving along back roads through Georgia on our way to the North Carolina mountains, listening to music and singing along with the encouraging words from a powerful praise song.

The next bend in the road brought one of the girls' favorite stopping places into view—McDonald's. This particular restaurant was set against a distant backdrop of the mountains rising before us and pointing the way to our destination. To recap, our two granddaughters, one of their favorite stopping places, an inviting view of our glorious mountains with all of us singing the powerful message of one of our great praise songs. It was an otherwise ordinary moment that turned eternal, giving us a glimpse of what heaven will surely be like.

And I didn't miss it. That time.

But I have. And so have you.

We often miss these moments while preoccupied with the busyness of getting ahead in the world, in our schools, and in our careers. We miss them in doing all of the social things that we feel we need to do so that we can gain acceptance as somebody important. Some of us miss them as we try to prove ourselves to others.

After Jesus was crucified, two men on the road to Emmaus were mourning His death. He had let them down—they thought He was going to rule Israel and everything would be fine. They didn't know that Jesus had been raised from the dead; and as they walked, Jesus joined them. They didn't recognize Him. But He walked with them and explained the Scriptures so they could understand.

And later when they recognized Him in the mealtime breaking of bread, they understood the eternal moment of which they had been part. The eternal Savior had broken into their everyday. "Didn't our hearts burn within us?"

No matter the darkness, disappointments, or difficulties, here's the truth—Jesus is walking with us, inviting us into eternal moments even today if only we'll look for them.

 IMPACT APPLICATION: Look around you for the eternal in the ordinary moments of every day of your life. That's where you'll meet Christ today and every day for all eternity.

CHIP, CHIP, CHIP

[Jesus] said, "I tell you the truth, unless you turn from your sins and become like little children, you will never get into the Kingdom of Heaven. So anyone who becomes as humble as this little child is the greatest in the Kingdom of Heaven." **Matthew 18:3-4**

WE HAD GATHERED TOGETHER around the dinner table in the kitchen with dear friends and our children who were visiting us for the day from Tampa. My granddaughter Hannah was, much to my delight, seated at my side, taking in all that was unfolding before her.

As our eyes met, and in the dearest, sweetest, most matter-of-fact voice she could muster, she exclaimed, "Granddaddy, you chew with your mouth open like I do!"—followed by a demonstration reflecting just one more behavioral trait that binds us together.

The idealistic innocence, trust, and honesty of a child of God—a child who observes the errant behavior of one who adores her and finds not something wrong but an endearing connection.

Yet while children view the world around them through the eyes of the God who created them, they don't often see it coming—the slow and steady chip, chip, chipping away of their idealistic fervor and passionate view of life and the world around them—by well-meaning parents, family, friends, teachers, and others.

We, jokingly at first, begin to call them "crazy" or "silly" for their idealistic views of the day and dreams for their lives or when they fall short of them.

Chip . . .

Our personal schedules begin to preempt the time we promised to spend with them when they were formed—the time needed to love, hold, play, and lovingly and consistently guide and nurture them so they can become all they were set aside to be.

Chip . . . Chip . . .

The labels we brush on them with our words stick in their hearts and then their idealism, trust, and honesty fade and begin to look a lot like ours.

Chip . . . Chip . . . Chip . . . Chip . . .

The late Urie Bronfenbenner, cofounder of Head Start, said, "The one indispensable condition for a child's successful upbringing is that at least one adult must have a deep and irrational attachment to him." To put it another way, every child must believe, feel, sense, hear, and see that someone is absolutely head over heels crazy about him or her.

Somewhere a child needs that from you—perhaps next door; down the street; in your community, state, or nation. Or perhaps standing by your side at this very moment.

IMPACT APPLICATION: The idealistic innocence, trust, and honesty of a little child—find it, nurture it, protect it, and spread it. Their lives depend upon it, and the life of our civilization depends upon it as well.

JULY 19

GIFTS FROM GOD

Her children stand and bless her. Her husband praises her: "There are many virtuous and capable women in the world, but you surpass them all!" **Proverbs 31:28-29**

AS THE VIEW outside my window continues to weave its tapestry of wonder, it reminds me of the blessing of a special person God gave me a few years ago. I suspect you may have one of these people in your life also. In my limited ability to describe them, I am led to a few observations:

- They're at times fragile and will cry at the drop of a hat—or the drop of anything, for that matter.
- Their feelings circulate just below the sensitive surface of what you think you see, easily erupting into roars of laughter or rivers of tears as they are touched by the joys and sorrows of others.
- They come with nicks and scars and wounds that you learn are at times unexpectedly and easily reopened.
- They see a world of right and wrong, harbor hopes and dreams, and honor you by allowing you to help nurture and achieve them.
- They view all of life with a contagious, childlike wonder, excitement, and appreciation.
- They hold the hopes and fears of their family in their hearts and courageously lay down their lives every day for their family's safety, security, and future.
- After a while they know they can count on you in the important things, but it takes a little while longer to trust you with their fears, heartaches, and disappointments.
- Beneath their usual cheery exterior, they can be haltingly shy, maddeningly independent, exhaustingly energetic, and unbelievably gifted.
- They see a world in need, children in pain, and lonely friends; and with undying loyalty, they reach out every day to brighten their lives.
- They come in all shapes and sizes, and they are all and always beautiful.

It must have been a beautiful day like today when she was born, a harbinger of her life and the bright blessing she was to be in our lives. She's the incredible mother of my two granddaughters, a dear friend of my bride (her mother-in-law), and the protective, supportive, and encouraging advocate of her husband, my son. He rightly praises her, and her two girls see her as their blessing.

Got one of these precious daughters-in-law? You're doubly blessed if you do. Care for them. Stand by them. Encourage them. Affirm them. Honor them. Celebrate them. Love them.

 IMPACT APPLICATION: Take time to honor your loved ones each and every day. God created them perfect, unique, and to be in relationship with you. Take time to help them discover their God-given purpose in life. You'll be glad you did.

MOMENTS AND PEOPLE
OF IMPACT

"I know the plans I have for you," says the LORD. "They are plans for good and not for disaster, to give you a future and a hope."
Jeremiah 29:11

OUR GODSON'S VOICE cracked as he shared news of the birth of his second child. So bright, so competent, and so strong as he served our country in the United States Air Force as a first lieutenant, Kevin's voice broke as he told me a son had been born to him, and his name was to be Timothy Scott Fletcher.

It was a humbling and joyful moment reminding me, through my own tears, of my unworthiness and inadequacy before one so pure as this tiny miracle of God with all the potential the Creator of the universe planted in his soul.

It had been one of those weeks of reflecting on those lives who have had and continue to have an impact on my life. A week of reflection on the life of a friend, Taylor—a doctor by training, now embraced in the arms of his heavenly Father— who delivered an incalculable number of God's tiny miracles like Timothy Scott. It had been a week of concern and exhilaration for a son and his family as an illness from many years ago recurred, then standing back to watch as our great God began to heal the illness and threw open doors and windows of opportunity where God meant for him to journey in his days ahead.

It was a week of learning of a nephew's ACL surgery, a gathering of family and friends at a sweet girl's graduation from high school, a fellowship lunch with a friend, an open house with many friends, and the celebration of twenty-five years of ministry by a pastor and his bride. It's been a week of the sad yet joyful reminder of the passing of a saint years ago—of my mother-in-law's walking among our lives before taking her place in that great cloud of witnesses encouraging and watching us from above. And it's been a week of planning to honor a precious daughter-in-law on her birthday as she celebrates one more year of touching the hearts of her family and friends.

In your own life, no doubt, you have similar memories of those moments and people who have walked with you for your good and God's glory, all orchestrated by the God who knows our every move and thought.

"'I know the plans I have for you,' declares the LORD, 'plans to prosper you and not to harm you, plans to give you hope and a future'" (NIV).

Thank the Lord for the blessings of impact He has provided through the lives of so many others. They are all a part of His plan to encourage you for your own life of impact.

IMPACT APPLICATION: Be thankful for the lives of others who have lived and shown you how to live a life of impact.

JULY 21

GOING FORWARD
WITH GOD

Moses did as the LORD commanded him. He sent out twelve men, all tribal leaders of Israel, from their camp in the wilderness of Paran.
Numbers 13:3

A TONE OF FRUSTRATION was apparent in a letter to the editor I read one morning, but a somewhat gratuitous comment in the letter was particularly bothersome. The writer scribbled these words: "Today's Americans haven't the courage or insight to venture off the couch let alone the vision to embark on something as terrifying as planning for the future."

At that moment, I thought of General Tommy Franks, who, at a morning CENTCOM briefing, was proudly explaining the missions of our Special Operations forces in Operation Iraqi Freedom as they set about assessing the danger and timing of their assignment, not with a mind-set of *whether* their objective could be accomplished but of *when*. Courage, insight, vision. Again I read, "Today's Americans haven't the courage or insight to venture off the couch let alone the vision to embark on something as terrifying as planning for the future."

At that moment, I thought of Joshua and Caleb and ten others sent by Moses on a forty-day mission into the Promised Land to assess the situation and to "see what the land was like, and find out whether the people living there are strong or weak, few or many" (Numbers 13:18).

The ten others who went with them, feeling more comfortable where they were and lacking courage, insight, and vision for the future, reported back to Moses that the objective would be impossible to achieve. But Caleb and Joshua did as they were asked and came back with full faith in the promises of their God and reported, with courage, insight, and vision: Go!

I wonder where we would stand if we were confronted with those conflicting reports—with Joshua and Caleb or with the ten naysayers? I wonder where we would stand if confronted with similar conflicting reports—for some decision in our lives impacting our futures.

I wonder about the valleys, heartaches, and challenges in your life. Do you believe what your sight, your feelings, and your present circumstances would tell you? Or do you believe in a God who casts an eternal vision for your future and who has always done what He promised He would do? Do you stand with the naysayers, or do you stand in faith in your God who says—go?

As I think about God's promises and about you, I realize the folly of those scribbled words in that letter to the editor. I realize that together and individually and with the eternal assurance that God holds the future in His hands, we can and will move forward into our future with courage, insight, and vision.

 IMPACT APPLICATION: When God sends us forth, there is no limit to our potential to do great things. What are you being sent to do—with God?

INDIFFERENCE—
NOT AN OPTION

Someone who does not know, and then does something wrong, will be punished only lightly. When someone has been given much, much will be required in return; and when someone has been entrusted with much, even more will be required. **Luke 12:48**

TO A LESS SENSITIVE and more indifferent soul, the occasion one evening a few years ago would probably have passed into history as a moment to just let her cry herself to sleep. But to Nathan, it was another moment to demonstrate his love for Hannah and the sacred value he placed on her and her feelings. As he entered her room and gently brushed away the tears on her cheeks, he could barely discern the words coming from her lips—"I miss my Mimi."

"Do you want to call her?" he asked.

"You call her, Daddy," Hannah offered as she calmed a bit, "and tell her I love her and other things you know I would want to say." Nathan could have let her cry, writing it off as the oversensitive outflow of a young heart, but he chose to engage with compassion. He cared at his and his daughter's deepest levels. He called.

I wonder how indifference sets into our lives. I wonder if we learn it as children from our parents. I wonder how we would recognize its stealthy approach—as it begins to change our priorities from those God lists as important to those which friends and society say are important.

Maybe indifference is a product of comfort and indulgence, or perhaps it's the end result of coming out on the short end of too many battles. I hope it's not an inevitable touchstone on our life's journey. Because one could see that its tentacles could imprison compassion behind the fences of self-centered lives, Godless families, indulgent communities, and isolated neighbors and countries.

But indifference isn't an option for Christians. Jesus makes it clear in the Parable of the Good Samaritan (see Luke 10) that we are to love our neighbors, and the definition of "neighbor" is broad and encompassing. Furthermore, He makes it clear that in the final judgment, we will be judged by how we treated the "least of these" (see Matthew 25).

No one is too small or insignificant to merit our attention and compassion. Indifference is never an option in the life God calls us to live with Him.

 IMPACT APPLICATION: History will judge us— both in the short and long term—as individuals, as parents and families, as churches and communities, and as a nation based on how we treated the least of those among us, and history must show that we developed a depth of caring that moved us at our deepest levels—to action, to service, to courage, and to hope for all the world.

JULY 23

ETERNAL DEPOSITS

The Spirit himself bears witness with our spirit that we are children of God. **Romans 8:16,** ESV

IT HAD BEEN quite some time since I had seen the movie *Mary Poppins*, but there I sat with my two granddaughters, engrossed in the music and characters of that classic movie as they paraded before us on the television screen.

Near the end of the movie, George Banks, father of Jane and Michael, with head bowed in defeat, walks slowly away from his home late one evening for a meeting at the bank where he works. He knows he will be fired when he reaches the bank—despite its having been his longtime place of employment. It is his only important identity in life, and it is about to be stripped from him.

And yet as he approaches this inevitable crisis of career, a crisis of conscience brews within him. Walking past lengthening shadows from the streetlamps, through shop-lined alleys and tree-covered walkways, past spires of buildings epitomizing success, he recalls the years of tears and smiles and the missed moments of his two little children's lives. In the grind of carving out his niche of success and self-esteem, the lives of his children have slipped between his fingers.

George Banks finally learns what is truly important and emerges from his crisis of conscience with a new and different definition of success. It costs him his job but gains him his life—the one that the God who created him intended for him to live. A life defined by his relationship with those most important people in his life and not by the things of life, the expectations of others, or a never-ending attempt to obtain the acceptance or affirmation of peers or parents who can't, won't, or don't know how to give it. A life whose success is measured not by things or by others but by the way his children describe him to others.

There was no one there to take a picture of us that day—eating marshmallow Peeps and watching *Mary Poppins* with my granddaughters wrapped in my arms and nestled securely in the chair with me—but I have an indelible portrait painted in my heart.

What choices are you making? Where do you find your identity? Are you finding your identity in success, which is fleeting? Or are you finding it by investing in those relationships with those closest to you, which last forever?

IMPACT APPLICATION: We have a choice. We always do. And it's a choice we must make again and again every day. We have in our possession the brushes and the paint. Which scenes of our lives will we create and remember?

JUST KEEP SWIMMING

After the earthquake there was a fire, but the LORD was not in the fire. And after the fire there was the sound of a gentle whisper. **1 Kings 19:12**

LYNDA AND I had taken our two granddaughters to the beach for a few days, and we designated one night as "movie night," selecting *Finding Nemo*.

Dory, you may remember, is the good-hearted, scatterbrained, lunatic-acting, blue-colored fish who befriends Marlin, the orange-and-white clown fish, in his search for his son, Nemo—who had been trapped in a diver's net and was seemingly destined to be lost forever.

Marlin is determined at all costs, even his life, to find his son. And Dory becomes his ally in the quest.

And she never loses sight of her goal, adopted from her new friend Marlin, to find Nemo. "Just keep swimming," is the encouragement she repeats over and over as she and Marlin pursue their prize.

The passage above is the culmination of a difficult time for the prophet Elijah. He is being pursued by King Ahab and Jezebel, who have had all the other prophets of God killed—and they are determined to add Elijah to that list. And so Elijah runs, not at all sure that God knows how bad things have gotten for him.

God tells him to go stand on a mountain. And while he's there, a wind comes by and then an earthquake and then a fire. God was in none of those, but instead He comes in the "sound of a gentle whisper."

What's going on in your life? Perhaps you're feeling under attack from all corners of your life. Some unjustified criticism has come your way. Or you're standing at a crossroads and are not sure which way to go. And in the midst of it all—whom do you listen to for your next steps?

Elijah learned that it was that "gentle whisper," the voice of God, that he needed to hear. And in addition to that "gentle whisper" of God in your life, who else in your life simply loves you because you are you? Listen to those voices too.

And through whatever we're going through, as we seek and listen to that "gentle whisper," remember those words of Dory to Marlin when she says over and over to "Just keep swimming. Just keep swimming."

Because that's what Christ says to each one of us as we swim on through each day of our lives and face the difficulties and uncertainties of tomorrow: "Just keep swimming."

He is with you. You can count on it.

 IMPACT APPLICATION: In the pressure cooker and difficulties of life, listen for that gentle whisper of the One who loves you most and "just keep swimming" with Him.

JULY 25

A SPLASH OF SUNSHINE

So may all your enemies perish, O LORD! But may they who love you be like the sun when it rises in its strength. **Judges 5:31,** NIV

"OH, GRAN, but you just cut them a few days ago!"

My elder granddaughter was staging a mild rebellion at the thought of having her play interrupted to trim her fingernails.

Nonetheless, she climbed on my lap and waited patiently while I carefully trimmed them. She trusted me never to trim so close that it hurt. I took that trust seriously. Holding her hands in the process, I could see characteristics in her fingers and hands of both her mommy and daddy.

I also saw the sunlight that emanates from her as she sat there. A light that follows her as she leaves and that shines on my life and those around her as she moves through her day. A light shared through her hands and the life of grace that God uses to bring light into, and life out of, the sometimes chaotic, tense, and dark rubble and ashes of my life.

It always happens when she is around or when I hear her voice. Perspective changes. Worries and frustrations about finances, relationships, deadlines, and things still on the "back burner" lessen. Eternal and godly priorities rise out of the valleys of the mundane and unimportant.

We need Deborahs in our lives, like the judge Deborah singing in the passage of Scripture above. The times of the Judges were dark and in many ways hopeless as the people turned away from God, but Deborah was a ray of light in a dark time. The people turned to the judges for deliverance from their enemies. And even when Deborah called Barak and empowered him to do God's work, Barak insisted that Deborah go with him, so important was her presence.

We need Deborahs, who by their lives and hands of grace bless those around them just by their presence, their gentle touch, and their caring ways. Deborahs of any age who light up the room and offer hope to those who need it, who serve God with hearts of compassion and charity toward those less fortunate, toward the least and the weak among us. Deborahs who with godly wisdom and idealistic, childlike fervor directed by their innocent love of God change our perspectives from the worldly and temporal to the eternal and lasting.

Look around. I'm sure you'll find them in many places, including and especially your children and grandchildren. Don't miss the moments to allow them to splash sunshine on your life.

"Oh, Gran, but you just cut them a few days ago."

She was probably right, but the moment really wasn't about nail trimming as much as it was about granddaddy just needing another splash of sunshine on his day and life.

 IMPACT APPLICATION: Look for—and cultivate— Deborahs around you, helping them bring light into the world.

ALL THINGS

We know that all things work together for good to those who love God, to those who are the called according to His purpose.
Romans 8:28, NKJV

MAYBE THIS IS A GOOD DAY for us all to remember the truth of that verse of Scripture.

It's a familiar verse, but in the midst of the challenges and uncertainties of the days that unfold before us, we need to make sure we have a good grip upon its truth, because our tendency is to head toward the exits and wonder which way to go next.

The apostle Paul—the same guy who was called Saul and who persecuted followers of Christ—wrote it. He was converted on the Damascus Road when Jesus appeared to him.

After that experience and being tapped as a disciple of Christ, we read in various accounts in Scripture that Paul's life was anything but what one might describe as "good." He was beaten, imprisoned, stoned, whipped, slandered, starved, and shipwrecked among other things. Good?

Yet Paul continued to reach for all his potential by sharing words of hope and conviction about what Christ had done and all that He would do. Was Paul a lunatic? Maybe, but history doesn't seem to record that he was. Zealous? Yes. Sold out? Paul knew that God was and had been with him through it all, behind the scenes, encouraging him and transforming every condition and circumstance into something for his good and for God's glory.

Notice in the verse that Paul says, "We *know*." He doesn't say, "We hope" or "We feel" or "Maybe." He says, "We know." God's loving involvement in our lives for good is unquestionable to him—as it is today for you and for me.

God promises to work out wonderful things in our lives. It's not a promise of "happiness" or "success" in all things, at least not as the world describes them. But it is a promise of the fulfillment of the eternal purpose of our lives and of deep satisfaction and fulfillment in the journey of a life aligned with God.

And notice one more thing Paul says: "all things."

Here's what we know through our own experiences with God and having learned through the experiences of Paul and others—"We know that all things work together for good to those who love God." In the good, the bad, the joyful, the painful, the disappointing, whatever—God works all of those together for good. And good as *He* defines it, which has to be a whole lot better than any good we can create.

IMPACT APPLICATION: Believe it: God will use "all things" that we go through—today, tomorrow, and every day of our lives—for our good and His glory.

JULY 27

THE RICHEST PERSON
IN TOWN

Suddenly, the angel was joined by a vast host of others—the armies of heaven—praising God and saying, "Glory to God in highest heaven, and peace on earth to those with whom God is pleased." **Luke 2:13-14**

IT IS AS DEFINITE for me as Christmas itself. Every year—without fail—I am certain to watch the movie *It's a Wonderful Life*.

The enduring message of the sacredness and value of our individual lives is made clear through the troubles and triumphs of George Bailey and the old Bailey Building and Loan he begrudgingly assumes stewardship over at his father's passing.

In the closing scene, George's younger brother, Harry—a war hero whose life was saved when he was a boy by George—has just learned of the Building and Loan's recent money troubles and flies home through a snowstorm to be with George and his family. When he arrives, he is not really surprised to see people from all around town gathering to share their money and lives to help out their friend George Bailey, the one who had through the years helped each of them.

Harry lifts a glass to toast his brother: "To my big brother, George, the richest man in town!"

What about you and me? Aren't we in the same position as George Bailey every day? Couldn't it also be said about us that no matter what we're going through, no matter our "status" in the meaningless pecking orders of society, that we are the richest people in town? Here we are, surrounded in life by the people and things that really matter and in some cases the memories of those people we still hold dear. So why do we allow temporary setbacks to paint the landscapes of our futures?

We have people in our lives that matter. People who love and care for us. People who need us and look up to us. People—in whatever number and relationship—who look to us, who listen to us, and whose lives are better because we are here and because our lives have been woven together with theirs, all as part of God's plan.

But we also have a Savior who came for us and who died for us so that we might live forever and who continues to live for us and intercede for us before the Father.

And for all of that, we should remember that each one of us is indeed "the richest man in town."

 IMPACT APPLICATION: I don't know what you will face in the days ahead, but I do know that you have a Savior. I do know that you have people who love and care for you, people who need you, people whose lives have been made better and whose lives will continue to be made better because of you.

TIE A KNOT AND HANG ON

After a while some of the Jews plotted together to kill him. They were watching for him day and night at the city gate so they could murder him, but Saul was told about their plot. So during the night, some of the other believers lowered him in a large basket through an opening in the city wall. **Acts 9:23-25**

THE APOSTLE PAUL was just three years on the job, yet it seemed as though his demise was imminent. Times were tough; the leaders of the day were after him; and no matter where he turned, it seemed he found himself facing struggles and troubles. And now it seemed as though the end was near—he was at the end of his options.

But then his friends, concerned about what might happen to him, came to him in the middle of the night and lowered him in a basket to safety through an opening in the wall, bypassing the city gate where the people were waiting to capture and execute him.

My bride, Lynda, expressed that story another way a number of years ago through her talent for cross-stitch. I was three years into practicing law, had just opened my own law office, and was unsure of what the future held. Upon arriving at the office early one morning, I found sitting on my desk a framed labor of love—a cross-stitch tapestry picturing a mouse hanging from a rope, apparently clinging desperately to his last hope—a knot. There it was—a knot tied at the end of the rope, saving him from what seemed to be an impending fall. There was also a phrase she cross-stitched on the canvas: "When you get to the end of your rope . . . tie a knot and hang on!"

I don't know what you're facing today. I don't know how long you've been facing it. I don't know the disappointments or heartaches you hold close. I don't know the failures or shortcomings you've experienced and can't seem to get beyond. I'll bet there are times when you can't even see past the glare of the problems shining directly into your eyes.

But I do know that there is someone who cares and whom God will use to deliver you through an opening in all the turmoil you face. Somewhere there is someone God will use to help you to hang on to the knot tied at what may seem at the moment to be the end of your rope. A knot that should remind you of God Himself—who you not only can and should always hang on to, but who is always hanging on to you.

 IMPACT APPLICATION: No matter what's going on in your life, wait just a moment longer. Look around, and you'll see someone who cares to help you. And you'll also see the knot, so hang on.

JULY 29

LIVE WHO YOU ARE

Let us run with perseverance the race marked out for us. Let us fix our eyes on Jesus. **Hebrews 12:1-2,** NIV

I AM PRIVILEGED to work with coaches and families in professional and inter-collegiate sports, helping them with contracts, placement, and professional and personal decisions.

There are regular moments when they have to make decisions as to which opportunity is the one they should follow. It's then that I help them remember who they are. I return to those priorities of their lives and match opportunities with them to make sure there is a fit. If not, it won't be long before they realize the decision was the wrong one. I focus not on what they do or have done but on who they are and should continue to be.

The focus of our lives should be on who Christ calls us to be, with and for Him. Who we are, in the midst of a world that is always asking what we have done lately, is the focus that brings depth to our lives and clarity to our decisions. Something inside us that recognizes the platforms we have been given—whether as husbands, coaches, parents, business executives, athletes, pastors, or church members—shapes the steps of our journey and who we are. It shows up in things like

- doing the right thing even when it may not be in our best interests;
- lifting lives to a brighter day;
- being a shining light, a positive influence for others, in the midst of difficult circumstances;
- raising a generation of healthy, affirmed, secure, and loved children with the confidence and assurance to step out into the unknown of their futures;
- glorifying God in everything we say, do, and think, whether we win or lose; and
- fixing our eyes on Christ, who first showed us the way.

If what we do is our focus, not only will there be times when we fall short and lose, but we will realize that we have ultimately failed. But if who we are is our guide, then along the way of striving for wins and losses, and experiencing both, we will become all we were created to be as our experiences shape us further into who we are, and the impact of our lives through the platforms of our lives will take on an eternal significance.

Then we will have succeeded—even in the midst of our losses.

IMPACT APPLICATION: The world around us focuses on what we do. But focus instead on who you are to build the life God intends for you to live—and make a difference with the platforms He has given you in the world.

THE REAL DEAL

Teach these new disciples to obey all the commands I have given you.
And be sure of this: I am with you always, even to the end of the age.
Matthew 28:20

IT'S A WONDERFUL PLACE we have all been at times in our lives, the world of
make-believe. Perhaps it's a place like Disney World or watching the illusions of
a magician like David Copperfield. Perhaps it's a movie in which everyone lives
happily ever after. Perhaps it's a story that moves us to tears. The world of make-
believe can be comforting. It's where we escape from the realities of the day into a
world of wishes, possibilities, and hope.

Maybe that's why many years ago, my two younger sisters, having just entered
their teen years, sat day after day in a movie theater to watch the original release
of *The Parent Trap*. From the first show in the morning to the last show at night,
all week one summer, they never moved, all for the price of one admission ticket
each day.

I thought that their behavior was strange until I saw the remake of the movie
later. That's when I realized that the movie had been a place of refuge for them, a
place of make-believe, where they could dream that things would turn out better
for them and their family than they seemed to be doing.

We've all gone there, to a place of make-believe. We feel better for a time as we
escape from the worry of financial problems, the heartache of a broken relationship, the pain of a child trying to find their way, or an addiction we can't seem
to shake. Perhaps we're still looking for some affirmation we never got years ago.

Yet inevitably, as we depart our movie theaters and other refuges of make-believe,
the light illuminates the reality that whatever was there before remains for us to face
again. And how do we deal with it, short of another retreat into make-believe?

By facing it, remembering we are not alone. We face our circumstances with
the one and only relationship that is not make-believe. He is the Real Deal, the
One who promises to be with you now and to the end of the world. Know anyone
else who can make that promise? There are many around us whose intentions may
be good, and they may give their life trying to fulfill that promise. But did they
create the heavens and the earth and all that is in them? Do they sit at the right
hand of God, waiting for us and cheering us on?

Make sure to take the hand of the One who is truly in control—with Him,
you can face anything.

 IMPACT APPLICATION: No matter what is before
you, you have a choice in dealing with whatever it is.
Face it hand in hand with the One who is the Real Deal.

JULY 31

PAINTING THE BLANK PAGES

Faith shows the reality of what we hope for; it is the evidence of things we cannot see. **Hebrews 11:1**

AS I ENTERED the upstairs room where I spend a good bit of time, the place my granddaughters call "Granddaddy's and our office," I reflected again on the paintings they had done in the past years on the easel in that room which always awaits their return.

One painting is fastened on the face of the easel. Three hang proudly across the mantle of the fireplace facing my desk; one is framed and hangs on the wall, and many others are kept in a neat stack on a cabinet in an alcove off the study.

It has been a while since my granddaughters and I have thumbed through all the paintings they have done. The last time we did, they recalled proudly every stroke, dash, and dot they had made on those initially blank pages. They had seen something there which they would not have seen on the pages in a coloring book. They had seen something on those blank pages from the nooks and crannies of their imaginations. Something fresh had made its way from the recesses of those intimate places, through their tiny fingers, to the paint-laden bristles of a brush, and onto a blank sheet of paper, where they began to tell those around them something of who they were, what they valued, and what they believed.

The roots of their faith, their beliefs, and their values were finding expression through those blank pages. There was no darkness or fear in those paintings, only light and hope. And the direction of their continuing formation will be determined moment by moment, not only through their imagination, but through the quality of their interaction with and encouragement from others, in addition to their environment.

Following that passage above, the writer of Hebrews recounts incident after incident of saint after saint, who demonstrated their faith by following their God without being able to see the end of the journey. They believed in and imagined a future painted by the hand of One who had proven time and again His faithfulness to them. Their lives and hearts were shaped by their faith in a God whose evidences of love were all around and whom they trusted to paint each new day of their lives.

As we approach the blank pages of our futures, do we approach them with fear or faith? Do we approach them believing in a God who has proven He can be trusted, or do we set Him aside and cower in fear of the unknown and unexpected? Faith or fear—how do we approach tomorrow?

 IMPACT APPLICATION: As we stand before the blank pages of our tomorrows, we can have faith in the God who created us to guide our hands and hearts as we paint the pages of each day.

REJOICE!

Always be full of joy in the Lord. I say it again—rejoice! **Philippians 4:4**

I WONDER if the apostle Paul's perspective about life would have been any different if he'd had a television set.

Probably not, since life was tough enough for Paul without hearing about all the other stuff that was going on in the world. It's a wonder he lived as long as he did—five floggings with forty lashes minus one; three beatings with rods; one stoning; three shipwrecks; robbed by bandits; danger lurking around almost every corner; often hungry, thirsty, cold, and without a shelter to rest his head, except during one of his many imprisonments.

I'm not sure anything he might have seen on television about what was going on in the world could have been bad enough to change the hope he carried in his heart. It seems that nothing could have or would have changed that hope to despair—nothing. Instead you could always find his words and life saying, "Always be full of joy in the Lord. I say it again—rejoice!"

I must admit that I have gone through periods where I haven't said that too often. It's probably because I have been watching too much of the local, national, and world news. If our children behaved, twisted the truth, and treated each other in the ways I have witnessed in some of those news reports, they would find themselves banished for life to time-out, at the very least. My expectations are always much higher, I guess, than they should realistically be. And we begin to think that what we are watching and hearing is the reality and center of our lives when it is not.

Paul suggests a better way to focus our hearts and minds: "Fix your thoughts on what is true, and honorable, and right, and pure, and lovely, and admirable. Think about things that are excellent and worthy of praise. . . . Then the God of peace will be with you" (Philippians 4:8-9).

Lynda seems to do that on a daily basis. I sometimes assume that she is just not engaged in what's going on around her. Wrong assumption. She is very aware but chooses to be engaged in much higher and loftier pursuits—such as what Paul says we should focus upon.

"Always be full of joy in the Lord. I say it again—rejoice!"

That's her. That's Paul.

And that should be us—you and me.

IMPACT APPLICATION: At the end of it all—no matter what goes on in the world around us that has absolutely no lasting or eternal consequence—Christ remains. Rejoice in Christ.

AUGUST 2

HARD-SHELL CHOCOLATE MOMENTS

If we knew how significant life's seemingly insignificant moments were to be, we'd probably spend more time enjoying them. **Anonymous**

IT WAS A THURSDAY NIGHT a few years ago, and I was at home with Lynda and our granddaughter, Hannah, eating ice cream covered with the Magic Shell chocolate topping, which hardens on cold ice cream. It was a wonderful evening.

While Hannah got every last bit from her bowl of ice cream, offering an occasional "mmmmmm," Lynda shared a moment from earlier that day when she and Hannah were sitting on a couch in a store in Tampa, waiting for Hannah's mom to finish some shopping. Hannah, completely unsolicited, had announced to her Mimi that she had "a happy heart." "You have a happy heart?" Lynda affirmingly asked, to which Hannah added, "Every day," as a tear formed in Lynda's eye. Tears of significance in the seemingly insignificant moments and places of life.

The next morning I made some reservations for an upcoming flight—and I made a new friend of the woman who was working at the Delta desk there in Salt Lake City. I truly believe God is behind it whenever I meet new people. During the course of considering the various options available for this flight or that, I told my new friend the story of our little girl with the "happy heart." From the other end of the line I could hear her words begin to choke with tears.

Just the day before, she shared, she had been sitting on a bench in the park with her six-year-old granddaughter, just passing the time of day—or so she thought. All of a sudden her precious little girl shrieked and pointed to a passing butterfly. "Look, Grandma! A butterfly!" They sat silently watching the majestic creature flit and float on the wings of the late-afternoon breezes. Tears filled her eyes when she realized it had been years since she had seen—really seen—a butterfly.

A touch of wonder seen through the eyes of her precious little girl while just sitting on an ordinary bench in an ordinary park. A touch of wonder found around a simple kitchen table in the presence of a chocolate-covered little girl who has a "happy heart every day." All serving to remind us that we serve a God who frequently hides Himself "from those who think themselves wise and clever" and reveals Himself "to the childlike" (Matthew 11:25). It's an amazing moment when we find significance and meaning in the seemingly insignificant details of life, and it's amazing how often a little child will lead us there.

IMPACT APPLICATION: Let me suggest that we be on guard for those significant moments, wrapped perhaps in simple brown paper wrappers, like ice cream and ordinary park benches, and found in our todays and every day as together we move on into all the wonder of the days ahead.

AFTER THE INTERMISSION

Jesus responded, "Why are you afraid? You have so little faith!" Then he got up and rebuked the wind and waves, and suddenly there was a great calm. **Matthew 8:26**

I DIDN'T KNOW ANN MARIE, but her tough, widowed husband couldn't choke back his tears as her life was replayed for the world to share on *Extreme Makeover: Home Edition*.

Ann Marie had died of cancer, leaving John and three young boys all alone. Her boys were so young that their memories of her would be filtered forever through others' recollections. What followed for them was a seemingly interminable intermission, a long period of inactivity and lack of direction, as they tried to find their way without her.

But after the intermission something happened. In the nursery of their new home, lying back and looking at the ceiling, her youngest son found his mom again in the shooting star flashing across a field of stars painted overhead.

Life's a lot like that. Periods of activity full of joys and heartaches, hopes and dreams, disappointments and distractions, followed often by intermissions of waiting, a loss of direction—lengthy and empty intervals of time, waiting and walking through some too-long valley. People we love die unexpectedly. We fall from grace in the midst of a weak moment. We lose a job we were well suited for. A relationship sours. A friend betrays us. A child can't find his or her way. It begins to rain and looks like it could last beyond our desire to care.

But as the Scripture above reminds us, that's never the end of the story. The disciples were in the midst of the storm but then the intermission came, and Christ had the last say. And that's the way it is for us when we go through whatever we face. It's never the end of the day; evening is still a long way off. Sophocles said it this way—"One must wait until the evening to see how splendid the day has been."

And inevitably, something always happens after the intermission. A little orphan girl named Annie finds a home with Daddy Warbucks. When Owl's house blows down in a "big wind," precious Piglet gives Owl his home, while Winnie the Pooh and Christopher Robin smile. Christ rose from the grave after He was crucified, dead, and buried.

Something always happens after the intermission. The day continues. The sun comes up. The stars shine. And even a little boy lying on his back in his new room captures the mom he never really knew in his heart as a shooting star glides before his eyes.

Something always happens after the intermission.

IMPACT APPLICATION: No matter what you're going through, it's not the end of the day. Don't quit; keep the faith. God is there, and He's not done yet.

AUGUST 4

JOE BROWN

Jesus said to his disciples, "Whoever wants to be my disciple must deny themselves and take up their cross and follow me. For whoever wants to save their life will lose it, but whoever loses their life for me will find it. What good will it be for someone to gain the whole world, yet forfeit their soul?" **Matthew 16:24-26,** NIV

IN ONE OF MY MANY OTHER CALLINGS, I coached baseball at the University of Florida. We were pretty good, too, going to the College World Series in Omaha, Nebraska.

To get to that level of consistent championship quality, we spent hours almost every day at the practice field, part of which involved my connecting with the lives of the players. It was part of my calling as their coach, mentor, and chaplain—maybe even as a disciple of God.

But we are called to be disciples in every setting, in every moment of our lives. We are Christ's ambassadors, touching whom Christ, and often no one else, would touch. The homeless, the hungry, the abused, the addicted, the helpless, the poor, the ill, and those simply needing a lift up in life. Children who go to bed hungry at night or frightened or who are all alone with no hope for a better tomorrow.

Maybe like this story of the town drunk and Joe Brown.

It seems that the little town had someone who always got drunk and had to find a place each night to sleep it off. But the town drunk had one friend. His name was Joe Brown. And every time this drunk lit up the town, Joe Brown was there to help him, to sober him up, to get him some coffee and something to eat, and to find him a place to sleep it off. Every time. No questions. No judgment.

And then a revival came to town, and Joe Brown invited his friend with the drinking problem to the revival. The man sat in the back of the revival tent after a long day of drinking and heard the evangelist say, "You can be different; you can change your life."

At the end of the service, an invitation was given to come down to the front for prayer. And so the town drunk made his way down and said to the preacher, "I want to change. I want to be like Joe Brown."

"No, my child," the preacher said. "You want to be like Jesus."

And the man asked, "Well, is Jesus anything like Joe Brown?"

Whom do we appear like to others around us? Are we Christ's disciples? Are we making a difference in the lives and the world around us?

 IMPACT APPLICATION: It's fairly simple: we are called to touch the world like Jesus, to make a difference in the lives around us, day after day, until we draw our last breath. How are we doing?

ANOTHER CHANCE— ANOTHER SHINING MOMENT

The angel said, "Don't be alarmed. You are looking for Jesus of Nazareth, who was crucified. He isn't here! He is risen from the dead! Look, this is where they laid his body. Now go and tell his disciples, including Peter, that Jesus is going ahead of you to Galilee. You will see him there, just as he told you before he died." **Mark 16:6-7**

MILAN, INDIANA, is a little town in which dreams, shining moments, and second chances were lived out over sixty years ago, all of which became the springboard for the movie *Hoosiers*.

Milan High School—a school of 160 students—won the state championship game in 1954, defeating Muncie Central (whose student body was about the population of *the entire town* of Milan) with a game-winning basket in the final seconds of the game. But it's in the shadow of the backboards where the real-life stories dwell.

That's the place we often overlook, where stories of second chances come alive and where dreams come true. According to the dramatized movie version, a coach, barred from coaching for hitting a player, was given a second chance. An assistant coach, down on his luck—also given another chance. The team's manager-player, who played sparingly up until then, in a critical moment was given a second chance. A team and a town—initially focused only on winning—were all given another chance to find more than just a state basketball title.

These stories are not at all unlike the story in today's verse. The same Peter who had on three separate occasions denied that he knew Jesus Christ as He was rapidly heading to His death on the cross is here given another chance. Christ was for Peter, and is for us, a place of second chances.

Need a second chance today? Well, here's the good news—second chances don't happen just in the movies. No matter what you've been through or how far down you seem to be feeling, as Jesus was there for Peter and His disciples, He is there for you and me. He stands ready to lift us to the light of a new day, into another shining moment.

With the same Jesus who gave Peter a second chance, you have another chance to change the way things are, to get up after you fall, or to change another life for the better. Reach for those second chances.

 IMPACT APPLICATION: Need a second chance? Today is the day. As with Peter and the other disciples, Jesus stands ready to give you a second chance.

AUGUST 6

ENCOURAGEMENT—NOT TOO FAR FROM HERE

Since we are surrounded by such a huge crowd of witnesses to the life of faith, let us strip off every weight that slows us down, especially the sin that so easily trips us up. And let us run with endurance the race God has set before us. **Hebrews 12:1**

ON HER OCCASIONAL VISITS to our home in North Central Florida—before she lifted off to heaven—Lynda's mom loved to sit in front of a blazing fire in our family room, even in the summer months when I would turn the air conditioner colder to simulate an environment warranting the blaze.

That was the way it was on her last visit with us. A year later, Lynda and I had moved in with her to care for her during her last weeks of life with us.

On one occasion during those last few weeks, a song was playing softly in the background as I sat next to her bedside. I realized I was sitting beside one of God's great saints—a saint who had held me, Lynda, her entire family, and everyone she met in her heart and would soon be part of that great cloud of witnesses cheering me and the rest of us on, as she had done all of her life.

She gave feet and hands to those words every day of her life, encouraging others and inspiring the rest of us by her example. That's what happened when she and our daughter-in-law got to know each other, and on that one occasion when Amy came to see her while Mother was visiting with us.

As the evening wore on, we noticed Amy was nowhere to be found until we quietly opened the door to Mother's bedroom. There, snuggled under the covers with this dear saint of ninety-three years was another younger saint—our precious daughter-in-law—softly rubbing Mom's head and gently whispering sweet words of reassurance to her until Mom gently slipped off to sleep.

The Scripture reminds us that "we are surrounded by . . . a huge cloud of witnesses" cheering us on as we "run with endurance the race God has set before us." And even in our most difficult moments, we can all recall those saints who have encouraged us and who have set a path for us to follow.

That must be why Mom loved those fires so much. She must have seen the light of God's love in the beauty of those crackling flames, a love she also felt in the hands, words, and heart of her beloved granddaughter-in-law.

As we too have saints cheering us on, we can cheer others on in their races.

 IMPACT APPLICATION: All around you there are those who need a saint in their lives. Someone to carry them through the valleys. Someone to touch them at their deepest points of pain and need. Someone to shine the light of God's love on their lives.

GET IN THE GAME

Can anything ever separate us from Christ's love? Does it mean he no longer loves us if we have trouble or calamity, or are persecuted, or hungry, or destitute, or in danger, or threatened with death? . . . No power in the sky above or in the earth below—indeed, nothing in all creation will ever be able to separate us from the love of God that is revealed in Christ Jesus our Lord. **Romans 8:35, 39**

OUR AMERICAN FLAG proudly waves in the morning breeze. The sight of it often floods me with an overarching hope for the future of my family, our nation, and the world.

Even more than that, together we find victorious hope in Paul's words to the Romans. They are words of promise for today and all our tomorrows. But they are not intended to suggest that we abdicate our responsibility to others but instead, with Christ in us, to care for others using the gifts with which we've been blessed.

We can't use that Scripture to stand on the sidelines, defaulting to a life of "what will be will be." Instead we must realize that the free will God gave to Adam and Eve He also gives to us, along with a call to us throughout His word to "get in the game."

There is too much at stake now and in the future to allow us to sit idly by and merely hope that all will go well. We need to stand firmly in our faith for the survival of values, knowing that evil won't simply go away and that the sacredness of young lives, the assurance of eternity for them and others, and the future of our great nation may depend upon our commitment and involvement.

And in that, we can draw strength and direction from these words from John F. Kennedy's inaugural address: "Ask not what your country can do for you—ask what you can do for your country . . . With a good conscience our only sure reward, with history the final judge of our deeds, let us go forth to lead the land we love, asking His blessing and His help, but knowing that here on earth God's work must truly be our own."

Yet even as we work to make our world a better place, we have the eternal assurance that no matter what we face, "neither death nor life, neither angels nor demons, neither our fears for today nor our worries about tomorrow—not even the powers of hell can separate us from God's love" (Romans 8:38).

Now that promise will sustain us! Amen and amen!

 IMPACT APPLICATION: If you're not already engaged with your community and the world around you, what simple step can you take today to begin? God's Kingdom will be enhanced and perhaps expanded as we get in the game.

AUGUST 8

PLATFORMS OF PROMISE

Moses my servant is dead. Therefore, the time has come for you to lead these people, the Israelites, across the Jordan River into the land I am giving them. I promise you what I promised Moses: "Wherever you set foot, you will be on land I have given you." **Joshua 1:2-3**

MY NEPHEW AND I had inherited the coaching honors of the previous season's last-in-the-league Little League baseball team of which my son, Nathan, was to be a new member.

We had gathered for our first team practice. As the players each meekly took their stance in the batter's box, I could see faces frozen in fear, eyes glazed over, knees knocking, and sweat pouring off their tiny hands, revealing an immediate concern that the ball was going to hit them.

Nothing I said could convince them they would be okay until—not totally accidentally—one of my pitches would gently plunk them on an arm, a leg, or a protruding backside. One by one they noticed that their arms and legs were still attached. And so they stepped back in the box, each time with more confidence than before. If they were going to do this, there would be times, impossible to avoid, when they would be hit, only to rise and try again.

It reminds me of Joshua. Moses has just passed from the scene, and God has selected Joshua to lead the Israelite nation. You can almost see Joshua, standing on the banks of the Jordan River, probably a little weary from the forty years of wandering in the desert, knees knocking, face frozen in fear, eyes glazed over, and palms sweaty as he realizes the new platform to which God has called him. But God reassures him of His presence and promises. Joshua takes his place in the batter's box and enters the Promised Land.

As each new day, month, and year unfolds before us, we will find ourselves standing afresh on the banks of a new promised land, realizing that our lives are yet unfinished. Let me warn you that if you decide to take a risk and get into the batter's box, you may get hit, and at times it will hurt. There will be times when you will be wrong, laughed at, and criticized. Guaranteed. Yet great achievement never comes without great courage. Great achievement will never come without getting plunked a few times in the arm, leg, or backside and getting up again and again.

By the way, did I mention that our team that year played for the league championship and finished second? Great achievement and courageous living can be yours, but only if you are willing to step into the batter's box.

 IMPACT APPLICATION: We know we aren't always going to succeed and will occasionally get hit, but God calls us to step into the promised land anyway because that's where the great things we dream of lie.

AN OCCASION OF BLESSING

When Isaac caught the smell of [Jacob's] clothes, . . . he blessed his son. He said, . . . "From the dew of heaven and the richness of the earth, may God always give you abundant harvests of grain and bountiful new wine. **Genesis 27:27-28**

AS WE AWOKE with our two granddaughters who were staying with us while a soft, steadily falling rain descended upon our neighborhood, a decision to have church at home seemed to be the order of the day.

After breakfast, our elder granddaughter, Hannah, introduced the worship service with a prelude from her piano assignments she had worked on the day before with Lynda, her Mimi, while Ellie Kate did her best to get into a mood of worship while looking for one of her new stuffed animals hiding somewhere around the house.

After the prelude, a prayer, talking a little about God, and a reading by Hannah from their *Jesus Loves Me Bible Storybook* about Jesus blessing the little children, Lynda and I, following the suggestion from the Scripture above, blessed each of our granddaughters. A blessing similar to Isaac's blessing of his younger son, Jacob.

Mimi began with Hannah by wrapping her arms around Hannah and telling her all that Hannah meant to her, reminding her of the times in her precious little life that she will always hold dear. Realizing that her Mimi was destined to go on and on until evening, I gently interjected some of my own remembrances of her life. Ellie Kate was next as we similarly shared our hearts with her.

Then we wrapped both girls in our arms and prayed—while they listened to each word we shared—that God, His angels, and all those He has entrusted to care for them would protect them, nurture them, and love them; that God would guide them along the path He has set before them; and that He would lift them to the glorious sunshine of all the promise He has placed in their lives and continue to grow them into all that He has created them to be.

It was a moment of blessing, a moment of affirmation for them. It was a special occasion. And it was a moment of profound impact for Lynda and me as well.

Something we should all consider doing regularly in our lives and families on rainy days or whenever.

IMPACT APPLICATION: Blessing our children, grandchildren, and others is always appropriate. But a blessing is not just an occasional thing. It must be a day-to-day occurrence in the lives of those whom God has entrusted to our care.

AUGUST 10

OFF COURSE? PRESS ON

I focus on this one thing: Forgetting the past and looking forward to what lies ahead, I press on to reach the end of the race and receive the heavenly prize for which God, through Christ Jesus, is calling us.
Philippians 3:13-14

I WASN'T FEELING SORRY for myself. Oh, maybe I was, at least a little bit.

I was in high school, and what little was left of my family life had just disintegrated. I was on my own. Standing there on that street corner, I had no idea what the next moment, let alone the next day, would bring. I wasn't thinking of my potential—I was simply trying to survive.

Of course, even though I didn't know Him too well at the time, God had His hand on my back. And through friends, teachers, loving classmates, and job opportunities that helped me earn enough to pay for rent, food, clothes, and medical bills, I made it through that season of life.

Paul experienced a lot in his life, both before and after his relationship with Christ formed. Before his relationship with Christ, his life was lived on Paul's terms. After he began his relationship with Christ, his potential to make a difference in the world was on Christ's terms.

And Paul's life wasn't always easy. But he learned that he could trust the One he served and that he had been given incredible potential, gifts, and opportunities to make a difference in the lives of others.

Through God's grace, we all have been given gifts and abilities—potential—to do what God has created us to do. We may go through seasons where the demands or disappointments of life knock us off course for a time from becoming all we were created to be—but the potential of our lives is still there.

Have we discovered that potential God has given us yet? Have we begun to push the envelope of potential within us to become all we were created to be? Do we strap on whatever potential we have to become all we were meant to be?

We have each been given one life. And the choice in how we live it is ours—but we will have one shot at living it. We can use it or waste it, but there's no doing it over. We can live each day fully or not.

So if you find yourself off course or ever begin to feel sorry for whatever has befallen you, don't allow the pity party to begin. Instead, take the first step off whatever street corner you're standing on. And then press on with God.

 IMPACT APPLICATION: No matter what we encounter, no matter how difficult the journey, God will help us to press on, to run and never look back.

HANDSTAND TRUST AND OPTIMISM

The LORD is my shepherd; I have all that I need. **Psalm 23:1**

I WAS HEADED TO THE BACK of the house from the kitchen. It requires that I pass through the family room. Ellie Kate was staying with me for a few hours and watching a movie while doing various acrobatic exercises.

"Gran," she said with a soft tone of expectancy while flipping up into a handstand, "please hold my legs." I reached out and gently grabbed the now upside-down girl around the ankles.

"Now lift me up." I obeyed dutifully, raising her head and hands a foot above the rug which was covering a hardwood floor underneath.

"Now, please walk around the room with me." I did, knowing that in a few days my lower back would probably remind me of this moment. But it's always worth it.

Trust. That made her want me to lift her and carry her around the room.

Fearless and not fully aware of the consequences to her head or neck if I dropped her, there she hung, upside down with only my grip securing her safety as we walked around.

Trust. Total dependence, in this case, on me.

Which leads to another character trait that will totally change our perspective—optimism.

An optimistic view in the midst of the peril of being dropped headfirst on the floor, which allowed her to take in the world around her with an expectancy of good.

And it was trust and optimism that allowed Ellie Kate to not only look at her new upside-down world but also embrace it and enjoy it—not giving a moment's thought to her safety, knowing that she would be all right.

It's the picture David painted in Psalm 23. It's a picture of trust. A picture to depend upon. A picture that allows us to embrace an optimistic and enthusiastic outlook of our life and whatever each day may bring our way.

But more than that it's a picture of a God who can be trusted, a God who can be depended upon, and a God who calls us, with Him, to an optimistic and enthusiastic view of life—because it is lived with Him.

I don't know what you went through yesterday that was less than encouraging. I don't know what you've gone through that may still be painting a picture of your view of God and your life. But when the past begins to paint the picture of our future—well, it's time to paint a different picture. We can learn from the past but should keep it in its proper place and not repeat it in our lives and the lives of others.

Trust and optimism—in the God who has our future.

IMPACT APPLICATION: Let that new picture of your life—the new view that trusts with an eternal optimism—begin today.

AUGUST 12

CHANGING TIMES

Jesus Christ is the same yesterday, today, and forever. **Hebrews 13:8**

SOME OF US MIGHT remember the words of Bob Dylan from years ago—"The times, they are a-changin'."

Today's reality for many of us is a bit more of the same. For a dear friend, it's a change from health to hospital because of a massive heart attack. For a nephew, it's a moment of career change as he graduates from the police academy, earning him the challenge and uncertainty of serving the community and confronting the troubles in our streets. For a couple strained to the breaking point, it's a changing relationship as the blade of divorce looms. For a beloved granddaughter, it's a change in a young person's view of immortality when faced with exploratory surgery for a problem of uncertain origin.

Everywhere we turn and in everything happening around us, the times are changing—too often spinning out of our control and beyond our reach as the clock strikes half-past some late hour. In the world, it is and has always been that way. Throughout history and to today, some would argue that the times are better, others that they are worse, but really they're just changing—and in the end are different. And too often uncomfortably different.

And where do we look for direction to find our way in these changing times?

Frederick Buechner once wrote, "All real art comes from that deepest self—painting, writing, music, and dance. . . . Our truest prayers come from there, too. . . . And I think that from there also come our best dreams and our times of gladdest playing."

That place of "deepest self." That place where the values that have guided us in the best of times and the worst of times have resided. A place where faith has restored us when the world came crashing in. A place from where our prayers are lifted with a sense of expectation and wonder as we survey God's creation all around us. A place of returning to all that is true and good, honest and childlike.

There's only one place where that is ensured for us—in Jesus Christ. As the writer of Hebrews reminds us, "Jesus Christ is the same yesterday, today, and forever."

Go there. Stay there.

 IMPACT APPLICATION: When's the last time you returned to that deepest place in your heart where all you know to be true, right, pure, lovely, admirable, excellent, and praiseworthy dwells? When is the last time, in the midst of whatever was going on around you, that you turned to the One who never changes and is always there—Jesus Christ? It's time. It's always time.

CACKLING LIGHT

You are the light of the world—like a city on a hilltop that cannot be hidden. . . . In the same way, let your good deeds shine out for all to see, so that everyone will praise your heavenly Father. **Matthew 5:14, 16**

YOU'RE REMINDED of it especially on glorious mornings but also on days that seem a bit less inspiring.

Light.

While my son Nathan and I were talking on the phone several years ago, I could hear my younger granddaughter, Ellie Kate, in the background cooing and jabbering away from the security of her daddy's lap. She probably got really excited when she realized at some point that her granddaddy was on the phone. So much so that when Nathan put the phone to her ear, she turned it loose!

Broken and loud, high-pitched and panting laughter—cackling, you might say—at the sound of her granddaddy's voice. If I had needed a dose of light in my day, she would have provided it. Instead, she increased the brightness of mine. Between moments of Nathan's and my own laughter, when he would momentarily reclaim the phone from Ellie Kate, the cackling would subside—until Ellie Kate and I would talk again, and the pure, bright light of excited utterances would come again.

I wonder when the true beauty and light created within each of us was last revealed in our own or someone else's darkness. Maybe it needs a gentle stoking to burn a little brighter for all the world to see.

In her recent book *And One More Thing before You Go*, Maria Shriver offers this advice from a speech her father, battling Alzheimer's disease, had shared several years earlier: "Break your mirrors! . . . In our society that's so self-absorbed, begin to look less at yourself and more at each other! You'll get more satisfaction from having improved your neighborhood, your town, your state, your country, and your fellow human beings than you'll ever get from your figure, your car, your house, or your credit rating."

It's easy to become absorbed in our own lives and problems—and the darkness that surrounds us. But Jesus calls His followers to be "the light of the world" for all to see.

In the days ahead, take a look around and find a few places where it seems the darkness may have set in, and then, in a mirror-breaking moment, let that light shine on the darkness in the world and in the lives around us.

IMPACT APPLICATION: Whether or not you find the days ahead sunny, joyous, or peaceful, let your light so shine on the people you meet that their lives can't help but be lifted into the glorious sunshine of all God intended them to be.

BURN THE BOATS

He said to the crowd, "If any of you wants to be my follower, you must give up your own way, take up your cross daily, and follow me. If you try to hang on to your life, you will lose it. But if you give up your life for my sake, you will save it." **Luke 9:23-24**

I HEARD A DEAR FRIEND share a story recently that may be part legend and part truth—regardless, it is worth embracing.

It seems that when Hernando Cortes landed in Mexico in 1519, it was with the view toward conquering and claiming the land for Spain (which he eventually did). However, when he and his band of roughly five hundred men landed, they realized they were outnumbered by a margin of over three hundred to one. And with that sobering knowledge, they stood there together—after having just taken their first steps onto the shores of Mexico. They arrived in eleven ships that were still anchored in the sea a short way off from the shoreline. The men's inclination, which they pleaded to Cortez, was to return to the boats and wait for reinforcements so as to avoid certain annihilation.

Instead, Cortez looked them straight in the eyes and said, "Burn the boats."

In the Scripture above, Jesus is similarly saying, "Burn the boats. Stop looking for a way out of what I am continually calling you to do. Follow Me. Stop looking for a bridge to safety, an escape route, or a comfortable assignment. Follow Me. Stop looking for a way to abdicate your duty. Follow Me. Deny yourself. Take up your cross daily. Follow Me."

We can all identify with those men standing on the shores of Mexico. In so many moments of so many of our days, we are confronted with obstacles seemingly too big to overcome or too tough to handle and face. It may be something unexpected occurring at the office. Maybe a relationship has soured and we just want out. Maybe circumstances have caused what has always been a dream to begin to seem like a nightmare. So we look for excuses that will allow us to turn away, to do something else, to escape, and perhaps in the process to simply save face.

But what is it that Christ would have us do? Is He still calling us to stand and press on? Does He still seem to be in the fray and perhaps we just need to hear His voice of encouragement reminding us that He is still there?

With Christ on our side, with Christ standing on whatever shore we've just landed on, we can "burn the boats" and head out in full commitment, knowing that whatever occurs with Him in charge will ultimately be for our eternal good and His glory.

 IMPACT APPLICATION: Follow Him, burn the boats, and watch what He will do!

LUKE

The man answered, "'You must love the LORD your God with all your heart, all your soul, all your strength, and all your mind.' And, 'Love your neighbor as yourself.'" **Luke 10:27**

AT THE START OF THE DAY, I reflected that our five-year-old basset hound, Luke, was probably sleeping in his nest at the veterinary hospital at the University of Florida, hooked up to a multitude of IVs designed to control and heal the disease which had dramatically threatened the promise of a long and normal life.

Or was that ever promised him? Or us, for that matter?

I had visited Luke each day of that week's exploratory surgery. I prayed with him, petted him, asked God to remove the tumor and to heal him, wiped drool from his face, kissed him, thanked the vets, and prepared to one day say good-bye. *Not now, though*, I remember thinking. *One day, in the distant future and after a long and normal life.*

I wondered when the last good-bye would be. I would want to make it special. But how could it be any more special than every moment we have had with him in the few short years he has blessed our lives?

If Luke had one day to live, would it look any different than the others? Would we do anything different than we have done every day of his precious life? Would it be filled with any less love and affection for him? Would it be filled with any less love from him to us?

When a teacher of religious law asked Jesus what he should do "to inherit eternal life," Jesus pointed to the law the teacher already knew. The answer was right in front of him: Love the Lord your God, and love your neighbor as yourself. When the teacher wasn't satisfied with this answer and asked Jesus who his neighbor was, Jesus told the man about a foreigner, a Samaritan, who gave life-saving service to someone left for dead, someone who couldn't repay him and who may have hated him if they had met in any other context. It was a life-saving act of love that Christ calls us to every day.

Loving God and loving others isn't something we save up for special occasions. It should be something that defines our lives at all times. Today, every day, every moment.

In some ways, when we know we will have to say good-bye, whether for a short time or a while, we feel like we need to mark moments as special to add the significance we think they deserve. But if we truly embrace a life of loving God and loving others in each moment, we can live without regrets—even if tomorrow doesn't come.

IMPACT APPLICATION: We're not promised tomorrow in our lives here on earth. Why not follow Christ's admonition and love God and love others?

AUGUST 16

A WALK IN THE WOODS

At that time Jesus said, "I praise you, Father, Lord of heaven and earth, because you have hidden these things from the wise and learned, and revealed them to little children. Yes, Father, for this is what you were pleased to do." **Matthew 11:25-26, NIV**

WHEN SUPPER, a few slides on the zipline, and a couple of games were behind us at the home of a relative, our two granddaughters eagerly exclaimed that they wanted to walk back to our house with us.

They led the way, trotting a few paces ahead of us, imagining themselves as beautiful thoroughbred racehorses. Smiling from our rear-guard position, we followed them home along the narrow lanes dotted with houses.

Less than halfway along the mile-and-a-half journey, Ellie Kate's younger and shorter-striding legs gave way to a ride on Granddaddy's shoulders for the rest of the trek. We did our best to keep up with Hannah as we trotted along at the urging of Ellie Kate's rider's crop. It was one of those moments where the miraculous broke in and took us by surprise.

But we often miss those miraculous moments because we're not looking for them or because we're looking for the drama of a Red Sea parting to qualify as a miraculous moment. God is always working supernaturally in our lives, causing miraculous moments to occur—in relationships, in noticing the wonder of His creation, or in lifting a life that needs it.

When was the last time you saw the miraculous in the common occurrences of your life? When was the last time you stopped long enough to look? When was the last time you spent a moment with a loved one and were given the gift of seeing the miraculous in the midst of the ordinary?

Moments like that don't cost you anything. You can't buy them, even though too often that's the way we think. They are all around us—and in the buzz and bustle of believing we are living the life we were meant to live, we miss them.

It is wisdom—godly wisdom—to see the miraculous in the common, because that is often where God hides it. It pleases Him to hide the miraculous "from the wise and learned"—or at least those who think they are—and to "[reveal] them to little children."

You won't find the miraculous in the places society would point you to. It isn't a by-product of intelligence, age, or authority.

But perhaps you will find it on a walk in the woods.

 IMPACT APPLICATION: Take the time to be quietly guided by the hand of the God who created you, and begin to see the miraculous in the common and everyday moments you will find everywhere.

GOATS ON THE ROOF

> We now have this light shining in our hearts, but we ourselves are like fragile clay jars containing this great treasure. This makes it clear that our great power is from God, not from ourselves. **2 Corinthians 4:7**

"LOOK, GRAN! They gave me a blanket and pillow and a bottle of water!"

Ellie Kate's amazed voice painted the picture of what she found neatly placed in her seat as we boarded the plane a few years ago to spend a few days in the mountains with her Mimi. Moments later she received her first Sprite while waiting to take off. Not too long after those experiences, she would discover the tray table in the arm of her seat, and when airborne, cover it with an array of snacks and drinks as she looked with wonder out of her window at the light shining on the clouds billowing just below us.

Then as we drove up the mountain, there was a required stop for my long-awaited introduction to "Goats on the Roof." It really was a joy to watch Ellie Kate pedal a stationary bike that sent a quarter's worth of pellets in a tin cup along a pulley system to four already-well-fed goats waiting on the top of one of the rooftops of this "must-stop" roadside attraction.

And then, in our few days together, I would experience other important moments, treasured moments from God, with her and Mimi. One such moment occurred as Ellie Kate came out of the bedroom one night in the mountains to say good-night one more time, and we talked about what we would do tomorrow. "Well," I responsibly began, "I first have to do my . . . and then I have some other things I need to work on."

"But Gran," she said, "you're supposed to be on vacation."

She had a point. And I had a change of attitude.

We get caught up in trying to keep up with our neighbors and the societal values of "more is better." Stuff still happens to us, things change, and people come and go. Things get confusing, people misunderstand us, and relationships strain. Disappointments, heartaches, and tragedies show us how fragile life and we are, as they often bring us to the point of despair.

But honestly, friends, in the face of my younger granddaughter's outlook on what is important and the reminders of the apostle Paul—of the treasure of Jesus Christ, the light shining within us, providing us with His all-surpassing power and amazing love—why do we worry?

What are we trying to keep up with that is worth more than Him and the blessings He has placed in our lives—like granddaughters and "Goats on the Roof"?

IMPACT APPLICATION: Go boldly into today and every day, knowing that the treasure of the light of Christ we have within us is what we really need to guide and direct our steps.

AUGUST 18

HOMELESS AT HARVARD

The LORD said to Samuel, "Don't judge by his appearance or height, for I have rejected him. The LORD doesn't see things the way you see them. People judge by outward appearance, but the LORD looks at the heart." **1 Samuel 16:7**

HE WAS CROUCHED IN A CORNER. A dirty hand stretched toward us from what was left of his ragged coat sleeve. It was perhaps the only space he felt he could claim as his own, just one of the too many empty faces lining the busy sidewalk in Cambridge, Massachusetts, begging for change to survive another day.

His location was a study in contrasts. A little more than a hundred feet away stood the noble gates to Harvard University, where our son, Nathan, attended law school. There was no way to avoid this man as Nathan and I walked along. It was more than disconcerting for those of us who had to pass this man's way every day, and for me it was a painful reminder of days gone by.

My thoughts drifted to a time years ago when I had been like him.

Yet I never took up a station to beg. I never let myself look like him. I never held a "Will Work For Food" sign that passersby could scoff at. But I understood the feeling of homelessness. Of being destitute. Penniless. Without family. All alone.

I was a teenager, trying to finish my last two years of high school. It never crossed my mind to squat on a street corner and beg for help. I was too concerned with what others might think. Instead I fought to survive by finding odd jobs—mowing lawns, pumping gas, bagging groceries, washing dishes—between classes, baseball, and basketball.

A chilly breeze interrupted my reflections, just when his face lifted and hand shook as he extended it in our direction. We couldn't pretend anymore that we didn't see him. We had seen his face, and he had looked into ours. *He'll only spend what I give him on a cheap bottle of wine*, I thought. It was a judgment I'm not proud of. It betrayed the state of my heart.

As we stood there on the cold sidewalk, Nathan broke the tension by sharing a word of wisdom and a compassion he has had for others as long as I have known him. "You know, Dad," he offered, "I think God is more concerned with the response of our hearts in the face of need than with our trying to judge what that man would do with our help."

Nathan and I reached into our wallets to share what was now in both of our hearts and touched the hand of a new friend. And in that moment, I believe, we touched the hand of God.

IMPACT APPLICATION: God calls us to touch the world for and with Him, not to judge it. Whose hand can you touch today?

DUCKVILLE

Those who trust in the LORD will find new strength. They will soar high on wings like eagles. They will run and not grow weary. They will walk and not faint. **Isaiah 40:31**

THE SUNSHINE HAD FILLED THE DAY, but I was having a little trouble seeing it that morning. I thought I knew why, but I still couldn't seem to get my eyes open wide enough to see it.

Søren Kierkegaard, a Danish philosopher, tells the story about a make-believe town where only ducks lived. It was Sunday morning in Duckville, and all the ducks were waddling down the street to the First Duckist Church. They waddled down the aisles, into the pews, and squatted in their seats. The duck minister took his place at the pulpit, and the church service began. The Scripture text for the morning was taken from the Duck Bible and read: "Ducks, God has given you wings—you can fly. Ducks, because you have wings, you can fly like the eagles. Because God has given you wings, no fences can confine you; no land animals can trap you. Ducks! God has given you wings!"

And all the ducks shouted together, "Amen!" And then they all got up and waddled out of church and back to their homes. Ugh! What a waste of a perfectly good Scripture, promise, day, and life.

Well, I've got to be honest with you, that was a bit like me that morning. In my better moments, I knew the sunshine of God's potential for my day was there—but I was not able to see, feel, or believe it. I wonder if you have ever been there. Ever had one of those mornings or days when you knew you should be flying through life the way God meant for you to do, but because of whatever problems were bothering you, you chose waddling instead?

A few years ago a friend of mine shared that when confronted with a problem that wouldn't seem to go away, he found that more often than not the problem was not the problem. What he found was the problem was his attitude toward the problem. And the result was waddling through life. Soaring would require remembering that "God . . . is able, through his mighty power at work within us, to accomplish infinitely more than we might ask or think" (Ephesians 3:20).

It's always our choice—waddling or soaring. In our better moments we know which God is calling us to. I suggest then that we embrace our better moments.

 IMPACT APPLICATION: The Scripture says we "will soar high on wings like eagles," so what's with the waddling? Soar!

AUGUST 20

MORE THAN
A DREAMER

If you keep quiet at a time like this, deliverance and relief for the Jews will arise from some other place, but you and your relatives will die. Who knows if perhaps you were made queen for just such a time as this? **Esther 4:14**

IT'S A HARD THING to stop and look within when we're so busy. Yet it's those moments of introspection, realizing that God has placed us here at this particular time for a reason, that tend to refine the quality of our tomorrows.

That's what Queen Esther had to do after Mordecai told her of Haman's plan to have all the Jews in the kingdom killed. She had to reflect: she could do nothing while the dreams of her people were snuffed out, or she could use her platform to take action.

We all have dreams, but they remain just that if we don't act on them.

Martin Luther King Jr. was felled by an assassin's bullet and died on April 4, 1968, in Memphis, Tennessee. He had a dream for his children and for children everywhere in our nation. And he held a mirror to our nation—getting each person to look within.

Our dreams may not require that we hold a mirror before the nation to show it a face of prejudice, injustice, discrimination, and unspeakable hatred, but our dreams will require action. Without it, they will die within us, along with the reason we were created to live at this particular time with the platforms we have been given. The music we were meant to play may never be heard.

What dreams do you have that you still carry around? Dreams for happiness, security, family, peace in relationships and the world, an end to injustice in your community, or brighter lives for those living nearby?

Perhaps you hold a dream to do something you may not ultimately be good at, but the fulfillment in knowing you tried will be exhilarating. Pursuing your dream, and stepping onto the platforms God may have set before you, will at least allow you to be able to check just one more thing off your list so you won't have to look back and say, "I wish I had done that."

Perhaps you hold dreams to see your children or grandchildren succeed in following theirs. Or perhaps you dream to do that one thing others have discouraged you from doing and have characterized as silly or a waste of time.

Martin Luther King Jr. had a dream. I have a dream. You have a dream. Maybe many.

So what are we going to do with them?

 IMPACT APPLICATION: We have all been created by God for such a time as this that we are living in. What are we doing with the dreams and platforms we've been given?

A WINNIE-THE-POOH KIND OF DAY

Trust in the LORD with all your heart; do not depend on your own understanding. Seek his will in all you do, and he will show you which path to take. **Proverbs 3:5-6**

IT CAN ONLY BE DESCRIBED as a Winnie-the-Pooh kind of day, blustery and uncertain. You're standing in the fairway, 180 yards from a narrow, elevated green sloping from back to front and guarded on the front and left by water and on the back and right by yawning bunkers.

An errant tee shot came to rest on the far left side of the fairway, now requiring an approach shot that must navigate around a majestic oak tree standing in your direct line of flight.

Years ago I would have surveyed that scene with only one acceptable outcome: the ball landing softly on the green and rolling directly into the cup.

But before making that shot, I suggest that you invoke what a good friend describes as the NATO principle: "not attached to outcome." The result is you will find joy in the journey. A journey of endless possibilities, of finding other paths to the same or a similar outcome, or perhaps of a different outcome than the one you had planned. A journey in which you notice all the blessings around you.

I'll bet you've already planned your "shots" for the week. Schedule set. People to see. Calls to make. Meetings to attend. Goals in place.

I wonder how far back in your memory you have to go to find that moment when all of your best-laid plans didn't work out as you had envisioned. Planning for tomorrow by using the gifts and abilities God has given you is necessary and important. But the outcomes of tomorrow, which you plan for today, are about as certain as holing out that shot I described earlier. The only thing certain about tomorrow is that God will be there to journey with you.

May I suggest a crisply struck six iron to get the ball gently on the front edge of the green? Oh, you did, but it rolled off the front slope and into the water? Not the outcome I would have intended either.

But did you notice the mother duck and her five babies paddling their way through the now rippling pond? When we are "not attached to outcome," we can better treasure the moments of beauty that are all around us, even when things do not go the way we had planned.

IMPACT APPLICATION: Our security for living comes not in knowing the outcome, not in planning for every possibility, but in going on the journey with God. We find security in knowing that no matter the unexpected twists and turns, we will be fine because we face them with a God who wants the best for us and is ultimately in control of it all.

AUGUST 22

IF TOMORROW NEVER COMES

Look here, you who say, "Today or tomorrow we are going to a certain town and will stay there a year. We will do business there and make a profit." How do you know what your life will be like tomorrow? Your life is like the morning fog—it's here a little while, then it's gone. What you ought to say is, "If the Lord wants us to, we will live and do this or that." **James 4:13-15**

RAINY DAYS SEEM to bring out that reflective spirit that dwells within all of us—at least they do that for me. Today is no exception as I sit here while rain falls softly outside my window and reflect again upon something I really don't like to think about.

If tomorrow never comes.

Books have been written about it. Songs have been sung from generation to generation to remind us. The lesson of that simple statement penetrates our hearts when loved ones leave us all too soon.

If tomorrow never comes.

From wherever the reminder enters our life, it always seems to cause us to pause, vowing to commit to change the way we approach the rest of today and all our tomorrows and the important people and things which are a part of them.

And yet when tomorrow does come, the urgency of the reminder seems to have waned, the penetrating clarity of the moment is forgotten, and our vow to change is set aside as simply another item on a long list of intentions. And then words like those of Jim Keller poignantly remind us to not let that happen: "Say what you want to say when you have the feeling and the chance. My deepest regrets are the things I did not do, the opportunities missed and the things unsaid."

Other reminders of the brevity of life often come when a trip takes me away from Lynda, when a time together with our children ends, or when the days slip by too fast when company is with us, knowing the day they will return home is just around the corner.

How do your reminders enter your life?

They often come in the aftermath of the scrambles of busyness, during which the important people, moments, and things are set aside, lost, and relegated to tomorrow. Our intentions are good, aren't they? We really will spend some time together, take a trip to somewhere we've never been, play a game as a family, read a book, and take a walk—tomorrow.

But what if tomorrow never comes?

Just something for us to think about—and to do something about—today. In case tomorrow never comes.

 IMPACT APPLICATION: If tomorrow never comes. The truth is that there will be that very moment for every one of us. Why not live today as if that moment were now?

JUMP IN A HOLE

These righteous ones will reply, "Lord, when did we ever see you hungry and feed you? Or thirsty and give you something to drink? Or a stranger and show you hospitality? Or naked and give you clothing? When did we ever see you sick or in prison and visit you?" And the King will say, "I tell you the truth, when you did it to one of the least of these my brothers and sisters, you were doing it to me!"
Matthew 25:37-40

HE WAS A DEAR FRIEND, teacher, and mentor to many. He was a great husband, dad, and granddad. And if you could have gotten him to sit long enough to watch one, Hal Ingman would have loved those home makeover television shows where the stories of families needing a hand up—and getting that hand up—are shared. That's what Hal, his children, grandchildren, Lynda, and Amy would have talked about had he not left this earth, and us, too soon over two decades ago. He was helping a young college student, a friend of his granddaughter, jump-start her car when his heart gave way. He never seemed to struggle with the question so many around us wrestle with each day: What will you do with the rest of your life? He was too busy living his by helping others live theirs.

Hal's life reminds me of the story of a guy who was walking along and fell into a hole. A doctor came by and looked down, and the guy asked, "Hey, Doctor, can you help me out of this hole?" The doctor filled out a prescription, tossed it into the hole, and went on. In a little while a minister came by. "Hey, Pastor, can you help me out of this hole?" The minister wrote a prayer on a piece of paper, tossed it into the hole, and walked on.

And then a friend came by; and when he heard the plea for help, the friend jumped into the hole. The guy who had fallen into the hole asked, "Why in the world did you do that? Now we're both in here!" To which his friend responded, "Yeah, I know, but I've been here before, and I know the way out."

Here's the question for you today: "What in the world will I do with the rest of my life?" Why not follow the example of our friend, Hal, and help that person who is standing right in front of you and, if need be, jump into the hole they're in to help them out of it?

 IMPACT APPLICATION: Know anybody who's fallen into a hole? Why not jump into their lives like Hal did every day of his life and help them out? If you're like me you've probably been there before and know the way out.

AUGUST 24

MASTER OF THE UNBELIEVABLE

Nothing will be impossible with God. **Luke 1:37,** ESV

THE MORNING BREEZES continue to float through the trees outside my window. Their mesmerizing movement through the branches carries an exciting message of hope that the unbelievable just may be believable. And may be just around the corner.

It just seems that way this morning. It seems it ought to be that way every morning. It seems that the God who created the world would want it that way all the time.

Maybe it's because I woke up this morning with a smile on my face thinking of my two granddaughters and their optimistic approach to life.

Maybe it's because deep down I know that is the way it should always be for our children and grandchildren. And maybe it's because I wish that that was the way it was for me as a child.

Why *shouldn't* it be that way for us for the rest of our lives? We may need to cast off the sour examples of some people in our past. We may need to forgive some of them and also decide we don't want to perpetuate those sour examples or treatment of others ourselves.

We may need to simply accept that the God who created us planted the seeds of believing in the unbelievable deep within our hearts. That the God who created us wove optimism into our being. That the God who created us created us in His image. We may need to remember that the God who created us walked on water, parted the Red Sea, healed the sick, brought people back to life, died for us, and then rose for us.

For what? So we will wander through life defeated, afraid, in a listless stupor from nine to five and on half-empty? I hope not. It's not the way He meant for it to be. Not on your life! And certainly not on His life!

I don't know what you went through yesterday or during times many years ago. It matters but only in that it is a part of history. We can either learn from it and keep it in its proper place—the past—or we can repeat it in our lives and the lives of others.

I don't know what you're facing today. But I do know that the God who created us makes the unbelievable believable.

Wow! That's unbelievable . . . almost!

 IMPACT APPLICATION: Let the winds blowing through your life remind you that God is a master of the unbelievable. Children have a way of seeing that—let's take a lesson from them and believe in the unbelievable.

NEVERLAND

You intended to harm me, but God intended it all for good. He brought me to this position so I could save the lives of many people.
Genesis 50:20

"SECOND [STAR] to the right and straight on till morning."

I wonder what J. M. Barrie had in mind when he penned those words in his classic book *Peter Pan*.

Here we are, standing together on the threshold of a brand-new day, and I wonder what's in our hearts waiting to come out. What Neverland have you longed to fly to? What is it you can't seem to overcome in your life that is holding you back from becoming all you can be? What mold or stereotype has the culture fit you into or dragged you down to? What music within you has yet to be sung? What flower planted deep inside you—by the One who created you—has yet to bloom?

Wherever it is, God has given you the key to get there. It's part of God's plan of hope and a future for your life. And He—going with you—has all the strength and power you will need to get there. We may fall a few times along the way, but the way remains clear: "Second to the right and straight on till morning."

When God gave Joseph dreams of his being elevated above his brothers, his brothers sold him into slavery in Egypt. But God continued to bless Joseph in Egypt, even after he was wrongfully put in prison, and placed him in a position of authority over all Egypt. And sure enough, when a famine engulfed the entire ancient world, Joseph's brothers came to Egypt, looking for food. Joseph was able to save their lives thanks to God working in and through Joseph's abilities and circumstances.

Joseph's brothers eventually feared that Joseph would seek revenge for what they did to him, but he told them, "Don't be afraid of me. Am I God, that I can punish you? You intended to harm me, but God intended it all for good. He brought me to this position so I could save the lives of many people" (Genesis 50:19-20). Joseph recognized that it was God who had given him his dreams, and it was God who—even in Joseph's years in slavery and prison—gave him the strength to realize those dreams.

We may not always feel God's strength carrying us through, but He has promised us, like He promised the apostle Paul, that "My grace is all you need. My power works best in weakness" (2 Corinthians 12:9). What dreams do you need to pursue today—in God's strength?

"Second to the right and straight on till morning."

Trusting God is the way. See you in Neverland!

 IMPACT APPLICATION: God stands ready to help you get to where He created and intended for you to be. He placed the key within your hands.

AUGUST 26

THE PRESIDENT
WHO BOWED

The LORD has made everything for His own purposes. **Proverbs 16:4**

IF THE STORY IS TRUE as it has been passed down through history, the twentieth president of the United States of America would have been extremely busy in this season, when children of all ages all across the nation return to classrooms to begin yet another year of formal education.

As legend has it, President James Garfield had what many viewed as a most unusual habit. Whenever he was approached by a little child while out walking, he would bow to the child with great respect and dignity. In that gesture, the president, who served for only eight months before falling to an assassin's bullet, was treating the child similar to a head of state or foreign dignitary. When asked why he felt it necessary to behave in such a fashion, he responded, "Because no one knows who's buttoned inside that little jacket or dress."

And it's true. No one knows the potential wrapped inside the body of a little child. No one knows the platforms that child will stand on someday as a leader of mankind; a pillar of our community, state, nation, or world; or something else.

By the same logic, no one knows the potential wrapped inside each one of us awakening this morning to a brand-new day. A "great day," as my bride described it, with a smile and lilt to her voice in her greeting to me on one of many mornings. She could give no particular reason why she said that, other than the reliable intuition of her heart that it was yet another day for each of us, full of opportunity and possibility.

She's right, you know. It's a great day for each of us to venture into those vast untapped areas of our lives. Areas that perhaps we have never even considered as being within our reach yet which lie within us. Pools of potential lying just beneath the surface of our awareness, waiting to be discovered yet too often clouded by the problems of our day, anxieties about our futures, personal or family concerns, troubles at the office and on the job, or financial stress.

I don't know what the rest of your life looks like. I don't know what the lives will look like of each of our children who are beginning a new year of school. But I do know that each of those lives—and yours—was created for a purpose by a perfect God who makes no mistakes.

It's a great day. Live it with all the possibilities within you.

 IMPACT APPLICATION: Were he here today, I am certain President Garfield would bow to each of you. In his stead, allow me to do so, acknowledging all the potential that God has placed within you.

ELLIE'S SAFE PLACE

You are my hiding place; you protect me from trouble. You surround me with songs of victory. **Psalm 32:7**

ELLIE KATE'S fourth birthday celebration lasted eleven days.

Eleven!

And at her request, the party's theme was Ariel from Disney's *The Little Mermaid*, her favorite princess at the time. Cake, balloons, invitations, and decorations—all Ariel.

When it was all said and done, however, she turned to her dad and announced, "Daddy, when I'm five, I want my birthday to be about *you*! I want your picture to be on my cake and on the balloons and cards and on everything!"

Then, turning to me, she exclaimed, "And Gran, when I am six, I want my birthday to be about you! Your picture on the cake and balloons and cards and everything!"

When she is with those two men she wanted to honor, she always feels safe and secure. She never is, or feels, threatened by them and never experiences or is threatened by any wrong or violence. She always is greeted by those two men with a smile, an instant hug, and a lift up onto a made-to-fit shoulder.

Two men in her life whom she trusts and views as "safe places," where she can always come when she feels anxious or scared or when things don't seem quite right and where she will be treated gently and respectfully when something needs to change. Places where she can throw an occasional tantrum, knowing that they won't throw one back at her. These special men love her with a love she can always feel in their words, smiles, expressions, and touch.

Don't you wish that was the case for every child God creates?

Perhaps there are those around you who need one of those "safe places" in their lives. Perhaps you are supposed to be, or can be, their safe place. Perhaps they *want* you to be their safe place. You can't just tell them you are—but instead they will know from the way you treat them whether you can be trusted to be that "safe place" or not.

Turns out our pictures weren't on her cakes when those fifth and sixth birthdays rolled around, but Ellie Kate shared all the affirmation we would ever need from her when she declared who she wanted her next birthdays to be about. It was a reminder and a call to always be a place she knows is there, a place where she can go, where she will always be loved, never harmed, always understood, gently guided and spoken to, and will always feel safe.

Whether or not people have one will make all the difference in their lives—for good or not—and for generation after generation after generation.

IMPACT APPLICATION: Perhaps someone you know—or have yet to know—needs a "safe place." Perhaps you can be that "safe place" they need.

AUGUST 28

NEVER ALONE

I look up to the mountains—does my help come from there? My help comes from the LORD, who made heaven and earth! **Psalm 121:1-2**

IT'S IN THE MORNING HEADLINES—all the stuff the print media tells us matters. Then we'll turn on our television sets and hear from local and national broadcasters about all that stuff that matters. Then on the way to work or an appointment, we'll hear from station after station on our radio about all the stuff that should matter.

Really? Is that the stuff that really matters?

If left to the voices in the world around us, we would spend hours in front of our television sets watching championship events in sports in the fall, winter, spring, and summer while our families keep themselves busy with other things, waiting for us to spend time with them. Or we'd watch politicians make promises on the floor of the Senate or House chamber or on the campaign trail that they have no intention of keeping.

And all the while we struggle to climb mountains or cross valleys before us. We try to find time in the midst of all that is going on for what we know are the important things of our life—God, family, and a satisfying career where we feel we're making a difference. And then we face the uncertainty of all that looms before us and wonder what really does matter.

I wonder, though, if what really matters most is that through all of that, we will never walk alone. Through all of that, we walk with a God who calls us to more than mindless enthusiasm for meaningless games, self-centeredness, worry, and fear. We walk with a God who calls us to truth, integrity, service, and hope. A God who knit us in our mother's womb and was with us when we were born. A God who knows what our childhood was like. He was with us on our best days and in our darkest moments.

With that assurance, no matter what we face or how much a world lost in meaningless priorities seems to be spinning out of control around us, we can remember, in the words of the song from Rodgers and Hammerstein's musical *Carousel*, "[we'll] never walk alone."

 IMPACT APPLICATION: What matters in life is that the God who was with you on your happiest days and in your saddest moments, the God who knows your unkept promises and your failures, is always with you. Never forget: you are never alone. Now that really matters.

LET THE SHRIEKING BEGIN

Dear friends, since God loved us that much, we surely ought to love each other. No one has ever seen God. But if we love each other, God lives in us, and his love is brought to full expression in us. **1 John 4:11-12**

FEW THINGS MEASURE UP to the spirit-lifting greeting I experienced the other day, and I would wish such a greeting for you every day. I was returning home from Tampa after spending the day with our son, Nathan, as he was getting a medical checkup. A trip anywhere around or through that area is never complete—or allowed—without getting another "fix" from a visit with our two gifts from God—Hannah and Ellie Kate—my two granddaughters.

As I walked in the front entryway of their home that evening, two-year-old Ellie Kate was the first to notice my entrance. The next scene was something approaching indescribable, even without the embellishment my heart holds now. Her eyes gleamed as an ear-to-ear smile broke across her face, and she began to shriek—and between shrieks, scream—"Gran! Gran! Gran!" and yes, "Gran!" over and over.

While she filled the air, and my heart, with her melody, she simultaneously jumped up and down, inching toward me before finally breaking into a full-fledged sprint with hands held high until she was safely nestled in my arms. The shrieking and laughter continued unabated, yet now mixed with an occasional hug and kiss.

Hannah heard the commotion from the other room and realized what was going on, and she burst onto the scene with her own screams of joy, jumping into my now-readied other arm while covering me with her own special brand of hugs and kisses. For five full minutes I held both girls in my arms, as my heart continued to fill, while they told me they loved me without once saying the words.

I wish that joy for you—and for everyone—but it is often a far cry from the way the world seems to operate. But maybe that kind of world, that kind of joy, begins with you and with me.

All I know is that I'm still smiling this morning. I can still hear the shrieks and can still feel the joy in my heart that Hannah and Ellie Kate showered me with that day.

Maybe it really can start with us. Who do you know who could use a spirit lift, a reminder that they are loved and welcome?

Let the shrieking begin!

IMPACT APPLICATION: Can you imagine what our days would be like if we started each of them with that kind of greeting? Can you imagine how someone else would feel after they were with us if we gave them that kind of greeting? Let someone know they are loved today.

AUGUST 30

SPACE MOUNTAIN

The LORD is my light and my salvation—so why should I be afraid?
The LORD is my fortress, protecting me from danger, so why should
I tremble? When evil people come to devour me, when my enemies
and foes attack me, they will stumble and fall. Though a mighty army
surrounds me, my heart will not be afraid. Even if I am attacked, I will
remain confident. **Psalm 27:1-3**

I HAD BEEN THERE BEFORE. The feelings were the same. The uncertainty, the anxiety about what was around the next bend.

It reminded me of what it felt like the first time we rode Space Mountain at Disney World in Orlando. Along the walls of the passageway where we waited and walked in the line approaching the beginning of the ride, there were strategically placed monitors flashing images of the ride that was in progress which I did my best to distract Lynda's attention from for fear she would bolt. After we were securely buckled into the car, the entry doors opened to reveal a complete absence of light, an environment of icy utter darkness in which you couldn't see your hand in front of your face, with cold air all too frequently laced with blood-curdling screams of other riders who also paid for this privilege of riding into the dark unknown.

The car began a slow ascent upward and then hurtled downward while throwing us to the left and right through turns which the darkness refused to reveal ahead of time. The screams, previously everywhere, now seemed to emanate solely from our car, providing an ironic assurance that my family was surviving this amusing ride. And then it was over.

I remember too many of those moments like Space Mountain in my life. How about you? Hurtling headlong into darkness and being thrown to the right and left by the circumstances and people of the world. And no matter how many times I remind myself that God is my light and must simply have me on the anvil, molding, shaping, and readying me for future purposes He is already aware of, the icy darkness of uncertainty still prevails.

There seems to be no immunity from these feelings creeping into our lives, but what we need to remember when they occur is that no matter what we face, no matter how many times we fall, the One David wrote about in the psalm above is there to lift us up: "The LORD is my light and my salvation—so why should I be afraid? . . . He will place me out of reach on a high rock" (Psalm 27:1, 5).

And as the ride screeched to a merciful end, the doors opened revealing the sunshine that was there all the time and the light of His marvelous love.

 IMPACT APPLICATION: "My light and my salvation." May we sense the certainty of the light of the Lord, as David did, in all of our "Space Mountains."

T-SHIRT MEMORIES

Every time I think of you, I give thanks to my God. **Philippians 1:3**

"SCOTT!" I had heard Lynda's urgent tone before, usually forecasting some impending involvement on my part. "I need you to go through these four bags of old T-shirts to see which ones you want to keep or give away."

Simple enough, I thought as I obediently climbed the staircase to begin what should be an easy enough task. Simple enough, that is, until memories began to wash over me as I went through them—college baseball coaching days at Santa Fe Community College and the University of Florida; the 1991 College World Series; Nathan's Little League, high school, college, and law school days; family trips; community service projects; and more. With my eyes now dry, I handed Lynda a short stack of ten shirts to give away, carefully carrying a seventy-plus armload of T-shirts and memories to a place of safety on an empty shelf high up in my closet. I just couldn't bear to let them go, and if you must label me anything, I choose to be known as an "incurable romantic."

Memories. Our connection to times gone by, indelibly etched reminders of our roots, family, friends, relationships, careers, joys, disappointments, and sorrows. Memories on our shelves, in our photo albums and videos, throughout the rooms of our lives, imbedded in the wrinkles of our faces and in the beats of our hearts. Memories that are ever increasing as time flies by. Memories of who we are and were and of things we are working on to change, and too many to count of moments and people which we cherish.

Our lives may seem to be flying by, but the gift of today remains the same as it has always been. And our memories will not be made in planning for our tomorrows, in reflecting on our yesterdays, or in dwelling on the years that remain. But our memories will be made in living and enjoying all the richness and fullness of today.

Our memories will be made in the extra moments of affirmation and nurturing we take with a loved one or a stranger, even when the moment is not easy. They'll be made in saying yes to our children or a friend when our arms are too weary. They'll be made, not in the T-shirts we gather, but in the time spent with family and friends digging deeply into this day for all it contains. Because the truth is that the T-shirts we carry into tomorrow, and the memories they embody, will well reflect the living of our lives today.

Those T-shirts I tried to purge that day—well, they're still there on the shelf in my closet. Memories.

 IMPACT APPLICATION: The memories we'll cherish and cling to in our tomorrows are made in our todays. Don't miss the opportunities to make them.

SEPTEMBER 1

TRUSTED TO MAKE
A DIFFERENCE

I know how to live on almost nothing or with everything. I have learned the secret of living in every situation, whether it is with a full stomach or empty, with plenty or little. For I can do everything through Christ, who gives me strength. **Philippians 4:12-13**

"GONE TOO SOON" might be one way to think of the precious life of Mallory Lynn Code, and I suspect that idea has crossed the minds of everyone who knew her.

Gone too soon. Perhaps, but not before she showed us how to embrace whatever confronts us—and refuse to let whatever it is define our lives, as she refused to let cystic fibrosis define hers.

Gone too soon. Maybe, but not before she touched the world around her with an infectious smile, an inspirational, zealous, and courageous determination, and a life-changing example of relying on the strength of Jesus Christ.

She lived a life that included being embraced by a loving family and an untold number of devoted friends. She joined her sister on two high school state championship golf teams, and they both attended college on golf scholarships at the University of Florida, where Mallory received her degree a year before her death. Mallory represented the United States twice, once on the Junior Ryder Cup team and once on the Junior Solheim Cup team. She played in and won many amateur USGA events.

"My life is perfect in almost every way," she shared. "I've got this awesome family, awesome friends, and an awesome relationship with the Lord Jesus. I've got golf, dance—everything. I don't want to be the little sick girl out there."

Mallory realized all that she had—despite one thing that caused her some problems—and leaned on God to provide her with contentment for wherever she was and strength to get through whatever she faced. And in that regard, what we may remember most about this precious, winsome warrior is her clear and bold voice proclaiming her faith in her Savior, the Lord Jesus Christ. It was through Him that she found the courage and strength to walk on. It was through Him that she found contentment in every situation, never desiring more or better—just Him. That was enough. That was the best.

Even her death didn't stop her from making a difference. As an organ donor, just hours after passing into the arms of her heavenly Father, she was able to provide a second chance at life to a recipient. It doesn't surprise any of us who knew her that she was still changing lives even then.

Gone too soon. Perhaps, but our lives are fuller and the direction is clearer based upon the path she set before us.

IMPACT APPLICATION: Mallory understood that God could use even the platform of a debilitating disease to bring people into a trusting relationship with Christ. How much more should you and I use our platforms for today and every day?

NON-PERFECT
PERFECT MOMENTS

I am counting on the LORD; yes, I am counting on him. I have put my hope in his word. I long for the LORD more than sentries long for the dawn, yes, more than sentries long for the dawn. **Psalm 130:5-6**

"SAFE!"

The call and signal by American League first-base umpire Jim Joyce was emphatic and immediate.

And wrong.

The runner for the Cleveland Indians, Jason Donald, was out by a half-step for what should have been the final out to Detroit Tigers' Armando Galarraga's perfect game. It would have been just the twenty-first perfect game pitched in Major League Baseball history and the first ever by a Detroit Tigers pitcher.

Yet watching Armando Galarraga's reaction after the call, you would never have known that he had just been unfairly denied a place in baseball history. Jim Joyce, after reviewing the play after the game, admitted he blew the call.

Officially it will not be recognized as a perfect game. Unofficially it always will be a perfect game. And the way the two central figures handled that non-perfect perfect game may very well always be recognized as one of baseball's perfect moments. A non-perfect perfect moment.

Joyce, a respected twenty-two-year veteran umpire, tearfully and apologetically admitted to everyone, but most importantly to Armando Galarraga, that he made a mistake. And Galarraga was calm, classy, and forgiving, treating Jim Joyce with respect the moment that it happened and in every moment thereafter.

It's almost as if both men were showing us how to behave when things don't go our way. It is almost as if they both knew there are more important things in life. Both were disappointed, but both seemed to point to the reality that tomorrow is a new day—that just like their lives are not defined by this moment, our lives won't be by similar moments.

Their handling of a disappointing moment reminded us all of something much greater than winning or achievements. They reminded us that in the day-to-day moments that unfold, we have a chance to turn non-perfect moments into perfect ones. Where—no matter what happened or happens to us—we move on, forgive, put life in perspective, and remember that there is much left to do. We remember the promise of today's verse. Circumstances come and go, but we can trust and hope in the Lord forever.

How we react in disappointment is one of the chief ways we reflect where our trust lies. Do we believe that our circumstances have the final word? Or do we believe what James writes: "Humble yourselves before the Lord, and he will lift you up in honor" (James 4:10)? What we believe has a huge impact on how we behave, especially when things don't go our way.

 IMPACT APPLICATION: The lesson of the "non-perfect-perfect moment" is that—no matter what we've gone through—we put our trust in God, who has different priorities than this world.

SEPTEMBER 3

SOFTBALL TRUTH

Jesus said to the people who believed in him, "You are truly my disciples if you remain faithful to my teachings. And you will know the truth, and the truth will set you free." **John 8:31-32**

MY ELDER GRANDDAUGHTER, Hannah, is a truth-teller.

It was probably her speed and trying to hit the corner of the base just right that resulted in a crisis of conscience during a softball game when she was younger. Attempting to score on another teammate's hit, Hannah rounded third base heading for home and eventually scored. The umpire and the other team's third baseman both said she had touched third base.

But she knew differently. And so she went to her "safe-and-wise place" for help. She knew that there the whole matter would be made right.

She told her daddy that even though the others said she had touched third base, she knew she hadn't. Between gentle sobs she told him what had happened and asked, "Who should I tell?"

She wanted to make sure the truth prevailed. She hadn't touched third. She felt locked in a lie and wanted to be free.

With the game having moved well beyond that moment, her daddy (another truth-teller of long standing) was unable to help her correct the situation. He also knew that the answer "it was up to the umpire" wouldn't assuage her feelings. And it's not the right answer anyway. The truth is always the right answer.

"Who can I tell?" Hannah wanted the truth to prevail. It's freeing. The truth was meant to gush from each of us as it does from innocent children. The truth is all they know.

Until they are taught the ways of the world, which demand conformity to rules of compromise—often just insidious little "white lies"—which allow our "games" to be played without too much interruption. Most sports require a suppression of the truth, not correcting favorable calls made in error. And it happens not only in sports, but also at the office, in our homes, and in our schools—little shortcuts, little lies, all "for the good of the game."

Wouldn't it be refreshing to see a player or coach simply stand up to say, "I missed third, and I'm out!" It would cost their team a run and maybe the game—but they would be free. And right, under the smiling eye of God. Wouldn't it be wonderful to watch a football coach come off the sidelines and say to the referee, "My player was out of the end zone when he caught the ball," or a baseball coach tell the umpire, "the ball the other team hit was a home run, not a foul," knowing it would cost his team the game?

The truth would set them free. The truth—the person of Jesus Christ—will set us free. It has that effect. And it could have that effect on those around us too.

 IMPACT APPLICATION: The truth will indeed set us free. Are there any areas you need to revisit and tell the truth in?

OBEDIENCE TO BLESSINGS

Moses protested to God, "Who am I to appear before Pharaoh? Who am I to lead the people of Israel out of Egypt?" God answered, "I will be with you." **Exodus 3:11-12**

AS I SIT HERE THIS MORNING, I remember the first time Lynda and I watched it together, during the first year of our marriage.

Year after year it ran from early Sunday evening all throughout the night and through the entirety of Labor Day with the host singing "You'll Never Walk Alone" to close the show at about 6:30 p.m. on Monday: the Jerry Lewis Labor Day MDA Telethon. It has brought hope to countless millions through the years, hope that has offered the probability for many dreams to come true.

People like Jerry Lewis took on the cause of MDA, and with God's help—no doubt—moved it as a mission that has blessed the lives of countless others.

Things happen for God's glory and our good—hope and blessings—when we answer the call to do what God calls us to do and continue to align our lives in obedience to Him and especially as it relates to touching the lives of others. It's in those moments when we sense hope filling our lives and the lives of others in the world that we begin to experience all the blessings God has in store for us.

In every act of obedience to God's call on our lives, there is a blessing just around the corner. In every act of obedience, there is the assurance of God's protection on our lives.

Moses didn't think he would be able to do what God called him to do—to lead the Israelites out of bondage and out of Egypt. But he did what God called him to do—he acted in obedience to God's call. And God protected and led him and the Israelites to freedom and safety, all the way to the Promised Land—to the land of milk and honey.

What is God calling you to do?

Because to not do what you know God is calling you to do is to settle for less. Less than what He wants for you; less than who you can be; less of the blessings God stands ready to heap on you and those around you.

IMPACT APPLICATION: What is it you know you should do that you know would move you closer to becoming the person God created you to be? Whatever it is—do it!

SEPTEMBER 5

MORE PRECIOUS THAN RUBIES

Who can find a virtuous and capable wife? She is more precious than rubies. Her husband can trust her, and she will greatly enrich his life. She brings him good, not harm, all the days of her life. **Proverbs 31:10-12**

SHE WASN'T AN ANSWER to my prayers, because back then I didn't pray for those kinds of things. Actually, back then, I didn't pray for anything. I didn't have that kind of relationship with God.

I'm just glad I wasn't listening in on what their conversation might have been like when God made His decision and told my bride-to-be about it years ago.

"Lynda," He probably said, getting her attention with a gentle tap on the shoulder, "he's the one I've chosen for you to marry."

He was pointing at me—a then nineteen-year-old who looked to be at least twelve and acted much the same age.

"Oh please, tell me you're kidding!" Lynda understandably might have responded. "Not him! I love him, but he's such a mess."

God said, "I know, but he needs you. He acts tough, but he's just trying to survive. He is a scarred and frightened little boy who needs someone he will eventually be able to trust, someone who will love him no matter what he does until he can begin to love himself and others—and Me. I have plans for both of you—but it begins with you."

With a clear sense of acceptance of His plan, Lynda said, "If you say so— okay—I'll do it."

I'm guessing that's how it must have begun—my relationship with my bride. A journey marked by hope, failure, disappointment, tears, laughter, heartache, joy, commitment, change, and growth. A journey blessed with a son, daughter-in-law, two granddaughters, godchildren, friends, pets, and opportunities to make a difference in the world around us. All stemming from Lynda's never-flagging commitment to the God of that conversation—and to me who He entrusted to her care.

A woman who has always thought it more important to hold her child, daughter-in-law, and grandchildren than to straighten up around her. A woman to whom God said, "Teach him to do the important things in life so I can use him to touch the world."

And she did.

From her I learned—slowly, I might add—that eternal happiness here and hereafter comes not from the accumulation of things but from the memories of times spent lifting, loving, and living with other children of God. I learned it's okay to be who God created me to be.

Proverbs says, "A virtuous and capable wife . . . is more precious than rubies." Are you valuing the special woman in your life today?

IMPACT APPLICATION: Take a moment to recognize all those around you—including your bride— whom God has given you to make a difference in your life. Thank God. Thank them.

HERE WE GO AGAIN

Even though the fig trees have no blossoms, and there are no grapes on the vines; even though the olive crop fails, and the fields lie empty and barren; even though the flocks die in the fields, and the cattle barns are empty, yet I will rejoice in the LORD! I will be joyful in the God of my salvation! The Sovereign LORD is my strength! **Habakkuk 3:17-19**

"HERE WE GO AGAIN." My friend's words were a reference to four hurricanes impacting the states along the Gulf of Mexico, as one hurricane took dead aim at the Florida panhandle and its neighbors. I had called to check on him as he and his family prepared, along with millions of others, for the impending impact.

My words this morning were no different from his, as with each new day the morning news brings an ever more numbing and often despairing revelation of the less-than-perfect world in which we live. A world filled with terror and natural disasters and where too many search aimlessly for some form of acceptance and hope, often in all the wrong places. We live lives marked by illness, rejection, worry, and feelings of insignificance in the face of what seems to be overwhelming odds and insurmountable hurdles.

I find myself guiltier than some of being overcome with worry and moved to tears for family, friends, and my fellow travelers facing the difficulties and storms of their days. Such moments fog my focus of what God has in mind for the rest of my life. Although brief and infrequent, they are moments devoid of His energy, absent His forward direction, and without an upward look at today and tomorrow.

Perhaps you've been there, where words like worry, fear, retreat, surrender, blame, and doubt infiltrate your heart rather than words like courage, perseverance, advancing, and hope. Natural? Sure. But not where we want to dwell with the time given to us.

What are you facing? What are you holding in your hand? A hurricane. The loss of a loved one. An uncertain job future. A sick or hurt child. Do you see His hand next to yours?

Look closer, and remember that we live with an unimaginably large God who is always with us. A God standing so close to us that His hair is blown by the same hurricane-force winds as ours and who walks with us through the valleys and over the mountains of our lives, always carrying our burdens and lighting our way.

"Here we go again."

Yet in and with Him, it really doesn't get any more exciting than that!

 IMPACT APPLICATION: What situation are you facing that you need to give over to God? Give it and your life to the God of the universe.

SEPTEMBER 7

ASPIRE TO BE
ALL YOU ARE

Among you it will be different. Whoever wants to be a leader among you must be your servant, and whoever wants to be first among you must become your slave. For even the Son of Man came not to be served but to serve others and to give his life as a ransom for many.
Matthew 20:26-28

"HANNAH, WHAT DO YOU WANT to be called when you are president?" I asked playfully, hoping to help my precious granddaughter touch the God-created potential within her.

"I don't know that I want to be president, Granddaddy."

"But I'll help you," I mused, anticipating my role as her chief of staff. Her shoulders seemed to lighten and toss back a bit with that assurance. "Okay," she committed as she and her Mimi walked back into the house.

Millions of us around the world watched as together we remembered a love for the ages. Time after time, as the week's activities unfolded celebrating the life and leadership of our fortieth president, Ronald Wilson Reagan, I had wished that Hannah had been sitting with me so I could talk to her about all that was happening and tell her all I knew about this man and the country he loved so dearly.

I wanted to tell her of a man of humble beginnings, with incredible potential like us all, whose life among us epitomized a love for the ages through a love of God, a love for America, and a love for his fellow man, always moving him to touch the common and see the spectacular in every human life and in every human heart.

He left us with much. He inspired us to so much more. Through his example of service in reaching down to touch and lift a child, to comfort a family, salute a soldier, pray for a man who wished him harm, stand for what he believed in, no matter the winds of opinion against him, open gates of opportunity, and tear down walls of oppression and so much more, we saw the majesty that is contained in the common moments of our lives. We were reminded of the potential that lay within each of us as he lit and relit the torch of the spectacular from the most common of moments to burn brightly within our hearts.

"So, Hannah, what do you want to be called when you are president?"

Lifting her gaze and with a gentle, self-effacing tone she offered, "How about just, President Hannah?"

Ah, the common touch of a servant heart.

 IMPACT APPLICATION: Who around you needs to be lifted to see the incredible God-given potential that lies within them, to aspire to all that God created them to be? Maybe you?

THROUGH THE DARKNESS

In him was life, and that life was the light of all mankind. The light shines in the darkness, and the darkness has not overcome it.
John 1:4-5, NIV

IT WAS A LONG WEEK. It seemed much longer than the seven days that ticked very slowly off the calendar. It was a dark week too.

The curtain of darkness lowered one night about an hour earlier than expected for that time of year. Timing is everything, and it seemed that it couldn't have been worse, as we huddled in our safe room on news that a tornado had been spotted heading in our direction.

Momentarily isolated from the outside world, we couldn't see or hear the rain pelting the already saturated ground while winds gusted to sixty miles an hour, testing the resolve of trees whipped to angles foreign to their usual upright existence. As I sat there, it was a moment which seemed eerily consistent with recent days where darkness seemed to cast its shadow around every bend in the road we had traveled.

I remembered the tears of joy ten days before that accompanied the birth of our second granddaughter, Ellie Kate, and then the darkness of her four-day fight for breath in the hospital's neonatal intensive care unit.

I remembered the joy as she continued to heal and was finally released to the arms of her mom and dad, who were anxious to introduce her to the light of her home.

I remembered the darkness two days later, as we learned that our elder granddaughter, Hannah, was on the way to the hospital in an ambulance after a car accident. I remembered the darkness in my son's eyes as he stood at the curb outside the hospital awaiting the results of the tests doctors had hurriedly conducted on the little girl he adored, struggling to make sense of it.

I remembered the tears of joy as my bride met us to share the doctor's report that the X-rays and test results were negative. I remembered the joy of watching a badly bruised and sore, but graciously spared, little girl return home for recuperation on a diet of Krispy Kreme donuts, boiled peanuts, and ice cream.

I hate to admit it, but I had forgotten that the Light that came into our world over two thousand years ago also came in at that moment on a dark night and into a dark world. I had forgotten that through the centuries that Light has shined through all the darkness of the world. And for brief moments, I had forgotten that in the midst of the darkness of that long week, that Light had never stopped shining. And that the darkness can never overcome it.

IMPACT APPLICATION: The sun replaced the darkness again this morning, but the Light had already overcome it. If you're in a dark place, remember the Light. It is always there.

SEPTEMBER 9

SILENT CLIMBS

Jesus often withdrew to the wilderness for prayer. **Luke 5:16**

EVER CLIMBED A TREE? It may be time to again.

As you ponder that for a moment, my seven-year-old son's smile continues to shine on me from a photo sitting a couple of feet from my shoulder. It's a snapshot of him from more than thirty years ago, sitting at a juncture of two limbs of a giant oak tree in his grandparents' front yard. Next to it is a photo of Hannah, his daughter, sitting in that same tree years later and smiling with much the same kind of angelic smile.

As I reflected upon the memories captured by those pictures, I thought about a recent request my granddaughter Ellie Kate made, asking me to help her up into the crape myrtle in our front yard so she could climb to a higher place and just sit, look, wonder, reflect, and do whatever else goes on in that precious little brain while sitting in a tree.

Do you remember those moments when you simply stood admiring the quiet strength and majesty of a tree or climbed one simply to sit and reflect, either in your backyard or somewhere along your journey?

There's something particularly peaceful, inviting, quiet, and almost sacred about those moments. Perhaps they start out as a part of childhood play or an adventure, as Lynda found as a child when climbing oaks and orange trees on the family nursery where her home was located. And sometimes it became for her a place to hide, to get away from it all, and to be silent for a time. The same was true for my daughter-in-law, Amy, as a ten-year-old. Her place of peace, refuge, and reflection was an evergreen tree that she had named after a friend of hers, a tree that Amy, as a child, would climb with regularity by herself. A safe place—to sit, to think, to reflect, and perhaps even to dream.

Perhaps, as Mother Teresa suggested, a tree is a place away from the noise and restlessness of our day-to-day lives—a place to find God. A place where we can reflect on the eternal and important things of our lives rather than on the things that are transient and unimportant. A place where we encounter God in the midst of all that is going on in our lives.

Climbing a tree can be a moment when we reach a place beyond where we are to where we begin to sense all the desires of our hearts. And perhaps through the efforts of our climb, as we attempt to reach for the stars, we will touch the hand of God.

 IMPACT APPLICATION: Where do you encounter God in silence? Go to that place today.

SPAGHETTI PROSPERITY

Prosperity is as short-lived as a wildflower, so don't ever count on it.
James 1:10, MSG

EARL LOVED his wife's spaghetti. As it turns out, Earl loved everything his wife cooked. Earl could hardly stand having to wait for every meal she cooked.

Earl was a longtime neighbor of some friends of ours. I don't know what he weighed the last time they saw him, but the story they tell of him is that when he was shot down over France in World War II as a belly gunner on one of our bombers on his last flight that day, he weighed 175 pounds.

Then ten months later, after serving his nightmarish sentence as a prisoner of war in a German stalag in Poland coupled with a six-hundred-mile march in the dead of winter across Poland to Germany on a not-always-steady diet of water and a couple of boiled potatoes each day, he weighed 118 pounds.

I don't know his weight the last time he checked. I don't know the number or names of all the medals he was awarded. But I know he loved his wife's spaghetti.

I thought about that as I leaned over to kiss Lynda before I went to sleep. I thought about that as I reflected on a recent car trip to Birmingham and back with my son. I thought about that as I reflected on the times I have held our youngest granddaughter in my arms. I thought about that as I remembered someone whose young bride had just been placed in hospice care. And I thought about that as I reflected on the pictures of homelessness, destruction, and seeming powerlessness experienced by victims of recent hurricanes.

I thought about that as I struggled to remember the last walk in the rain I took with my bride, the last sunset I noticed, when I last touched someone in need or helped a neighbor, the last time I appreciated a butterfly's gentle flight, when I last felt the breeze blowing through my hair, or the last time I gave priority to the "important" things in life that deserve my attention over the "urgent" things that too often receive my attention.

Too often we define prosperity by fleeting things like money, power, status, or achievements. And as James points out in today's verse, prosperity like that "is as short-lived as a wildflower"—it is fragile and could desert us at any moment. The key to the good life is not the things we usually chase. Rather, it is honoring God and basking in the blessings He has freely bestowed on us.

Chief among the blessings Earl delighted in was his wife's spaghetti. May we all, in the adversity we face and amid the noise competing for our attention, find similar blessings in our own lives.

 IMPACT APPLICATION: What we so often define as prosperity is fleeting. Delight yourself in God and the blessings He has given you.

SEPTEMBER 11

REMEMBER ABOVE ALL

God elevated him to the place of highest honor and gave him the name above all other names, that at the name of Jesus every knee should bow, in heaven and on earth and under the earth, and every tongue declare that Jesus Christ is Lord, to the glory of God the Father. **Philippians 2:9-11**

I CAN ALWAYS SEE IT from where I sit at the desk in my upstairs office. The inscription printed below the picture of the twin towers that once stood as the World Trade Center, shimmering golden as they reflect the sun, is a reminder of what occurred there those many years ago and a commitment that it should never happen again—anywhere.

I know what the inscription says without having to read it:

On Saturday, September 8, 2001, three days before our National tragedy, a group of Bayonne residents took a harbor cruise. As the sun sets on Manhattan, an Alabaster City gleams. The reflection of our World Trade Center in the glistening harbor is representative of America the Beautiful's "Sea to Shining Sea." This photograph is one of the last amateur photos taken of our glorious skyline. May it serve as a reminder of our resolve for enduring peace at all costs.

There are some things you can never forget. There are some things you *should* never forget. There are some things you *must* never forget. The resolve is oft supported with words, and even as time passes, it needs to be supported with action. But the path to a future of a secure and enduring peace is still muddled at best.

Will we ever forget the Judeo-Christian values, foundations, and traditions of who we are as a nation or forget those who have stood in the gap through the centuries to protect those values, foundations, and traditions? Or will we forget the promises each generation makes to the one before it—to carry the torch of freedom forward with honor and respect? Or the promise one generation makes to the next—to hand them a nation better than the one received? And will we remember that, at the end of it all, Jesus is the name above it all? Above all that has occurred, does occur, and will occur—Jesus is Lord and remains on the throne.

Among all the images we can recall, the image and promise that God is above it all should give us all an everlasting hope for today and our tomorrows—and on through eternity.

IMPACT APPLICATION: As we remember September 11, 2001, amid all the dialogue, rhetoric, and posturing of the day, we would do well to remember that above it all, God is still in charge; and Jesus is the name above all names.

UNITED IN GOD

If my people who are called by my name will humble themselves and pray and seek my face and turn from their wicked ways, I will hear from heaven and will forgive their sins and restore their land.
2 Chronicles 7:14

DAWN WAS BREAKING as I retrieved the morning newspaper and posted the American flag in its holder on the side of our house. And as I reentered our house, I found my thoughts drifting to a statement by a dear friend whom I heard quoted again the day before. A couple of days after the attacks on our country on September 11, 2001, marking the beginning of a new and different type of war, the Reverend Billy Graham's daughter, Anne Graham Lotz, was interviewed by Jane Clayson.

She asked Anne, "I've heard people say . . . 'If God is good, how could God let this happen?' To that, you say . . . ?"

Anne responded with these sobering words: "I say God is also angry when he sees something like this. I would say also for several years now Americans in a sense have shaken their fist at God and said, God, we want you out of our schools, our government, our business, we want you out of our marketplace. And God, who is a gentleman, has just quietly backed out of our national and political life, our public life. Removing his hand of blessing and protection. We need to turn to God first of all and say, 'God, we're sorry we have treated you this way and we invite you now to come into our national life. We put our trust in you.' We have our trust in God on our coins, we need to practice it."

As I sat in my study later, preparing some notes for my upcoming sermon at a local church, my thoughts drifted again to that defining moment in our history. In the aftermath of those horrific attacks, national unity was reinvigorated, and the real priorities of our lives seemed to become much clearer. And there was a massive sprint to the roots of our faith and a sense of unity in our land.

Of course, no one desires for disaster to strike, and no one wants for our country to mourn like it did when we were attacked. But in all times, and certainly at times when it seems like the nation is falling apart, we need to remember our roots and draw closer together in our shared connections. And what unifies us as Americans? Our freedom, of course; but also our historic and foundational faith in God.

God forbid that we should ever endure more attacks like those we faced on September 11. But whenever we face national trials, difficulties, or seemingly defining moments in our journey as Americans, we should be moved once again to humble ourselves, to repent, to pray, to seek God's face, and to renew our commitment to God.

United in God. United in freedom. God bless America.

IMPACT APPLICATION: Pray today for peace and revival in our nation and that we would be united together in freedom, seeking God.

SEPTEMBER 13

SPRINKLE

You saw how the LORD your God cared for you all along the way as you traveled through the wilderness, just as a father cares for his child.
Deuteronomy 1:31

THE DIGITAL PICTURES which were taken did their best to capture the moments of their time together at the Girl Scout daddy-daughter dance. But even the pictures couldn't capture the gleam in her daddy's eye as he painted the picture of Ellie Kate making her way through the crowd at the dance to receive what she described afterwards as the award she and her daddy won dancing together. It was a door prize—but you can tell her that at your own peril. To her, she and her daddy won the prize while dancing together.

Is there a powder we can sprinkle on our children and grandchildren to keep them from growing up? Is there a shelter we can house them in to protect them from the cold winds which will inevitably blow through their lives?

Oh, how I wish it were like that daddy-daughter dance for all children! Where children felt they were deeply loved all the time. Where children would catch a glimpse of God's love for them through those entrusted with their care. Where the voices of those close to them connect them to the quiet voice of a God who is always pursuing them.

Maybe it's we adults who need a powder someone can sprinkle over us. Some of us would just need a dash, and some of us would need to be covered from head to toe. A powder to keep all of us well-meaning caregivers from trying to mold our children into something they're not. A powder to keep us from teaching our children by our actions and words that we would rather be with others than with them. A powder to prevent us from subjecting our children to the same system of "earned love" we may have experienced as children—rather than modeling the example of the unmerited love of God.

Our children grow up like too many of us—impersonating someone they're not. Someone they were not created to be. And no matter how many church services, Sunday school classes, or functions they attend, they too often have trouble hearing the voice of God whispering to them. And so they seek approval through what they do, what they wear, what they have, and what they look like—until the still, small voice of God becomes silent in their lives.

God cares for us the way a father would. All of us who are fathers would do well to mirror God's example in the care of our own children.

Maybe there's a powder. Or maybe there's a daddy-daughter dance. Maybe there's just you and me. Let's care for our children and grandchildren as God cares for them.

 IMPACT APPLICATION: What would it look like for you to care for your children as God does? Live like that today.

A PRECIOUS GIFT

The Spirit of God has made me, and the breath of the Almighty gives me life. **Job 33:4**

THE VALUE OF A HUMAN LIFE: Is it precious and with value impossible to calculate or something less?

When I was an adjunct professor at a local community college a number of years ago, my students regularly had to wonder what relevance the study of cases involving issues of school busing and desegregation and murder on the high seas had to a community college course on business law. If they did wonder that, they did so privately. After all, since I was their professor and immediate arbiter of value, their final grade remained in my control, and they didn't regularly complain.

But one such case caught their attention. The facts were compelling in that historic case. On July 5, 1884, Dudley, Stephens, Brooks, and a seventeen-year-old boy, Parker, were cast away in a storm on the high seas 1,600 miles from the Cape of Good Hope and put into an open lifeboat from their lost vessel. For twenty days they had no food except two tins of turnips and a small turtle they caught and no water except such rain as they caught in their oilskin capes. On the twentieth day, Stephens, with the approval of Dudley and the dissent of Brooks, killed Parker, who at the time lay helpless, weakened by famine, and ill. The devilish deed provided nourishment for the remaining three until they were picked up by a passing vessel four days later.

The verdict of the English Criminal Court in the case of *The Queen vs. Dudley and Stephens* (December 9, 1884): murder. In reaching its decision, the learned court, through Lord Coleridge, chief justice, shared this: "To preserve one's life is generally speaking a duty, but it may be the plainest and the highest duty to sacrifice it. . . . [Otherwise,] who is to be judge of this sort of necessity? By what measure is the comparative value of lives to be measured? Is it to be strength, intellect, or what?"

Life is a gift from God to be used for His glory, our good, and as Jesus' parable of the Good Samaritan reminds us, the good of others around us. What are you doing with your life today? What are you doing today for the good of others? When others look back after your time here, what difference in the world will there be because God gave you the gift of your life?

Life is a precious gift. Don't waste yours, and do what you can to protect that gift in others.

IMPACT APPLICATION: Our lives are a precious gift from God to be used for His glory, our good, and the good of others. Your life is a precious gift set in place by God for this time in history. Embrace that gift to leave the legacy God intended you to leave when He created you.

SEPTEMBER 15

THE ONLY ONE
I SEE IS YOU

One day some parents brought their children to Jesus so he could lay his hands on them and pray for them. But the disciples scolded the parents for bothering him. But Jesus said, "Let the children come to me. Don't stop them! For the Kingdom of Heaven belongs to those who are like these children." And he placed his hands on their heads and blessed them before he left. **Matthew 19:13-15**

I WOULDN'T HAVE MISSED IT for the world. I had to change some plans when I heard about it—but as with anything involving my granddaughters, my plans always get changed to be with them.

The school that our granddaughters attended had scheduled its annual Spring Art Showcase, during which they present a night of music and art put on by the students to benefit the continuing good work of the school's fine arts department.

Hannah, our elder granddaughter, participated with her class in a powerful instrumental rendition of "Jesu, Joy of Man's Desiring," and Ellie Kate's class performed a number of pieces including "Books of the New Testament," which Ellie Kate sang passionately.

At the conclusion, I went to each of them individually and told them that what they did was wonderful, that they were wonderful, and that I couldn't take my eyes off them as they were performing.

And then I asked six-year-old Ellie Kate, "Ellie, tell me, was there anybody else up there singing besides you?"

She looked puzzled at first and then smiled and hugged me when I explained to her that she was the only one I could see.

I asked a similar question of Hannah, who was eleven at the time, at the conclusion of the concert. Again, a slightly puzzled look for a moment, and then a wide smile broke across her face. She knew what I meant and also responded with a hug.

That's how Jesus Christ views not only my granddaughters, but also all of His children everywhere around the world. Actually, He would enlarge the focus to include all of His children, of all ages, everywhere around the world so that they, too, feel as I try to make my granddaughters feel—special, precious, unique, loved, beautiful, wonderful, and secure. That means you, too.

How about that child near to you? Has it been a while since that child or grandchild has felt the touch of Christ on their life, perhaps through your presence, your smile, a gentle touch, or an affirming word? How about someone else of any age around you or whom you meet?

"[Jesus] placed his hands on their heads and blessed them."

IMPACT APPLICATION: When was the last time you knew Christ was looking at only you? Go ahead, look up—into His eyes looking at you!

BEING LIKE HER—
WITH HIM

If you faithfully obey the voice of the LORD your God, being careful to do all his commandments that I command you today, the LORD your God will set you high above all the nations of the earth. And all these blessings shall come upon you and overtake you, if you obey the voice of the LORD your God.

Deuteronomy 28:1-2, ESV

I WANT TO BE LIKE HER. In the most basic and important of ways, I want to be like her. And if it's not asking too much, to have her precious smile and sparkle that fills her life too.

You would too, if you knew her.

She simply wants to please God. She loves Him. She talks about Him. She reads about Him. She talks to Him. She wants to do what He wants her to do.

Somewhere in the midst of her journey, Ellie Kate, like her older sister, began to know about God and became His child. And ever since, her desire to please Him has grown in ways nothing short of delightful to watch.

She wants to please Him. She wants to honor Him. She wants to do what He would smile upon. At her tender age, she is not always sure what that looks like. But her heart wants to please Him—and so at times she needs guidance from those He has entrusted to care for her.

She cares that others know that God loves them. She cares that others feel good about themselves and feel included and special. And because of the state of her heart, the Scripture above forecasts what she has to look forward to in her life—a life full of God-appointed blessings that will come upon her and overtake her.

I want to be like her. In the most basic and important of ways, I want to be like her. And have the smile and sparkle in her too. And the blessings would be nice.

What about you? Where is the focus of your heart today? What do you hope for and dream of in life? What are you struggling with? What tragedy has just hit? What news has shaken you to the core? What are you seeking in life?

Maybe you have a granddaughter, grandson, or child like Ellie Kate. Someone with a childlike purity and innocence that seeks God and wants to serve and be like Him. Be like that child. And together, let's do our best to keep these children like that, shielding them from the "cold water" of a world that seeks to rob them of their innocence.

I want to be like my little granddaughter, so I need to seek first the God whom she seeks to honor and please. And follow her example.

What about you?

IMPACT APPLICATION: Why not let the Scripture above, and my youngest granddaughter, guide your next steps? Seek first after God.

SEPTEMBER 17

THE RACE—
GOD'S GOT IT!

I believe in God, the Father Almighty, the Maker of heaven and earth, and in Jesus Christ, His only Son, our Lord. . . . I believe in the Holy Ghost. . . . Amen. **The Apostles' Creed**

HERE WE GO AGAIN. Ready to get back on the track and ride through the week believing we will make it, hoping it will be better than the last and trusting that we will have the strength to get to the end.

A few years ago, the vast majority of the horse-racing world believed that Big Brown would win the Kentucky Derby in only his fourth career race, even starting from the most distant outside post position in a field of twenty. They were right. They were almost wrong, though, as a courageous filly named Eight Belles ran a courageous race before horrifyingly breaking down after the finish line.

Here we are in another week, wondering what to believe today and in the days that will come. Will a door close we had hoped wouldn't? Will a relationship be lost because we can't unpack the baggage accumulated through the years? Will an innocuous skin blemish turn into something more serious or a flutter in our chest require surgery? Will our children understand that it's not about their worth when someone hurts their feelings? Will a loved one unexpectedly breathe their last?

It's not a race for the fainthearted. The track is crowded and at times narrow, dirt is kicked in our faces, the finish line seems a long way off, and we're not sure we have the stamina to make it, let alone take another step. Yet it's a journey we must make.

And in the midst of our doubts and difficulties—while wondering what, if anything, there is to believe in—we need to start by remembering that we are not here by accident. There is a divine destiny to it all—from the starting gate to the finish line   and there is something to believe in while we're on the track and all along the way down the homestretch of our lives . . . however long that is to be.

So, here we go. Ready? No? Not so sure? Maybe? Not quite yet?

Maybe this will help us to get ready and to get back on the track for today and all the days ahead. As you prepare for the day and the week, strap this on to believe in while you ride through this week and the next and the next.

The God who created you knows what He is doing; He is still on the throne; He loves you; and He will never leave you.

What else do you need? Believe it! Believe in Him! Have a great ride!

 IMPACT APPLICATION: Believe it all along the way. Draw strength in its truth. Strength to start the day. Strength to pick yourself up after you fall. Strength to hang on.

SPIRIT OF INDOMITABILITY

The LORD your God is going with you! He will fight for you against your enemies, and he will give you victory! **Deuteronomy 20:4**

IT WAS TO BE his final tournament and turned out to be his final match. He lost in the third round to Benjamin Becker, who stood cheering him with the rest. Having won the match, Becker knew he would advance to the next round in that year's US Open, but his applause and tears were in sadness and respect for the passing of this remarkable elder statesman of tennis.

Andre Agassi. Why were we drawn to him and others like him? Perhaps for some of us, it's his ability, which earned him sixty singles titles and eight grand-slam titles throughout his career.

Perhaps it's all the charity work he has done for children, raising tens of millions of dollars for at-risk youth. Perhaps it's his respect through the years for those who now stood and applauded him as he always bowed to all four sides of the stadium after a match.

But I suspect there is something greater about this man that draws us to him. You could always see it in the steely determination of his eyes. It was marked at every twist and turn, injury and setback, by a determination, perseverance, and unyielding and unconquerable approach to all he could be.

Very simply we were drawn to his indomitable human spirit. For those of us who watched his last match over a decade ago, we strained and fought with him as he struggled to move, to return a serve or volley, or to reach a lob to which his aging tennis body objected, trying to carry his dream into just one more moment. There was no quit in him.

In our better moments we remember that we, too, have that indomitable human spirit. It's how we were made. It's how we should live. In Andre Agassi's efforts we caught glimpses of it in our own lives. We have had cold water poured on our lives and dreams in the form of defeats, the unbelief of others, or circumstances beyond our control. Cold water we have usually overcome. But cold water that at times has begun to form into unbelief.

You can see it every day in the faces of those who never smile, who always assume the worst, and who look for what's wrong in every moment. I wonder if you've ever seen it in the mirror. If so, change it now because it's not the way we were created to live.

A legacy of indomitability at any age, at every age. It's a God thing. Smile and claim it.

 IMPACT APPLICATION: With God's Spirit within us, we can and should move beyond all that would slow us down or stop us. The journey ends only when it ends in His heavenly arms.

SEPTEMBER 19

WATCH THIS SPACE

I don't mean to say that I have already achieved these things or that I have already reached perfection. But I press on to possess that perfection for which Christ Jesus first possessed me. **Philippians 3:12**

"WATCH THIS SPACE."

Those words can't help but raise the expectations of all who pass by. It's a marketing technique used to positively fill an empty billboard while generating interest from advertisers to use as an advertising space, which a passerby may be looking at in the days to come.

But more than that, it points us to the promise of tomorrow—that our next day will be even better than today.

Watch what happens. Watch this day. Watch this life. Watch the difference.

That's the promise of Scripture. That's the promise of eternity. That's the promise of a God who sent His Son for us, so that through a relationship with Him, we might be assured that no matter how good today is, the best is yet to come.

Virginia Clark, the beloved mother of dear friends, left us with a testimony of love for the least of those around us and an example of courage in life that told us that no matter what you face, you should face it with a smile for all the world to see.

And Keli McGregor, a beloved husband, father, and friend to many and president of the Colorado Rockies Baseball Club, left us with a testimony that demonstrated every day that life is not about us but about others and that what we are supposed to do with whatever God has given us is to make the lives of those around us better.

I suspect if we listened closely, we would hear them both telling us that there is still much to do. I suspect they would want to tell us that retirement is never an option in the Kingdom of God, that the fear of tomorrow which tends to freeze us today is less than it's made out to be, and that personal comfort—to the exclusion of living lives of impact for God—is something to eschew.

Through those two precious lives, we could see and hear the words "Watch This Space" emanating from them—painting a picture for us of what was yet to come. And for those of us who knew them and others like them, that space was always filled to overflowing—the next day and the next and the next—with the very best that God created their lives to be.

Of course, there are others who come to mind now as we reflect together. How can we best remember all of them?

By living. Fully.

Fill your space with a life well lived for God and others.

 IMPACT APPLICATION: What will fill the space on your "billboard" for the entire world to see—the rest of today, tomorrow, the next day, and then the next?

HAVE WE FORGOTTEN?

Remember this and keep it firmly in mind: The LORD is God both in heaven and on earth, and there is no other.
Deuteronomy 4:39

LOOKING ACROSS the landscapes of our nation and world, I have begun to wonder, *Have we forgotten?*

On Wednesday, October 17, 2001, Representative Roscoe Bartlett of Maryland addressed the US House of Representatives: "Of the first 108 universities founded in America, 106 were distinctly Christian, including the first, Harvard University, chartered in 1636. In the original Harvard student handbook, rule number one was that students seeking entrance must first know Latin and Greek so that they could study the Scriptures: Let every student be plainly instructed and earnestly pressed to consider well, the main end of his life and studies, is, to know God and Jesus Christ, which is eternal life; and therefore to lay Jesus Christ as the only foundation for our children to follow the moral principles of the Ten Commandments."

We couldn't possibly forget that heritage from my son's alma mater, could we? Have we forgotten?

Representative Bartlett went on to note that *The McGuffey Readers* were used for more than one hundred years in our schools, with more than 125 million copies sold. Among its many lessons is this: "Do you see that tall tree? Long ago it sprang up from a small nut. Do you know who made it do so?" Its answer to the student: "It was God, my child. God made the world and all things in it. He made the sun to light the day, and the moon to shine at night. God shows that he loves us by all that he has done for us. Should we not then love him?"

In 1963, the Supreme Court ruled Bible reading unconstitutional in our public school system. It reasoned that "if portions of the New Testament were read without explanation, they could and have been psychologically harmful to children."

Have we forgotten?

Representative Bartlett noted also that French historian Alexis de Tocqueville published *Democracy in America* in 1835 following his visit to America in 1831. He shared: "I sought for the key to the greatness and genius of America. . . . But not until I went into the churches of America and heard her pulpits flame with righteousness did I understand the secret of her genius and power. America is great because America is good; and if America ever ceases to be good, America will cease to be great!"

Have we forgotten?

IMPACT APPLICATION: Throughout the history of our country God hasn't gone away, but perhaps we have turned away. Perhaps it's time to remember and turn back.

CHERISH THEM
ONE MORE DAY

Love each other with genuine affection, and take delight in honoring each other. **Romans 12:10**

I DON'T KNOW WHEN LYNDA and Og Mandino would have met, but he must have known her. He, at least, had to be thinking about her, or someone like her, when he wrote what has been Lynda's "rule number one" for life: "Beginning today, treat everyone you meet . . . [with] all the care, kindness and understanding you can muster, and do it with no thought of any reward."

Og Mandino may not have known her when he penned those words, but I have watched her for over half a century live out those words in her life for all the world she touches. Words each of us would do well to consider for our lives.

Through the years, I've watched her sacrifice her health, wealth, and personal convenience for children, her granddaughters, godchildren, her parents and mine, and every member of her extended family and mine. It never mattered to her if her efforts were appreciated because she didn't do it for appreciation, only love.

I've watched her devote time to friends who often didn't notice, but she devoted it anyway. I've watched her holding a dying child in her arms at an AIDS clinic, frail, with empty eyes as she just wrapped him in her arms, rubbed his head, kissed his face, and then cleaned him and her suit up after he threw up on both of them, only to wrap him in her arms once more. I've felt her love, loyalty, support, and encouragement in the valleys of my life, often when I least deserved it, lifting me to the mountaintops God intended for me to climb. I've watched her recite verse after verse of Scripture about the love of God for others without ever uttering a word.

Recently we celebrated another of Lynda's birthdays. My daily and selfish prayer is that we celebrate many more. The world needs her, her family needs her, her friends need her, and I need her. Funny, but if you asked, she couldn't tell you the last time she felt she had done something that touched a life because it doesn't stand out as unusual or different to her; it's simply a way of living for her. She doesn't keep a list and has never sought acknowledgment or reward. Her heart holds all the reward she ever needs as she warmly remembers the lives around her.

Got someone like this in your life? Cherish them and learn from them.

 IMPACT APPLICATION: Who in your life has lived a life like the one set out above that perhaps you have taken for granted? Embrace them, encourage them, and then embrace their example—the world needs more of the love they share. And, thank God for them.

THE OTHER SIDE OF THE WALL

In the beginning God created the heavens and the earth. **Genesis 1:1**

WE'VE ALL HAD THOSE QUESTIONS put to us before from our children. You know, the ones you can't answer or don't want to think about, so you try to dismiss them. Maybe we've given an answer just acceptable enough to deflect the question so the conversation can move on to something else.

Ellie Kate's question seemed to come from nowhere. We weren't talking about anything related to what she asked. We were just hanging out in the kitchen, laughing and doing things you don't usually do unless blessed by a visit from precious granddaughters. And then four-year-old Ellie Kate hung her question in the air.

"Gran." And then she paused to make sure she had my attention as she finished the climb onto the kitchen counter. I could tell from the inflection in her voice something serious was on the way.

"Yes, Sweetie." I readied myself for what was coming.

"Gran, how was God born with nobody?"

Brief outlines and catchy phrases related to scientific theories danced through my head. I even thought for a moment of sharing my "Brick-Wall Theory" to prove that God is and has to be the real deal, always has been, and was here to create it all in the beginning. Simply stated—if you go out as far as you can into the universe, reach or envision what you think to be the end, and then, in your imagination, build a brick wall at that spot, what would be on the other side of the wall? That has the potential for keeping me up at night, until I remember God. What is beyond the wall *has* to be the same as what is on this side of the wall—God—something so infinite and extravagant that it is beyond explanation.

I took a moment and responded, "I don't know, Sweetie." I then added, "That's what's so great about God—somehow it happened. One day He can answer your question about how He was born with nobody."

No deflection there, I hope. Just an honest admission of ignorance stemming from a total lack of knowledge.

I'm sure in the days ahead Ellie Kate will continue to amaze, bewilder, and challenge us with the questions she hangs in the air for us to ponder. Answers will come.

Maybe not today. One day. One day.

God—yesterday, today, every day, and for all our days.

 IMPACT APPLICATION: We won't ever have all of the answers now. Rather than get stuck on things we can't answer, stay focused on the important things—a life well lived and lives touched and changed.

SEPTEMBER 23

AN ATTITUDE OF HOPE

We have this treasure in jars of clay to show that this all-surpassing power is from God and not from us. We are hard pressed on every side, but not crushed; perplexed, but not in despair; persecuted, but not abandoned; struck down, but not destroyed. **2 Corinthians 4:7-9,** NIV

WE FIRST NOTICED a problem when she bumped her head into a chair leg. The next day the vet discovered that our twelve-year-old basset hound Pansy had blood clots in her eyes obstructing her vision. We left early from our vacation in the mountains to have her examined at home at the University of Florida veterinary school, where we learned she had incurable lymphoma. With chemotherapy she would have six to twelve months left. She didn't seem to be in pain, slept a lot, moved deliberately, and yet wagged her tail when she saw us.

In her own way she carried an attitude of hope in the face of her cancer. Even though she is no longer with us, I am still learning a lot from this wonderful gift from God.

Each one of us carries a certain attitude, a certain approach to life. An attitude completely unique to each one of us, which has been shaped, both positively and negatively, by an assortment of events, people, and circumstances. And an attitude that colors the world we live in and paints a picture for each one of us of either sadness or happiness, hate or love, anxiety or security, defeat or victory, worry or faith, despair or hope.

When life hits us full in the face, whether in our families, our relationships, our work, or our walk of faith, our attitude will either demonstrate a power and a hope that braces us to stand firm against all we face, or reflect an emptiness and despair that sends us into retreat in the face of our adversity.

It's all in our attitude. All in our approach to each and every day of our lives, each and every minute, second, moment of our existence on God's earth. Our attitude has been shaped throughout our lives, but most importantly, today, no matter what has happened to us before, we can choose to claim a life-changing, transforming, eternal, and growing relationship with the Father through His Son, Jesus Christ.

In the face of adversity, most of us will seldom experience what the apostle Paul experienced. But despite that, he chose an attitude that he expressed in the Scripture above. An attitude of hope that claimed that, with Christ, he might be knocked down in life, but he would never be knocked out.

An attitude of hope.

IMPACT APPLICATION: You have a choice each day to carry whatever attitude toward life you choose. No matter what you face, with Christ in your life, you can carry an attitude of hope.

PRAYING FOR CHANGE

For God so loved the world that he gave his one and only Son, that whoever believes in him shall not perish but have eternal life. **John 3:16**, NIV

"THE DIFFERENCE BETWEEN a lady and a flower girl is not how she behaves, but how she is treated . . . [Professor Higgins] treats me like a common flower girl, and always will. But I know that I shall always be a lady to Colonel Pickering."

The recollection of that statement by *My Fair Lady*'s Eliza Doolittle about the way Colonel Pickering, versus Professor Higgins, treated her shattered my thoughts those many years ago. I was preparing a talk that Eliza's statement made me realize was nothing more than empty words. About two hundred people would be gathering in a few days at a local church for a Valentine's Day sweetheart dinner to hear a word of love and encouragement for their marriage—from a hypocrite.

Just moments earlier I had prayed—once again—with all the sincerity I could muster that God would change something about my bride I couldn't accept. I have to confess that I prayed like that a lot back then about things that seemed to annoy and frustrate me.

As I continued to wrestle, rationalize, and struggle to find a message of encouragement for those who would soon gather, one of the most familiar of all verses landed with a thud in my heart: "For God so loved the world that he gave his one and only Son, that whoever believes in him will not perish but have eternal life."

I read it again: "For God so loved [me] that he gave his one and only Son. . . ."

And then one more time: "For God so loved [Lynda] that he gave his one and only Son. . . ."

It was a moment that moved me to tears and to pray for forgiveness. The sorrow I felt of moments missed enjoying the beautiful idiosyncrasies of her creation hung heavy in my heart. The moments of laughter, tenderness, and acceptance missed because of my self-centered view of the way things should be hung heavy in my heart.

I prayed again, this time that God would change not her but *me*. I prayed that He would change my perception of her God-ordained value, just as she was, just as He had created her. I prayed that He would change my heart to accept *all of her*, with all her radiant beauty, grace, and differences.

And His answer to my prayer brought a smile to my face, laughter in my eyes, and appreciation in my heart.

 IMPACT APPLICATION: We should pray daily, thanking God for the gift of our loved ones, praying also that He continue to change us until we fully appreciate how precious they are, just as they are.

SEPTEMBER 25

RIDE, CALVIN, RIDE!

I focus on this one thing: Forgetting the past and looking forward to what lies ahead, I press on to reach the end of the race and receive the heavenly prize for which God, through Christ Jesus, is calling us.
Philippians 3:13-14

IT RESONATED A BIT LONGER than all the other tripe I hear on talk radio when someone commented the other day—"We live in a cynical world. A tough world of competitors willing to step on and over you to climb the ladders to success."

So, how's your day going so far in the midst of this world?

We won't hear quite as much about Calvin Borel—jockey and dreamer—now that his horse Street Sense didn't win the Triple Crown. And that's a pity because Calvin Borel's life paints a picture of stark contrast to the one painted by that talk show commentator's remark.

Calvin Borel, over forty years old, standing 5'4" and weighing 114 pounds, looks as though he has lost all his teeth. He articulates his feelings in words that at times expose the eighth-grade education he received. Still, he is a jockey beloved by everyone. With his exemplary work ethic, he overcame broken legs and ribs, a punctured lung, a spleen removal, and a coma, riding horse after horse in race after race chasing a dream—in what some viewed as clearly out of his reach.

Dropping out of school after the eighth grade to pursue his dream and living in poverty in the bayous of Louisiana, he rode barefoot and often without a helmet unless one could be borrowed, just to follow his dream, his passion. The son of a sugarcane farmer, he rode races on the bush tracks near his home of Catahoula, Louisiana, light years from a ride around Churchill Downs and the Kentucky Derby.

Yet years later, after riding in locations most of us have never even heard of, let alone been to, in claiming race after race on poor mounts that could barely find the track let alone cross the finish line, Calvin rode Street Sense to victory in the Kentucky Derby. Even the queen watched as this common, everyday man fulfilled an uncommon dream.

The truth is that we do live in a somewhat cynical and tough world. We often get discouraged when we feel like someone else is doing all we ever dreamed of doing. As the years go by, we begin to believe that we'll never reach that moment we have long dreamed of. That may be true, but should it stop us from trying anyway? Or as Calvin might put it—ride anyway!

IMPACT APPLICATION: In the face of all the adversity and cynics, with the passing of time and the distinct chance that we may not make it, why not get on the horse and give it a go anyway?

WATCHING
THE CALENDAR

A child is born to us, a son is given to us. The government will rest on his shoulders. And he will be called: Wonderful Counselor, Mighty God, Everlasting Father, Prince of Peace. Isaiah 9:6

WATCHING THE CALENDAR.

In addition to millions of excited children the world over, my daughter-in-law, Amy, is watching the calendar until Christmas, Santa Claus, the baby Jesus, and presents. It's not just Santa Claus or the presents themselves, which Amy shakes for clues as to their contents or surreptitiously inquires about. It's not just the majesty of the moment in that squalid manger of so long ago which captures her childlike heart and causes her eyes to twinkle even more than they usually do as she reflects on the meaning of it all. In addition to all that, it's the love that enfolds her from all those who love her all year long and remind her again at this miraculous time of year how special she is to so many.

One of my many reminders of Amy sits not too far from me on the credenza next to my desk. It's a manger scene she gave me a number of years ago. I leave it up all year long, ready for my granddaughters' periodic visits and rearranging of the figurines. In addition to those we normally expect to see in the manger scene—Mary, Joseph, the baby Jesus, sheep, camels, shepherds, and wise men—there sits a little toy dog in a yellow plastic chair with a red stocking cap on its head and a green wreath around its neck from their daddy's Playskool set when he was a child. All of them have come to visit the baby in a manger, to reflect, to wonder, and perhaps, like us, to seek something more.

When was the last time you stopped and visited the manger? When was the last time you quietly looked into the face of the baby and remembered who He came for? When was the last time you heard yourself say the words of worship "O come let us adore Him, Christ, the Lord"?

Watching the calendar all year long. There is an undercurrent of excitement that was whispered by Isaiah to his people long ago—"For unto us a Child is born, unto us a Son is given . . . Wonderful, Counselor, Mighty God, Everlasting Father, Prince of Peace" (NKJV).

Isaiah was saying, "Don't give up; something more is coming."

"For unto you is born this day . . . a Savior, who is Christ the Lord" (Luke 2:11, ESV).

It's not just a lowly manger, but a birthplace filled with a love that enfolds us every day throughout the year; a hope that transcends all our sorrows, disappointments, and loneliness; and a majesty that holds our eternity.

IMPACT APPLICATION: The manger—now that's a place worthy of a visit, today and every day of the year and for the rest of our lives.

SEPTEMBER 27

LIGHT THE WAY

You are the light of the world—like a city on a hilltop that cannot be hidden. No one lights a lamp and then puts it under a basket. Instead, a lamp is placed on a stand, where it gives light to everyone in the house. In the same way, let your good deeds shine out for all to see, so that everyone will praise your heavenly Father. **Matthew 5:14-16**

IT BECAME PITCH BLACK in an instant that night. My granddaughter Hannah was busy upstairs in the playroom. Outside the winds were howling, with lightning cracking all around so that it was easy to see the deluge of rain dumping on the neighborhood. It was a spooky kind of night.

And then the lights went out everywhere, and I heard Hannah's frightened scream from upstairs. Anticipating a problem, I had earlier retrieved a few flashlights, just in case. Holding one above my head with the light piercing the darkness, I ran from the kitchen toward the frightened voice coming from upstairs.

When Hannah's eyes saw the light, her voice calmed. And as she followed the light down the stairway to me and to the rest of her family, all the fear of the earlier moment subsided. The darkness was gone.

Light has that kind of impact on us. Light has that kind of impact on others. And light has that impact on the darkness. It rekindles hope.

Jesus calls each of us "the light of the world." Think about that for a moment and what it can mean to others if we let it shine in the darkness of the world, the storms, and the problems in those lives all around us. You and me, light and hope for others. You bet. Jesus said it.

A number of years ago Elihu Burritt wrote, "No human being can come into this world without increasing or diminishing the sum total of human happiness, not only of the present but of every subsequent age of humanity. No one can detach himself from this connection . . . everywhere his presence or absence will be felt—everywhere he will have companions who will be better or worse for his influence."

Who knows? When you shine your light, you may start a firestorm of others lifting their own lights high for still others all over the world. I suspect it will also rekindle hope in your life. Funny how that seems to work. And in the process, the darkness won't stand a chance.

IMPACT APPLICATION: We have a choice. No matter our circumstances, we have a choice. We can wait in the shadows of our own moments of darkness for a light from somewhere or for someone else to come, or we can be a light for others. A light that will pierce their darkness and rekindle their hope.

THE WONDER OF YOU

When I look at the night sky and see the work of your fingers—the moon and the stars you set in place—what are mere mortals that you should think about them, human beings that you should care for them? Yet you made them only a little lower than God and crowned them with glory and honor. **Psalm 8:3-5**

AUGUSTINE WROTE, "People travel to wonder at the height of mountains, at the huge waves of the sea, at the long courses of rivers, at the vast compass of the ocean, at the circular motion of the stars; and they pass by themselves without wondering."

Now there's a thought that will ruminate for a while in the cavity occasionally occupied by my brain. Interesting, though, that such an ageless human malady doesn't seem to affect our children or grandchildren, who with eyes wide open explore not only the wonders of God's creation all around them but also the wonder of God's creation that is them.

Until, dare I say, they grow older like some of us, and we've had a chance to throw enough cold water on their little minds of wonder. That's not how the Creator intended it to be, for them or for us.

Too many of us all too often wander through life drawing away from, instead of tapping into, the potential God has placed in our lives. The reasons we recite are many and seemingly justifiable on the surface, yet they are all rubbish. And all of them block the potential placed within us that when fully realized and utilized, would cause us to soar to exhilarating heights where we are sure to catch a glimpse of His smiling reflection. Too many of us come to the end of our days never having reached our full, God-given potential.

In our better moments we know that that is what God intended for each of us to do with the privilege and wonder of the life He created and entrusted to us. To live life to the fullest. To reach for all we can be, to reach for the heavens.

So as you travel the world and the life God has given you, don't miss the mountains or the huge waves of the sea; experience the long courses of the rivers, the vast compass of the ocean, and the circular motion of the stars. But while you do all of that in this journey God has given you, don't miss the wonder of you.

The God-created wonder He has designed to be uniquely you.

IMPACT APPLICATION: The wonder of His creation—you and me. No matter what we have done with it before, the key question and choice for each of us is, *What will we do with it today and every day for the rest of our lives?*

SEPTEMBER 29

SLIPPERY SLOPES

You will know the truth, and the truth will set you free. **John 8:32**

A NUMBER OF YEARS AGO, as the morning unfolded with the first of the year's tropical storms approaching, destined to dump refreshing rain across a parched landscape needing renewal, a headline I saw moved me to wish for heart renewal. I remember it was one of Saturday's sport section headlines: "Tiger Trumps MJ as Favorite Male Athlete."

Conducted annually by Harris Interactive, an online poll determined that for the first time since 1993, Michael Jordan had fallen out of number one to be replaced by Tiger Woods as the most popular male athlete. Included in the top ten were two other names of note—Kobe Bryant and Barry Bonds—causing me to wonder who you and I might select. What standards would you use if you were polled? Ability, positive impact, character, years of sustained performance?

I was reminded of an interview of Dan Rather during the episodic coverage surrounding the end of his long and notable career. The discussion revolved around values one should embrace in journalism and life in general. The questioning narrowed its focus to honesty as a value one might consider worthy of a career and life well-lived, when Dan Rather made this assertion: "I think you can be an honest person and still lie about a number of things." I sat stunned in the wake of his comment.

What values guide your life? How many of us would knowingly adopt that phrase to characterize an honest person? Yet it's a slippery slope easier to begin to descend than you think. What values guide your life? What are the "rules of the road" that govern how you treat people and make decisions and that guide you in the midst of the most important crossroads and moments of your life? Are they tied to the absolute truth and hope of the risen Christ or to the relative temperatures of the day? Are they the values embodied in the example of God Himself, or are they tied to political correctness, academic freedom, personal autonomy, convenience, creativity, and expression, where "what is right for me" trumps "what is right"?

Select carefully. You may never make a "favorite" list, but remember that at the end of it all, right and truth will always triumph, will always result in freedom, and will always get you safely home.

IMPACT APPLICATION: The truth of the risen Christ directs us to the truth in all things—stay at the top of any slope you face with that.

STEPPING OUT
WITH PASSION

I still belong to you; you hold my right hand. You guide me with your counsel, leading me to a glorious destiny. **Psalm 73:23-24**

REMEMBER THAT LAST PROJECT at the office you were sure you could never do or get done on time? You were defeated from the start.

Remember that time when someone forgot to recognize your birthday? You were hurt for the day. How about when you watched the evening news and were sure the world was going to blow up at any moment? The clouds encircled you, despite the sunshine trying to break through.

Maybe you're still finding it hard to forget some of the childhood admonitions that broke your spirit and put you on a downward spiral. Things like "You've never been a good test-taker" or "I wish you were more like so-and-so" or "You'll never amount to much." The saddest part of statements like those is that over time they tend to color our early view of our heavenly Father. And they tend to sap us of the passion and will to step out because we are unsure of the result. And so we find ourselves at a life-changing fork in the road, trying to decide which path to take, and we decide to sit in the corner, waiting for a sign that never comes. Passionless. Frozen in fear with the prospect of failure looming before us.

I suspect that if we tabulated the number of times we allowed our thoughts to run in a negative direction instead of a positive one when faced with a view of the next steps of our lives, we would see that the enemy to all we were meant to be was not out there somewhere but was really lurking inside us. Inside, where we may have learned to see the glass as half empty instead of half full. Where no matter what we face, we tend to dwell on the worst that could happen in every situation, rather than on all the possibilities. And so we too often take the easy way—or no way—rather than risking failure.

Maybe you've never been there. Good. Just guard against the creep of the enemy who will rob you of all you were meant to be.

But for those of us who have been there, well, it's a new day, and the rest of your life is before you. And it's your life, not what someone else has said it should be. It's the life He created you to live with passion. And it's right there before you. Claim it for yourself today.

Step out. With passion.

 IMPACT APPLICATION: One day at a time, step out with passion into all He created you to be. And remember as you do that He will be right there by your side, urging you on and holding you by His right hand all the way.

OCTOBER 1

FALL

For everything there is a season, a time for every activity under heaven. . . . Yet God has made everything beautiful for its own time. He has planted eternity in the human heart, but even so, people cannot see the whole scope of God's work from beginning to end. So I concluded there is nothing better than to be happy and enjoy ourselves as long as we can. **Ecclesiastes 3:1, 11-12**

A COLD FRONT BLEW through our area and swept across the southeast ushering in the season of fall with its cooler temperatures and brisk breezes. At about the same time, our two granddaughters, a young friend, and my sister Randi, here for a visit, swept through the playroom and other parts of our home leaving behind them the signs of their wonderful invasion.

After we spent some time straightening up, the rooms were returned to some semblance of neatness. The only thought that came to my mind was *I wish it were still filled with toys and games and with them.*

I have found that I tend to feel that way a lot during this season of my life.

Maybe that's why, as the pages of the calendar continue to turn so quickly, fall has become my favorite season. It seems to be a more reflective time. The myriad colors of the changing leaves paint vividly the emotions of the time and the season. The air is cooler. The breezes are more brisk and yet gentle as they touch and blow through your hair. The holidays are just around the corner, when pages will be added to the albums of family memories.

I suppose it comes with the territory—getting a bit older, that is. And with it more moments spent in times of reflection.

Fall. It's a season of life that everyone—of any and every age—should embrace throughout their whole life. It's a season when the important things seem to come into much clearer focus. A time to be reminded that the important things are not simply to be remembered or embraced in the fall of our lives, but in every season.

I was made to believe earlier in life—and for a time bought into it—that there would be time later to see my family. There would be time later to spend with my spouse, child, and friends. I rationalized as moments now forever gone passed me by.

Today it's different. "Never again" is the theme for me and the rest of my days. But "never again" seems to come with the territory of getting older.

Enjoy the most glorious of seasons, reflecting on the most meaningful moments and memories to be made. Live them now.

 IMPACT APPLICATION: Reflect on what is truly important. Why wait until the fall of your life, or later, to reflect on the things and people that truly matter? Tomorrow may be too late.

400—TOGETHER

I planted the seed in your hearts, and Apollos watered it, but it was God who made it grow. It's not important who does the planting, or who does the watering. What's important is that God makes the seed grow. **1 Corinthians 3:6-7**

ON JANUARY 19, 2013, Coach Billy Donovan won his four hundredth basketball game as the head basketball coach at the University of Florida. He had also previously won thirty-five games while head basketball coach at Marshall University. And the Saturday afternoon game that put that capstone on his long string of victories was a performance worthy of the achievement.

To those who have followed him, this achievement was no surprise. To those who love him, there was gratitude for the health, opportunity, and ability God had given him to reach this point. And from the focal point of the achievement—Coach Donovan himself—there was humility and deflection.

In a series of cordial exchanges in the postgame media gathering, at one point a reporter asked what it felt like to reach such a milestone and at one school—not common in the history of the sports world. Without a moment's pause, Billy responded exactly the way those who know him would expect. "I don't look at them as my wins. I look at them as University of Florida wins."

He went on to elaborate that there are so many people, players, and coaches who share a part of all these victories. Some, he pointed out, were in the stands today. So many other past University of Florida teams he led had also contributed their share, which when accumulated through the years resulted in reaching this milestone—together.

It's no surprise that Billy Donovan has been so successful through the years. His success is not about him. No matter how many others want to focus on what occurs on the hardwood court as his accomplishment, he refuses to allow the focus to remain on him. Instead, he is always giving others the credit, others their due, and others the respect he holds for them.

And those who know him best know that the main source he credits for any of his successes, on and off the court, is the God who loves him and the passion of his commitment to grow more and more each day through his personal relationship with Jesus Christ. A relationship which continually calls him to being all he can be, to becoming the best person that God created him to be—as a man, husband, father, coach, friend, mentor, lifter, and encourager of others around him.

Can you imagine what the world would look like if more and more of us took that approach to life?

 IMPACT APPLICATION: Give credit where it is due—to others and the God who is in control of it all. Then to honor Him, be the best you can be wherever He plants you.

OCTOBER 3

CONTRASTS
OF IMPORTANCE

The King will say, "I tell you the truth, when you did it to one of the least of these my brothers and sisters, you were doing it to me!"
Matthew 25:40

IT WAS A LONG WEEKEND of contrasts between the important and unimportant, the humble and arrogant, sunshine and showers, memories and hopes, blessings and struggles, and—well, it was a long weekend of contrasts. You've had them.

Somewhere it included changing my granddaughter's diaper and observing a new head football coach, praying his focus would always remain beyond self, both inside and outside a stadium that each night casts its shadows across the lives of children who will go to bed hungry, abused, and without a chance for an education. In the meantime, I remember thinking of my godson and the son of a dear friend—second lieutenants both—standing ready for flight duty, at minimal pay, so that we might sleep quietly and safely in our beds at night.

Just another weekend of contrasts.

Somewhere in the midst of the weekend there was time spent with my daughter-in-law and neighbor as we watched my son teach my elder granddaughter the intricacies of baseball. We were watching my alma mater sweep undefeated through the NCAA regional baseball tournament, hoping that the players and their coaches realized that the fame, the game, and the outcome didn't really matter that much unless they embraced the platform they had been granted to positively impact the lives of others. After all, the roar of the fans will eventually fade if wins don't continue, injuries and aging will beset the players, losses will result in changes of personnel, and then the opportunities to use the platform they have had may be forever lost.

Just another moment of contrasts.

A longtime friend, Bob, would have loved that his Gators had won the regional baseball tournament. Bob would have been there—he never missed—but instead, those of us who attended his funeral were reminded of how he had touched our lives through the years. He didn't have wealth or political influence. He hadn't climbed to the top of any corporate or coaching ladder, but he would have known what to do for others if he had. He achieved no notoriety, but his word was always good, and he always wanted to know how you and your family were doing. He simply touched a lot of lives and now rests in the arms of his heavenly Father.

It has been a weekend of contrasts.

 IMPACT APPLICATION: Every day of our lives is filled with contrasts between the important and unimportant. I wonder which we will see, which we will grasp, which we will act upon. The purpose of our lives will be defined by our choices.

THE UNCOMMON PATH

I am about to do something new. See, I have already begun! Do you not see it? I will make a pathway through the wilderness. I will create rivers in the dry wasteland. Isaiah 43:19

"GRAN! GRAN!" It's how Ellie Kate tries to rein me back in when I am waxing on about something she asked but clearly missed the point she was trying to make.

"But Gran! Gran!"

There is an urgency to our younger granddaughter's little voice that would lead an outside observer to believe that if only I would stop listening to my own voice long enough to hear hers, there is much on the line here, much I could learn, and much I really need to hear to point me in a different direction and on a different path.

But it's not always easy because the common course of our lives is one of familiarity and comfort and often has been dictated by the rules of the world we live in, rules to which we have become all too accustomed or resigned. We follow the usual and common paths.

And then we tend to instill that common course into the next generation and the next—molding them into our own image, often living through them the lives we wish we had lived.

And so their journey begins to look a lot like ours. They tend to smile as we do—or don't. They tend to react to things, positively or negatively, the way we do. They tend to see who they can become as we see that for their lives. Often the same way others saw it for ours. They tend to try to live up to what our expectations of them are, usually dictated by our journey or the values of society. The templates of how we, and society in general, lived our lives are laid upon theirs—and too often they simply follow wherever the path we set out in front of them leads.

That's not the way God intended it to be.

We were meant to live uncommon lives of significance. Lives like no one else, because by His design, we are like no one else. We were meant to follow Him where there is no path and blaze the trail that only our lives can blaze.

I can almost hear that voice of God screaming down from above—"Scott! Scott! Not that way! Scott—this way—follow me!"

It's my choice to listen. It's my choice and yours to live the common lives that the world lays before us or the uncommon lives that God intended for us to live.

"Gran! Gran!"

I'm listening, sweetie. Finally, I'm listening. Thank You, Lord!

 IMPACT APPLICATION: The path is clear: live the uncommon life—the life of impact and significance that God intended when He created you and only you, and leave the trail and impact for good that He intended, that only you can leave.

OCTOBER 5

BEGIN THE CLIMB

Let all that I am wait quietly before God, for my hope is in him.
Psalm 62:5

YOU HAVE HAD THEM BEFORE, I'm sure, those quiet still mornings before anyone else is awake. Special mornings where your thoughts drift to somewhere you haven't been in a while, before the news begins to filter in for the day and as the sun gently tiptoes across the yard. Mornings where you've felt energized and uplifted by all the memories from your yesterdays, the reminders of the blessings already of today, and the hope in all your tomorrows. You're ready for the day, ready to climb.

Since I didn't have a driver's license at the time and was living on my own, I don't remember exactly how I got there. The ticket to the movie cost me a night's wages from washing dishes at the all-night diner down on the beach. I was a junior in high school as I sat there all by myself in a theater full of people, captivated by the story line and music of *The Sound of Music.* And much like one of those quiet mornings, it touched something in me as it still does today these many years later.

At one point, the lyrics and musical score of the song "Climb Ev'ry Mountain" soared across the screen, lifting the viewers and me to a realization of all the potential of a brand-new day.

You couldn't help but be lifted toward the dreams long embedded in your heart. You could sense the strength building within you that would enable you to overcome even the most difficult of times you have faced or to commit to climb whatever was before you. You couldn't help but reflect on your dreams and begin to climb toward the ones that really count.

Perhaps today it will encourage us to climb toward those dreams that are still sitting on ready, toward relationships that need to be restored, toward lives to be improved, and toward people to be loved just as they are and lifted to all they were created to be. Perhaps you could begin to climb toward building deeper relationships with your children and grandchildren and other family members, friends, and neighbors. Perhaps you could begin anew the climb toward making a difference in just one life and then another and another.

And perhaps today you will begin to climb hand in hand with the One who is always there, waiting, watching, encouraging, and climbing with you toward a life He is calling you to, toward a life that changes the world around you, one life at a time. Perhaps even your life—for all eternity.

IMPACT APPLICATION: Each day is a new opportunity to climb with Him toward all He has placed on our hearts and to become all we were meant to be. Begin the climb today.

GROUNDED
IN HIS LOVE

Your roots will grow down into God's love and keep you strong.
And may you have the power to understand, as all God's people
should, how wide, how long, how high, and how deep his love is.
Ephesians 3:17-18

HIS WORDS from a few years ago continue to resonate in my thoughts as the sunshine sweeps across every morning. As I was reflecting on them, our godson and his family happened to be with us for a day, and during the course of one of our conversations, he mentioned how fast time seems to be passing. Tell me about it.

For it seemed like just yesterday that our godchildren and their families, as well as our children—Nathan, our son, and Amy, our daughter-in-law—were married. And at that moment our son and daughter-in-law were celebrating their nine-teenth wedding anniversary—a journey that has had many mountaintops and, as with all journeys, a few valleys. A journey where in the good times, like us all, they have had to recheck and reclaim their values, and in tough times they realized they had to draw close to them. A journey where at all times they have had to remember who they are and from where they came, as they have been exposed to the influences of other people, institutions, and a shifting society.

The words I was remembering are those of a dear friend and mentor who taught me something I have never forgotten. He happens to be a federal judge. That has been his profession for over four decades. His calling, though, has been to live a legacy that lifts the lives in the world around him.

It was during lunch one day when he told me that, wherever you find yourself, whatever you face, whatever you have done or are planning to do, always remember the best of your roots, the best of where you came from, the best of who and whose you are, and most important, that you are God's child and your roots go down deep into the soil of His love for you, whether you realize it or not. It will serve to stabilize and then redirect you. Words for my son and family and for my godson and his family as life speeds along.

Even though the Judge and I don't spend as much time with each other as in times before, those words continue to influence my life and day-to-day decisions. Through those words that day, as well as others since, his steady influence has rippled through my journey for the good of those others who are always close, whether family and friends or those others who have come into my life.

 IMPACT APPLICATION: Focus on and ground yourself in God's incredible love and those other encouraging, uplifting, and affirming roots of your life for today's travels and tomorrow's dreams.

OCTOBER 7

BEING A MAN

Look at my Servant, whom I have chosen. . . . He will not fight or shout or raise his voice in public. He will not crush the weakest reed or put out a flickering candle. Finally he will cause justice to be victorious.
Matthew 12:18-20

IT'S A SAD REALITY of life that as men try to be the spiritual head, supporter, and strong rudder of their families, while also setting their course in a world that respects only résumés, trophies, and trinkets representing wealth and achievement, we too often miss becoming all that God created us to be as men. That is, some of the characteristics woven by God into us are suppressed by a society bent on the temporal and transient rather than the eternal.

So our nature to be sensitive, vulnerable, and honest with who we are and what we feel is often undeveloped and unshared with others behind our personally constructed walls. And when we keep the walls up, we also become unapproachable by all those around us who need a place to learn and land.

I've seen too many dads who never hug or kiss their children and never say, "I love you," rationalizing that this was how they were raised. I might ask, as I heard a famous talk show host ask someone once, "So, how's that working for you?" And how do you suppose it's working for those who are looking to their fathers or grandfathers or uncles or other men in their lives for all that it means to be a man? We've all been to way too many funerals where children and families walk away crying, not just for their loss at that moment but for all the lost years never really getting to know that man who had occupied such an important place in their lives.

Maybe it's time, no matter your age, to open up, to become all that God created for you to be—not just a supporter, protector, husband, father, and friend, but all that He created you to be as a man, including the sensitive, vulnerable, and deeper parts of you—allowing you to experience all the fullness of life God intended for you to experience and intended for those around you to enjoy.

And if you need a little assurance to take this leap of faith, to open your life up, to let the walls down a bit, to let others into all those other areas of your life as you begin to allow the more sensitive and emotional sides of who you are to show, remember that no matter what may happen, the One who created you will never leave you and will always love you.

 IMPACT APPLICATION: Why not stop being something we're not and stop trying to hide who we are and simply be all God created us to be—with all of our strengths, weaknesses, courage, emotions, sensitivities, creativity—in the platforms of influence He brought into our lives?

A BLESSING THREE TIMES OVER

Jesus called a little child to him and put the child among them. Then he said, "I tell you the truth, unless you turn from your sins and become like little children, you will never get into the Kingdom of Heaven. So anyone who becomes as humble as this little child is the greatest in the Kingdom of Heaven. And anyone who welcomes a little child like this on my behalf is welcoming me." **Matthew 18:2-5**

STRANGE AS IT MAY SEEM, as I wrapped myself in a warm robe to let the dogs out on a cold, clear morning, my thoughts were on a precious little girl a hundred and thirty miles away, wearing a warm sweater or jacket matching the required school uniform as she headed to her first-grade class with one of her parents.

Hannah, my elder granddaughter, had called me three times in the last two days to wish me a happy birthday. The first call was left on the answering machine Saturday, the night before the magical day, in words etched forever on the machine and my heart.

"Happy Birthday, Gran!" Followed immediately, not by the traditional "Happy Birthday to You," but instead in her very own passionate arrangement of John Philip Sousa's "The Stars and Stripes Forever," which she knew would touch her Granddaddy's patriotic heart.

On my birthday the next morning, she called again, catching me before Sunday school with another "Happy birthday, Gran!" and then a much-welcomed litany of her plans for the day.

Then, finally and later that evening, after what I learned was a long and tiring day of bike riding, sand pouring into her hair at the playground, and other general and important play activities, she made one last call, just to make sure I knew she cared. She called from the warm folds of her clean bedsheets and a blanket, moments before falling asleep and after a bath and deep-scrub hair shampoo to ask if I'd had a good day with Mimi. She was a bit sad, though, because her bike had gotten wet under the sprinkler. She was relieved after Mimi and I assured her it would be fine.

I can't remember what happened the rest of those days around my birthday that year, but it was a birthday weekend I'll never forget because my precious granddaughter wanted to make sure I knew she loved me.

Happy birthday, indeed. Jesus talks about the reward of welcoming children on His behalf in the Scripture above, but there is great reward in the welcome that children show to us as well. Don't miss opportunities to cultivate relationships with all the children in your life.

IMPACT APPLICATION: They melt your hearts and they grow too fast. Don't miss a moment with your children, grandchildren, godchildren, or others— those are sacred times. And if you have missed a few too many, it's not too late to begin making memories today.

DO YOU HEAR THE PEOPLE SING?

Dear friend, don't let this bad example influence you. Follow only what is good. Remember that those who do good prove that they are God's children, and those who do evil prove that they do not know God.
3 John 1:11

ON CHRISTMAS MORNING one year, my daughter-in-law, Amy, handed me a package and asked me to open it while everyone's attention was on me. There, lying within the folds of the tissue paper, were orchestra-level tickets to the upcoming musical production of *Les Misérables*. It was the fifth time we've seen this glorious and heart-wrenching tapestry of the struggles between good and evil, which mirrors the struggles of our society as a whole, while embracing the underlying premise that together we can, and should, reach beyond our circumstances toward a divinely intended purpose of becoming all we were created to be.

Published as a book in 1862 and introduced as a musical in the 1980s, this gripping plea for social change took shape in Victor Hugo's heart following an incident he witnessed on the streets of Paris in 1845. An impoverished man was arrested for stealing a loaf of bread to feed his family within an arm's length from a beautiful woman of affluence riding comfortably in an ornate carriage. While he was arrested, she rode on secure in her insensitivity to his plight and secure in the distance of concern for others, which society had branded as tolerable between the classes. It was a condemning contradiction of the times. We dare not let the story of those times so long ago be true of us today. Or so we would hope.

The musical ends with the stirring challenge by the entire cast to answer the call of God to us all to make the world a better place for all people, as we hear—

> *Do you hear the people sing lost in the valley of the night?*
> *It is the music of a people who are climbing to the light. . . .*
> *Do you hear the people sing? Say, do you hear the distant drums?*
> *It is the future that they bring when tomorrow comes.*

A casual observer would think the gift I received was simply tickets from a precious daughter-in-law to see a simple story, a simple yet powerful musical. Yet they are so much more. They were yet another divine and much needed reminder in the story of the duty, challenge, and responsibility to become more than we are and all we can be for God and for all the world.

 IMPACT APPLICATION: Life carries in its purpose for us the duty to reach out to others and to help them become all they were meant to be. To do less is to live less, and we will be judged, as we are watched from above, by the way we treat the least of those who walk among us.

ADDING VALUE

Above all, clothe yourselves with love, which binds us all together in perfect harmony. **Colossians 3:14**

WEBSTER'S NEW WORLD COLLEGE DICTIONARY defines *influence* as "the power of persons or things to affect others, seen only in its effects." Of course the world is full of example after example of lives influencing others—for good or not.

And we only have to turn on the local or national news to catch glimpses of those who sadly influence generation upon generation to turn from the best of who we are and can be. Yet every now and then, someone comes into our lives to influence us to take yet another step in the direction of becoming the best we were meant to be.

You may be able to count them on one hand. People who, by their wise influence, add value to our lives in many different ways. People who set forth values to which we should turn, aspire, and return. There may be more people like that in your life than that of some others, and we can call them by all sorts of descriptors—mentor, friend, bride, husband, mother, father, son, daughter, grandchild, godchild, brother, sister, teacher, coach, Gran, Mimi, and others. But just holding those titles alone does not qualify them as those who have or will add value to your life.

Be aware of those people around you who add value to your life. Seek those people out and make them a part of your life. Stay close to them. Stay close to the ones who see the God-given potential in you, who see all you can be and never try to tempt you away from who you were created to be. Never let those positive influencers get too far. Allow their positive, life-changing, and wise influence to flood over you every day. Cling to the ones who will add value to your life, and then allow their influence to ripple through you to others whom God has placed in your life to impact.

With those value adders in our lives, we then will find ourselves moved to do the same for others, so that we might be the positive influence for someone we know or someone we meet today. That's the picture we should want to see—ripples upon ripples of adding value to the lives around us, generation after generation after generation. We will be adding value to their lives—by our example, our words, our actions, by our very lives.

 IMPACT APPLICATION: There are those in the world who take away things in our lives, and there are those who add value to our lives. Surround yourself with those who add value to your life, and then be one to others.

OCTOBER 11

ROLLER COASTERS

Do not fear, for I am with you; do not anxiously look about you, for I am your God. I will strengthen you, surely I will help you, surely I will uphold you with My righteous right hand. **Isaiah 41:10, NASB**

I WOULD BE HARD PRESSED to list any roller coasters as favorites. I haven't been on many, and I don't usually choose to ride them. There are some beauties out there, to be sure: Fahrenheit in Hershey, Pennsylvania; Cyclone in Coney Island, New York; Black Mamba at Phantasialand in Germany; Leviathan in Canada's Wonderland; Kingda Ka at Six Flags over Jackson, New Jersey; and Revenge of the Mummy at Universal Studios in Orlando, Florida.

I'll ride a roller coaster occasionally, but I don't like them much. That should come as no surprise when you realize my favorite rides are It's a Small World and Soarin' at Disney World.

The ups and downs, twists and turns, loops, corkscrews, boomerangs, inverted turns, and figure eights are not things to which the human body was meant to be subjected. But that's not my concern—whiplash, pulled back muscles, and the like can all be resolved with treatment, rest, and a good massage. It's that one loose bolt that didn't get tightened by a tired construction worker that can cause the whole thing to come unhinged.

Life is a lot like that. Twists and turns, figure eights, inverted days, and loose bolts causing things to fall apart without warning, with all of those contributing to an uncertain and at times scary journey.

Here's where it gets better, though—when Christ is in the front car. The twists and turns are still there. You'll still have to go through the figure eights and loops and corkscrews. And the ride will at times be uncertain and scary.

But with Christ in the lead, we know how it will end. We know that not only is He with us as we buckle in and as we climb to the top of the first leg to experience the first big out-of-control drop and while we hang on for dear life as we rocket around curve after curve and loop upon loop, but He is also waiting for us as we glide into the end of the ride.

I'm not sure what you've been experiencing lately on the roller coasters you've been riding. I'm not sure what disappointments or heartaches you've been through. But here's what I know—no matter what the ride has been like or will be like, the God who created you was with you at every bend, rise, drop, and turn and will be with you the rest of the way.

And He'll be with you on all the rides ahead, in all the days ahead, and all the way into eternity.

 IMPACT APPLICATION: In the midst of whatever roller coaster you're on, look around. God is either running the controls or sitting in the lead car.

CHANGE YOUR PARADIGMS—CHANGE YOUR LIFE

The thief's purpose is to steal and kill and destroy. My purpose is to give them a rich and satisfying life. **John 10:10**

IN HIS BOOK *The Seven Habits of Highly Effective People,* Stephen Covey defines *paradigm* as "the way an individual perceives, understands, and interprets the surrounding world. A mental map." Christ suggests our paradigm for life should embrace His words of an "abundant life," now and forever.

I wonder what the paradigms of your life, or of your children, or of the people in the world around you, look like. I wonder if they resemble this one made by Ken Olsen in 1977 when he was President of Digital Equipment: "There is no reason for an individual to have a computer in their home."

Paradigms—how we view ourselves, others, and the world—affect the platforms of influence we have been given. It's how others, especially our children, learn from us how to view themselves—through the paradigms we teach them. Our paradigms influence whether our lives and those whom we influence and are called to bless will be ordinary or extraordinary. They impact how we will walk through our todays, and they set the road map for our tomorrows. They often determine whether we will embrace each day to the fullest or shrink back in fear as the morning breaks.

Old and comfortable paradigms often freeze us from attempting the extraordinary, perhaps for fear of failure, an unwillingness to leave the comfort of our daily routines, laziness, or failure to take responsibility for the gifts our Creator has given us. We give others around us who look to us for direction and wisdom all sorts of excuses as we cling to old ways of doing things, but deep down inside, where it gnaws at our soul, we know the truth and reasons that hold us back from becoming all He intended.

What extraordinary things are you missing in your life, or with your bride or child today, that you will never have a chance to enjoy again because you're doing the same thing you learned growing up or throughout your life?

What extraordinary things are others missing from their lives because you're focused on filling your own trophy case, decorating your own comfortable home, and assuring your own level of ease and comfort?

What extraordinary things are you missing in your life because you're afraid to step out of the daily "eight to five" routine that provides the security of a salary, benefits, and, dare I say in many cases, boredom?

Change your paradigms—change your life. Start by embracing the abundant life Christ calls each of us to.

IMPACT APPLICATION: Change your view to align it with God's, and make your life extraordinary in and with Him.

OCTOBER 13

GOD, HERE I COME!

[Jesus] said: "I tell you the truth, unless you change and become like little children, you will never enter the kingdom of heaven."
Matthew 18:3, NIV

THE MORNING'S BREEZE had ushered in a few days of what would be the last of the cooler, spring-like temperatures for that year. Much different than the oppressive heat of the previous day, which provided the backdrop for this scene of never-ending and total trust.

Standing at the edge of the pool, our younger granddaughter Ellie Kate, time after time, wide eyed and smiling, issued fair warning with the words "Granddaddy, here I come!" and leaned headlong into a graceful belly flop, breaking the surface of the water not too far from my waiting arms. Deep end, shallow end, with me looking or almost looking. Here she comes.

Fearless and not fully aware of the consequences of her inability to swim and her innate need for air, she jumped. Scary. Yet inculcated at this point in her young life was the knowledge that as long as she saw me nearby, she knew I'd be there and fully trusted in my ability to secure her safety.

Hers is a simple approach to life. Free from the tentacles of pride and unconcerned with social status or the opinions of the world, children the world over like Ellie Kate and her sister, Hannah, quickly learn to depend solely upon those they can trust—their parents and grandparents—as places of refuge and safety.

It's the picture Christ painted in the Scripture above of the complete dependence upon, and surrender to, God that is necessary to enter His Kingdom, to be great in His Kingdom, to be His servants for all the world. A dependence marked with a simple approach to life. A dependence that requires us to use the knowledge, gifts, and abilities—the wisdom—He has created within us to make decisions that honor Him and not us.

A dependence that announces, "God, here I come!" knowing and trusting that He will be there to catch you.

A simple approach to life—like that of a child—for all eternity.

IMPACT APPLICATION: It is something which is not intrinsic in our nature—giving up control and being dependent upon someone else. But to become all who God created us to be, that is what we must move toward—complete and absolute dependence upon and surrender to Him and His will for our lives. The neat thing is that God has proved He can be trusted with our lives.

GOD WILL
SEE US THROUGH

I hold you by your right hand—I, the LORD your God. And I say to you, "Don't be afraid. I am here to help you." **Isaiah 41:13**

LUKE, OUR BASSET HOUND, is gone now. But I remember the day when I watched our gentle puppy limping outside one morning, wondering what the little guy was thinking. We'd been told he had a problem with the growth plates in his left front leg. I wondered how much pain he was feeling and why it didn't seem to get any better. And yet he just seemed to push on through it, although slower than before. I wondered how much longer he had before someone unsuccessfully tried to persuade me it would be pointless to allow him to go on.

As I continued to watch my courageous little friend navigate the side porch steps despite the pain that was readily apparent in his gait, the words of Tom, the trainer from the movie *Seabiscuit*, began flooding my thoughts: "You don't throw a whole life away just 'cause he's banged up a little."

Tom, a has-been horse trainer, had defiantly offered those words as reason enough to save the life of a horse no longer useful for racing because of a fractured leg. And from that moment on, Tom, together with an owner struggling to overcome the pain of the past, an abandoned young boy, a defeated jockey named Red, and a small, fifteen-hands-high horse named Seabiscuit, became the unlikely catalyst of renewed hope for millions of Americans struggling to survive and overcome the difficulties that had beset them in the Great Depression.

For a number of reasons, our country turned the corner back then, as we have so many times before and will again when we must in the future. But in part we rode into a bright new day on the back of a once beaten, broken, and crippled horse named Seabiscuit, who captured the hearts of a struggling nation and inspired millions to reach beyond their banged-up lives, find their purpose once again, and become all they were created to be. And, in that, inspired them to become who they were meant to be—and to reach out to touch the face of God.

And the God of Isaiah will do the same for us each day of our lives, even if we are banged up or beaten up and no matter what obstacles we face or difficulties we are going through. Every day.

In his own way, Luke lived that, pushed through each day, and left a memory still blessing the lives of those who knew him.

IMPACT APPLICATION: No matter what we are in the midst of, God is there, and God has a purpose for us as we go through it with Him.

OCTOBER 15

YOU'RE NOT DONE

The whole law can be summed up in this one command: "Love your neighbor as yourself." **Galatians 5:14**

IT HAPPENS EVERY YEAR when the leaves begin to turn and the weather eases toward tolerable—the fall sports spectacular. An eclectic hodgepodge of amateur and professional sports sure to delight and dominate those most discriminating of households. Football, hockey, golf, volleyball, soccer, and for the true sports connoisseur, the Major League Baseball playoffs culminating in the October blessing known as the World Series. If you love it, it's a glorious time. If you love someone who loves it, you're a saint.

And in the midst of the season, the memory of a man nearly blind is staked in my consciousness. His name is Hal McCoy. He made his mark in life as a respected Cincinnati sportswriter. As I understand the story, he experienced a stroke in the optic nerve of his right eye, and his vision began to blur. He continued with his left eye serving the demands of his job until one year later the blurriness hit his good eye. The result was that he was functionally blind for the profession he had known for over thirty-one years. He felt he couldn't go on, and so he was ready to quit.

Enter the young third baseman for the Cincinnati Reds, Aaron Boone, who refused to let him quit. Together they found ways in which others could help Hal gather the information his now blurry eyes no longer allowed him to, so he could devote himself to the crafting of stories that captured the personalities and events in the world he so loved.

A few years later, Hal McCoy was inducted into Major League Baseball's Hall of Fame, the crowning achievement of our national pastime. All because of a God who gave him the gift of wordsmithing and the gift of a young man named Boone, who refused to let him throw away what he still had left just because of a little blindness.

What about you? You may be "blind," but what do you have left? You may have something blocking the path you had so carefully laid out before you. What seemingly immovable obstacle lies before your week, your month, or the rest of your life? What mountain has suddenly blurred your highway of hope?

Although real, they truly are only a temporary blur in the vision for your future which the God of all creation holds for you. Or perhaps you know someone who needs a "Boone" in their life, and you can be that person.

Whatever it is, you're not done! Get on with it—today and for the rest of your life.

 IMPACT APPLICATION: The world is in desperate need of the gifts God has given us, no matter how blurry things might seem to you now. You're not done; keep going!

BEING REAL

Then Jesus wept. **John 11:35**

THE WORDS CAME OUT that morning in bursts through streams of tears as I sat trembling on the edge of our bed.

"Lynda, quick. Go get Nathan, right now!" I knew it was time.

Immediately she understood and dismissed, in her usual stride, the abrupt tenor of my voice. She knew I was still trying to learn how to be the father that I longed and needed to be. It had been a journey of fits and spurts, trial and error, and through the example of others, especially her, I was being guided to be the better father that I should be.

"Hurry up, hurry up, go get Nathan!"

The moment took on urgency in my mind because a few days earlier Lynda had shared with me that our then seven-year-old son had come quietly to her with a heavy concern. He wondered if his daddy ever cried, because in the seven years since his birth, he had never seen me cry. She knew it was part of my carefully maintained and protective hedge she had finally been allowed behind but where very few others had ever been allowed to venture. Not even him.

And so as I sat there on the edge of our bed crying for reasons unimportant today and long since forgotten, I decided it was time to let one of the protective walls down. Through those tears, I knew it was time to let Nathan see me—real, feelings exposed, vulnerable, and sensitive. It was a risk I needed to take for him and for me and a leap of faith for one who always kept those feelings—which might expose a weakness or a chink in the armor of my image as a man—well hidden.

Steeling my emotions within a keyless vault had served to protect me through the years from further harm, which I had experienced as a child, but in the process, I was now learning, it had made me less of a man than my Creator had intended for me to be. Nathan needed to experience all of what being the man God was creating him to be was like.

And as we held each other, with his Mom watching approvingly, our now mutual tears turned to smiles and then laughter, as a pathway through my hedge began to open for him and others.

IMPACT APPLICATION: God created us to have an impact like none other in our families, among friends, in our careers, and in all the places of our lives. But to have the impact He created us to have, we must be authentic, and that at times is demonstrated by a willingness to share our fears along with our hopes, our disappointments along with our joys, and our sadness along with our happiness. To be real.

OCTOBER 17

FACING ALL OF LIFE

We are hard pressed on every side, but not crushed; perplexed, but not in despair; persecuted, but not abandoned; struck down, but not destroyed. **2 Corinthians 4:8-9,** NIV

A FEW YEARS AGO the behavior of Luke, our five-year-old basset hound, began to change, indicating to us that he was not feeling well. It came upon him rather quickly, and subsequent tests by the veterinarian would show that he had cancer that would soon thereafter take his life. Yet on that cool, crisp morning when I was letting him out, he mustered all the spring in his step he could find and bounded down the steps and outside. It was inspirational to watch him continue to use whatever potential he had remaining.

Hubert Humphrey, the former United States senator from Minnesota and vice president, was a similar inspiration to others in and throughout his life. Near death, he whispered a truth for the ages: "It isn't what you've lost, it's what you've got left that counts."

The apostle Paul, imprisoned, cold, hungry, shipwrecked, beaten with rods, and flogged over and over, reminded us in those words set out in the Scripture above that no matter what we face, our potential through Christ is undiminished to deal with what is before us. We are crushed, despairing, abandoned, or destroyed in life only if we allow ourselves to be.

Paul's words are a powerful, eternal reminder that no matter what we have been through in life and what we are facing, our life isn't over yet. Whether we've been whacked with cancer, are losing our way, or are experiencing one failure after another; whether relationships are lost or we find ourselves suffering through seemingly endless surgery after surgery, living with mental or physical illnesses that tend to stop a family in its tracks; whether in looking back with regrets and wondering where all the years have gone and what we have done with them or reeling from a mistake that happened all too recently—through all of that and more, the message of God and the examples of so many like the apostle Paul call us to push on, press on, and live on with Christ in the lead. Thank You, Lord!

When life is getting you down today, when you are feeling overwhelmed, remember that you are only defeated if you allow yourself to be. And with Christ in the lead—we never are defeated.

"Luke, so you want to go out again, already?"

Atta boy!

 IMPACT APPLICATION: No matter what difficulties you may face in life, remember that with God leading the way, there is always more for you to do with and for Him. Always.

LIVING A LIFE
OF "WE DID"

Teach us to realize the brevity of life, so that we may grow in wisdom.
Psalm 90:12

IT WAS A MEMORABLE WEEKEND that reminded me "we did" is a much better recollection than "we meant to." After a weekend visit that included wandering in the hallways and rooms of our hearts and home, our son, Nathan, and his then four-year-old daughter, Hannah, departed for home, leaving us poorer by their absence but richer with a bag full of memories.

If my recollection serves me correctly, "we did" play baseball in the backyard three times, play basketball on the patio twice, and eat barbecue dinner with Hannah's other grandparents and our godson before his trip to Italy. We swam three times, once with our basset hound puppies, made a card for Hannah's mom, and opened four homemade cards her mom had made for Hannah to open each day that she was gone.

Throughout the weekend, "we did" eat sausage, eggs, waffle sticks, SpaghettiOs, some boiled peanuts and ice cream with sprinkles, chocolate shell, and whipped cream. We grilled hamburgers for one dinner and enjoyed sliced turkey with mustard for another.

"We did" watch as Hannah squirted whipped cream into her daddy's mouth, followed by a pizza dinner and discussion about Jules Verne's *20,000 Leagues under the Sea*. She and I read Winnie the Pooh's *Blustery Day* and *The Big Honey Pot Rescue*, painted three vivid pictures with sparkly poster paints after sketching one with pastels, and walked among the gardens to smell the flowers and clip a tiny handful of gardenias for a vase on our kitchen counter. She walked five minutes on the treadmill at the brisk pace of two miles per hour at a fifteen-degree incline, took a wild roller-coaster golf cart ride with me over the hills and mounds around the golf course, and spent a good bit of each day feeding the tiny puppy, Lily, while sitting in her crate with her.

"We meant to" was not invited to be a part of our lives that weekend. Yet all too often, for too many of us, "we meant to" has left a trail of regrets woven in and through our lives. Things we can't do anything about now but which leave us with an empty bag of memories. Here's the bottom line—don't do it again. Adopt a "we did" attitude for your life, and then do the important things with the important people of your life every chance you have to do them. You will never regret it, and even more important, neither will they.

Live today as though it is the only day you will be given. If you feel a "we did" moment coming on, just do it!

IMPACT APPLICATION: Life was meant to be lived with all the important people and sacred moments God has given you—so live it.

OCTOBER 19

KNOCKING DOWN BARRIERS

Don't become so well-adjusted to your culture that you fit into it without even thinking. Instead fix your attention on God. You'll be changed from the inside out. . . . Unlike the culture around you, always dragging you down to its level of immaturity, God brings the best out of you.
Romans 12:2, MSG

"YOU SEE THINGS; and you say 'Why?' But I dream things that never were; and I say 'Why not?'"

George Bernard Shaw's words make up one of the great statements about the life I believe God calls us to live. With the opportunities we have before us to make a difference in this world, He calls us to reach for what we believe things should be in the world and within the lives around us.

Our son, Nathan, was five when we became convicted that despite the Civil Rights Movement and the elimination of "separate but equal" from our culture— at least by the rule of law—we still had a long way to go as a society in knocking down the artificial barriers we had erected between us—based on skin color, gender, economic status, and the like. The barriers which kept so many from reaching their full potential and realizing their platforms of influence.

And so Lynda and I established a rule, which we honor to this day as a family, that we would not describe anyone by their skin color. If we saw three boys standing in a group—one who happened to be African-American ("Black," back then)—and you wanted to point him out for some reason, you did so by saying that he was "The one in the middle," or "The one with the red shirt on," or "The tall/short one"—whatever—just not skin color.

It was amazing to watch Nathan grow, always looking for something more in the people he saw, rather than simply their outward appearances, and never describing anyone by skin color. Interestingly, and sadly still today, if you listen closely to people speaking, they will seldom refer to skin color if the person is white but will far too often refer to skin color if the person is not, as if to fit them into some predetermined mold or stereotype.

What's inside you longing to come out? What mold or stereotype has the culture fit you into or dragged you down to? What do you dream of that never was? What flower planted deep inside you by the One who created you has yet to bloom? What dream smoldering within your heart has yet to begin to burst into flames?

We have before us the opportunities to make a difference in the world. Maybe it begins with asking "Why not?"

 IMPACT APPLICATION: When will you begin the journey to the way things should be? When will you help someone else begin theirs? Why not today?

THE WHAT OR WHY OF LIFE

If we look forward to something we don't yet have, we must wait patiently and confidently. **Romans 8:25**

THE SIGNALS OF FALL were everywhere. The breeze seemed brisker and cooler. Our American flag seemed to billow with more purpose from its post outside our home. Major League baseball playoffs began their trek toward the World Series. And college football fanatics saw the fallibility of humanity in their favorite teams.

That particular week five of the top-ten-ranked college football teams in the nation lost all jockeying for a shot at the national championship. Those heading into the weekend games ranked number 3, 4, 5, 7, and 10 all lost. They showed up, kicked off, ran, and passed the football up and down the field for three-plus hours—and lost. And for many fans of those five teams, their world came crashing in. Their hopes for a national championship were dashed. Winning is the key— and they lost. Or did they?

It really depends on why they are doing what they are doing.

If it's all about what they do, the result, the score, the win, the ultimate championship—then indeed, they lost. But if by some chance it's about something more, something deeper, perhaps bowing to considerations of why we do it, then even in the loss, they may have won—even though the result will still appear in their season record as a loss.

The head coach of one of the five teams that lost had this to say: "The phrase I was taught as a young person is *the soul of a man is exposed when you get hit in the face.* I don't want to overdramatize a loss in football with some of the major issues in life. But the soul of a man isn't exposed when you pick up a [championship] crystal bowl and put on a championship ring. A lot of people can do that. It's when you have to rebound from some adversity."

There you have it. The soul—something deep within us that guides our next step in life. Something inside us that, when faced with a future where the end is always unclear, empowers us to take the next step anyway. Something inside us that defines why we do everything we do.

Could it be God's hand of direction, pointing the way toward the purpose of our lives?

Think about that the next time fall hits and you're trying to get into the national championship game or whatever you are reaching for. Think not about *what* you are doing, but *why* you are doing it.

IMPACT APPLICATION: We all do a lot of stuff we can use to answer when asked about what we do. What would we answer if we are ever asked *why* we do what we do? In those answers you will begin to find God's purpose for your life.

OCTOBER 21

HITTING THE FLOOR WITH PASSION

Light is sweet; how pleasant to see a new day dawning.
Ecclesiastes 11:7

I'VE HAD THOSE MORNINGS when there were enough easy ways to hit the snooze alarm over and over, when I was so tired and had no desire to face the day. I knew it before my feet hit the floor. No excitement, no passion, no desire to open my eyes to the brand-new day God was setting before me.

I wonder; when was the last time you felt excited about waking up in the morning? Today? Yesterday? Can't remember because it's been so long? Maybe you used to be excited, but then that tragic day came when you lost a loved one? Or maybe it was before the doctor's words that there was nothing more that could be done, hitting you like a sledgehammer? Or before you lost your job?

I don't know what the reading on your excitement meter is today, but I do know that no matter what it reads, no matter what you're going through or where you find yourself, there is One who is excited to see you today. We call Him by many names—Father, Wonderful Counselor, Mighty God, Emmanuel, Prince of Peace, Jehovah. But I would suggest that there is one name He loves to hear above all others from your lips—Abba, or Daddy, the most intimate of all names we can call Him. The name that shows Him you know how excited He is to see you today and every day, as you awake or sleep quietly under His protective gaze each night or as you return home to Him through each thought and through every day of your life.

Something got you down today? Feel as though you're on the downward slope of your life on earth? Perhaps you're starting something new or facing some uncertainty, something that seems a little scary and you're not sure you can handle. Do yourself a favor, and remember that the God who created it all is the One who gave you this day and stands ready to walk and run with you through it. Feeling a bit empty and without passion and excitement for the day? Let the God who created you fill you with His passion.

Then go out and do yourself and someone else another favor: share that passion with them.

It will make all the difference in their life and in yours.

 IMPACT APPLICATION: Every day with the God who created you is a day of excitement and a day to be passionate about. Every day is also a day to share that passion not only with Him, but with all those around you.

I WISH I HAD DONE THAT

The thief does not come except to steal, and to kill, and to destroy. I have come that they may have life, and that they may have it more abundantly. **John 10:10,** NKJV

I WASN'T READY for what Nathan said when he called me one day a few years ago. We had always encouraged him to write—a gift he has demonstrated since he was a teenager.

"Dad, I'm thinking about talking with Coach Dungy about writing a book about him. What do you think?"

I fought back feelings of worry—as best as I can remember, they would have been expressed, "Really? It will take so long to do that, and then you have to hope you can get a publisher. How will you be able to support your family in the meantime?" Those particular words of a concerned father remained unspoken.

Instead, I listened while he told me about his dream. He had some savings and felt a calling to write a book about his dear friend Tony Dungy and his life—the ups and downs and the values that have guided his journey—a book that would glorify God and bless and encourage people as they lived their lives. When he had finished, my response was, as it has consistently been in similar situations: "Try to minimize the moments in your life where you will look back and say 'I wish I had done that.'"

It was not an easy road for him in those initial years, but he never lost sight of the dream God had placed in his heart. And through many starts and restarts, prayers and encouragement, working in ministry in his local church to support his family while still pursuing and waiting for God's timing, and even friends "paying forward" what someone had done for them earlier in their lives, the book *Quiet Strength: The Principles, Practices, and Priorities of a Winning Life* became a reality, and other books followed.

The journey wasn't easy, and circumstances came up that could have stolen that dream many times.

What is trying to steal your dream? Your joy? Your hope? Perhaps someone has criticized what has been laid on your heart for you to do. Perhaps past failures tell you that you're sure to fail again. Perhaps it's worry or feelings of inadequacy or despair at the current circumstances of your life. Perhaps your time is spent on climbing the ladders the world says you should.

Yet Christ came that we might have life and have it more abundantly. Who do you think puts those dreams in your heart? And who do you think tries to steal them?

Follow your dreams. God will guide, protect, and walk with you as you do.

IMPACT APPLICATION: Align your heart and desires with the God who created you and follow the dreams He has placed in your heart.

OCTOBER 23

ETCHING LOVE IN THEIR LIVES

He returned home to his father. And while he was still a long way off, his father saw him coming. Filled with love and compassion, he ran to his son, embraced him, and kissed him. **Luke 15:20**

SEVERAL YEARS AGO Nathan returned home a bit earlier than expected from a trip. Expecting to surprise Amy and Hannah with his early arrival, instead he caught them still out running some errands in preparation for his return. He was unpacking in the back bedroom when his heart quickened as he heard their car pull into the garage and the door to the house open. Then he heard the rapid patter of little footsteps heading his way and his daughter's precious voice as she ran to greet him, calling to him over and over, "Daddy, you will be so excited to see me!" And he was, and he will always be.

When was that last time you felt someone was excited to see you? When was the last time someone felt you were excited to see them? Is there someone who needs to know that you are excited to see them today? A child. A niece or nephew. Your bride. An elderly person. A friend. A neighbor. A student. Someone you coach. Someone you work with each day. Perhaps even someone you have not in the past felt all that excited about seeing each day or any day.

Nathan's daughters know that their daddy will be excited to see them each and every day, that his heartbeat always quickens a beat or two when he knows he's about to see them again. They know that about their mommy, too, and me and their Mimi and many others.

It didn't happen overnight, but over and over their daddy indelibly etched his love for them in their lives. He etched it through his excitement for them, with his smile, the lilt and lift of his voice, the ever-present affirmation of his words, the always gentle and protective touch of his hands, and his constant presence in their lives.

The etching happened in the mornings as they awoke, during play and planting flowers in the yard, while on their "date night" together. He never missed a moment to etch his love on their hearts while reading together, eating together, splashing in puddles together, traveling together, in moments when they were happy and moments when they were not.

In every moment of their lives, he etched the words in their hearts—"I am so excited to see you."

God is similarly excited to see us, even more so when we come to see Him.

Who needs to feel your excitement about them today? Etch it on their lives.

 IMPACT APPLICATION: We each have the power and ability to impact the lives of others to glorify God. Their lives will be better for it, and so will ours.

FACING THE SCARY MONSTERS

I lie awake thinking of you, meditating on you through the night. Because you are my helper, I sing for joy in the shadow of your wings. I cling to you; your strong right hand holds me securely. **Psalm 63:6-8**

EVERY NOW AND THEN the scary monsters seem to return.

I was reminded of that a few years ago as our granddaughter Hannah expressed concern to her Mimi that she thought an R.O.U.S. (Rodent of Unusual Size—from the movie *The Princess Bride*) may have infiltrated the normally safe space under her bed. As her Mimi inspected the area to remove any such intruder, secure the space, and allay her fears, I made a mental note to thank her parents for exposing her tender innocence to that image, and others, at her age. (Only kidding.)

Yet even when scary monsters on occasion do rear their ugly heads, Hannah is beginning to know where to go for help in handling them. Whether an R.O.U.S. or similarly envisioned creature from the world of make-believe, monsters in the shape of anxieties about tomorrow or in the form of guilt over something she needs to get off her mind, or concern over some other fog she can't seem to wrap her brain around to get clarity or peace about, she is learning where to go for help, security, and peace.

As we prayed with her that night, she thanked God for being with her, for knowing that He was bigger than all the scary monsters and anything else that bothered her and that He would help her. She asked that He stay with her that night, as He always does. It is clear she was learning where to turn for help in dealing with R.O.U.S.'s and other monsters of the day and night.

How about you? Where do you turn for help in dealing with the monsters of your days and nights? Where do you turn for help with an addiction that you can't seem to get past? Where do you turn for help with the feelings of desperation and emptiness that consume you from the loss of a loved one? Where do you turn when you're trying to find the passion that will fill each day with significant productivity? Where do you turn when you can't seem to get over something in your past that is tying you down and holding you back from becoming all you were meant to be?

May I suggest that you take a suggestion from a little girl whom God sent our way many years ago and let Him help you to deal with those scary monsters?

IMPACT APPLICATION: Life is full of scary monsters to deal with. But there is One who is in our corner who is bigger than them all. Turn to the God who is always there with you and loves you, and turn those scary monsters over to Him.

OCTOBER 25

WORLD SERIES ROSES

Don't copy the behavior and customs of this world, but let God transform you into a new person by changing the way you think. Then you will learn to know God's will for you, which is good and pleasing and perfect. **Romans 12:2**

YOU CAN TELL FALL has officially arrived with the start of World Series baseball.

And to this day Lynda says she doesn't remember the brown paper bag hanging from my left hand on that fall day in the first year of our marriage.

It was October 1967, the first game of the World Series. Lynda and I had been married in June and honeymooned along the east coast.

My perennial favorites, the long-suffering Boston Red Sox, were about to square off against the mighty St. Louis Cardinals. My supervisor could sense that my attention was elsewhere and graciously told me to go home and watch the game.

Before driving home, I stopped, knowing I shouldn't, at the grocery store and bought a six-pack of Hamm's beer. It was a period before I stopped drinking alcohol. The six-pack cost eighty-five cents, which was more than our budget could afford.

So there I was driving home for the game, beer in a brown paper bag next to me and with guilt steadily rising within me. When a florist shop popped into view, I stopped and purchased two yellow roses. Feeling slightly better, I headed home with my one-dollar bribe lying on the seat alongside the paper bag with its illicit contents, realizing that I had now spent almost two dollars that we couldn't afford.

Lynda saw me pull in and rushed to greet me at the door. All she saw were the two yellow roses I pushed toward her face with the accompanying greeting, "Happy World Series!" She beamed at my distraction and never said a word about the beer, and in typical fashion, my Red Sox lost game one.

But the tradition of the roses, now a dozen yellow ones given on the first day of each World Series, has continued without blemish for forty-nine years, despite its worldly beginnings. It was perhaps a selfish beginning to a glorious tradition and annual symbol of renewal of a lifetime commitment to a precious gift from God.

As only God can do, He transformed a bad decision into a loving tradition and eventually removed a destructive habit, making me a new person. Traditions like that, no matter their beginnings, when aligned with God, are to be cherished and nurtured, moving us toward the lives of impact God has designed us to live.

 IMPACT APPLICATION: The traditions of our faith, of our country—even traditions of World Series roses—demand that we require better of our lives each and every day, all under the transformative hand of God.

OUR HEISMAN TROPHIES

The Life-Light blazed out of the darkness; the darkness couldn't put it out. . . . The Life-Light was the real thing. . . . We all live off his generous bounty, gift after gift after gift. **John 1:5, 9, 16,** MSG

AS EVERY COLLEGE FOOTBALL SEASON winds down, the headlines across the nation begin to talk not only about winning championships and bowl games or setting passing and touchdown records, but winning the Heisman Trophy.

For what purpose? For what ultimate good? To use the platform it offers to positively influence the lives of "children of all ages" in the world.

That's it. And that's enough, despite what other reasons the world may give for its purpose.

Perhaps the winner of the Heisman Trophy each year will do the same thing that folks like Brian Clark and Phil Pharr did when they were living lives that modeled a standard of faith, integrity, and service for our son Nathan, while Nathan—age ten—stood nearby, idolizing them just because they were football players. They got Nathan's attention because they were college football players, but they helped to set the direction of his life because of the character of their walk. And for their influence, Lynda and I remain eternally grateful.

So what are you doing with your own "Heisman Trophies"? You don't see them in your trophy case? Look around at your roles—perhaps Dad, Father, Son, Husband, Grandparent, Friend, Teammate, Employer, Employee, Coach. See them now? Opportunities to leave a legacy.

The Heisman Trophy presented each year at the end of a season of magnificent accomplishments will sit in a glass case at some university gathering "oohs" and "aahs" from those passing by and even an occasional particle of dust. Yet it can represent so much more than recognition for what was achieved by one person in one football season.

Perhaps, just perhaps, it is the beginning of an opportunity of what can be achieved in the world around us. Brian and Phil understood that. Nathan—because of their influence and the ongoing influence of others—understands that.

Perhaps, just perhaps, it will become a platform to change lives for good, to help others become all they were meant to be, and to point them to the One over all. Used for anything else, the Heisman Trophy simply becomes a twenty-five-pound bronze statue in a case. Used to change the world, it becomes a light blazing in the darkness, pointing the way to all we were meant to be, pointing the way to the One True Light that still blazes in the darkness.

What will each of us do with our "Heisman Trophies"? What will be the legacy of our lives?

IMPACT APPLICATION: We all have "Heisman Trophy" roles and opportunities to impact others' lives around us, leaving a legacy only we can leave. All for the good of others and for God's glory.

OCTOBER 27

MAKE IT PERSONAL

He will answer, "I tell you the truth, when you refused to help the least of these my brothers and sisters, you were refusing to help me."
Matthew 25:45

IT SEEMS MORE PERSONAL this morning. The sky outside my window continues to darken. It seems more personal this morning, as I remember her face from a few days past.

She seemed troubled as she stepped from the public bus which had pulled to a regular route stop in front of me. Frantic almost. Her hurried gait seemed almost energized by fear. Perhaps she was returning from work, going home to a troubled situation. She hitched her bag once more over her shoulder as she scurried to cross the street behind my now-stopped car.

What was her life like? Was she rushing home to children? Was she married? A boyfriend? Stable? Abusive? The worried wrinkles in her face betrayed years of living beyond her real age. It seemed more personal now as I realized that she was once a little girl with the whole world in front of her. I wondered if she was living out any of her childhood dreams. It didn't seem like the world had been kind to her, and her haggard look made me terribly sad on her behalf.

It just seems more personal now. Perhaps it's a fatherly instinct. Maybe it's an authentic sensitivity to the vulnerability of the defenseless, of any age, sharpened on the anvil of personal childhood experiences. Maybe it's a descending and ominous awareness of the reality of a culture that too often sees its highest and best use in the luxury of personal comfort, in an escape to retirement, or in an ever-increasing climate of self-promotion, while turning a blind eye to the need in our world and the growing statistics of generation upon generation being lost in a downward spiral of self-destruction, hopelessness, and washed-away dreams.

It just seems more personal now, having seen that woman walk past my car. But you know, it's always been personal, yet somewhere along our journey with too many self-centered days, we lost our way, our real purpose, and we lost sight of that frightened little girl, now a woman getting off the public bus, while still carrying those childhood dreams but now they're only in her baggage of memories labeled "what might have been."

Isn't it really time for it to be personal, to see the responsibility and opportunity each of us has to make a difference in this world? With the platforms and opportunities we have, take it personally and make a difference today before it's too late.

IMPACT APPLICATION: When the plight and interests of others is foremost in our minds and hearts and we act to make a difference in those lives, we begin to approach our highest and best use for which God designed us.

MORE TO LIFE

Seek the LORD while you can find him. Call on him now while he is near. **Isaiah 55:6**

WE KNEW THAT the victorious head coach of Super Bowl XLI was a nice guy. And so was the head coach who came up just a bit short. Both of them finished a long way from last.

That Super Bowl between the Indianapolis Colts and the Chicago Bears was a game marked by riveting story lines and participants striving after the ultimate prize in professional football. Yet for Tony Dungy and Lovie Smith, that game was not the "end all, be all" in their lives. In a joint statement printed in *USA Today* issued a few days before the game, here is what they had to say: "On Sunday, one of us will be world champion. It's the ultimate goal—but we know that there is more to life than football. Even when you have achieved the ultimate, something better lies beyond."

More to life than football or sports? In this culture?

Did they mean to suggest that the Super Bowl championship will not satisfy? You've got to be kidding. Well then, how about winning the national championship in college basketball? Or the national championship in college football? Or both, like the University of Florida did a few years ago. Surely that must be the pinnacle in our journey to find fulfillment and satisfaction in life? There are fans, alumni, followers, coaches, athletes, boosters, and sports administrators everywhere who think so.

In another setting before that Super Bowl, Coach Dungy added this to his pregame comments: "A personal relationship with Jesus Christ is the only way I've found true peace, joy and forgiveness."

I wonder if you've found what you think you're looking for. Or perhaps you think you found it once but laid it aside for other pursuits. I wonder if you're feeling fulfilled each day—or instead find yourself tossed and torn by the events and circumstances all around you. Perhaps you find yourself living a life where your happiness quotient is determined by the wins and losses of each day.

Well, if any of that defines your life, perhaps you need to look somewhere else. Perhaps you need to look where Tony Dungy and Lovie Smith point their lives. That's where you'll find the ultimate prize—in a relationship—or renewed or restored relationship—with the risen Christ.

Tony Dungy may have been presented with the Vince Lombardi Trophy for winning Super Bowl XLI, but the truth is that he won it a long time before that when he learned about what really matters in life—a relationship with Jesus Christ.

IMPACT APPLICATION: Ultimate fulfillment is available through a personal relationship with Jesus Christ. In Him we find our purpose and the greatest victory in all of life.

WINDMILLS

The thief's purpose is to steal and kill and destroy. My purpose is to give them a rich and satisfying life. **John 10:10**

I GUESS IT WAS ABOUT 6 A.M. when the morning stillness was broken by her crying on the monitor in our bedroom. Our granddaughter Hannah was spending that weekend with us. Our son, Nathan, was representing the Tampa Bay Bucs at the National Football League Draft that weekend, and his wife, Amy, had traveled with him.

As I climbed the stairs to Hannah's room, I knew it would be good for her if she could sleep a little longer. Lynda was always good at getting her back to sleep, but I told Lynda I'd go and check on her. As I arrived at her bedside, Hannah advised me of the problem. Nemo, her new plush fish toy, had fallen out of bed, and Hannah was worried because she couldn't find him. With all the wisdom and care the situation required, I tucked Nemo under her arm.

Fresh from another child-rearing success, I eased into my office, where my gaze fell on the figurine of Don Quixote, which Lynda had given me after Christmas. I remembered the wonderful evening, recounted by Nathan on the phone, that he and Amy had just had in New York. Dinner and the Broadway play *Man of La Mancha*. His voice resonated between the tension of sadness and inspiration created by Cervantes as he depicted scenes emanating from the time of the Spanish Inquisition of the 1500s and created a character for the ages, who in the destiny of his own mind marches forth to right the wrongs of the world.

With the faithful Sancho Panza by his side, he crusades against all that has held others down—tilting at windmills, thinking them to be giants, and trying to turn peasant "women of the night" into "fair ladies," especially one he finds charming, Aldonza, whom he renames Dulcinea. The story is of human faith, survival, innocence, honesty, and courage.

And I thought of a friend I had spoken to not too long before whose wife was tilting at the windmills of a recurring illness. I wonder what windmills some of you might be jousting with today. And then the above words of Christ come to mind.

He was talking about the abundance of a life's journey that points both to the depth of living now and the length of living in eternity with Him. It is a life's journey that is not without problems and pain, and it is clearly not a life that denies or runs from the wrongs, sorrows, foes, weariness, ups and downs, and seemingly impossible dreams we will face. Instead, it is a life that faces them straight up and courageously, changing the world for the better.

 IMPACT APPLICATION: There we see it—God's purpose for our lives is to live a rich and satisfying life. How do we do that? With Him in the lead.

WE HAVE MET THE ENEMY—HE IS US

Don't copy the behavior and customs of this world, but let God transform you into a new person by changing the way you think. Then you will learn to know God's will for you, which is good and pleasing and perfect. **Romans 12:2**

I REMEMBER YEARS AGO reading a quote from the *Pogo* cartoon strip: "We have met the enemy and he is us." That's true—way too often. It may have been true in the you and me of yesterday. But I have a sense that it doesn't have to be that way in the you and me of today and of all of our tomorrows.

And as we, from wherever we find ourselves, step into something new in our lives—whether it be a new venture, New Year, new relationship, new career choice—the underlying message of that phrase is clear now because it points out the insidious difference between the way we too often have been programmed by the world to look at ourselves and the way the God who created us looks at us. It's all about the potential and hope He intends for us to claim in His plan for our futures. And that's what the apostle Paul says in the passage of Scripture above.

If we stop for a moment and give Pogo his due, we can see that very quote played out every day all around us. We can see it playing out in the partisan bickering of our nation's elected leaders, arguing issues to secure their power rather than to do what is in the best interests of our country and world. We see it in successful businesses, professional associations, and even religious organizations, disintegrating on the altars of greed and power. We see it in the lives of children and families, losing their way somewhere along the road society paves as the path to success. We see it in people like you and me, never reaching their full potential despite our incredible, God-given gifts and abilities.

If we're painfully honest with ourselves, we will see that we meet the enemy every day, and it really *is* us and so often the view we hold of ourselves. And often that view comes from the world around us, which we allow to determine who we are or should be.

Let's start again. Let's take a look at our portrait that the God who created us has painted. Let's remember as we do that He created us unique with incredible potential, gifts, and abilities like no one else. And let's also remember that He makes no mistakes—we are who we are for a reason. His reason.

 IMPACT APPLICATION: The God who created you and me is brilliant, purposeful, loving, faithful, and caring in all He does. Embrace that truth as you step into a brand-new day with Him.

OCTOBER 31

APPOMATTOX, GOD, AND US

Be sure of this: I am with you always, even to the end of the age.
Matthew 28:20

THE AIR WAS THICK the day a detour from my scheduled trip led to a respectful walk over the grounds of the Appomattox Court House National Historical Park in Virginia. It was the last stretch of a three-day journey reconnecting and researching ideas with family and friends.

As I walked around, I couldn't help but wonder what that day must have been like on April 9, 1865, when Ulysses S. Grant and Robert E. Lee met on those grounds to end the painful, tragic, and bloody hostilities known as the Civil War. For me, this detour was a time of reflection, remembering the roots of our past that have served to shape and influence who we are as a nation and a people today. And it led to a moment of personal reflection for me, remembering those who have crossed my path during the journey of my life, who have stood by me and shaped who I am.

Many come to mind—my bride, her parents, our families, our son, daughter-in-law, granddaughters, siblings, godchildren, coaches, mentors, and friends. So many, too numerous to mention and even too numerous to remember—one brushstroke at a time painting the portrait of who I am today.

We all have people in our lives who have stood by us and inspired us. We've needed them and wouldn't be the same without them. We've all had those moments when we've reached rock bottom, when we feel we've hit the depths of despair, when we've compromised the values we know we should live by. We've all had those days when we feel we can no longer lift our heads heavenward to see the sunshine just beyond the rainbow, when we have lost our way and forgotten who we are and who we were created to be, and when we feel so insignificant that we wonder whether anyone, anywhere, cares at all. And, no doubt, we'll have them again. It's at times such as those that we need to remember all those who have painted the portraits of our lives.

But there's One greater than all of those who created and sent others to cross our paths and help to shape our lives. He was there when we were created and with us on the day we were born. He was with us on our most difficult days and most joyous moments and will be with us in all the days of our futures. He is responsible for painting the beautiful portraits of our lives.

 IMPACT APPLICATION: When you find yourself at times struggling in your life, which will happen, remember those who have been a part of your journey and remember and claim the promise of the One who has loved you since the beginning of time.

GRANDDADDY'S GIRLS

Children are a gift from the LORD; they are a reward from him.
Psalm 127:3

IT WAS A MOMENT MISSED.

My elder granddaughter, Hannah, had learned to ride her bike a week earlier with her parents, her younger sister, Ellie Kate, and her Mimi all in attendance. I had just left to return home, not knowing that bike riding was in the plans and that this momentous occasion was about to happen.

And I understood that she took off riding for hours as they cheered her every start, stop, and turn until exhaustion brought her bike to its place of rest for another day. Of course, if I had known, I would have stayed; instead, it was left to my imagination to paint the picture of "Granddaddy's Girl" climbing another mountaintop on the way to growing up.

Later that evening as she and Mimi were preparing for bed, Mimi went on and on about how glad she was that she was there to see Hannah's first-ever moment of riding her bike all by herself without the training wheels. Hannah took it all in, pleased with her accomplishment, and then offered a response born of a sensitive heart that knew how much she was loved. "Poor Gran," she offered. "He's so sad he didn't get to see me ride." She knew innately how much I would have wanted to be there.

Those words demonstrate a few things my granddaughters know to be true about their "Gran." They know

- that my heart skips a beat every time I see their faces;
- their granddaddy is excited to know everything they do;
- they don't have to do anything special, or prove themselves, for me to want to hold them; and
- they "hung the moon" in my heart the moment we learned they were on the way.

And undergirding those feelings are some things I know to be true about precious children, grandchildren, or godchildren everywhere. We know that they are God's children, given in sacred trust to parents, and special others, to respect, nurture, care for, and love. We know that God has created them unique, with special gifts and abilities, knowing that their generation would need what He gave them to offer to the world. We know that God created them in His image and wired them with a thirst for Him. And we know that in each of them, God wrote a great and unique story in which each new page brings continued excitement, wonder, and blessing to the reader.

Granddaddy's girls, and so many others, are a gift from God for you and for me.

IMPACT APPLICATION: Pray that God would faithfully surround our children, grandchildren, and godchildren with a ring of angels to watch over them in every moment of their lives.

NOVEMBER 2

MAKING US BETTER

He will wipe every tear from their eyes, and there will be no more death or sorrow or crying or pain. All these things are gone forever.
Revelation 21:4

RILEY ROOSTER came to trust me within the first twenty-four hours of my visit with some dear friends in their home on the top of a knoll in the picturesque township of Topsham, Maine. For the remainder of my visit, their youthful golden retriever waited outside my bedroom door, ready to overwhelm me each day with his ebullient personality.

A few years thereafter, another dog just like Riley endeared himself to me much more quickly. *He had to,* I thought, as I found him all alone in the median of one of our neighborhood roadways on my way home. I'm still not certain what possessed me to approach this eighty-plus-pound golden retriever. He could have taken me to the ground in one nervous leap. But I couldn't leave him out there all alone.

His long blond hair, although wet, muddy, and matted, still flowed a bit like a lion's mane. I left the car engine running, standing nervously behind the open car door in case a quick exit was warranted.

He was obviously lost, confused, and exhausted, but his now-wagging tail betrayed that he was glad to find a friend, and he wasted no time in jumping into the front seat of my car, mud and all, to go wherever new friends go together. I would learn, when we were able to reunite him with his owner the next morning, that his name was also Riley.

We spent the night together—Riley, Lynda, and I, along with our three basset hounds—after our dogs shared some of their food, treats, water, and one of their softest beds.

Riley Rooster and the Riley of that night in the median touch the very best of our humanity. They make us better and more as God created us to be. Dogs (and other animals) have a way of doing that. They possess an incredible ability to open your heart anew to those very best places that may have begun to gather dust through the years and all the stuff of life. That should come as no surprise, since dogs are one of God's purest creations.

Funny, mischievous, loyal, patient, and forgiving, they're the ones meeting you at the door, so glad to see you at the end of a long day when no one else seemed to notice all day long.

Will Rogers once said, "If there are no dogs in Heaven, then when I die I want to go where they went." He has no doubt found that he can have the best of both blessings—heaven and his dogs—in eternity. My God—animal lover that He is—really intended it to be that way.

IMPACT APPLICATION: God created them on the sixth day because He loved them and loved us. Through their passion for life, they inspire us. Through their grace and forgiveness, they humble and teach us. And through their presence, they love us.

INVOLVED FOR AMERICA

The authorities are God's servants, sent for your good. . . . So you must submit to them, not only to avoid punishment, but also to keep a clear conscience. **Romans 13:4-5**

THIS MORNING I reflected on the recent civil, peaceful, and record turnout on Election Day, highlighting and underscoring the very best of our traditions, values, and heritage.

And that is what our son Nathan wanted our granddaughter Hannah to embrace as he picked her up at school that afternoon to head to his polling place. He had thrown his hat in for a vacancy on the Cheval West Community Development District in Lutz, Florida, hoping to contribute in some meaningful way to the betterment of their community. As a part of the process, he sat near the polling place with his sign to answer questions from prospective voters and neighbors, which might help them cast a more informed vote.

Not one to miss an opportunity to be a part of the moment, Hannah, wearing her "Future President" T-shirt I bought her a few years earlier, crafted her own impromptu sign, adorned with a beautiful flower of multicolored petals, a figure that resembled a mouse, and the words "Vote for Daddy." Together they sat there for hours with their signs and conversations until the polls closed at seven o'clock, watching America at its very best, interrupted only by Hannah's short nap. Weary but feeling fulfilled, they headed home to share with her mommy and sister, Ellie Kate, the excitement bubbling in her heart from this—her first participation in the election process and the affairs of the United States of America.

While some threaten to leave, others line up by the millions to enter a nation where freedom empowers each of us to reach beyond reality to where our dreams invite us to go. Millions attempt by any legal means possible to enter a place where they can become anything their hearts long for and where together we challenge the impossible and then do it again and again. A place where brave men and women throughout the centuries have stepped forward for us, vowing to protect with their last full measure of devotion a land they love.

This great nation has once again risen out of its struggles and turned its eyes toward the heavens to glimpse all that it can be and all which God created it to be. Yes, we have our differences, but as one candidate for the presidency so eloquently reminded us in his concession speech a few years ago, "There are no winners or losers, only Americans."

By the way, the result of Nathan's election: 461 to 461. He won on a draw of cards at the office of the Supervisor of Elections the following week.

IMPACT APPLICATION: God calls us to be involved in His Kingdom work, and His Kingdom work is everywhere we can make a difference for Him. That includes performing our duties as citizens of this great nation.

NOVEMBER 4

PLUGGED IN

A final word: Be strong in the Lord and in his mighty power.
Ephesians 6:10

MY ELDER GRANDDAUGHTER, Hannah, and her daddy went to a Krispy Kreme donut shop for dessert after dinner one night while my daughter-in-law was at a meeting. Hannah's donut selection was a nourishing chocolate cake with chocolate icing and sprinkles. As they sat eating their donuts and sharing a container of milk, her daddy, Nathan, began to point out to Hannah the elaborate nature of the "Hot—Fresh—Now" lighted sign that was flashing over the counter, signaling that a freshly prepared batch of donuts was ready for sale and consumption.

According to Nathan, the sign was intricately constructed with wires and complex gadgetry, and as I gathered from his comments, its operation was well beyond his ability to understand. Yet as he tried to point out the elaborate circuitry of the flashing neon sign to his daughter, he wondered aloud how it could possibly light up the way it did.

"Well, I know how it lights up, Daddy," she proclaimed. With a wave of her arm, reminiscent of the Creation story, she pointed to a receptacle on the nearby wall with an electric cord attached and declared, "It's plugged in," as she scraped more chocolate icing and sprinkles from her donut.

So, how are things where you are? Enjoying dessert, or still trying to deal with the main course? Is your family okay? How about your career? Is it still on track? Is everything properly plugged in and in order with no serious challenges ahead? Do you have all the power you need readily at hand?

Or is there an illness in your family that isn't getting any better? Or are you in the midst of a job change and have no idea what the future holds? Have you just noticed that your children are bigger and older than you remember the last time you had the time to look? And who's that person sitting across from you at the breakfast table? Are you trying to plug your extension cords into every energy source you can and instead finding that the circuit breakers are tripped?

I have a suggestion for you, to which my granddaughter Hannah alluded. Plug into the ultimate source of power and purpose for your life. A source that will provide you with all the peace, purpose, power, and fulfillment your life will ever need. It may not result in what the world says you need—as a matter of fact, I would venture to say the world's results for your life would fall woefully short of the power I'm suggesting. But you will begin to find fulfillment, satisfaction, and meaning in your life and all the blessings that are yours to enjoy.

And that source is Jesus Christ.

IMPACT APPLICATION: Plug into the ultimate source of power for every day of your life—Jesus Christ.

HOLY GROUND

If you give even a cup of cold water to one of the least of my followers, you will surely be rewarded. **Matthew 10:42**

TIME SPENT with our granddaughters always seems to cause me to reflect on the important things of now and then. One particular time I remember is when my elder granddaughter Hannah and I were watching reruns of *Mr. Rogers* and eating snacks.

"He's nice," Hannah chirped softly, as Fred Rogers tied up his colored Keds, zipped on his out-of-date sweater, and gently shared the melody—"It's you I like, / It's not the things you wear, / It's not the way you do your hair— / But it's you I like. / The way you are right now, / The way down deep inside you." I believed him, and many others through the years have believed him, even that one little girl, now a grown woman, who thanked him in New York City as he was there to be awarded for a lifetime of achievement about a year before he died.

It seems that as a little girl, not much older than our granddaughters, she had been terribly abused. But each day she had a safe room in her house where she would watch Mr. Rogers and listen to him tell her—just her, she thought—that he liked her, she was pretty, and she was special just the way she was. It was almost "make-believe" for her, but his reassuring words carried her through her daily torment until she was older and able to finally free herself. And even though forever scarred from the abuse, she survived because of those words of encouragement and hope every day from that TV screen to her through the years. Today she lives a life of purpose, meaning, and sensitivity for others.

With tears in his eyes as he recounted the tale shared with him by that woman, Mr. Rogers said that he felt as though the airwaves that existed between him and that little girl over the years had been "holy ground," affirming, loving, and holding her. And they had been just that. He didn't know the little girl at the time, but he was simply doing what he felt he was called to do.

"It's you I like, / It's not the things you wear, / It's not the way you do your hair— / But it's you I like. / The way you are right now, / The way down deep inside you."

It's still quiet around here, but in the solitude of my memories, I can't help but wonder where God has set that "holy ground" for you to touch family, friends, coworkers, or perhaps that person you just passed on the street who needs you in a time of disappointment, difficulty, and despair. Mr. Rogers is gone from us now, leaving his example with those of us who still remain, but his message and impact may be able to live on through us.

 IMPACT APPLICATION: Every moment of every day of every life presents an opportunity to have a sacred impact in someone's life. Why not have that impact in the world around you today?

PRECIOUS MOMENTS

You should clothe yourselves instead with the beauty that comes from within, the unfading beauty of a gentle and quiet spirit, which is so precious to God. **1 Peter 3:4**

AS THE MORNING ROSE around me, I could visualize the easel as I made my way up to my study at the top of the stairs. And sure enough, there it stood at the far end of the study in an alcove framed by bay windows and bookcases, illuminating my slowly awakening consciousness. And it still proudly displayed the painting my granddaughter Hannah had created for her Mimi during her last visit with us.

My thoughts drifted to an earlier time with Hannah. She was painting at that same easel with her artist's apron hanging large around her. The brushes were furiously whipping through the air with poster paints, glitter paints, and watercolors, all boldly painting hope, brightness, and love on what began as a blank page. A few feet away, I was at my desk watching out of the corner of my eye while rummaging through the dictionary for some new word for the day.

"Hi, Granddaddy!" she sparkled between brushstrokes.

Lifting my eyes and thoughts from the dictionary, I found myself stammering for just the right word to express my feelings for that life of incredible potential standing before me. I stuttered.

In my lapse and without missing a paint stroke on the canvas in front of her, Hannah interrupted my halting attempts for the right word by interjecting, "Precious, you mean. Right, Gran?"

Yes, that's what I meant—precious. She'd heard me call her that many times before. Precious. Something of great price or value. Costly. Something of inestimable value, impossible to quantify, irreplaceable. Yes, that's what I meant.

"Hi, Precious."

In today's Scripture, Peter talks about what is precious to God—the beauty that comes from within. It can be tempting to chase things that boost our external appearance—status, possessions, looks, notoriety. Even good things like volunteering or giving to charity can lose their value if we do them for how they make us look to others. God looks at the heart, and He cares about "the unfading beauty of a quiet and gentle spirit," one that does the right thing, even when it isn't being noticed.

Precious. It's not about what you do. It's about who you are. It's about all you can be for yourself and those you hold dear. And it's about the One who values you above all else.

 IMPACT APPLICATION: Have you been using the wrong standard for what's important? Focus today on what God finds precious—who you are inside.

THE GOD OF HOPE

After waiting another seven days, Noah released the dove again.
Genesis 8:10

NOAH WAITED AND WAITED amid the floodwaters that surrounded the ark, and he stretched his eyes as far as he could see in every direction. He waited for a desperately needed glimpse of hope that even some small patch of dry land on the horizon would provide. It would seem that he and the others of the day had been given a bad break.

Gehrig was thirty-seven years old when he died on June 2, 1941. Upon his retirement from baseball two years earlier, Gehrig, the heroic and talented first baseman for the New York Yankees—nicknamed the Iron Horse for his 2,130-consecutive-games-played streak—uttered these immortal words, which remain indelibly etched in our collective psyche: "I consider myself the luckiest man on the face of the earth. . . . I might have been given a bad break, but I have an awful lot to live for."

Dying from ALS, he was elected to the Baseball Hall of Fame the same year he issued that ringing reminder of gratitude and hope. He spoke words of hope that have echoed in the recesses of our hearts every time they are reheard in the years since they were first spoken.

We've all been there. Maybe we're there now. Once we felt that there was so much potential ahead, and now we're feeling lost. Flooded by mounting bills and just trying to make ends meet each day, tension in the next steps of our career with no prospects of a job anywhere in sight, classes we're taking in school that we just don't understand, anger at some health problem that looks like it's here to stay, or a disconnect with a spouse. We've looked for a bit of sunshine, and all we see is water, water everywhere. We don't necessarily need a solution, but a little ray of sunshine, a little ray of hope, would be nice. But then the darkness seems to descend again on our day.

But while we're wondering when, if ever, the floodwaters will subside and the sunshine will return, take a look with me at the next verse in Genesis: "When the dove returned to him in the evening, there in its beak was a freshly plucked olive leaf!" (8:11, NIV).

The dove brought more than a leaf to Noah. It brought hope—hope that this watery journey would soon end. Hope that Noah's dreams of dry land were not in vain. In our better moments we know that our hopes for a better day are also not in vain.

 IMPACT APPLICATION: No matter what we are going through, the God of Noah sends us His hope.

NOVEMBER 8

PRICELESS MOMENTS

Now I am giving you a new commandment: Love each other. Just as I have loved you, you should love each other. **John 13:34**

IT WAS JUST AN ORDINARY MOMENT. Just another one of many trips into the attic. I hadn't planned it, but being a bit impulsive as I stood near the entry door to the attic, I decided to do a bit more purging of some accumulated stuff. It became another one of those much-needed learning moments in my life.

As I stood there paging through the dust-covered spiral-bound handbook of inspirational quotations I had just rescued from one of many boxes earmarked for the trash, a smile crept across my face. The words "Dad—I thought you might enjoy. 1/4/89—Nathan" had been written inside the front cover.

My son hadn't given me that particular book for my birthday or any other special occasion that I could remember, but it was just simply another one of those many priceless moments where he has reached out in love to me.

As I continued to thumb through the pages of that little book, my thoughts drifted to that series of MasterCard commercials that used to be popular. You couldn't help but smile when they flashed across your television screen. It must be that they touched some longing deep within us or some warm memory of the past or perhaps stirred some fervent wish for our future.

As I read on in that gift from Nathan, I remembered Lynda driving to Tampa on numerous occasions to help Amy out and to see our granddaughters. I thought how much I would love to see their faces, read their thoughts, and feel their heartbeats quicken when they saw their Mimi come to their door in Tampa.

Borrowing a page out of the MasterCard playbook, I might describe Lynda's trip and the memory-making moment this way:

- A full tank of gas—$42
- Driving two and a half hours on a crowded interstate—exhausting
- Keeping the trip a secret from her granddaughters—unlike Mimi
- The look on her granddaughters' faces when Mimi's car pulls up to the curb—priceless.

I don't know what you see when you look back on life—warm memories or regrets. I'm pretty sure you can't do anything about them now, even if you wanted to. Yet the life we have left is still ahead of us, and the moments before us are ours to use anyway we wish. Why not make them priceless?

 IMPACT APPLICATION: Henry Drummond reminds us that "You will find, as you look back upon your life, that the moments that stand out, the moments when you have really lived, are the moments when you have done things in a spirit of love." Live today in a spirit of love.

HAND LIFTERS

As long as Moses held up the staff in his hand, the Israelites had the advantage. But whenever he dropped his hand, the Amalekites gained the advantage. Moses' arms soon became so tired he could no longer hold them up. So Aaron and Hur found a stone for him to sit on. Then they stood on each side of Moses, holding up his hands. So his hands held steady until sunset. As a result, Joshua overwhelmed the army of Amalek in battle.

Exodus 17:11-13

LOOKING BACK NOW, it seems fairly obvious. And were I not so busy, I would have noticed they were there all the while—people quietly and consistently supporting what I was doing.

Prior to this moment in Scripture, Moses had been running on adrenaline for some time. Although he always felt ill equipped to do what God had called him to do, he had trusted God's leading and led the Israelite people out of slavery in Egypt.

And in leading them toward the Promised Land, Moses became weary, not only physically but also emotionally from the strain of responsibility, constant criticism from the Israelites, lack of support, and lack of commitment to the vision God had set before them.

And when Moses needed strength in helping Joshua in the battle against the Amalekites, Moses found it in his brother Aaron and longtime companion Hur. They simply came and held his hands up—one on each side—so that he could direct and encourage Joshua in the battle.

We've all been there, something in our lives beginning to take its toll on us physically and emotionally. Maybe it's as a leader in your home. Maybe at work as an employer, a supervisor, or an employee. Perhaps it's in a position of leadership at church or within charitable organizations or in sports.

Wherever it has been, you know that at some point we all need an Aaron and a Hur to encourage us, sustain us, and lift our hands and our spirits. Lifters who will remind us that we're okay, we're on the right track, and who will shine a light on the way we were going when the vision grows dim. And we need to be a lifter for others as well.

There have always been people helping to hold my hands in the air. And I'll bet if you stopped and thought about some of those exhausting and difficult moments in your life, you, too, would remember those who have been there, helping to hold your hands up.

It makes you want to never throw in the towel, knowing there are others who will help to keep your hands high in the air as you become all who God created you to be.

IMPACT APPLICATION: Who's lifting your hands up? Whose hands are you helping to lift?

NOVEMBER 10

WORTHY

When people do not accept divine guidance, they run wild. But whoever obeys the law is joyful. **Proverbs 29:18**

MY THOUGHTS DRIFTED to the words of a dear friend recounting her trip to Washington, DC, and the day she stood in a gentle rain before the memorial remembering the 58,209 patriots who gave their lives during the Vietnam War. The raindrops mixed with her tears as they also cascaded over the names etched on the granite walls of that solemn memorial.

And as we pause each year around the activities of this Veteran's Day to honor those who have stood in the gap for us and for this great land across the ages—and still do today—we pause to remember the sacrifices they have made so that we and others might continue to live in the warm breezes of liberty, justice, and freedom. This great experiment—America—was discovered and founded upon a firm reliance on God and maintained upon the sacrificial lives of countless numbers of heroes through the ages. It has and must continue to stand as a beacon of hope for all the world. A country woven together under the heritage of lives who have given everything for us so that we might not only live in freedom but be able to reach out to the good of each other and for the hope of others around the world.

Yet I wonder sometimes if we get it. I wonder if our vision for tomorrow remembers the past. I wonder if some of us would change our behaviors if we stopped to reflect on those who have gone before and on the last full measure of devotion they willingly gave—and continue to give today. Would it make a difference in how we lived our lives, treated our neighbors, or served our country and world if we remembered how they lived—and died—for us? I wonder if we are worthy of what they have done for us.

Call me naive, perhaps way too idealistic, but I dream of a country and a world where all people are free from government or other oppressive intrusion in any form and, instead, where children of all ages everywhere have the opportunity to use their own God-given potential to find hope for the future intended for their lives in the break of each new dawn.

To remember that "with a firm reliance on the protection of divine Providence, we mutually pledge to each other our Lives, our Fortunes and our sacred Honor."

 IMPACT APPLICATION: It's really up to us how long liberty and freedom will prevail, but the truth is that it has always been up to us and will be for all of our days to come.

STANDING IN THE GAP

We know what real love is because Jesus gave up his life for us. So we also ought to give up our lives for our brothers and sisters. **1 John 3:16**

IT WASN'T UNTIL about ten years after serving in the US Air Force during the Vietnam War that I remember hearing the words *Thank you.* Until then, my fellow servicemen and I were often ridiculed for our service. But that night, things changed. Lynda and I had attended a Fellowship of Christian Athletes banquet in Gainesville, Florida. At the conclusion of his remarks, the speaker asked all the veterans to stand and be recognized—first from World War I, then World War II, then the Korean War, and finally the Vietnam War.

At first I didn't stand until Lynda nudged me. And as I stood slowly and noticed that she proudly kept looking up at me, tears streamed down my face— born of the memories of so many who were now gone and of the pain and rejection by so many around us who disagreed with the war and ridiculed those answering a call to duty during that time. I stood.

It was the first time since I had served that any positive recognition had been offered. And it became a defining moment for me—a moment long overdue; a recognition that I, and so many others like me, held a sacred designation in the annals of American history: veteran.

We are at the juncture of yet another defining moment in the journey of our nation. A moment where we honor our veterans while the very foundations of who we are as a nation are being challenged and attempts are being made to strip those foundations away—the very foundations our veterans stood in the gap to preserve.

And the challenges are coming from many quarters. Recent polls would suggest that the vast majority of Americans cherish the important foundations of our nation and that God has always been a cornerstone of those foundations. Americans are standing up to give loud voice to those long-held beliefs. That they are doing so is yet another defining moment for our nation.

The veterans we honor each year are veterans of the United States of America— nothing else, nothing less, and nothing more sacred than having stood in the gap for our country, families, and the God we serve and upon whom this great country was established.

May God continue to bless all those veterans who stood and stand in the gap for this great nation, and may God continue to bless the United States of America.

IMPACT APPLICATION: The foundations of this great nation are rooted in the transcendent concepts of liberty, freedom, a government of the people, and a firm reliance on God. Those veterans we honor knew that when they stepped forward and said, "Send me," and they deserve our respect.

NOVEMBER 12

STAND AGAIN

Give to everyone what you owe them: If you owe taxes, pay taxes; if revenue, then revenue; if respect, then respect; if honor, then honor.
Romans 13:7, NIV

"YOU NEED TO BE there at 5:30 tonight!"

I had just returned from a trip and had, in all honesty, forgotten that this was the night when my granddaughters, along with the rest of their classmates, were to be a part of a Veteran's Day celebration at a local church, where the presence of their two granddaddies—veterans—was required.

There has never been a moment when we have stopped as a nation to honor those who have sacrificed so much for us and our great country when tears haven't welled up in my eyes.

It happened again as our granddaughters and their classmates remembered the veterans who were present that evening at that ceremony. And as we pause this week, and especially on Veteran's Day, we do so to honor those who have stood in the gap for us and for this great land across the ages and to this very day. We pause to remember the sacrifices they have made, and continue to make, so that we might continue to live in the warm embrace of liberty, justice, and freedom.

America was discovered and founded upon a firm reliance on God and on the sacrificial lives of countless numbers of heroes throughout the ages, and it has stood and must continue to stand as a beacon of His hope for the entire world. We will pause to remember a country founded upon the belief that in the commonality of our lives under God—whether in suffering or good fortune—we are called to be a lighthouse for each other and the world, to reach out to others in need, and to do all we can to ensure that no one lives in fear or in want of freedom.

There are times in our history—both recent and past—where it seems we have forgotten how we got here. Where we have forgotten our divinely inspired roots. Where sounds of discord drown out the quiet penetrating melody of taps or the lyrics and passion of our nation's honored hymns.

And in the midst of all that we have been through and will go through, we would do well to stand together hand in hand again in every town, city, and state, from coast to coast throughout this land, and honor those veterans who have stood for us and for this great nation.

IMPACT APPLICATION: We can never afford to forget. There is too much at stake. We can never forget the legacy of those who have gone before us and sacrificed so much so that we might live in freedom today. They have given so much *for* so much.

SHIBBOLETH

Jephthah captured the shallow crossings of the Jordan River, and whenever a fugitive from Ephraim tried to go back across, the men of Gilead would challenge him. "Are you a member of the tribe of Ephraim?" they would ask. If the man said, "No, I'm not," they would tell him to say "Shibboleth." If he was from Ephraim, he would say "Sibboleth," because people from Ephraim cannot pronounce the word correctly. **Judges 12:5-6**

MY ELDER GRANDDAUGHTER, Hannah, and I were together in the family room of our home, where I was quietly watching her play. It must have been an ever-so-slight glint from the rays of the sun off the side of my head that caught her attention. The next thing I knew, her tiny hand was gently brushing through the hair on the side of my head, followed by a tone of sweet concern in words hairdressers must use. "Granddaddy, your hair is gray."

My thoughts returned to a day years earlier, lying on the bed looking at the ceiling after "celebrating" my mid-century birthday, wondering where had it all gone and so fast, what had I done in those passing years, and what would I do in the years ahead?

In the passage set out above, the people of Gilead had just defeated Ephraim and seized the fords around the Jordan to prevent their escape. To ensure they did not escape, they selected a password that would be difficult for Ephraim's people to pronounce. If the Ephraimites attempted to cross out of the confinement of the society that now governed them, they were asked to say "shibboleth." However, if they said "sibboleth" instead, the differences of heritage and dialect would be revealed, and they would be identified as the enemy and summarily executed.

More broadly, *shibboleth* has become a term for testing the borders of something. What is in, and what is out? Which brings me to today's question: What is the shibboleth of your faith? What is the shibboleth that will define the rest of your life?

We will not find it in the rearview mirrors of our mistakes or regrets, in religious rituals and rules, in the huddles or prayer groups we attend, or by aligning ourselves with the judgments and biases of a culture that demonizes our differences.

But perhaps the shibboleth, the rudder, the criterion which should set us apart for the rest of our lives will be found in a relationship with the living God and His Son Jesus Christ, through the guidance and life-changing power of the Holy Spirit.

My hair may be gray, but that isn't the criterion that defines me for Hannah. It's Christ and everything He calls me to.

Where is your identity found?

IMPACT APPLICATION: What is the shibboleth that defines your faith? Let it be the saving relationship you have in Jesus Christ, and let that relationship be reflected in all you do.

NOVEMBER 14

PUT ME IN, COACH

This is my command—be strong and courageous! Do not be afraid or discouraged. For the LORD your God is with you wherever you go.
Joshua 1:9

IT WAS A BEAUTIFUL MORNING when Lynda and I started our trip that would take us to spend a few days on Hilton Head Island, South Carolina. Along the way she tolerated my putting the song "Centerfield" by John Fogerty on repeat and playing it for our four-hour trip to Hilton Head. Lynda had long ago come to accept this quirk of mine, which she has identified as caused by a missing gene.

"Put me in, Coach, I'm ready to play, today. . . ." Its message of can-do and discovery, of pushing the boundaries, of reaching beyond, risking, and trying resonated with me, as it does with many in our society today. Pushing the boundaries, reaching beyond, and taking a risk to do something you've never done before. But what if I drop a fly ball? What if I strike out? What if I fail at the new job? What if I don't succeed?

In the context of reaching for our potential and the exhilaration we would feel if we reached it, there is the chance we might also experience disappointment and setback, even disaster or tragedy. Certainly that was the experience of some of the crews of our space program, as we all were devastated by the explosion of the *Challenger* after its launch in January 1986 and the disintegration of the *Columbia* on its return in the skies over Texas on February 1, 2003.

Yet those crew members pushed and demanded to be put in the game because they knew that the greater tragedy was to not go, to not risk, to not reach, and to simply live out their lives in comfort and convenience.

Sounds a bit like the choices we face, doesn't it? Choices between moving toward uncertainty and risk—or not. Yet even confronted with the tragedy of defeat, the real tragedy would be allowing the potential disappointments, disasters, and loss of comforts and convenience to freeze us where we are with significant years of living remaining. The real tragedy would be allowing the risk and fear in the uncertainty before us to prevent us from going where we should go and from reaching toward our fullest potential in the process.

Put us in, Coach, we're ready to play to the end of the day—every day for the rest of our lives.

 IMPACT APPLICATION: Today is that day to do that which you have held off doing for any number of reasons. Today is the day to risk and reach to become all you can be—to reach your fullest potential—with God leading the way.

IT COULD BE DIFFERENT

Today in the town of David a Savior has been born to you; he is the Messiah, the Lord. This will be a sign to you: You will find a baby wrapped in cloths and lying in a manger. **Luke 2:11-12,** NIV

JUST A LITTLE OVER a month away, and it could be different this year. Really. It will probably depend on where we look as we move through the next few weeks. But really, it could be different this year.

"You will find a baby wrapped in cloths and lying in a manger."

Just a little over a month away, and the crushing busyness of the season has already begun. The Friday after Thanksgiving will bring newspaper inserts of sales you can't miss, stores opening at midnight and other ungodly hours and welcoming bargain hunters, and lines forming for days to take advantage of electronic once-in-a-lifetime games. It's called "Black Friday," signifying a retailer's reliance on that particular day to put their "bottom line" into the black—dollarwise—for the year. Really. But it could be different this year.

"You will find a baby wrapped in cloths and lying in a manger."

Just a little over a month away, and somewhere children are going to school in clothes unwashed for weeks—the only clothes they have. Black Friday isn't an event for the head of their household for obvious reasons. Yet it's still just over a month away for them, too. But it could be different this year.

"You will find a baby wrapped in cloths and lying in a manger."

Just a little over a month away, and somewhere a person is looking to find enough money to buy another car or house for their collection. It's the only place they know where to look to feel better. Really. But it could be different this year.

"You will find a baby wrapped in cloths and lying in a manger."

Just a little over a month away, and soon households will put up lights for the season (or are already doing that), climbing trees and onto rooftops—the sparkle the lights will give off adds something to our hearts. Lights that could remind us of the one true Light, if we stopped long enough in their reflection to see where their rays were pointing. It could be different.

"You will find a baby wrapped in cloths and lying in a manger."

Where will we look? Will we see those others around us whom He came for as well—perhaps even to help them to a better place?

It could be different this year—why not? Maybe it will depend on you and on me and what we decide to do today.

 IMPACT APPLICATION: It could be different. It will all depend on where we look. As we look toward the coming Christmas season, let's keep our eyes focused on Jesus Christ.

OUR LEGACY
ALONG THE WAY

Good people leave an inheritance to their grandchildren.
Proverbs 13:22

THE LEGACY he is leaving began long before that moment. However, when my godson, Kevin James Fletcher, was commissioned as a second lieutenant in the United States Air Force after graduating from the Air Force Officer Training School, his legacy took on new direction and impetus. It continues to this day as he lives the legacy he will leave.

We all remember their names—Clark, Williams, Hall, Wilson, Harrison, Jefferson, and Hancock—who along with forty-nine others signed the Declaration of Independence over two centuries ago. And they did so, knowing full well that as they signed that noble document, it would mean the death penalty if they were captured by the British. These were not wild ruffians, but men of means, men with education, and men of profound character who valued liberty more than they valued their own lives and whose legacy has impacted the lives of so many in so many places since those moments of commitment years ago.

His name was Shutruk-Nakhunte, king of Anshand and Susa, sovereign of the land of Elam. He lived around 1158 BC in the area of the Mediterranean. Don't bother looking—you probably won't find him in the history books, and it was unlikely he was remembered in the hearts of any of his peers. He lived a life devoid of character and contribution and a life remembered only by an accidental few for reasons ignominious. The reason is suggested in this quote from the movie *The Emperor's Club*—"Great ambition and conquest without contribution is without significance."

His name is Tom Landry. He lost more Super Bowls than he won of the few he participated in during nearly thirty years as head coach of the Dallas Cowboys. But his contributions to our world continue to be reflected in the lives of people he has touched from every walk of life. He was a man of profound character who realized that the life he was given was not for himself alone but to be used for the good of others.

What will our legacies be? Will they be reflected by the plaques on our walls, the trophies on our mantles, the dollars in our bank accounts, the wins in our careers, or the titles or positions we have held?

Or will they be reflected in the people we have helped, the friends we have stood by, the children we have lifted, the courage we have shown in the face of injustices we have confronted, the selfless service we have rendered, or the imprint we have left on the world?

How will we be remembered? That answer will be found in the contribution and imprint we made in the lives around us along the way.

IMPACT APPLICATION: We are leaving our legacy every day. What will it look like at the end of this time on earth?

SEIZE THE DAY

The very credentials these people are waving around as something special, I'm tearing up and throwing out with the trash. . . . Yes, all the things I once thought were so important are gone from my life. Compared to the high privilege of knowing Christ Jesus as my Master, firsthand, everything I once thought I had going for me is insignificant—dog dung. **Philippians 3:7-8,** MSG

TALK ABOUT A REAWAKENING, a paradigm shift. I wonder what caused Paul to see his life differently, to see now as "dog dung" everything he had previously valued. Perhaps he had just read the obituary page of the local paper and realized he didn't know one name listed. Perhaps he was suddenly overwhelmed with his own sense of mortality and reflected on what he had done in and with his life. But the real story is that he finally realized the abundant life God had meant for him to live. It was literally a life-changing moment for him.

There are some words engraved on a paperweight sitting before me in the center of my desk: "What would you attempt to do in life if you knew you could not fail?"

Every morning my glance at it energizes the passions in my heart to live this day in such a way that in looking back I won't have to say, "I wish I had . . ." Today my glance brought back memories of *Dead Poets Society*, a movie from some time ago.

You may remember the scene. Mr. Keating (Robin Williams) walks past a row of students in his class and beckons them to follow him into the hallway. Standing before the trophy case in the hallway, he asks one of the students to read a page from their poetry text—

Gather ye rosebuds while ye may, Old time is still a-flying.
And this same flower that smiles today, tomorrow will be dying.

With that thought floating through the hallways of their minds, they stare transfixed into the faces in old photographs of basketball and football teams, faces that once reflected the same hopes and beliefs as theirs, yet hopes and beliefs that, in too many cases, went unfulfilled. The boys realize they don't know anything about the people behind the faces except that they are gone. "Fertilizing daffodils," Keating muses. Keating begins to plant a life-changing shift for the boys, and for those of us watching who have now been drawn into the scene, by whispering, "Carpe diem, carpe diem, seize the day, make your lives extraordinary."

That's the message of Christ to each of us—seize the day. Allow Him to fill you with passion. Nothing halfway or halfhearted—seize the day with Him.

 IMPACT APPLICATION: Each day is a gift that deserves every ounce of the passion God has placed within us. Release it each day and see what extraordinary things God can accomplish through you when you do.

NOVEMBER 18

LEAVING A LONG SHADOW

Yes, I am the vine; you are the branches. Those who remain in me, and I in them, will produce much fruit. For apart from me you can do nothing. **John 15:5**

IT'S NEVER AN ORDINARY walk down our front driveway to retrieve the morning paper. The world always seems so alive. Today was no exception as I paused for a moment in one of our front porch rockers to think about Lynda's dad. It was an intentional moment—a tribute of respect in a way—to a man I love.

Recently we remembered his birthday, although he's been gone now for nearly twenty-two years. As I sat there, slowly rocking and reflecting on the memory of his understanding smile and spirited laughter, I could sense his shadow moving across every bed of flowers and the shrubs and trees.

He didn't plant any of them, but through his influence and love of nature which he passed on to Lynda, I could see his shadow in everything I surveyed. Whether daylilies or wax begonias; pink and white impatiens; flame-red azaleas; camellias; oak, red maple, dogwood, redbud, or crepe myrtle trees; and so much more, his influence in her life was everywhere. He was and would be proud of the shadow she continues to cast in so many ways for so much good.

The same influence and love of nature found its way into the DNA of our son and granddaughters. Lynda's dad would talk to Nathan about such things as he held him on his lap as a newborn and then as he grew to climb trees in dad's yards at home and in the mountains. He was always proud of Nathan, and he would be today as Nathan continues to follow his heart to change the world for the better.

The impact of this great man still looms over so much and so many lives and casts a long shadow for good. An influence and example to emulate.

Perhaps this influence was born out of his love and respect for nature. Although he never said it this way, I suspect he could see in me, and others, the same thing he saw in his beloved flowers and plants—all of which would eventually bloom and grow: potential. He saw it everywhere and in everyone. And when no one was looking or aware of what he was doing, he would quietly water, prune, fertilize, and nurture that potential in all of us—just as he did in his gardens.

His long shadow seems like it's everywhere in my life. Maybe you know someone in your life like that. Maybe we need to make sure our lives are casting a long shadow of impact for good around us.

 IMPACT APPLICATION: It should never be an ordinary walk into each day of our lives. We should be about casting shadows of influence and impact in the world around us.

RISING OUT
OF THE CLOUDS

I pray that your hearts will be flooded with light so that you can understand the confident hope he has given to those he called—his holy people who are his rich and glorious inheritance. **Ephesians 1:18**

THE SCENE BURNED in my heart: two women, citizens of two nations, rising from their seats in the gallery of the US House of Representatives at the State of the Union address, reaching to embrace each other for the very first time, perhaps for something more, perhaps for something better.

The election had taken place just a few days before, and the picture was etched in my brain of the Iraqi woman pushing two fingers proudly in the air—the universal symbol of victory—with ink staining one, signifying she had just cast her vote for freedom, the first time she had ever voted. She and millions of her fellow Iraqis went to the polls with clear skies—except under a different cloud that they knew hovered above them, the threat of death if they went. And yet they still went in numbers beyond any estimation, person after person, family after family, each receiving their badge of freedom in the form of an ink-stained finger.

Eleven years earlier Safia Taleb al-Suhail's father was assassinated by Saddam Hussein's regime. And there she stood as a guest in the gallery of the US House of Representatives, the leader of the Iraqi Women's Political Council, with an ink-stained finger signifying her vote cast for freedom just a few days before.

And now this woman, a representative of one nation, is hugged by another woman. One year earlier, in the battle to free Fallujah, Janet Norwood's son, Marine Corps Sergeant Byron Norwood, gave his life so that Safia could cast her vote for freedom. And Janet Norwood stood in the same House of Representatives gallery with her husband, Bill, to honor the memory of her son and all those who had stood and fallen with him in this struggle for freedom.

Two women and two nations, now standing together, along with many others, rising out of the ashes of oppression, reaching toward something more, reaching upward and beyond for the freedom and potential to be all we were created to be.

May God continue to bless the United States of America, and may God bless the future of people everywhere who are simply seeking freedom to reach the potential God has placed within them. May we enjoy the liberty we have and with it feel the duty to work for the liberty of those who yet need it, so that we may all have opportunity to reach the potential God has placed in us.

IMPACT APPLICATION: The God who created all of this the world over couldn't have intended any less for each of us but to reach for and embrace our fullest potential.

NOVEMBER 20

A PROUD HERITAGE—I CAN ONLY IMAGINE

Remember the days of long ago; think about the generations past. Ask your father, and he will inform you. Inquire of your elders, and they will tell you. **Deuteronomy 32:7**

I CAN ONLY IMAGINE what it must have been like. It may have been a day that was gray, drizzly, and dark with no light to guide them as they set out across the seemingly endless expanse of the dark waters of the North Atlantic. They left clinging to a thread of hope for a better life for themselves and their children, which they had heard about from the rumors running through the streets of their beloved homeland.

The Poland my maternal grandparents knew as children was gone under the tyrannical boot of Communist domination, and so they embarked on a journey with no assurances and only the possibility that the whispers they had heard were true.

I can only imagine what they were feeling as they saw the Statue of Liberty standing majestically before them as they entered New York harbor and what went through their minds as they endured the integration process at Ellis Island. I can only imagine the determination, integrity, and faith it took to envision the boardinghouse they started in a small town on the tip of Long Island.

I learned as I grew older that they were not educated people, and that surprised me. To a little boy, they seemed to know everything and courageously embraced the values of their faith to overcome all that was before them, even the paralyzing stroke my grandpa suffered as I watched him get the car ready for what was to be our early morning fishing trip.

Looking back, I hope I showed them I was always proud of them and of the heritage their lives built into mine. I can only imagine where and who I might have been without their reaching for the stars. I can only imagine where and who I might have been without the faith and determination they demonstrated as they boarded that ship ready to take them so far away from all they had known and loved, for something better, something more, something that would allow them to become all they were created to be.

We can run from who we are. We can try to be something we're not or wish we were like someone else. And if we do, we will never become all that we ourselves were created to be. Standing proudly, though, as individuals and as a country, on the foundation of our heritage as we reach for the stars, is how we find we will become all we were meant to be.

 IMPACT APPLICATION: We have all spent too many years of our lives trying to be someone else. And by doing that, we run from whom God created us to be. Proudly embrace and run to who you are.

THE CORNERSTONE

God is building a home. He's using us all—irrespective of how we got here—in what he is building. He used the apostles and prophets for the foundation. Now he's using you, fitting you in brick by brick, stone by stone, with Christ Jesus as the cornerstone that holds all the parts together. We see it taking shape day after day—a holy temple built by God, all of us built into it, a temple in which God is quite at home.
Ephesians 2:19-22, MSG

I OFTEN ASK MYSELF the questions, *Who am I? What path should I be on in order to become all I should be? Where should each day begin? Where should decisions I make today begin? Where should I look for guidance in my relationships?*

Where does direction come from? There are a lot of self-help books available and more each year with (purportedly) all the right answers to getting from here to where we think we want to be. Where do we look for wisdom to know when to throw aside some things that are hindrances and embrace others that may be helpful?

What should our priorities be? Should they be different than they were yesterday because of changes in the world or because of financial changes in our lives? Or should they remain the same? Are they worthy of being embraced, or were they wrong to begin with?

Where do we go to determine which career choice to place our ladder against to begin climbing? How many ladders should we have positioned on various walls? How will we know if we were right and whether to keep climbing or to stop and move our ladder to another wall? Should we give any credence to what the world holds out as success?

The problem when we lack direction is usually our focus. Too often we are beginning in the wrong place. We will never get to a place of peace and clear direction by focusing on ourselves.

I realize the conclusion I am about to share is obvious to many of us, and you probably already know the right response, but it bears repeating. For help with uncertainty, we should begin with the Cornerstone—Jesus Christ. We should always make sure that the Cornerstone is firmly in place and then allow Him to direct and guide our decisions, steps, thoughts, planning, career choices, and dreams.

And then with patience, we should allow that living Cornerstone to build the walls of who God created us to be.

IMPACT APPLICATION: You can begin to build your life a multitude of different ways, climbing all sorts of walls, according to all the dictates and examples of society. But the only way you will become all you were meant to be is to build your life on Jesus Christ.

NOVEMBER 22

COLD FRONTS, SNOW FLURRIES, & ROUGH PATCHES

The LORD had said to Abram, "Leave your native country, your relatives, and your father's family, and go to the land that I will show you." . . . So Abram departed as the LORD had instructed. **Genesis 12:1, 4**

A COLD FRONT came through this past week, setting some records for low temperatures in various parts of the country. And it still seems a good bit colder outside as this morning continues to unfold.

Many of us have been here before. We're in the midst of fall; and with winter approaching rapidly, we know things won't be getting any warmer for a while. Snow is expected today and throughout the week in the Northern Rockies and other parts of the High Plains states. And the weather forecasts are suggesting that the roads will be a bit rougher this morning in the East and Midwest, with rains expected in parts of the Southeast.

Yet it's warm and safe and secure within the walls of our home as the day begins. A place I want to stay awhile longer or all day if possible. Not having to face all that is before me today. Ugh! Anything but that.

You've been there. We all have. We don't want to leave the warmth and security of where we are to face what we know is waiting out there.

Life is a lot like that. We wake up on days throughout the year facing cold fronts, snow flurries, rain, and rough patches in the road before us. They often come wrapped with different names like unanticipated changes in career direction, a job loss, major projects past due, relationships on the brink of falling apart, our children losing their way and falling under the pressure of the wrong crowd, the mortgage payment past due and the bank account empty, friends not being who we thought they were, an illness descending upon a loved one, and needing to move or change but the risk seems too great.

Cold fronts will blow through. Rough patches will test our comfort and hope. Snow flurries will "white out" and blur our vision and direction and often freeze us into inactivity and complacency. Rains will temporarily wash away the roads before us, and at times it seems the dreams we believe are at the ends of those roads.

But we were created for so much more than to stay in the warmth and comfort of our shelters. And so with God leading the way, we choose to go, to get out, to be all we can be, every day.

Cold fronts, snow flurries, rain, and rough patches on the road ahead? Go—with God!

IMPACT APPLICATION: We were created to live. We were created to blossom, to rise out of our bud, out of what seems to be the warmth and secure comfort of where we are. We were created to leave and live, to reach, and to go.

A MOOD AND MOMENT OF THANKSGIVING

I have learned the secret of living in every situation, whether it is with a full stomach or empty, with plenty or little. For I can do everything through Christ, who gives me strength. **Philippians 4:12-13**

IT MAY BE that the mood of the day is still being painted by the memory of that man holding a sign of protest on the street corner. Maybe it lingers by the headlines in today's news about continuing trouble in the Middle East. Maybe the mood of the day is painted by the lingering confusion and rubble of storms that have hit various parts of our nation and people. Or maybe it's just the seemingly insurmountable mountains in our lives.

And yet it's Thanksgiving time. As we enter this holiday season, I can't help but believe that no matter where we find ourselves, a mood of honest reflection will serve to remind us to embrace moments of thankfulness and give us a reason for hope. We can be reminded of these truths:

- In the midst of our daily discouragements, disappointments, and failings, God's blessings are all around us—in a beautiful sunrise bursting with promise for the day, a newborn baby's cry, a grandma's wrinkled smile as she wraps her arms around her precious grandchildren, a table full of food, or a blazing sunset gracing our sitting together one more time as family and friends.
- We are blessed with true friends, who remain friends through everything, even the hard times.
- We can make the most of the time we have with our families. I was reminded of that again by a note from my granddaughter Hannah during a visit a number of years ago. The envelope was decorated with shamrocks, and the note inside was adorned with four hearts—blue, orange, purple, and green—and the following words: "Can we eat thanksgivening food together? I hope we can. I can't wait to see you next time I do."

My hope for you and your family—for all of us—is that we might not only be reminded anew of those moments and people for which we should be thankful, but that in the midst of whatever our week and day will bring, we will embrace with grateful hearts those fresh moments of blessing provided by the One who knows us best and loves us most.

IMPACT APPLICATION: In the midst of all the other moods being painted around us in our lives, nation, and world—paint instead a mood of thanksgiving and appreciation for all the blessings in your life. Paint such a mood that for today and the rest of your life it will carry you victoriously through each day and into the hope of all your tomorrows.

NOVEMBER 24

AN ATTITUDE OF GRATITUDE

Give thanks to the LORD, for he is good! His faithful love endures forever. **1 Chronicles 16:34**

LYNDA LEFT BEFORE I returned from a business trip. She, my daughter-in-law, Amy, and our granddaughters drove to Highlands, North Carolina, to await Nathan's and my arrival for a Thanksgiving Day gathering.

The note Lynda left for me said: "I can't wait for you, Nathan, and the dogs to get up there with us! Remember what happy times await us at Thanksgiving and how much it means to our children to have us all there. XOXO"

Thanksgiving—that most distinctive of American holidays—is a time when we pause to reflect and give thanks. It is a time to express gratefulness, to reflect upon the past, to embrace the blessings of the present, and to lift praises for God's faithful guidance through all the circumstances that have made up our lives.

On the first Thanksgiving, back in 1623, the governor of the Plymouth Colony, William Bradford, led the people in offering gratitude. I share his words to help us also rekindle the spark of gratitude:

> Inasmuch as the great Father has given us this year an abundant harvest of Indian corn, wheat, beans, squashes, and garden vegetables, and has made the forests to abound with game and the sea with fish and clams, and . . . He has protected us . . . has spared us . . . has granted us freedom to worship God according to the dictates of our own conscience; now, I, your magistrate, do proclaim that all ye Pilgrims, with your wives and little ones, do gather at ye meeting house, on ye hill, between the hours of 9 and 12 in the day time, on Thursday, November ye 29th of the year of our Lord one thousand six hundred and twenty-three . . . to . . . render thanksgiving to ye Almighty God for all His blessings.

The glory, power, and significance of that first Thanksgiving is not because it came out of prosperity, but because it came out of adversity. And in that adversity our ancestors dared to thank God, not for what He would do for them in the future—but for what He had already done for them. Indeed, my dear Lynda was right that these are and should be happy times—for there is much for which we can be thankful.

Most important, Thanksgiving is a time to look beyond this world and to remember our beginnings, and, with a true spirit of humility and an attitude of gratitude, remember the Creator from whom all blessings flow.

IMPACT APPLICATION: Thanksgiving should move us to an attitude of gratitude, as it moved those who have gone before us, for all the blessings from God that we enjoy.

THE WAY IT WAS
MEANT TO BE

He came into the very world he created, but the world didn't recognize him. **John 1:10**

IT WAS A THANKSGIVING gathering as it was meant to be, with our family gathered together, temperatures in the fifties, a fire in the fireplace, the sky just as blue as it should be, and a table full of food for which to also be thankful. And then lifting prayers to the Creator of it all, with our granddaughters' only additional wish—that it would snow.

How was Thanksgiving for you? Was it as it was meant to be?

And now what? Black Friday. Cyber Monday.

Really?

You've got to be kidding. And what is sad is that there are way too many of us who actually listen to and arrange our lives so as to line up with those commercialized obstacles to all that is good. What is the result? We ingrain the same behavior and values into the generation coming in behind us.

And we wonder and sometimes express surprise at what our children learn from all that is going on around them. Merchandizing madness. Commercialized chaos. Things. Self-indulgence. Stuff. Indeed, what will they learn from a society that has begun to accept less as more, okay as best, and doing whatever you feel good with, instead of becoming all that God created you to be?

But hold on for a minute, because in the midst of the ceaseless noise clamoring for our attention, there is good news—our annual moment and sacred reminder of the Good News that is just around the bend and heading our way at light speed. It came as the first Christmas gift—wrapped in a human life and presented to all of mankind in a manger inside a stable behind an inn in the little town of Bethlehem.

How will this season be for us? The choices are clear.

Like the changing temperatures from fall to winter, the contrasts around us are clear and compelling. Amid the desperate needs—homelessness, poverty, neglect, loneliness, orphans, addictions, confusion, and despair; amid the prevailing standards of success established by society to which we too often aspire—money, power, accolades, nice homes, rubbing elbows with the right people in the right groups—we see the babe of Bethlehem, the gift from heaven, and are reminded that, as Jesus said, "It is more blessed to give than to receive" (Acts 20:35).

The contrasts are clear. Will we see them? Will we recognize the baby in the manger?

How will Christmas be for you and me?

Will it be a Christmas that is how it was meant to be?

IMPACT APPLICATION: We are fast approaching the celebration of that moment when God came to earth to show us a better way, to show us the way to life eternally with Him—but also to show us a life that can make a difference in this world here and now. Let's follow the better way—it's our choice.

NOVEMBER 26

THANKSGIVING SURPRISES

Always be joyful. Never stop praying. Be thankful in all circumstances, for this is God's will for you who belong to Christ Jesus.
1 Thessalonians 5:16-18

HER VOICE PENETRATED the quiet of the morning all the way to my upstairs office. "Scott, quick! Come here! Hurry!"

I've yet to learn whether the excitement in Lynda's voice foretells a problem or a celebration, but in either circumstance I respond quickly—especially, as then, when we have one of our granddaughters staying with us. So I hurriedly made my way, two stairs at a time, down the staircase to the voice calling from below.

Arriving at the scene in the downstairs powder room, heart still pounding, I was greeted by a cheering Mimi and a smiling Ellie Kate, who was still sitting on the potty. Ellie Kate's excited words filled my ears—"Gran, Gran—tee-tee in the potty."

I am grateful for her life. Remembering her time in the NICU following her birth, I am grateful for her health. I am thankful for all the healing moments of her life leading to this moment—and for all the other magnificent moments and circumstances of her life.

Thanksgiving. The season is upon us again. That most distinctive of American holidays. A time to pause, reflect, and give thanks. A time of grateful—and, where needed, forgiving—reflection upon the past, embracing the blessings of the present and lifting praises for the overarching faithfulness of God through all the circumstances that have made up our lives. Thanksgiving is a time when the simple tends to become the magnificent, while all we thought was important fades into the background. And it's a time of hope for all the future that God has in store for our lives.

I don't know all the circumstances of your life—past, present, or future. Perhaps you feel a little like the guy in the photo a dear friend sent me the other day—parachuting into a lake surrounded by and full of alligators. Perhaps that's been your week or the one you think you're facing. I don't know.

What I do know is that through it all, and after it all, family, friends, and the faithfulness of God will provide the most magnificent and memorable of moments, while all the rest, at some time or another, will fade into the background. Magnificent moments of thanksgiving—and maybe even, if you're really lucky, a "potty moment" like the one Lynda and I experienced that morning—to cherish for all eternity.

 IMPACT APPLICATION: It's always a time to recall God's faithfulness and to reflect on the simple blessings of your today and every day, and a time to reclaim anew all the hope He has planned for your future.

A SUCCESSFUL SPIRIT

[Scrooge said,] "He has the power to render us happy or unhappy. . . . his power lies in words and looks; in things so slight and insignificant that it is impossible to add and count 'em up: what then? The happiness he gives, is quite as great as if it cost a fortune." **Charles Dickens,** *A Christmas Carol*

THIS PASSAGE FROM DICKENS'S classic illuminates the first crack in Scrooge's plan for success, a plan that would result in coffers of gold—and a waste of his life. The visit from the first spirit that Christmas Eve was his first glimpse into the truth that happiness is not determined by fortunes. It's determined by things as simple as adding value to others' lives.

There was a time when the football world was convinced Tony Dungy would never achieve the success that marked the "great ones" in the world of professional football. But I would venture to say that he has been in that category of "great ones" for a long time.

Just ask the likes of Lovie Smith, Herm Edwards, Mike Tomlin, Rod Marinelli—all became head coaches in the NFL because Tony Dungy added value to their lives. Ask hundreds of other coaches and front office personnel; ask his friends and family whose lives have been shaped and nurtured by a man whose values are not guided by the things of the world but by whether God is smiling down on what he does. Ask all those whom Coach Dungy gave a chance somewhere along the way. And if you look closely, you will often see that it was at his personal or professional expense.

The measure of his "success" has come not from winning football games or from getting to Super Bowls. That road is littered by the lives of many others who have been there and have never learned the real lesson of success. Real success that comes wrapped with a smile from God is achieved through a courageous, caring, and sacrificial life that is more concerned about leaving a positive imprint on the lives of others than about one's own position or success. Real success—Tony Dungy style—comes when you realize that somewhere along the way, someone saw your potential and gave you a chance; that each and every person is a creation of unlimited potential, whom you now have an opportunity to mentor, mold, and bless; and that one day you will not be remembered by the size of your house, bank account, or trophies gathering dust on the mantle.

But you will be remembered by the lives you have changed for the better.

IMPACT APPLICATION: Help as many people as you can, as often as you can, to become all they were created to be by giving them a lift up to pursue their dreams.

NOVEMBER 28

WITHOUT A DOUBT

The one sitting on the throne said, "Look, I am making everything new!" And then he said to me, "Write this down, for what I tell you is trustworthy and true." **Revelation 21:5**

IT WAS EARLY as I peered through my upstairs office windows into the darkness. In a moment, I would hear the sounds of our puppies downstairs, with one fewer precious voices joining the chorus.

And as the darkness slowly gave way to the light, my thoughts drifted again to the gut-wrenching numbness of twenty-four hours earlier as Lynda and I found our beloved basset hound, Pansy, lying silently, breathlessly, and peacefully on our kitchen floor. The pain and emptiness of her loss is intense, but we wouldn't have missed it for all the world, not a moment, not a memory, not one waggle of her tail, bounce of her step, or beat of her faithful heart.

And so we claim His promise—"Look, I am making everything new!"

A promise of a God who always keeps His promises. The promise of a God who surrounded Adam with animals in the Garden of Eden; who when He delivered Noah from the Flood surrounded him with animals; and who, when His Son was born in a meek and lowly stable, surrounded Jesus with animals.

In *Holiness in Hidden Places*, her book about heaven, Joni Eareckson Tada shares, "If God brings our pets back to life, it wouldn't surprise me. It would be just like Him. It would be totally in keeping with His generous character. . . . Heaven is going to be a place that will refract and reflect in as many ways as possible the goodness and joy of our great God, who delights in lavishing love on His children."

And so we claim that promise for our family and for yours and for all of our "Pansys" with which you, and we, have been and remain blessed.

Robert Louis Stevenson put it this way: "You think dogs will not be in Heaven? I tell you, they will be there long before any of us."

His point is clear, and I believe that my God has provided a way for both—us and Pansy (or whatever name you choose to call your pet)—into a place more glorious than all the best of His creation we have witnessed thus far.

Now, as our numbness morphs into hope, all that's left for me to do is to try to live up to the kind of person our precious Pansy thought I was.

I'm going to need help.

 IMPACT APPLICATION: Thank You, Lord, for Your gift of these precious creatures.

GRANDMA'S POACHED EGGS

They are like trees planted along the riverbank, bearing fruit each season. Their leaves never wither, and they prosper in all they do. **Psalm 1:3**

MY PATERNAL GRANDMOTHER was really too elderly and settled as a widow to take on five children to raise. She lived all by herself in a small house in Waukegan, Illinois. But I suppose she realized that if she didn't take us, strangers would, and that didn't sit well with her.

There wasn't much I could point toward to know what was right. Truth for me then was whatever got me through the day. I was ready to drop out of school, get a job pumping gas, and generally begin making my way in the world. Thank goodness drugs weren't in vogue, I didn't have any money to buy alcohol, and I was too afraid to violate the law. I wasn't rebellious—only God knows why—just angry and aloof. And I trusted no one. So it was strange that something as innocuous as a poached egg in the hands of someone like Grandma could begin to change all of that. But it did.

She was a passionate, tough old bird, as the expression goes, with a raspy and at times high-pitched voice. It was to become the first voice in a long time that I could trust. For it was Grandma and her poached eggs which slowly penetrated the veil of anger and helped me to get to a better place. At least she and her poached eggs got me through the ninth grade without dropping out.

I wonder if you've ever had one. A real poached egg, not those fake things you see made in elaborate and expensive pans that come out perfectly round. That's not the way life works. That's sure not how my life worked, and that's not how Grandma made her poached eggs.

It was a Friday tradition when we lived on South Gretta Avenue with her, and we all looked forward to it. I can still see Grandma, standing over that gas stove, spoon in hand, swirling the near-boiling water in her old cast-iron skillet to create a vortex in the center of the water into which she would gently slide a fresh egg, only to watch it emerge minutes later—not in fragments but as a whole pristine white egg, ready to be laid on a piece of buttered toast she had prepared earlier.

The stability of Grandma's presence in my life and the Friday tradition of a poached egg helped me through a difficult time in my life. My grandma was, in the language of the Psalms, a tree "planted along the riverbank"—strong and secure. Honor the "trees" in your life, and strive to be a source of security for those around you.

 IMPACT APPLICATION: Our passion for life, for what is right, and for those around us has immense, life-shaping energy to change lives. Remember that and then change a life.

NOVEMBER 30

KEEP DREAMING

He gives power to the weak and strength to the powerless. Even youths will become weak and tired, and young men will fall in exhaustion. But those who trust in the LORD will find new strength. They will soar high on wings like eagles. They will run and not grow weary. They will walk and not faint. **Isaiah 40:29-31**

THEY WERE MY LAST THOUGHTS as I finally fell asleep that night a few years ago and my first thoughts as I awoke the next morning, preparing for the time together this week with my granddaughter Hannah. Painting, reading about Winnie the Pooh and Piglet and Junie B. Jones, snacks, playing with her daddy's toy farm and castle, running the train, some snacks, laughing, talking about important things, playing with the puppies, swimming, a few snacks, taking bath with floating toys, cuddling stuffed animals, reading bedtime stories, saying her prayers, and, oh yes, another snack.

Maybe we'll talk about her dreams of what she wants to be when she grows up and maybe, just maybe, I'll tell her about Shaun Micheel. "Who?" she'll ask. I'll probably tell her that, like her daddy when he was a little boy who taped his dreams on the mirror in his bathroom, he was somebody who also had dreams when he was a little boy, and as he grew older, he kept believing in them and reaching for them, and on one particular Sunday, one of those dreams came true.

Standing 162 yards from the pin in the eighteenth fairway of Oak Hill Country Club in Rochester, New York, with a seven iron in his hand, Shaun Micheel, forgetting he was 169th in the world rankings of golf, nailed it to within three inches of the cup to become the champion of the Professional Golfers Association of America tournament. The PGA was the last major tournament of the year, and with that victory Shaun joined an unlikely group of first-time winners of golf's four major tournaments. It was a victory for dreamers everywhere.

What do you dream of for your future? What dreams do you have for your life, your family, and your world? What dreams do you have for brighter days that have had too much "cold water of reality" poured on them? What dreams do you have that have been abandoned or put on the back burner because of the troubles and disappointments of your day? Perhaps you're living one of your dreams, but your grip has loosened amid human and worldly distractions, shortcomings, and disappointments.

But wait a minute. Hold on to that seven iron in the middle of your eighteenth fairway, and read again those words spoken by the prophet Isaiah, inspired by the Dreamer of dreamers.

"Hannah, let's have another snack. We'll need all the energy we can muster to reach for our dreams and become all we were meant to be."

 IMPACT APPLICATION: You can soar like an eagle or not. The choice is always yours.

A FRESH START

A thief is only there to steal and kill and destroy. I came so they can have real and eternal life, more and better life than they ever dreamed of. **John 10:10**, MSG

LYNDA'S DADDY—one of the great men in my life—used to walk through cemeteries regularly. He did this considering the lives memorialized there to help him reflect on where he himself had been and who he was as he set his sights ahead.

Such a walk—reading sentiments etched on grave markers by the hearts of loved ones left behind—always causes me to wonder if Christ's words set out above became real in the lives of those who are remembered there.

Did the journey of their lives reflect an eternal perspective? Was the journey of their lives as the Good Shepherd intended—or just "good" with all the usual trappings of the "good life" espoused by society, if even that? Did they just exist through the days along their journey? Or did they live the life God created them to live and which Jesus called them to live?

I wonder if they ever knew—and more important, *believed*—deep down that they were God-created "one-of-a-kinds." I wonder if they ever felt that they were the most important person in the world—to at least one other person.

What about you? Do you believe that you are a God-created, one-of-a-kind original? Do you believe that the hand of the Creator has shaped you with gifts, abilities, interests, and motivations in combinations and magnitudes that no one else has? Do you believe that you are called by your Creator to a life of purpose that is more than just "good" but rather to a life with an eternal perspective that is, as today's verse describes, real, more, full, better, and abundant?

Or has the thief destroyed those beliefs along the way, perhaps even insidiously before you were aware of your surroundings and what was going on in your world? Have you been led to believe that you are common, regular, and really no different from anyone else—nothing really special? And instead of nurturing, encouraging, and sacrificing for all that was unique and wonderfully created in you, have those thieves instead reshaped you into the image of others?

Where are your dreams? Are they in full flight? Or are they abandoned, killed, or destroyed? Have you failed so many times that you just don't want to try again? Do you believe you can do all things through Christ who strengthens you and created you (see Philippians 4:13)—or is that just another nice-sounding Scripture?

IMPACT APPLICATION: Embark on a fresh start today that follows the path God intended for you to walk. A fresh start that reclaims all you were meant to be. A fresh start that begins with a saving relationship with Christ.

DECEMBER 2

RUNNING RIGHT

Let us run with endurance the race God has set before us. We do this by keeping our eyes on Jesus. **Hebrews 12:1-2**

DESPITE THE NAGGING NAYSAYER voices emanating from my knees and ankles, running a marathon remains an aspiration, although it has moved considerably down the list of things that matter most. This morning's cool wintry breeze stirred afresh my thoughts of running. It stirred my thoughts of Ron and Denise, too.

Ron is a friend of mine, a wonderful man with a wonderful family. A football coach. The very person you would want leading and shaping the lives, character, and integrity of young men in the caldron of societal pressures that all too often place little value on those qualities.

Denise was a friend of mine, a wonderful woman with a passion to touch the hearts of others for her Savior. Lynda and I attended the memorial service celebration for her several years ago. Denise was the very person you would want around to point out the things that matter most in life. She was thirty-five.

Theirs are lives run with perseverance, much like that required when running a marathon. Lives lived expecting and longing for what's next, focusing on the things that matter most, like family, friends, touching lives, building character, and demonstrating courage in the face of the adversity, disappointments, and obstacles they face.

The Greek word for "race" is *agon*, from which we get our word *agony*. It signifies a match or a race in which endurance and determination must overcome those moments in any race when we get cramps in our legs or a stitch in our side, when we "hit the wall" with the burning temptation to throw in the towel and sit on the sidelines. But hearts fixed on Christ fight through all of that, running with perseverance the race of our lives fixed on what matters most—Him.

I don't know what you're facing—illness, broken dreams, the loss of a loved one, a career off track, or a relationship that is lost or struggling. Maybe the wind seems to be whipping into your face and your knees and your ankles are aching and your legs are wobbly. No matter, because our encouragement and example come from the One who has run the race before us and cheers us on every day of our lives.

At the end of your days, will what matters to you *most* be the notoriety you achieved in your profession and the money you made, or will it be the family and friends gathered at your bedside and those held in your heart as you slip into the arms of your Creator?

Run your race today with Christ in the lead.

IMPACT APPLICATION: Run your race and live your life so that you enjoy today the people and things that will matter most today and at the end of your days.

DIVINE INTERRUPTIONS— BLESSINGS FOR LIFE

Encourage one another daily, as long as it is called "Today," so that none of you may be hardened by sin's deceitfulness. **Hebrews 3:13,** NIV

IT WAS AN UNEXPECTED TELEPHONE CALL and a welcome interruption waking me from a light sleep early one evening that week. A week that had been eventful and full, jarring and joyous. A week of things with my family that served to transform my perspective—actually, *correct* my perspective would be more honest—from one that had become painfully self-centered and inwardly focused earlier in the week. The call would continue to make that much-needed change for me—as conversations with him usually did.

I knew his voice as soon as he spoke. I had been blessed to meet Bob and his young son "accidentally" years earlier on the driving range of a golf course in Hilton Head, South Carolina, as I unwound from the stresses of a long day of lectures at a national medical conference. I was about to hit another practice shot with my eight iron when I heard him whisper to his son, "Now watch this." I prayed I could just hit the ball at all, now realizing I was being watched. I did.

A few swings later, as is my nature, I walked over to meet this soon-to-be lifelong friend from Mobile, Alabama, and his son—now years later a United States Air Force Academy graduate and US Air Force fighter pilot. Though my friend is a medical practice administrator of some note, his claim to fame was as the marshal (yellow helmet and all) at the tee of the par-3 twelfth hole of Augusta National Golf Club each year for the Masters Golf Tournament. (He recently retired after thirty years of service.)

Through our years as friends, we have shared stories, books, meals, golf moments, Augusta, reflections on our nation and our mutual service in its defense, politics, and memories of friends come and gone. We have checked in when storms seemed to be threatening one or the other. And we have been there to share with each other the things that mattered most to us in the deepest recesses of our hearts—our families.

His call was a welcome interruption—a divine interruption—helping me to refocus on those around me who needed me—my bride, son, daughter-in-law, and two granddaughters—precious creations of God. The woeful festivities of my self-imposed pity party ground to a halt as our hour-long conversation continued to unfold, redirecting me to embrace the important.

Do you have friends who encourage you and redirect your focus when you've lost the way? Treasure them, and by their example, strive to be that encouraging friend for others.

IMPACT APPLICATION: If you ever find yourself in a self-inflicted pity party, I pray that you may be blessed with an unexpected and welcome interruption—of a divine nature—from someone like my friend Bob.

DECEMBER 4

ROLE MODELS

I, a prisoner for serving the Lord, beg you to lead a life worthy of your calling, for you have been called by God. **Ephesians 4:1**

AS I MEANDERED the curves of the driveway while making my way back to the house with the morning newspaper, I could see Lynda's handiwork blooming amid resplendent beds of coleus, impatiens, and begonias. She's been given a gift for creating warmth, welcome, charm, and a sense of hope in the simplest settings of God's creation. It's a platform that she uses well.

Returning to the front door, I noticed the headlines of the sports section read "An Unlikely Winner." Ben Curtis, the champion golfer of the British Open, ranked 396th in the world as the week began and was in his rookie season on the PGA tour with no top-ten finishes for the year and a local caddie who asked, "Ben who?" when he was hired to carry his bag for the tournament. The polite twenty-six-year-old bested a field of the very best golfers in the world to claim the coveted Claret Jug and a platform he only dreamed of before his final putt dropped into the cup on the eighteenth green.

Time will tell if he uses it well, for occupying that same front page was the most recent story in the saga of another fall from grace. Say it ain't so, Kobe! With a platform in sports rivaling that of Michael Jordan and Tiger Woods, Kobe Bryant joined the growing list of role models who are falling into the seemingly sweet temptations of the world around us. And we—our society, people young and old alike—can't afford the loss. Generation after generation aspires for something more in life, for values that last. And instead, while looking up to those we admire, often for other reasons, we watch as so many tumble from their platforms.

On a smaller but no less powerful scale, each of us all too often falls from the platforms of influence we have been given. Trying to rationalize those falls, we use excuses with our spouses like "needing a place to let our hair down" or with our children like "I'll stop doing that when they get older" or "I'm an adult, and it's legal for me."

Paul tells us to live a life worthy of God's calling. And in Matthew's Gospel, Jesus calls us to let our light shine before others in such a way that they may see our good works and glorify our Father who is in heaven (see Matthew 5:14-16). Our platforms—of whatever size—are meant to influence others for their good. Be careful of how you use them.

 IMPACT APPLICATION: What's your platform? Gardener? British Open champion? NBA All-Star? Teacher? President? Author? Parent? Grandparent? Husband? Friend? Whatever platform you've been given, use it well for the good of those who are watching and to the glory of the One who gave it to you.

DECEMBER 5

SNOWCATS

I can do everything through Christ, who gives me strength.
Philippians 4:13

THE SIGNS SAID "Beware of Snowcats." At approximately five feet high and eight feet wide, you couldn't miss them. Large warning signs were strategically placed on the sides of the ski trails of Buttermilk Mountain in Aspen, Colorado. After three days of skiing, our then ten-year-old son, Nathan, pointed to one of the signs as we were riding the ski lift and asked, "Daddy, have you seen one yet?"

"Seen what, Nathan?"

"A snowcat!" Further discussions with my young son revealed that the "snowcats" he believed the signs referred to were of the mountain lion, snow leopard, or comparable dangerous animal variety.

But here's the key for you and me to remember—despite believing that at any moment a mountain lion or leopard could leap out of the trees and bushes while he skied down the slopes, Nathan never stopped skiing. His courage in the face of "danger" taught me a lot that day about the strength and courage that is within us to deal with whatever we might face in life.

But if your journey has been anything like mine, you've faced your share of "snowcats"—real or imagined. Whether facing the loss of a loved one or a much-needed job or facing an illness that has reared its ugly head again. Perhaps you are still trying to help your children find their way in the world or wondering what your real purpose in life is.

Taking your cue from Nathan on facing your "snowcat," maybe you will have the chance to finally change that one habit you should have changed a long time ago. Or maybe you will mend a fence, build a bridge, or lift a life that needs lifting—and maybe in the process find that yours is lifted also. Maybe you will realize that there is no reason why you can't do this or do that—whatever it is you have always dreamed of doing.

Maybe you will realize that you may not always get where you set out to go, that you may fall short too often to keep count, or that you may have to keep your eyes on too many warning signs at times—but you are not locked out of potential and possibility. And all it may take to accomplish things you've only dreamed of until now is a bit of courage that allows you to just keep on skiing past all the problems, obstacles, and uncertainties you will face.

And maybe in the process you will even come to realize, as the apostle Paul did, that all the courage we will ever need is available in and through a relationship with Jesus Christ.

 IMPACT APPLICATION: I don't know what "snowcat" moments you are facing, but my encouragement is to keep skiing, knowing that God is with you.

DECEMBER 6

FRIENDS FOR LIFE

Where two or three gather together as my followers, I am there among them. **Matthew 18:20**

ONE OF MY MOST PLEASANT of recollections always brings a smile to my face for many reasons, including how God is always at work in the lives of His children. It occurred at a local spot known as Dale's Hamburgers over thirty years ago with a dear friend. He remains a close, dear friend, one of those friends who are part of a small, trusted group you can count on one hand. Those few who never leave you, who carry your burdens while you help them carry theirs, who forgive you, and whose friendship is not tied to what you can do for them or some expectation that you will fill some void in their life.

Colonel Timothy P. Fletcher, United States Air Force, now retired, is a graduate of the University of Florida. He is personable, bright, has unshakable faith in his Lord, and is humble. He possesses a Daniel-like integrity. At Dale's that day, he was uncertain of the next step in his life. It must have been the hamburger I was eating that provided a momentary burst of wisdom as I wondered aloud: "Tim, have you ever thought of going into the service as a career?"

His response began a journey marked with remarkable accomplishments—a journey with his bride and family, a journey of twenty-eight years around this country and world serving his nation with honor. His retirement ceremony—just one more moment of recognition and accolades to add to a legacy of a distinguished career—was a few years ago. It was emceed by one of his sons (and one of our godchildren), Major Kevin James Fletcher, United States Air Force.

Two friends one day, simply sharing a meal together, that set the course of the rest of his career and led to his son's choice of a career as well.

Not every meal with friends is a momentous occasion. You won't always hash out decisions that will set the course of your life. And the advice I gave him that day doesn't feel like it was my own—it came from two friends trusting the Lord together.

But you also never know when momentous conversations will happen. You can't manufacture them, and they only happen once you've made and cultivated deep friendships.

Who is your "Tim," someone you can share life with, whose opinion you respect, and who can encourage you in your life and faith? Such friends are rare, but they are truly a gift from God.

Tim is the same today as when we first met and as he was during that lunch at Dale's—a steadfast friend through all the ups and downs of our journey together. And I have the continuing privilege to call him friend.

 IMPACT APPLICATION: Cultivate your deep friendships, and value the time spent with your friends. It just may change your life—and theirs.

A REBEL AT HEART

A child is born to us, a son is given to us. The government will rest on his shoulders. And he will be called: Wonderful Counselor, Mighty God, Everlasting Father, Prince of Peace. **Isaiah 9:6**

WE'RE MOVING QUICKLY NOW, past a period of thanksgiving and reflection and into the season referred to as Advent, meaning "coming," or as I heard a friend refer to it not long ago, as the season that "reminds us that Christ has already landed and is on the move." My friend's reference is spoken like a true rebel, a true follower and believer in the One whom Isaiah referred to as Wonderful Counselor, Mighty God, Everlasting Father, Prince of Peace.

While Isaiah was going through his list of possible names, I wonder why he didn't also refer to Christ as "Rebel." Maybe when Isaiah wrote those words more than seven hundred years before the birth of the Babe of Bethlehem, he didn't know that Christ would in actuality be a bit of a rebel. Perhaps he could have used something like "Raging Rebel" or "Jolly Rebel" or "Loving Rebel" or "Beautiful Outlaw," as John Eldredge referred to him in his book by the same title. Perhaps Isaiah should have included one of those names because, upon honest reflection, that's exactly what Christ was, and what He is, and what He will be in all the days ahead—a rebel.

And He is on the move.

From the quiet birth of a gentle baby, unnoticed by those scurrying around to obey a census decree, who would have thought He would have grown to be such a rebel? And the truth is that nothing today has changed. He calls us out of our comfort zones and into the world, just as He stepped out of His comfort zone when He walked among us.

Certainly you remember what He did while He was here on earth. Who in their right mind would have dared call the religious leaders of the day hypocrites and a brood of vipers, or thrown the moneylenders out of the Temple? Who would have been found eating with tax collectors and other such sinners? What self-respecting Jewish man in that day would have met with and spoken to, in broad daylight, a Samaritan woman as Jesus did? Who would make crooked limbs straight and the blind to see? Who would have called people to help others, even at great personal sacrifice? Who would have touched a leper, healed on the Sabbath, or brought dead people back to life? We may not like it, but we have to face the fact that the Babe of Bethlehem—Jesus—was a rebel.

It seems that our world could use some of those rebels following Jesus right about now. But, even more than that, we could use Him.

IMPACT APPLICATION: Jesus "came" into the world and turned everything upside down. Put on your leather jacket; it's time to be a rebel and engage the world with the same passion that Jesus did.

DECEMBER 8

WHAT DO YOU NEED?

The angel reassured them. "Don't be afraid!" he said. "I bring you good news that will bring great joy to all people. The Savior—yes, the Messiah, the Lord—has been born today in Bethlehem, the city of David! And you will recognize him by this sign: You will find a baby wrapped snugly in strips of cloth, lying in a manger." **Luke 2:10-12**

LYNDA AND I WILL GATHER again this year with our family to open the gifts we have for each other.

And before we look in our stockings or open our gifts, we will sit down together to read certain Scriptures, including the verse set out above from the Gospel of Luke.

And I will cry a gentle tear again.

I will cry with the reminder of what God did for us by sending His one and only Son as the baby born in Bethlehem. I will cry with gratitude, knowing that if God had not sent His Son—for me—my world and life would be so much less than it is, if I were alive at all. I will cry with the knowledge that my bride, son, daughter-in-law, and two precious granddaughters are secure in their relationship with Christ and that they will grow to love Him even more as He continues to demonstrate His love for them evermore.

Christmas can be an emotional time as we remember the loss of a loved one now gone at this Christmas for the first time, a discouraging time with hurried lives leaving things undone and people untouched, or a depressing time as the sadness and heartache of bleak Christmases past rears up again in our memories.

But Christmas is a time when we remember that God came as the babe of Bethlehem to a world in need—and said to the world, "What do you need?" The shepherds came, and the wise men followed—and He asked them, "What do you need?"

And as you come, reaching out in praise and in need, see if you don't see the tiny baby reaching out His hand to you, to hold you, to comfort you, to lift you in whatever your moment of need.

Christmas is here once again. Look closely as you come. Look closely to see if you can see the Christ child reaching out His hand—do you see His tiny hand reaching out to you? It is—now, as it always has and as it always will.

Come to the manger. Come to the babe of Bethlehem.

Now that should make you cry—for joy.

 IMPACT APPLICATION: Christmas is here again to remind us that no matter what you and I need, you and I will find it now, right here, in a manger in a stable, in the person of the babe of Bethlehem.

LISTEN FOR THE BELLS

Look! The virgin will conceive a child! She will give birth to a son, and they will call him Immanuel, which means "God is with us."
Matthew 1:23

THE LIGHTED PLASTIC SANTA—now more than forty years old—is positioned once again as he has been each year since our son was born. Now scratched and faded from the many years, he still shines brightly next to the little Christmas tree in the alcove of the bedroom specially designed for our granddaughters.

Each year Ellie Kate makes it a point to hold that plastic Santa snuggly in her arms and whisper over and over, "I love you, Santa." Words of belief and hope. Words forecasting and embracing something magical and inexplicable that will surely happen soon.

Her actions remind me of the little boy in the book and movie *The Polar Express*.

It is Christmas Eve, and the little boy tosses and turns in his bed, waiting for the sound he has always been sure will come: the ringing of the bells from Santa's sleigh. Uncertainty has crept into his mind, though, because earlier that day a friend insisted there is no Santa. The bells had stopped ringing for that friend. But the little boy believes deep down that the bells will still ring for him. And by the time the story ends, they have—because he believed.

Of course, *The Polar Express* is a fictional story, but it points to a deeper truth and a deeper story: "Look! The virgin will conceive a child! She will give birth to a son, and they will call him Immanuel, which means 'God is with us.'"

Believe in the virgin birth? Hear the bells ringing? Hear the voice of the prophet from so long ago?

What about God becoming man? Hear the bells? Hear the cry of a baby in a manger in Bethlehem?

In a world spinning out of control, what is there to believe in? It seems as though there's not much that we can or would want to believe in; certainly nothing that you or I would want to stake our lives—or our family's lives—upon.

I heard the bells ring again not long ago as I watched our two granddaughters during a church Christmas festival. They were laser-focused, always trying to find Jesus. They found Him as a baby in a manger, then a young boy, and then a man—always believing, in the midst of everything else going on around them, that He was there.

What is there to truly believe in?

Worldly gain? Not likely. Santa Claus? Perhaps. Family loyalties and long-term friendships? Now you're getting closer.

Immanuel, God with us? You've got it!

Immanuel—God is with us! Now *that* is something we can believe in—today and for all eternity.

IMPACT APPLICATION: As we approach the celebration of Christ's birthday, listen for the bells and for the cry of the baby in a manger. Do you hear them?

DECEMBER 10

ONLY WITH GOD—
A VIRGIN BIRTH

"Joseph, son of David," the angel said, "do not be afraid to take Mary as your wife. For the child within her was conceived by the Holy Spirit. And she will have a son, and you are to name him Jesus, for he will save his people from their sins." . . . When Joseph woke up, he did as the angel of the Lord commanded and took Mary as his wife.
Matthew 1:20-21, 24

IT HAD TO HAVE BEEN a strange experience for Joseph.

From the little we know of him, Joseph was a righteous, law-abiding, hard-working, and understanding man. He was engaged to Mary, and under Jewish law, they could not be intimate until they were married. So when he found out Mary was pregnant, in order to save his reputation and to spare Mary public embarrassment, he decided to divorce her quietly. But then he had a dream in which an angel gave him another option, God's option and purpose in all of this:

> Joseph, son of David . . . do not be afraid to take Mary as your wife. For the child within her was conceived by the Holy Spirit. And she will have a son, and you are to name him Jesus, for he will save his people from their sins.

Joseph has a lot to teach us about listening to God in our decision-making. As we consider his story, we can ask ourselves: *Where are we headed? Why are we headed there? How will we behave along the way? And what will we do when we get there?*

In other words, what is our purpose in life? And do the steps of our journey reflect that purpose?

Joseph was heading toward Bethlehem because of a census requirement. And he was traveling with a woman he was engaged to marry, who was pregnant—as only the Lord would know how. Joseph traveled based on a dream, believing in an angel, believing in a strange thing God was doing.

And what was Joseph's response to all of what God was doing and what the angel said was before him? "Are you nuts, Lord?" No, that's not what he said. Maybe that's what we think he should have said. Maybe that's what we would say.

But take a closer look at Joseph. He's the one always standing quietly in the background of manger scenes. Even though he may not have understood everything, his response was always one of humble obedience. He knew he always wanted to live out God's purpose for his life.

We're in the home stretch, dear friends. Get ready—God is doing something strange yet amazing for you and for me and for all the world.

 IMPACT APPLICATION: We begin to live as God intended when His purpose becomes our purpose, knowing that He always wants the best for us.

MAKING ROOM

While they were there, the time came for her baby to be born. She gave birth to her firstborn son. She wrapped him snugly in strips of cloth and laid him in a manger, because there was no lodging available for them. **Luke 2:6-7**

AS WE APPROACH the celebration of Christmas once again and as presents begin to find their way under the tree around the manger scene, you can't help but wonder what that day must have been like so many years ago.

If we could listen across the centuries, I would imagine that we'd hear the tramp of millions of feet, all traveling to various parts of the world, all in obedience to the command of Caesar Augustus. It was a busy time, and the streets of Bethlehem were crowded, literally overrun with people milling about, talking, trading, waiting to be enrolled, and waiting to be taxed.

All of the rooms were taken, and so we see Joseph and his wife forced to find shelter in a stable. Welcome to Bethlehem, Holy Family. Welcome—to a filthy, damp, cold manger.

It's symbolic of what would happen to Jesus throughout His ministry. There was no room for Jesus in the inn. Throughout His life, the welcome was the same; there never seemed to be room. There was no room in the Temple or the courts, because the people didn't understand His message, His ministry, or who He was. That has been the case throughout history—in many people's lives there has been no room for Jesus.

One reason Christ is crowded out might be because of what John suggests in his Gospel—that a darkness exists in the world. It's a darkness that entered the world in the beginning of history, and it's an ever-present darkness that invades our own lives, where we, too, experience uncertainty, bitterness, jealousy, despair, depression, guilt, shame, disappointment, and failure. Yet it's a darkness that the light of God's magnificent invasion of our world overcame more than two millennia ago and can overcome once again in your life and in mine.

Maybe the innkeeper or other people throughout history didn't leave room for Him because they didn't recognize the importance of the moment—just as we tend to do. We, like that innkeeper, often miss the mighty, the powerful, the tremendous evidences of God, because He chooses to hide Himself in the meek and lowly, in the quiet, gentle ways of a babe in a manger, and in so many other blessings in our lives which we often overlook. He's coming again.

May I suggest that we stop and make room for Him?

 IMPACT APPLICATION: Will we make room for Jesus this year—under our trees, in our hearts, and in our lives? Will we make room for Him today, tomorrow, and throughout eternity? If we do, it will make all the difference in our lives and the world around us.

DECEMBER 12

FOLLOW THE LIGHT

The wise men went their way. And the star they had seen in the east guided them to Bethlehem. It went ahead of them and stopped over the place where the child was. . . . They entered the house and saw the child with his mother, Mary, and they bowed down and worshiped him.
Matthew 2:9, 11

WE WERE SURROUNDED with the story of the life of Christ through the spectacular pageantry, music, and narration of "The Promise of Christmas," presented by Idlewild Baptist Church in Lutz, Florida.

Our two granddaughters didn't need the drawing pads and markers their daddy brought to help sustain them through the two-plus hours of the pageant—they were mesmerized by the entire presentation. Ellie Kate, four, was seated on her daddy's lap, and sometime after Jesus' birth in Bethlehem while other characters were onstage she asked, "Daddy, where is Jesus?"

Nathan responded, "He'll be back in a minute, sweetie."

"But Daddy, I want to see Jesus!"

There it is. That moment of clarity in the midst of whatever is going on in our lives. That same moment of clarity the three wise men experienced as they simply followed the light shining down from the star to where the Christ child lay. They wanted to see Jesus. And when they arrived, they looked past everything else and fell down and worshiped him!

Craning her neck to see past the heads of the people seated in front of her and the distraction of folks trying to find their seats in the darkened worship center, Ellie Kate searched to see Jesus throughout the pageant. She simply tried to "follow the Light."

It's that simple. That's what you and I need to do today and in all our tomorrows.

Yet too many things filling our days tend to cloud and distract us from that simple mission of following the Light—the one true Light. Too many of the problems and worries of the day and the anxiety about tomorrow obscure our gaze from the Light. The economy is in the doldrums, a loved one has been in an accident, an illness is not responding to treatment as the doctors thought it would, the memories of Christmases past haunt us—with an emptiness for loved ones we miss or heartaches from things we can't get beyond.

Sadly, our journey to find the Light is occasionally clouded by those who mean well but who place layer after layer of religious dogma, rules, and regulations on the "Light." In those very places where people come believing they will find clarity, healing, and hope, too often they find instead thickening clouds preventing them from seeing the Light.

"Daddy, I want to see Jesus!"

It was one of those unexpected moments of life-changing clarity from a little child.

 IMPACT APPLICATION: It's that simple. That's what you and I need to do today and in all our tomorrows. Are you following the Light? Make following the Light your overarching passion.

COUNTING THE DAYS

A child is born to us, a son is given to us. . . . He will rule with fairness and justice from the throne of his ancestor David for all eternity. The passionate commitment of the LORD of Heaven's Armies will make this happen! **Isaiah 9:6-7**

TWELVE DAYS UNTIL CHRISTMAS.

I told Lynda that I didn't have time to put up a real Christmas tree. But then my granddaughters insisted otherwise and took me to pick one out. We ended up with *two* trees: one five feet tall—small enough for Ellie Kate, with a little help from Gran, to easily put the star on top; and the other, which Hannah insisted on, so that we would have enough room to hang all the ornaments we've accumulated.

So we went from one real tree that we have traditionally put up for over forty-four years to considering no tree to now having two real trees. Lynda just shook her head and smiled as we moved furniture around to fit both trees within the confines of our cozy family room. Ten days to go.

One of the ornaments is a collection of four pieces making up a manger set—the baby Jesus in a cradle, Mary, Joseph, and a little lamb. It needs to be hung carefully so you can see them together and so they are all looking at Jesus. I usually do the honors. But this year Ellie Kate insisted she hang them and on her little tree to boot.

As I suggested, they were all looking at the baby Jesus; but they had their backs to the rest of us. Mary, Joseph, and the little lamb didn't want to be distracted by any of us onlookers, Ellie Kate explained. Mary, Joseph, and the little lamb wanted to see just the baby Jesus.

Eight days to go.

There is an undercurrent of excitement, anticipation, and expectation in the world around us and for good reason. Isaiah whispered it to his people long ago: "A child is born to us, a son is given to us. . . . He will rule with fairness and justice from the throne of his ancestor David for all eternity. The passionate commitment of the Lord of Heaven's Armies will make this happen!" (Isaiah 9:6-7).

Seven days to go. I can see the meaning. I understand. Christmas is all about Jesus. Christmas may have taken place in a lowly manger, but it's the birthplace of the King. It's filled with a love that will enfold us every day throughout the year, a hope that transcends all our sorrows, disappointments, and loneliness, and a majesty that holds all of our eternity.

Five days to go. Do you see it coming?

The birth of our Savior, Christ—the newborn King!

IMPACT APPLICATION: When was the last time you stopped and visited the manger? Perhaps a little more time around the manger with family and friends is what you need this year.

DECEMBER 14

THE LIGHT FOR US

The Word gave life to everything that was created, and his life brought light to everyone. **John 1:4**

THE CHRISTMAS SEASON is here! And none too soon. The Light that John spoke of in his Gospel is arriving—finally! Hearts seem brighter, and our steps seem lighter. Or do they?

Maybe you have heard of D. J. Gregory. He was born with cerebral palsy and with underdeveloped lungs and entangled legs. Doctors told his parents he would never walk and would be confined to a wheelchair for the rest of his life. His parents didn't buy that prognosis, and five surgeries later—before the first grade—D. J. moved from crawling, to two crutches, to one, and then finally to a cane to support his labored, painful walk. The light of hope shined a bit brighter.

D. J. could actually compete in golf, although he had to hit the ball with one hand while maintaining his balance with the other and his cane. By his own admission he wasn't very good, shooting an average score between 105 and 115 per round. But the light grew brighter.

And he played, and with that attitude coupled with his passion for golf, he embarked on the remarkable adventure of walking every hole of every round of every PGA tournament held in 2008—just to prove to himself and others that he could. Forty-four tournaments in forty-five weeks; 180 rounds of golf following different touring pros each week; 3,256 holes and more than 900 miles—with blistered toes and feet and falling on many occasions—he gained the respect and admiration of every player on tour. D. J.'s light was shining brightly, encouraging those around him.

Yes, Christmas is coming. Finally! The Light of Christ for all to see. It is a Light that changes our lives and the world.

And the Light John spoke of is always here. It's a Light that has steadfastly shone through all the darkness of the world. It's a Light that shines over and through all the nicks, scars, underdeveloped lungs, and entangled legs of our lives, illuminating all the potential God has placed within us.

It's a Light that we particularly remember at this time of year. And it still shines brightly for us today. Christmas is coming, reminding us once again that Hope is here. Always.

Christmas has come—not just for a few weeks of every year like this one, but it has come for every day of our lives.

 IMPACT APPLICATION: Let that Light put a spring in your steps, a sparkle in your eyes, and a fire in your hearts, not just in the days ahead in this fast-approaching season, but in every day through every year of your whole life.

DECEMBER 15

SANTA CLAUS AND OTHER WONDERS

The angel reassured them. "Don't be afraid!" he said. "I bring you good news that will bring great joy to all people. The Savior—yes, the Messiah, the Lord—has been born today in Bethlehem, the city of David!"
Luke 2:10-11

WHEN DID YOU STOP BELIEVING?

As our precious granddaughter lay there, taking in the Christmas scene before her in the bedroom, she caught me by surprise when she asked, "Gran, is there really a Santa Claus?"

I figure this is as good a season as any for true confessions, so here it is. Long ago, and in the spirit of continuing to develop his character and establish a relationship of trust and truth-telling in his heart, I told our son what I had been told as a child. I wanted him to be able to say I had always told him the truth about everything. I couldn't "lie" to him anymore.

And so I told my son there was no Santa Claus. I didn't want to wait for some irreverent urchin to break his heart full of wonder. I broke it instead.

The "truth" about Santa Claus is just another in a long litany of reality checks that the self-proclaimed learned, wise, and mature among us impose on the idealistic spirit God created that urges us to believe in the possibility of the impossible. I suppose these reality checks begin when we lose the game we should have won, when someone we trusted hurts us, when a teacher labels us as low achievers, or when a parent calls us a name we hadn't heard before. And sadly, so sadly, we allow those things to define our futures.

The problem is this—I really don't know whether there is a Santa Claus. How do I know there is no Santa Claus? Just because I haven't seen him? How do I know there is no toy factory at the North Pole? Just because I haven't been there? How do I know there are no elves? Just because I haven't tasted their hot chocolate?

Similarly, how do we know we'll fail again if we don't pick ourselves up and try? How do we know a relationship won't work if we don't take the first step to see if it will? How do we know friends won't feel better if we don't reach out to touch them in their moment of need? And how do we know we can't achieve what we dream, to reach for and perhaps even touch the stars, if we don't try, if we don't reach beyond where we are?

What about you? Do you believe in the wonder, majesty, and possibility of the impossible?

 IMPACT APPLICATION: Believe in the impossible—with Christ. None of us will reach our full potential without it.

DECEMBER 16

WHERE ARE WE HEADING?

It came to pass in those days that a decree went out from Caesar Augustus that all the world should be registered. . . . So all went to be registered, everyone to his own city. Joseph also went up from Galilee, out of the city of Nazareth, into Judea, to the city of David, which is called Bethlehem, because he was of the house and lineage of David, to be registered with Mary, his betrothed wife, who was with child.
Luke 2:1-5, NKJV

EVERY YEAR IN OUR MARRIAGE, we have gone out to secure a real Christmas tree, even during the growing popularity of artificial trees. And ever since they were old enough to go with us, our granddaughters have assisted in the selection process.

Recently the usual tree lot had fewer trees. By the time we got there, only a handful of smaller ones, about six or seven feet, remained. Our family room usually has one about ten feet tall to accommodate the many lights Lynda and the girls enjoy, as well as all the ornaments we have collected through the years.

But there we were, and as I was about to suggest we look elsewhere, Lynda, Hannah, and Ellie Kate proclaimed, "Here's the one!" As I walked toward them, I noticed the tree was about six feet tall. It seemed tiny and probably a bit lonely, since it was one of the last trees on the lot. But it was cute, especially with the three girls smiling where it stood. As I reached them, our two granddaughters exclaimed, "It is a baby one, Gran, like the baby Jesus."

The Scripture above points out that Joseph and Mary were heading back to the small town of Bethlehem to be registered. And that is where it happened. Where God's plan to save the world was born—through a tiny baby in a dank, dark stable.

Where are you heading in this most exciting of seasons—a season always filled with anticipation and joy? Anticipation and joy, at least, is what I see coming out of the hearts, eyes, and words of those two little girls who selected a smaller Christmas tree that year—in honor of the baby Jesus.

Where are you heading? What are you running after? What do you love most? All of us are running after something. Too often we find we're running after possessions, money, and trophies. Too often we find we're about our image, our reputation, and recognition. Trust me, when you get what you want, you may not feel as satisfied or fulfilled as you had hoped you would be. And in the process, you may overlook Jesus, who should be at the center of our thoughts.

This season, run to the manger. Look past what the world says is biggest and best. Run to the baby Jesus.

 IMPACT APPLICATION: We're heading to the manger to see the baby Jesus. What will we do with Him when we get there?

WILD TURKEY MOMENTS

When they saw the star, they were filled with joy! **Matthew 2:10**

THE THREE WISE MEN followed the star until they reached Bethlehem—the birthplace of the King. Tradition tells us that they would have seen sheep, lambs, and donkeys. But there is no indication they saw any wild turkeys.

I was still a little groggy—tired from moving for the first time in twenty-eight years—but I was awake enough to see a wild turkey walking very slowly about fifty yards away. Pansy, our elderly basset hound, watched with me, for some reason suspending what would have been her usual desire to bark.

As silly as this may seem, it was a special moment for me. I can almost describe it as a God-appointed moment because all the urgent things on my agenda—and there were many—were forgotten. I sensed the presence of God, and I sensed that God was taking that brief moment to teach me again about the important "wild turkey" moments of my life. And in case I needed a final reminder, He sent Hannah to me later that day.

Our then-two-year-old granddaughter "helped" with all the unpacking. First, Hannah would check out all the rooms and secret passages in the house to make sure they had sufficient space for her to play. Then, she would provide Lynda and me with a "wild turkey" moment in the midst of our unpacking. Just as we had our arms full of dishes or towels or were carrying a box that seemed to weigh one hundred pounds, Hannah would find one of us and lift her arms toward us—signaling that she needed to be picked up and held. It was a God-ordained "holy moment," and we put down what we had in our hands to pick up the precious child of God standing before us. The reward was always the same: a head nestled on our shoulders and a hug that seemed to be a direct gift from God.

Have you had any "wild turkey" moments lately? Or perhaps you haven't recognized them in the midst of your busyness and daily "got to make a living" schedule. When they saw the star, the wise men recognized the moment had come—the moment that had been prophesied.

The wise men probably didn't see any wild turkeys on their journey, but in their moment, in the face of a tiny baby, they saw the King of kings. And that moment is here again. He has come with outstretched arms to embrace us where we are and to take us where we ought to be—on our knees by the side of the manger—to worship and dwell with the eternal Hope of the world for the rest of our days.

IMPACT APPLICATION: Stop. Listen. Find divine guidance for your journey in those unexpected places and "wild turkey moments."

DECEMBER 18

THERE IS STILL ROOM

[Mary] brought forth her firstborn Son, and wrapped Him in swaddling cloths, and laid Him in a manger, because there was no room for them in the inn. **Luke 2:7,** NKJV

DESPITE WHAT YOU MAY THINK, I really don't have it all together. None of us do, you know. And never does it become more apparent than at this time of year, when, despite having long ago come to grips with a difficult childhood, the remnants of painful memories linger.

I can remember most of the forty-five places I lived before my eighteenth birthday, but I can't remember a Christmas in the seventh grade. I can remember almost dropping out of school in the ninth grade to start a career at the local gas station in Virginia, but I don't remember a tree or presents that year. I can remember lying in bed my junior year with a fever, swollen glands, and a broken heart as my younger brother and sisters were told they would get no presents that year because the money was spent on my medicine. I can remember working three jobs my senior year in high school, living on my own, paying room and board—no Christmas, no presents, no one attending my graduation, and definitely no God in the picture. It was the worst of times, and I couldn't have cared less whether there was any room for Him in the inn.

Have you noticed in the picture albums of your memories that heartaches are included too? Have you noticed how they seem to be amplified during this holiest of seasons, despite our having turned the page and put an end to the self-appointed pity parties of years past? The memories linger and at times gently haunt our hearts. Have you noticed how the troubles of today seem especially troublesome and painful? Have you noticed how the uncertainties of the future seem reflected in every single twinkling light and ornament hanging from the tree you finally got up? Have you noticed also that after all of that, there seems to be little room left in your heart for Jesus?

The passion for the season, the flame of passion for life, is at a low flicker or has gone. But in our better moments we know that God is still here. Through all of that in the past, He still watched over us, shepherding people in and out of our lives to help—until we could get to a place where we made room for Him in our lives.

Remember this, in the midst of all the heartaches of the past and the challenges and disappointments of today—"She brought forth her firstborn Son. . . ."

For you and me. What else do we need?

 IMPACT APPLICATION: No matter what we've been through, the passion to live the life God intended for us to live begins when we make room for Him in our lives. Do it today.

NICKED A BIT,
BUT STILL SHINING

The Word gave life to everything that was created, and his life brought light to everyone. The light shines in the darkness, and the darkness can never extinguish it. **John 1:4-5**

THERE BELOW ME stood our Christmas tree clothed in three thousand miniature lights of blue, green, purple, yellow, and red, dancing and twinkling onto every surface around the room.

Each year, after I put all the lights on the tree, Lynda and I will begin to decorate the tree with the ornaments we have gathered through the years. The ornaments all hold memories of family and friends, marking special moments, events, and travels, as each one is gently unwrapped to take its place among the branches. Two very special ones—the first ones Lynda and I bought together for the first Christmas of our marriage—will also be making their usual appearance.

Mine—blue and white checked and a bit nicked and faded—will be hung somewhere near the middle of the tree, its usual location. Lynda's—once a soft green with a snow-capped-gold covering, now wrapped in cellophane in hundreds of tiny broken pieces caused by a fall of some twenty years ago—will be nestled snugly among the branches nearby. Both showing years of living, perhaps even reflecting the ups and downs of our journey together.

Those ornaments paint a piece of the picture of our lives. We may find life at times a bit faded and broken in places. A bit tired from the passing of the years and stressed due to the uncertainty of tomorrow. Or you may find yourself a bit anxious wondering where the money will come from to pay next month's bills, let alone to put a few presents under the tree. For one of you, that deep-seated loneliness has set in again because a loved one who filled your days with joy is now gone from your side.

But before you allow yourself to stay there, before you allow the darkness to set in, look at that scene again with those two weary, faded, nicked, and broken ornaments. Do you see it?

Two ornaments—faded, nicked, broken, and weary. True. But still there, wrapped in the secure, warm glow of the lights of the season. Lights shining in the darkness of our family room, like that one true Light that came into our dark world over two thousand years ago. And John reminds us in this simple passage that the Light is still here for us today, and the darkness has still not—and will never—overcome it.

 IMPACT APPLICATION: No matter what is going on in your life, remember that for today, tomorrow, and always, the Light that all the darkness of the ages will never overcome is here for you and for me for all eternity.

DECEMBER 20

STABILITY
IN THE MANGER

They were terrified, but the angel reassured them. "Don't be afraid!" he said. "I bring you good news that will bring great joy to all people. The Savior—yes, the Messiah, the Lord—has been born today in Bethlehem, the city of David!" **Luke 2:9-11**

WE BOUGHT IT the first year we were married for one dollar from the local Firestone store—our first Christmas album together. And every year, after our real Christmas tree is selected and put up with the lights in place so all is readied for the placing of the ornaments, we start decorating as the second song on the album, "We Need a Little Christmas," begins to play.

It's a spirited song and a joyous tradition that brings an immense measure of stability to our lives. The same stability that happened each year, when Lynda, Nathan, and I would get up early and drive to her parents' home as the entire family gathered for Christmas Day, where we would find Uncle Bob and Candy already at the stove cooking bacon, sausage, and eggs. Aunt Marilyn, Lynda's sister, wandered around with a video camera and a bank of blinding camera lights, capturing the memories of the family eating breakfast and opening presents together and of Lynda's daddy painstakingly opening every gift with his pocket knife to preserve the wrapping paper he would never use again.

The same stability that happens today in our home. When our children and grandchildren arrive on Christmas morning, the Christmas story in Luke is tearfully read, and our two granddaughters' eyes grow wider as they view the scene painted by Scripture.

And ever so slowly, each year, the purpose of our lives becomes clearer. It's always about Christ.

I don't know what's going on in your life right now. I don't know the pain of the past you may be carrying with you into this season of light. I don't know what the future holds for you. But I'll let you in on a secret. Through it all, today and tomorrow, Christ has come, and He cares. And even more than that, He continues to stretch out before us the purpose of our lives.

Old Christmas carols, Christmas trees, twinkling lights, memorable ornaments, family gatherings, and friends on the phone all add to the richness, tradition, and stability of our lives. But from where does the real and lasting stability come? Where is the anchor that grounds us and helps us to a clearer focus on the real purpose of life, which helps us weather the storms of disappointments and the capricious winds blowing across an uncertain future?

It's found only in the Good News of the birth of Jesus Christ.

IMPACT APPLICATION: You will find real purpose for the living of each day in the angel's message of Good News of the birth in Bethlehem. Embrace that birth in the midst of whatever is going on in your life.

CLOSER TO THE LIGHT

The Word gave life to everything that was created, and his life brought light to everyone. The light shines in the darkness, and the darkness can never extinguish it. **John 1:4-5**

AS LYNDA AND I BEGAN to depart that sacred ground more than forty years ago, with stained glass windows and saintly statues of Saint Jude's Catholic Church towering majestically above, we looked back and saw him stop at the end of the pew. He knelt on one knee, facing the crucifix hanging above the altar in the front and made the sign of the cross reverently upon his head and shoulders. "In the name of the Father, Son, and Holy Spirit. Amen," we heard the boy whisper.

Our four-year-old son, Nathan, had probably observed me "genuflect" as I left the pew a few moments before him and, as impressionable little boys will do with their dads, he parodied my ritualistic observance of the hanging Christ. In that moment, I scanned the recesses of my memory to dredge up some meaningful purpose for leaving the pew in such a manner, beyond just the tradition I had begun as a child. I was certain Nathan didn't know, and so as he sat between us in the front seat of our car as we traveled home, I asked him about that moment we had witnessed a few minutes earlier.

"When you do that, do you get closer to God?" he asked. Anticipating his next comment with excitement, I said that you certainly could be closer to God in that moment.

"Well then," he smiled, "I just wanted to be closer to God." It was clear then who in the car understood. And it wasn't me.

Years and years of wandering in and out of Catholic, Episcopal, Methodist, Baptist, and other churches with membership classes, buildings, pledge cards, meetings, and programs had left me no closer to the Truth espoused that morning by our little gift from God. And it wasn't until a few years later that the love of God through Christ penetrated my heart.

As together we enter this Advent season, we approach again the celebration of that moment so long ago when that Light, which shines through the darkness, came to dwell among us in the person of Jesus Christ. The whole purpose of John's Gospel was to turn that light of hope a little brighter and remind us that no matter what we face, what we're going through, what disappointments, failures, and heartaches we have suffered, there is a light that shines through and that all the darkness of all those moments cannot and will not overcome that one true Light.

Once again it's time—it's always time—to draw close to that Light.

"In the name of the Father, Son, and Holy Spirit. Amen."

IMPACT APPLICATION: Draw close to the one true Light, to the God who loves and adores you, to the Christ who came for you.

DECEMBER 22

FROM THE PALACE TO THE MANGER

Herod called for a private meeting with the wise men, and he learned from them the time when the star first appeared. Then he told them, "Go to Bethlehem and search carefully for the child. And when you find him, come back and tell me so that I can go and worship him, too!" After this interview the wise men went their way. And the star they had seen in the east guided them to Bethlehem. It went ahead of them and stopped over the place where the child was. When they saw the star, they were filled with joy! **Matthew 2:7-10**

IT WAS CHRISTMASTIME, and we were busy with all the usual preparations, but we were in the palace and missing the manger. That is, until our granddaughters intervened to help us with the tree decorations.

Our elder granddaughter, Hannah, put ornament after ornament on the tree, creating a densely populated belt of her favorites at a perfectly outlined little-girl height. In the meantime, we watched as Ellie Kate, two years old at the time, crawled under the tree with her head up into and surrounded by the branches of the tree and strings of twinkling lights.

"Oh gosh!" she quietly murmured again and again as the lights danced in her eyes. And then, with her gaze fixed, her words quieted and she sat motionless in the moment. "Baby Jesus," she quietly and reverently exhaled.

"Baby Jesus, Gran. Baby Jesus, Mimi."

She had found the set of hanging figurines of Mary, Joseph, a lamb, and the baby Jesus in a cradle, gently swinging in the tree amidst the loving activity of two little girls and us. We looked at the figurines with Ellie Kate and Hannah as together four hearts paused in worship. With Ellie's help, we had left the palace, followed the star, and found the Savior.

The wise men had heard that the baby was born, the One they call the King of the Jews. They went to Jerusalem to the palace of Herod to find Him. They went to the wrong place.

That's what we do—looking and staying too long in the palace. We look for happiness, success, and satisfaction in all the wrong places. We look for the extravagant and the worldly.

Our careers demand our time and our lives while we sacrifice our families on the altar of our search for contentment and success. We struggle with decisions when all the while the star hovers above us, waiting for our glance to point us to the only answer. We decorate our lives with ornaments and trinkets and numb our sadness, disappointments, and pain with stuff, looking for answers that never come.

Leave the palace. Go to the manger.

IMPACT APPLICATION: The stuff of the palace will entice us, but what is in the manger will save us and sustain us.

ONE CLEAR SIGN

You will recognize him by this sign: You will find a baby wrapped snugly in strips of cloth, lying in a manger. **Luke 2:12**

IT WAS ABOUT THIS TIME OF YEAR, a number of years ago now, that Lynda, Nathan, and I visited longtime dear friends stationed with the United States Air Force in Munich, Germany. Being a fairly observant and bright baby boomer, I noticed at some point along the drive on the way to their home from the airport that all the road signs and advertising billboards were written in German, an all-too-obvious revelation that seemed to impress only me. Despite the fact that I personally could not understand the information and directions the signs provided to get us to our destination, we arrived safely at our friends' home.

Our friends could read the signs.

I wonder what one unfamiliar with the "language" would think today were they to drive about and observe the activities going on around us during this rapid approach to Christmas. I wonder what the signs would tell them about the direction of our journey. I wonder if they would know where we were headed as they watched people and neighborhoods busily decorating their homes with trees, lights, and ornaments or saw shopping malls packed to overflowing.

I wonder if they would be able to tell the direction we were headed as they watched communities around our nation remove manger scenes from the public square. I wonder if they would know where we were headed as they entered stores, only to be greeted with a rousing "Happy Holidays."

Yet were they to take a moment to cut through all the glitz and glamor of decorations, the hustle and bustle of busy shoppers, and the attempts by communities, stores, and political leaders to create a universally acceptable "language" for the season, the observer would eventually find the sign that points them in the right direction and to the real reason for it all:

"The Savior—yes, the Messiah, the Lord—has been born today in Bethlehem, the city of David! And you will recognize him by this sign: You will find a baby wrapped snugly in strips of cloth, lying in a manger" (Luke 2:11-12).

Despite all the contrary signs throughout the ages and today, that is the one clear sign that matters now and for all eternity and will make all the difference in our lives when we arrive there.

IMPACT APPLICATION: No matter the signs all around us, there is only one sign that truly matters, one sign that offers the clear and only direction for where we are headed—the Christ child lying in a manger.

DECEMBER 24

MAGIC OR MIRACLE?

The angel answered, "The Holy Spirit will come on you, and the power of the Most High will overshadow you. So the holy one to be born will be called the Son of God." **Luke 1:35, NIV**

MAGIC? MIRACLE? WHICH IS IT?

Be honest now—the first time you heard the Christmas story, you wondered if or maybe even thought it was magic, didn't you? Or was it a miracle, an event that contradicts known scientific laws and is thought to be due to supernatural causes?

It seems as though an individual could rationalize and explain that a belief in either might produce the end result, but only one will produce the life-sustaining claim to hope. And what about all the evidences after the virgin birth of the Christ child as a boy and then an adult—teaching, healing, saving, dying?

You have to admit, it was a mighty strange way to save the world. To send a baby through a virgin girl. Yet whether we believe it to be just something that occurred by some inexplicable means—magic perhaps—or believe it to be the hand of God in His plan to save the world makes all the difference in the approach to our todays and tomorrows. And, even more important, it will make all the difference in the days of our eternity.

Look back at your life's journey. How did you handle the difficult times? Did your actions and feelings—when the money ran out, when you lost a loved one, when illness hit, when a child lost his or her way, when a relationship ended, or when a career path was closed—reflect a belief that what God did way back then was a miracle or was something else? Did you cling to hope or cringe in the face of uncertainty?

Do the responses and reactions to the circumstances of your life reveal a depth of faith and belief in a God who really did send an angel and the Holy Spirit to a virgin girl? Do they reveal a depth of faith moving us to believe that—even though it seems to be a very strange story indeed—it is a story for the ages that only the God of the ages could fashion?

The depth and stability of our faith in difficult times reveals, it would seem, how we view what He did way back then. Was it a sleight of hand or a supernatural act?

Here we are approaching Christmas once again. Christ is born. It is a time to reflect once again on the God who sent His Son as a tiny baby, through a virgin birth, to save the world and to save you and me.

What do we really believe?

IMPACT APPLICATION: Think about that first Christmas. Magic or miracle? What we really believe will make all the difference for all our todays, our tomorrows, and our eternity. Miracle!

CRADLED IN LOVE

The Savior—yes, the Messiah, the Lord—has been born today in Bethlehem, the city of David! **Luke 2:11**

PERHAPS YOU WERE STILL ASLEEP or preoccupied with other early morning wanderings, preparations, and responsibilities. I wonder if you noticed the light of this morning's dawn breaking bold in hues of orange and gold and warm across the previously darkened sky introducing the clear, crisp, cold light of the day.

I couldn't help but be reminded again through that glorious array of early-morning colors of the approach of Christmas. In the hustle, the bustle, and busyness of my days; in the press of other priorities, problems, or perplexities of the past; in the hour-by-hour, day-by-day pile of moments—the approach of that magnificent light of the babe of Bethlehem had been relegated to the status of slipping by.

It happens all too often, not just at this glorious time of year but during the daily crush of our lives, where we miss or shut out that moment that can make all the difference. But then a reminder invades our lives.

It happened to my bride several years ago. Looking for almost any reason to travel to Tampa to visit our children and, of course, our only granddaughter at the time, Hannah, Lynda drove down to help our daughter-in-law Amy make some final preparations for Christmas.

As children of all ages love to do at Christmastime, one evening, Lynda and Hannah bundled up after dinner for a grand tour around the neighborhood where our children lived to experience the Christmas lights that had painstakingly been hung by their neighbors in preparation for this season.

As she described it later, it was a glorious time as she saw again and afresh through the eyes of our granddaughter the beauty of the lights surrounding their every step. Lynda was reminded through the excited utterances of Hannah that indeed a light was invading us again, a light of hope, power, love, and peace for all the ages and for her.

Following their return home, Hannah came to her Mimi as she was taking off her coat, reached up, cradled Lynda's face in her tiny hands, like those of a baby, and looked straight into her eyes and said, "Merry Christmas for you, Mimi!"

And that's what's happening again for each of us—a light has come into the world through a baby in a manger. A light of love and peace, of power and hope.

The angel said, "The Savior—yes, the Messiah, the Lord—has been born today."

Merry Christmas for you, Mimi!

Merry Christmas for you! And you! And you!

Merry Christmas for us all and for everyone who will take Him into their hearts today and every day and for all eternity.

 IMPACT APPLICATION: The Light from the cradle is here—and we dare not ignore it because it can make all the difference in our lives now and for all eternity.

DECEMBER 26

THE HIDDEN
HAND OF GOD

"My thoughts are nothing like your thoughts," says the LORD. "And my ways are far beyond anything you could imagine. For just as the heavens are higher than the earth, so my ways are higher than your ways and my thoughts higher than your thoughts." **Isaiah 55:8-9**

CHANGE. It's usually something we endure and not necessarily all that well. Perhaps it would be a whole lot easier for us to endure if we knew what life looked like at the end of the change. Sometimes change paralyzes us so much that we don't realize the platform the change has created.

You've probably experienced it. A move. A new job. No job. A death in the family. An empty nest. Going from the comfortable and certain to the uncomfortable and uncertain.

It seldom seems easy to wander through. No matter our age, we're not quite as malleable as we'd like to believe we are. We don't often like the idea of feeling like clay in the Potter's hands. And so we tend to rebel, push back against, run from, or attempt to stall any change knocking on the front doors of our lives.

Maybe it's because we've been burned before with other changes in our lives. Maybe we're running on empty, exhausted, feeling used up, finished, defeated, or retired. Maybe a relationship has changed or will. Maybe an illness has reared its unwelcome head once again. Maybe we're just afraid to leave the temporal security of our man-made existence. Maybe we feel like we're being called to a place where not only can we not see the light at the end of the tunnel, but we also can't find the tunnel. Maybe, for whatever reason, at this point in our lives, we find ourselves struggling simply with changing from one day to the next.

And then, maybe—it's because we worry more than we trust.

Maybe—as a friend put it recently—it's because in the midst of whatever change is going on in our lives, we tend to forget to trust the "hidden hand of God," which is guiding and directing the change for His glory and our ultimate good.

What change are you facing in your life?

May I suggest that you approach that change with the belief that it is an opportunity to reconnect with the "hidden hand of God"? May it be a time when you allow the "hidden hand of God" to mold you more and more into all He intends for you to be.

The "hidden hand of God"—something in which you and I can always and forever trust in the midst of all the change we experience.

 IMPACT APPLICATION: View change—it will come—as an opportunity to allow the hidden hand of God to mold you further into all He created you to be and to increase your platform of opportunity to impact others for His glory.

YOU'RE VERY, VERY WELCOME, GOD

We thank you, O God! We give thanks because you are near. People everywhere tell of your wonderful deeds. **Psalm 75:1**

THERE'S A SPECIAL PLACE we have taken our son, daughter-in-law, and grand-daughters on occasion for retreat and vacation in Sea Island called the Cloister. It is family oriented and located in a beautiful setting among the marshlands and beaches of that area of southeast Georgia.

During one visit, Lynda and I had just finished wrapping our eldest grand-daughter into the soft, fluffy folds of her bed and praying her into another night of rest, when her daddy stole into our room to do the same. By the way, it's only a real vacation for Mimi and me if the two girls can sleep in our room each night. Consistent with that wish, our younger granddaughter was already fast asleep in another part of our room.

As her daddy approached, Hannah lifted the bedcover, showing him how she had just finished praying and had invited God into her bed next to her. As he lay down next to her, and after she reminded him that he was lying on God and prob-ably needed to move over a little bit, she explained that after God had said thank-you to her for inviting Him into her bed, she had said in return, "You're welcome."

But then she realized that maybe she should have said, "You're very welcome" because He is God. And then she was off to the races, explaining to God, in the presence and embrace of her Daddy's attentive audience, that "Well, you're God, so I should have said, 'You're very, very, very, very, maybe a thousand times, very welcome!'"

Her points were clear; her purpose was rock solid. She had welcomed God once again into her life, specifically into her sleep-time, and knew that God was with her and would be with her throughout her nighttime and throughout all the days and nights of her life. And knowing that reminded her that God is very, very, very, very, maybe a thousand times or more, very big and deserving of all her thanks and praise and welcome into her life.

What is our view of God in the quiet moments of our lives? What is our view of God in the busy moments of our lives? When is the last time we've said "thank you" or "you're welcome" or simply spent a few minutes talking with Him?

Doesn't it seem obvious and as natural as a little girl's view that God should be very, very, very, very, a thousand times, very welcome in our lives?

IMPACT APPLICATION: In our quietest moments and in our busiest moments, we need to remember that the God of the universe is bigger than all we face and is with us not only as we sleep, but also to walk with us and help us through our days.

DECEMBER 28

LYNDA AND BERNARD

This is the message you have heard from the beginning: We should love one another. **1 John 3:11**

IF YOU'RE BLESSED to know my bride, Lynda, then nothing good you hear about her will surprise you, especially this story. This story is illustrative about how her life and love has changed lives through the years and in particular the life of one boy named Bernard.

Bernard was a football player at Eastside High School with our son, Nathan. Bernard lived in what our community refers to as the east side of town, which some viewed as the less affluent side of town.

It was Football Parents' Night at Eastside. At halftime the players were to be introduced alphabetically by their last names and then escort their parents across the center of the field. Bernard had no father living at home. His mother said she hoped to come so Bernard could escort her across the rain-soaked field at halftime. It had been raining through the first half of play, and the field was wet and muddy.

As they got to the Ws in the alphabet, we were getting ready to line up and were about to be introduced, while Bernard still waited. His time to have been introduced had long since come and gone. He stood there all alone, waiting, looking hopefully in the distance toward the parking lot for a sign of someone coming that would signal to him how important he was. But no sign came. His mother hadn't come.

Seeing him in tears at the door of the locker room with mud all over his uniform, his helmet hanging at his side and his head hanging even lower, Lynda stepped out and held out her other arm to Bernard and said, "Bernard, you and Nathan will walk with me tonight as my two sons."

Arm in arm, the three of them walked across that rain-soaked field as a family, with me walking dutifully and tearfully behind them.

In that simple loving act, Bernard saw his importance, his own value and worth. To Lynda, his value was not determined by what other less sensitive people saw, but by what God saw. God saw a person of worth and value, and so did Lynda. His burdens of rejection were left at the door of that locker room because in that moment Lynda's act cut through his pain and said to him, "Bernard, I love you, and I'm here for you." The impact that moment had on his life was immeasurable.

For years after, Bernard would call the house, and after a polite talk with me, would ask to speak to "Mom."

That simple act changed his life.

 IMPACT APPLICATION: We are called over and over by God to love one another. Today and every day, look for those moments when you can love and lift someone to the place God wants them to be.

WHOM DO YOU TRUST?

The LORD is my rock and my fortress and my deliverer; My God, my strength, in whom I will trust; My shield and the horn of my salvation, my stronghold. **Psalm 18:2**, NKJV

WHEN OUR TWO GRANDDAUGHTERS were fairly young, they began to trust the God who created them, as they trusted their parents and grandparents. What they are continuing to find as they grow in those relationships, especially with God, is that in that trust, they have not been let down. In that trust, they will realize that they are precious—not just with spoken words but with the sacrificial deeds of those they trust.

But sadly that's not always the case. Parents, grandparents, and others who should have loved, protected, defended, encouraged, made us feel special, and built us up haven't done that. And as a result, they have clouded our view of the God who stands ready to secure us in His heavenly arms.

We tend to think God is a lot like them. It's natural since they are the authority figures in our lives. And that is simply not true. So in too many cases, we've got junk to get over and bad memories to get past before we can let down our defensive walls of self-protection and leap into the arms of that loving God in complete faith that He will be there.

And here's a place to start. We can all remember that one person who at some time in our lives has been that example of trust, love, and protection for us. It may be a parent. It may be a grandparent. Good. But it may be someone else. Someone who by their example gave you a glimpse of the loving nature of the God you can trust to always provide for you and who always wants the very best for you. Start there in catching the view of the God who waits for you. Start there in developing that eternal relationship with the God you can trust to catch you when you fall or when you take a leap of faith. You will find that He is the God who will never leave you and will walk with you for the rest of your journey.

And then, when you're ready, boldly announce "God, I'm here and ready to go!" He'll be there to catch you, hold you, lift you, and walk with you—in the shallow and deep ends of your life, the rocky rapids, the turbulent storms, and the dark nights that haunt your soul.

He'll be there. Set everything else aside and trust Him.

 IMPACT APPLICATION: In various degrees, we all find it hard at times to trust God. But the God who created us is ready when we can finally leap in faith into His arms. You'll be pleasantly surprised at how strong those arms are and at how soft the landing will be.

DECEMBER 30

WHERE DO THEY FIND KIDS LIKE THIS?

Direct your children onto the right path, and when they are older, they will not leave it. **Proverbs 22:6**

IT WAS ONE OF THOSE GRUELING DAYS we all must surely experience at times, having gone through and dealt with a number of issues throughout the day. I had just settled into our family room chair for the evening when I heard, "Does Daddy know this?" Lynda's words pierced the quiet of my thoughts and heart. Lynda was on the phone with our son, Nathan, learning that his long-awaited eye surgery was in the morning. We had talked about it, but I had forgotten the date. I picked up the phone, listened, laughed, worried, and then prayed for him, the doctors, the nurses, and any other sources of comfort that would come to mind. Thankfully, it went well.

Two days later, we attended the wedding of Kevin, a young man I had coached years earlier in baseball. I had also coached his two brothers, Greg and Ken, his groomsmen. They had all done well in school and gone on to play baseball in college, as had my son, who also had participated with and against these three young men in high school and American Legion baseball. Now all were involved in successful professional pursuits. Greg still carried the cross in his pocket I had given him years earlier.

As I reflected on those young men, these words flooded my thoughts: *Where do they find kids like this?* It wasn't an original thought. I had heard the story recounted by Martin Savage, one of our courageous reporters embedded in one of our American overseas military operations where he followed the exploits of our brave and passionate young soldiers living out their personal call to defend this nation. My thoughts returned to my son with his passionate heart to help folks who are down on their luck and less fortunate than others.

Where do they find kids like this? We find them in the cities and suburbs, in the regions of snowcapped mountains, rugged wilderness, and golden fields of waving grain, in small towns and big, in every nook and cranny of this great land. They follow the passion God placed in their hearts and touch and build the lives of others around them.

Where do they find kids like this? They're gifts from God—in our homes, neighborhoods, and schools—entrusted to parents and grandparents and extended family and others to teach, nurture, grow, and inspire others to be all they were created to be.

Each day we have the opportunity to encourage "kids" like this. May God help each of us in this pursuit.

 IMPACT APPLICATION: Every day we have the opportunity to turn up the flame of passion in those young folks around us whom we are entrusted to help grow. Look for the opportunities to grow them into all God created them to be.

WE HAVE BEEN TO THE MANGER

The angel reassured them. "Don't be afraid!" he said. "I bring you good news that will bring great joy to all people. The Savior—yes, the Messiah, the Lord—has been born today in Bethlehem, the city of David!"
Luke 2:10-11

THAT'S WHAT I WANT US to reflect on today. On this day so close to another Christmas celebration, I'd like for us to not just read those words above again with our eyes or listen with our ears to the words of the angel, as recorded by Luke, spoken so long ago:

> Fear not: for, behold, I bring you good tidings of great joy,
> which shall be to all people.
> For unto you is born this day in the city of David a Saviour,
> which is Christ the Lord. (Luke 2:10-11, KJV)

I'd really like for us to hear those words with our hearts so that as we continue on in the weeks ahead, into the New Year and beyond, the people we come in contact with in the weeks, months, and years ahead will know where we have been. People we see and who will see us, people we talk to, touch, work with, and live with will know that we have been with Jesus.

They will know we have been to the manger.

They will sense something different in us.

And I would like us to move on from this moment and to sense and remember that this Christmas celebration has not just been any day, any experience, any celebration, any Christmas, but that we have been with Jesus. And that because of that experience, an experience available to us every day of our lives, our lives are different and our approach to all of the ups and downs of life, its valleys and mountains, the joys and sorrows, will be different—when we remember where we've been and who we have been with. And to remember that it is a celebration, at the manger, that is available to us each day, not just at that wonderful time we recently celebrated at Christmas.

We've been to the manger, and we have been with Christ.

And all the world will know. Because they will sense something different in us, something fresh and new. And renewed hope for our lives, for theirs, and for all the world.

IMPACT APPLICATION: It's a season of reminder—where we remember that moment when Christ came into the world for you and for me. And He is here for us—to visit, to embrace, to walk with us—each day. To the manger every day—and people will know where we have been and where we are going every new day of every new year—with renewed hope.